In the western Christian tradition, the mystic was seen as having direct access to God, and therefore great authority. Dr Jantzen discusses how men of power defined and controlled who should count as a mystic, and thus who would have power: women were pointedly excluded. This makes her book of special interest to those in gender studies and medieval history.

Its main argument, however, is philosophical. Because the mystical has gone through many social constructions, the modern philosophical assumption that mysticism is essentially about intense subjective experiences is misguided. This view is historically inaccurate, and perpetuates the same gendered struggle for authority which characterises the history of western Christendom.

This book is the first on this topic to take issues of gender seriously, and to use these as a point of entry for a deconstructive approach to Christian mysticism.

CAMBRIDGE STUDIES IN
IDEOLOGY AND RELIGION 8

POWER, GENDER AND
CHRISTIAN MYSTICISM

CAMBRIDGE STUDIES IN IDEOLOGY AND RELIGION

General Editors: DUNCAN FORRESTER *and* ALISTAIR KEE

Religion increasingly is seen as a renewed force, and is recognised as an important factor in the modern world in all aspects of life – cultural, economic, and political. It is no longer a matter of surprise to find religious factors at work in areas and situations of political tension. However, our information about these situations has tended to come from two main sources. The news-gathering agencies are well placed to convey information, but are hampered by the fact that their representatives are not equipped to provide analysis of the religious forces involved. Alternatively, the movements generate their own accounts, which understandably seem less than objective to outside observers. There is no lack of information or factual material, but a real need for sound academic analysis. Cambridge Studies in Ideology and Religion will meet this need. It will give an objective, balanced, and programmatic coverage to issues which – while of wide potential interest – have been largely neglected by analytical investigation, apart from the appearance of sporadic individual studies. Intended to enable debate to proceed at a higher level, the series should lead to a new phase in our understanding of the relationship between ideology and religion.

A list of titles in the series is given at the end of the book.

POWER, GENDER AND
CHRISTIAN MYSTICISM

GRACE M. JANTZEN

John Rylands Senior Research Fellow
University of Manchester

CAMBRIDGE
UNIVERSITY PRESS

Published by the Press Syndicate of the University of Cambridge
The Pitt Building, Trumpington Street, Cambridge CB2 1RP
40 West 20th Street, New York, NY 10011–4211, USA
10 Stamford Road, Oakleigh, Melbourne 3166, Australia

First published 1995

Printed in Great Britain by Woolnough Bookbinding Limited,
Irthlingborough, Northants.

A catalogue record for this book is available from the British Library

Library of Congress cataloguing in publication data

Jantzen, Grace.
Power, Gender and Christian Mysticism / Grace M. Jantzen.
p.   cm. – (Cambridge Studies in Ideology and Religion; 8)
Includes bibliographical references (p.   ) and index.
ISBN 0 521 47376 4 (hardback) – ISBN 0 521 47926 6 (paperback)
1. Mysticism.   2. Women mystics.   3. Sex – Religious aspects –
Christianity.   4. Power – Religious aspects – Christianity.
1. Title.   11. Series.
BV5083.J36 1995
248.2′2′082 – dc20   94–44562   CIP

ISBN 0 521 47376 4 hardback
ISBN 0 521 47926 6 paperback

To Ann

In the name of us all
Let there be peace and love among us.

May the skies be clear,
And may the streets be safe.

In the name of us all,
Let there be peace.
(Summerville 1972, adapted)

'Hence this book. It is "unfinished." No theology, no book, is ever enough. *Only justice is enough*, and if any book can help us along this common way, may it be read and taken to heart.' (Heyward 1982: iv)

Contents

		page	
List of illustrations			x
General editors' preface			xi
Preface			xiii

1	Feminists, philosophers and mystics	1
2	Mystics, martyrs and honorary males	26
3	The mystical meaning of scripture	59
4	Mystical theology and the erotic other	86
5	'Cry out and write': mysticism and the struggle for authority	157
6	The visions of virgins: spirituality and sexual control	193
7	Heretics and witches	242
8	The language of ineffability	278
9	Conclusion: mysticism and modernity	322

References	354
Index	380

ix

Illustrations

1   *Creation and Fall*. Bedford Book of Hours, British   *page* 46
    Library.
2   *The Temptation of Adam and Eve*. Psaltery, St John's
    College, Cambridge.   66
3   Lollard Bible. Cambridge University Library,
    MS Ee. i. 10 fol. 6iv.   185
4   *Eucharistic Christ and Charity*. Wallraf-Richartz
    Museum, Cologne.   210
5   *Hildegard Receiving her Visions*. Biblioteca Statate di
    Lucca, *Liber divinorum operum*. MS fo. 9r.   226
6   *Waldensian Heretics*. Frontispiece to the French
    translation of Johannes Tinctoris, *Tractatus Contra
    Sectum Valdensium*, fifteenth century. Cabinet des
    manuscripts, fonds, français 961. Bibliothèque
    Nationale, Paris.   257
7   *Hildegard's Vision of the Cosmos*. Biblioteca Statate di
    Lucca, *Liber divinorum operum*. MS fo. 9r.   272

General editors' preface

In the early 1970s it was widely assumed that religion had lost its previous place in Western culture and that this pattern would spread throughout the world. Since then religion has become a renewed force, recognised as an important factor in the modern world in all aspects of life, cultural, economic and political. This is true not only of the Third World, but in Europe East and West, and in North America. It is no longer a surprise to find a religious factor at work in areas of political tension.

Religion and ideology form a mixture which can be of interest to the observer, but in practice dangerous and explosive. Our information about such matters comes for the most part from three types of sources. The first is the media which understandably tend to concentrate on newsworthy events, without taking the time to deal with the underlying issues of which they are but symptoms. The second source comprises studies by social scientists who often adopt a functionalist and reductionist view of the faith and beliefs which motivate those directly involved in such situations. Finally, there are the statements and writings of those committed to the religious or ideological movements themselves. We seldom lack information, but there is a need – often an urgent need – for sound objective analysis which can make use of the best contemporary approaches to both politics and religion. Cambridge Studies in Ideology and Religion is designed to meet this need.

The subject matter is global and this will be reflected in the choice both of topics and authors. The initial volumes will be concerned primarily with movements involving the Christian religion, but as the series becomes established movements involving other world religions will be subjected to the same objective critical analysis. In all cases it is our intention that an accurate and sensitive account of religion should be informed by an objective and sophisticated application of perspectives from the social sciences.

This work constitutes a stimulating, scholarly and wide-ranging feminist analysis of the ways in which 'mysticism' has been socially constructed in different ways at different times, and is implicitly bound up with issues of authority and gender. Following Michel Foucault, and applying his ideas to mysticism, Jantzen maintains that what matters as mysticism will reflect the institutions of power in which it occurs. For Jantzen, as for Foucault, history may be seen as a struggle between competing power blocks struggling for domination, while from within the mystical tradition (and especially out of the experience of female mystics) have come creative efforts at pushing back the boundaries of institutional power. By utilising a deconstructionist approach, and deploying the widest variety of materials, from all eras of Christian writing, the author is able to show convincingly that women's mystical experiences were regarded as threatening by those in positions of religious authority and were continually subject to social control. Her primary motive in so doing is to counter what she sees as the detrimental effects of the current social construction of mysticism, which has reduced mystical experience to its personal and psychological dimensions alone, thus deflecting attention away from any political and social dynamic it may have.

Preface

This book has been a long time in the making, and I have accumulated many debts. About twelve years ago, I began to develop a long-standing interest in Christian mysticism and spirituality at both a personal and a professional level. I began to write a book about what we could draw from Christian mystics regarding philosophical questions such as evidence for the existence of God, the mystical core of religion, and above all problems of evil and questions of justice. When I looked at what philosophers and theologians say about mysticism, however, it soon became apparent that they were often quite inaccurate as to the actual mystics of the Christian tradition. In fact, a standard practice was to take William James' account of mysticism, written at the turn of the century, as adequate description, and to go on from there without going back to primary sources except perhaps to cull juicy quotations to support a position taken on other grounds. The more I read of the mystical writers of the Christian tradition, the less acceptable such a practice came to appear. I saw an ever-increasing gap between their concerns and those of contemporary philosophers writing about them. I decided that I would not add to the books on mysticism which take little notice of actual mystics; and chose, as a preliminary, to make as careful a study as a non-medievalist could of medieval mystical writing, focusing on one person, but also trying to understand her in a wider context, both socially and in terms of the western mystical traditions reflected in her work. That is how my book on Julian of Norwich (1987) came to be written.

The reasons for choosing Julian as a case study were multiple. She had lived in England; thus it was easier for me to explore her historical and social context than would have been the case had I chosen a continental writer. She wrote in a language I could read in the original; and her writings fit comfortably between the covers of a single book. She lived almost at the end of the medieval period; in her writings could be traced strands of several of the major mystical traditions of western Christendom. The most significant factor, however, was her gender. Although at the time I began my study of Julian my feminist consciousness was very low, it was important to me to study the life and work of a *woman* mystic, one to whom I instinctively felt a sympathy based on shared gender.

Though the book on Julian is written from a determinedly Christian perspective, the writing of it began to reshape my thinking about the Christian tradition and the relation of gender and power within it: the institutional church seemed, increasingly, to have a lot to answer for. So, however, did modern philosophy as it seemed to me. When I turned from case studies of medieval mystics to philosophical and theological writings about mysticism, I found myself increasingly perplexed. On the one hand, there has been over the past ten or fifteen years a mushrooming of philosophical interest in mysticism and religious experience, with steady publication of new monographs and journal articles. On the other hand, any competent undergraduate can quite easily show that what philosophers say or assume mysticism is like bears little resemblance to actual historical mystics of western Christendom. Such misrepresentation might be understandable if philosophers were not particularly ·interested in the subject of mysticism; but what is going on when there is so much putative interest, and yet people who would normally insist upon meticulous scholarship are not giving attention to primary sources?

Growing feminist consciousness enabled me to approach my continuing research with a hermeneutic of suspicion: perhaps it was not only philosophers writing about mysticism, but even those who were presenting histories of mysticism who were operating with an understanding shaped by centuries of the power of patriarchy; and perhaps it was this which operated to blind contemporary writers to what mystics were saying. This suspicion was sharpened by a four-year appointment to the

Canadian Royal Commission on New Reproductive Technologies. Though on the face of it this assignment was poles apart from consideration of medieval mysticism, the total immersion in the interface between rigorous academic thinking and policy formation in the world of power politics made me see the relationship between power and knowledge in a wholly different light. I began to take serious notice of who are the beneficiaries and who are the victims of systems of power/knowledge. In the case of new reproductive technologies, the beneficiaries are those with powerful vested interests: pharmaceutical companies, big science, big business. The victims, too often, are women, children, aboriginal people, disabled people, ethnic minorities.

The glaring interconnection between power and gender which had been forced on to my attention in the study of new reproductive technologies and health care markedly shifted my focus in thinking about mysticism as well. In early and medieval Christendom, after all, there was an overt link between the knowledge of God gained through the mystical life and the authority which could be claimed on the basis of that special knowledge. When I looked again, it was possible to trace a series of major changes in the understanding of what counts as mystical; and in every one of the changes there was a gendered struggle for power and authority. This book is an account of some of those struggles, and an analysis of their philosophical implications.

We are no longer living under the sacred canopy of the medieval era: people who say that they have mystical experiences are not likely to be given vast political and financial authority on the basis of the knowledge of God which they claim. Religion has been discarded as a public force: we could say that of all the privatisations, the privatisation of religion has been one of the most thorough and the least remarked, even though it continues to shape secular consciousness in ways that are often unconscious. At the same time religion, and especially religious experience, has become far more available to women – women who, in idealisation though not in reality, are also private, and are the primary keepers of house and home. A connection can be traced between the domestication of women and the domestication of religion such that claims to religious experience become permissable for women in direct proportion to the decline of overt public importance of religion. And I have argued in this book that one of the reasons why philosophers of religion often ignore the primary sources of mystical writings and their social and cultural locatedness is that if these were to be taken into account, then it would be necessary to recognise the web of knowledge, power and gender which a study of those sources exposes: knowledge and power which, in the modern era, was largely transferred from the church to the academy.

If I am right, then most current philosophical writing about mysticism is misguided, asking questions and dealing with issues in ways that are not only inaccurate to mystical writings but also using the resulting distortion to bolster philosophical and theological positions which the mystical writers themselves would have repudiated and which must now be read as central to the totalising enterprise of modernity. Furthermore, such philosophical writings are, I argue, also actually perpetuating the gendered struggle for authority under new, secular guise. Those who seek for justice must become aware of the ways in which the language of the mystical has been appropriated by philosophers and theologians, whose discourses of power work, often unwittingly, against women and oppressed groups; and we must reclaim the dangerous memories of mystical writers, especially women, which enable our discourses of resistance.

My first thanks go to Ann Peart, who has partnered me and this book in many ways throughout its writing. She has read and commented on every chapter, many of them several times, and has literally 'heard me into speech'. For being herself, for our shared struggle for justice and truth, for all her practical and intellectual help, this book is dedicated to her with much love and gratitude. Our grandbaby Elizabeth, and her mom Jill Arthur, have cheered our lives and made inescapable the effort for a more just future. The Women in Theology group of which we are a part has been a source of strength, as has been the St Hilda Community and the informal group of women who meet together at Websters in Womenspace. For helping to birth my feminist consciousness I owe a great debt to Janet Morley. Ann Clarke has been an insightful counsellor and friend. The members of the

Canadian Royal Commission, as well as our support staff, had more to do with this book than they are ever likely to know; and I am grateful for the experience of four years of thinking and working together. One of the special delights of frequent trips to Canada was reconnection with my cousins Gloria and Vern Neufeld-Redekop: some of the preliminary thinking around issues of mysticism and gender was first presented to a group of people who met in their home, developed in Bev Harrison's study at Union Theological Seminary, and presented again to a group of people taught by Carol MacCormack at Bryn Mawr: my thanks to all of them. Stewart Sutherland first encouraged me to make a serious academic study of mystical writers, even though that was an unusal thing for a professional philosopher of religion to do: Keith Ward later affirmed me in that study. Deborah Padfield read and typed early drafts of some of the chapters, and has been a friend throughout, as have Richard and Doreen Padfield and Beth. Jeremy Carrette made perceptive comments on a first draft of the book: it was he who first suggested the phrase 'technologies of patriarchy' to describe what happened in the changing social constructions of mysticism in western thought. For comments on particular passages, and for helpful guidance, friendship, bright ideas, loans of books and articles, and saving me from many mistakes, I wish to thank Peter Byrne, Brenda Gillon, Graham Gould, Mary Elisabeth Moore, Susan Hardman-Moore, Anna Claire Mulder (for helping me see that 'a resentful woman is divine'), Patrick Sherry, Terry Tastard, Mark Wynne and Theo Zweerman. Many audiences, academic and non-academic, have heard sections of some of these chapters; their questions and comments have helped to shape the final result. As always, I owe a particular debt to my students. Alex Wright and two anonymous readers from Cambridge University Press made perceptive and affirmative comments for which I am grateful.

Earlier drafts of sections of some of the chapters have been published elsewhere: in particular, material from chapters 1 and 9 in *Hypatia* (Autumn 1994); chapter 4 section 3 in *Eckhart Review* (Spring 1994); material from chapter 8 in *Religious Studies* 1989 and 1990; material from chapter 3 in *King's Theological Review* (1988) and from chapter 9 in the same journal (1990).

CHAPTER I

Feminists, philosophers and mystics

> The important questions to be asked by theology ... are:
> who should do theology, and where, and in whose interest,
> and for whom? (Metz 1980: 58)

What is mysticism? Is it an experience of direct communion with
God? Or is it a human phenomenon, at its best benign piety and
at its worst muddle-headed fanaticism claiming divine authority
for intolerant behaviour? Is mysticism something shared by all
world religions, which could serve as a link between different
ways of life and belief? Or is the idea of a mystical core of religion
misguided – perhaps yet another of the totalising discourses of
modernity? What does mysticism have to do with justice? Is
mystical experience private and subjective, or does it have
political and social implications? Is mysticism related to gender,
perhaps especially available to women? Or is feminist mysticism
impossible; is mysticism essentially patriarchal?

Implicit in all of these questions is an agenda of power. The
fascination of the subject of mysticism is not, I suggest, simply a
fascination with intense psychological experiences for their own
sake, but rather because the answers to each of these questions
are also ways of defining or delimiting authority. The connection
of questions of power to questions of mysticism is obvious as soon
as one stops to think of it: a person who was acknowledged to
have direct access to God would be in a position to challenge any
form of authority, whether doctrinal or political, which she saw as
incompatible with the divine will. It is obvious, too, that if
defining mysticism is a way of defining power, whether institutional or individual, then the question of who counts as a mystic is

of immediate importance. From the early days of the Christian church, struggles for authority were prominent; and throughout the medieval period, the struggles increased. It was crucial to the ecclesiastical establishment that those who claimed knowledge of the mysteries of God should be contained within the structures of the church, since the power of the church would be severely threatened if it should be acknowledged that access to divine authority was possible outside its confines.

In modern times, the issues of power in relation to mysticism have shifted less than we might think. If, for instance, mystical experience (or religious experience more generally) were to be trusted, this would provide an authoritative basis for knowledge of the existence and nature of God: if this were to be established and acknowledged, it would accord enormous authority to those whose experience was deemed to be veridical. Or, from another perspective, if mystical experience could be delimited as private and subjective, this would be a way of ensuring that it did not have to be taken into account by those making social and political decisions: religion could be kept out of politics. If mystical experience were seen as gender-related, especially available to women, and at the same time also as private and subjective, then this could be used to reinforce stereotypes of women as the spiritual nurturers of humanity while keeping both women and spirituality firmly domesticated.

It is a commonplace of postmodern philosophy that knowledge and power are interconnected, and that an investigation of what is allowed to count as knowledge can never be far removed from an investigation of power relations. It is a commonplace of feminist thinking that any investigation of power relations soon reveals issues of gender. Putting these two commonplaces together, it becomes reasonable to suppose that answers to questions of what mysticism is and of who counts as a mystic, though they will not be constant, will always reveal interconnected struggles of power and gender. They will, in other words, turn out not to have the neutrality and objectivity about them which modern philosophical discussion of them regularly assumes.

In this book I wish to explore the connection of power and gender in the definition of mysticism by investigating a series of situations in which the struggle over who should count as a mystic is apparent. Apart from its intrinsic interest, this exploration has two aspects. First, it is intended to undermine certain modern philosophical assumptions about mysticism, which I will outline in a moment. Secondly, it is meant as a contribution to the feminist project of deconstructing patriarchal paradigms of power while celebrating the lives of women of spirit who carried forward alternative visions, often at great cost to themselves.

Both of these aspects are necessary, as I will show in more detail below. Contemporary philosophers are seduced by a particular picture of mysticism, inherited largely from William James, which involves them in a stately dance of claims and counterclaims about experience and interpretation, language and ineffability, credulity and doubt. The movements of this dance are by now well defined; but what is hardly ever noticed is how little resemblance they bear to the things which preoccupied the medieval men and women whom they themselves would consider to be paradigm mystics. Nor is it at all usual for modern philosophers discussing mysticism to pay close attention to the issues of power, let alone gender, which I suggest are essential to adequate analysis.

Whereas philosophers of religion have paid a great deal of attention to mysticism (albeit in my view to a conception of it which owes more to modern philosophical ideas than to classical mystics of the Christian tradition) feminists have hardly paid attention to it at all. There have been important studies of gender-related issues such as food and fasting among medieval women mystics (Bynum 1987a), and also of individual women mystics (Jantzen 1987; Newman 1987), which I shall draw upon in the chapters which follow. There has also been considerable interest in specifically women's spirituality, whether as part of the Christian tradition or as pagan or goddess spirituality (Conn 1986; Fischer 1988; Plaskow and Christ 1989; Spretnak 1982). But there has been virtually no attention paid to the way in which the delimiting of mysticism through the centuries was crucial to maintaining male hierarchical control in church and society, let alone to the ways in which issues of power and gender are intertwined in contemporary philosophical discussions of mysticism. Clearly, feminists have much to gain from pondering the ingredients which have gone into the construction of mysticism, both historically and in the current philosophical agenda.

In the remainder of this chapter I shall first discuss in more detail some current philosophical perspectives on mysticism, clarifying and substantiating the claims I have just made regarding the misguidedness of much philosophical preoccupation with mysticism. I shall then turn to a brief consideration of postmodern philosophy, particularly that of Foucault, who offers useful tools for examining issues of power and gender, and a model for the deconstruction of the notion of mysticism. However, I shall also point out some of the limitations of Foucault from a feminist perspective, and conclude the chapter with a discussion of the feminist philosophical methodology that will be used in the remaining chapters.

I THE PHILOSOPHICAL PICTURE

Contemporary philosophers of religion have a clear idea that mystical experiences are private, subjective, intense psychological states. Whatever else is open to question about mysticism, this, at least, is assumed. This is true in spite of the fact that it is a commonplace among contemporary writers on mysticism that the word is notoriously difficult to define.

For example, Nelson Pike in his *Mystic Union* (1992) concentrates wholly on the variety of intense psychological states which he believes certain mystics have described as union with God. Pike takes seriously the need to look at primary sources, and spends time trying to analyse the various stages of mystical development as presented by Teresa of Avila, which he then uses as a basis for his philosophical discussion about the relationship between experience and interpretation in mystical experiences. However, since he has already assumed that what is of fundamental importance is the experiential psychological states of the mystic, his whole account is focused upon those states and their similarities and differences. He never asks whether this is the right focus, or whether it might seriously distort what the mystic herself considered to be essential.

At one point, to be sure, Pike comes very close to seeing that his concern is not the concern of the people whom he is discussing. In his Preface, he asks, 'What, then, do we find when we turn to the primary literature?' and in response he says,

Comments about the states of union are often embedded in contexts in which mystics are less concerned to describe features of mystical phenomena than to extol the majesty of God, decry the sinful states of the soul, warn against the dangers of deception, etc. (1992: xii)

Exactly so; we shall see ample evidence of this in the chapters that follow. But instead of taking this as a warning that the project of philosophical analysis of mysticism strictly in terms of psychological states might be misguided, Pike simply takes it as adding to the difficulty which a philosopher who discusses mysticism must face. The central question which he sets himself is, 'What is it to experience union with God?' And he immediately adds the following gloss: 'More precisely, what are the experiential or phenomenological features of the various experiences traditionally included in the union class?' (x). Union with God is simply *assumed* to be a subjective psychological state. Accordingly, there is no consideration of moral issues, for example, let alone of the social and political context in which certain people were allowed to count as mystics while others were not. It is as if Teresa of Avila, as well as Jan van Ruusbroec and Eckhart and other mystics whom he discusses, could have 'experiences of God' that could be known and identified as such without any reference to the ecclesiastical and social climate in which they were living, and can usefully be analysed by a modern philosopher of religion strictly in terms of the psychological phenomena involved.

Similarly, Bernard McGinn, in a long theoretical appendix to his *Foundations of Mysticism* (1991) cites a variety of writers, among them Dean Inge (1925), Cuthbert Butler (1967) and Louis Dupré (1987) all of whom deplore the lack of precision and consequent misuse of the term. Nevertheless, McGinn proceeds to outline major philosophical, theological and psychological approaches to mysticism since the beginning of the nineteenth century. It soon becomes clear that although he too would wish for a more precise and consistent usage of the word, McGinn, like most of the authors he considers, from Ritschl (1887) to Von Balthasar (1982) and from William James (1960) to Philip Almond (1982) sees mysticism essentially in terms of intense, private, subjective experiences, and that it is these experiences whose significance must be studied if we are to grasp the meaning and value of mysticism. Indeed, what is striking is that although the evaluations of mysticism among the writers he cites range from complete dismissal and contempt to enthusiastic endorsement, there is virtual agreement that what they are talking about is an intense psychological state, whether described as direct experience of the presence of God, or as visions, locutions or other extraordinary phenomena. It is this direct experience upon which McGinn himself chooses to focus, even though he recognises the problematic nature of the terms he uses. As he puts it,

Rather than trying to define mysticism (any simple definition of such a complex and controversial phenomenon seems utopian), I prefer to give a sense of how I understand the term by discussing it under three headings: mysticism as a part or element of religion; mysticism as a process or way of life; and mysticism as an attempt to express a direct consciousness of the presence of God. (xv)

It is clear, however, that the third of these three headings must be the decisive one. Without the idea of a 'direct consciousness of the presence of God' McGinn would hardly consider any process or way of life or element of religion as mystical. It is the implicit incorporation of that direct consciousness, and hence a psychological state, into the other headings that makes it appropriate to consider them as aspects of what may be meant by mysticism.

This assumption of its subjective and psychological nature is a regular occurrence in the current philosophical discussion of mysticism. John Hick, in *An Interpretation of Religion* (1989: 165) discusses the question of whether the mystical experiences of adherents of various world religions are at their core the same: he does not question the basic understanding of mysticism as centrally involving a subjective state of consciousness, usually brief in duration, and quite different from ordinary consciousness. Similarly Michael Stoeber, in his interesting search for a mystical theodicy, characterises an 'authentic' mystic as one who 'grants the experiences extraordinary status as a central premise of his or her life' (1992b: 80). Again, most of the contributors to Steven Katz's new volume on *Mysticism and Language* (1992) assume that mystical experience is an intense subjective state: the discussion is not about that, but about the extent to which such a state is expressible in language. These recent authors are only following a long line of writers, among them Anthony O'Hear (1984), J. L. Mackie (1982) and Richard Swinburne (1979) who, ever since William James, have seen mystical experience as essentially involving the four characteristics of ineffability, noetic quality, transiency and passivity (James 1960: 367), even while fundamentally disagreeing with one another about the significance of such experiences.

I have argued elsewhere that this characterisation of mysticism bears little resemblance to what was considered important by those who are taken as the paradigm mystics of the Christian tradition: people like Bernard of Clairvaux, Eckhart, Julian of Norwich and John of the Cross (Jantzen 1989; 1990). It is relatively easy to show that as Nelson Pike suspects, the preoccupation of modern philosophers with the alleged intense psychological states of consciousness is a serious distortion of what the mystics themselves desired or held important. And a little further investigation reveals that much of the modern construction of mysticism derives from an attempt to circumvent Kantian strictures on epistemology, strictures whose effect would be to render veridical religious experience impossible.

Kant's understanding of rationality and his theory of knowledge stands at the summit of what can be termed the Enlightenment project. In his view, human knowledge can never extend to knowledge of things as they are in themselves; the best we can hope for is accurate knowledge of things as they appear to us. Knowledge of ultimate reality, including knowledge of God, must therefore remain forever beyond human capability: we can never circumvent the categories of our perception which entail that any human experience will be seen strictly in their terms. The price of the Enlightenment project of making the human subject the centre and foundation of all knowledge is that knowledge of transcendent reality is forever foreclosed.

Postmodern theorists have taken this centrality of the rational subject as one of the most objectionable aspects of modernity; and much has been written about 'the death of the subject'. Whether this is to be welcomed or not is another question: feminists in particular have reason to be wary of announcements of the 'death of autonomous man' in a world in which autonomous women have hardly had a chance to be born (Braidotti 1991; Flax 1990b). I hope to return to that discussion on another occasion; for the moment, what is significant is that contemporary Anglo-American philosophers of religion remain largely untouched by postmodern concerns, and conduct their discussion of mysticism, wittingly or not, under the long shadow of Kant. Central to their definition of mysticism, therefore, is the work of Schleiermacher and William James, who tried to retrieve religious and mystical experience from Kantian strictures by seeing such experiences as unique, intense, subjective states of consciousness occurring 'on the verges of the mind' (James 1960: 406), different from normal consciousness and thus escaping Kant's critical theory. Not all modern philosophers acknowledge their indebtedness to Schleiermacher and James; but it is clear that without their emphasis on the subjectivity of religious experience generally and mystical experience in particular, contemporary discussion would be very different. I will return to these points in chapter 8.

The classical mystics of the Christian tradition had not read Kant, and their preoccupations were quite different from what one might think if one read only modern philosophical discussion of mysticism. Even when mystics did speak of experience, what they were focusing on was something much broader and more nuanced than is captured by the characteristics given by James and accepted by subsequent philosophers. Moreover, they cannot all be piled into one monolithic heap, as though their experiences and concerns were all very much alike. As I shall show, even the idea of who should count as a mystic and what should be seen as genuine spirituality changed greatly within western Christianity. Furthermore, the evolving understanding of the mystical was inextricably linked with evolving gender relations; and in this as in so much else, men in power made the rules, often in ways that would increase their own authority at the expense of women. In fact, as we shall see, female mystics were much more concerned with visions and locutions and intense experiences than were most male mystics. Indeed, the disparagement of intense experiences on the part of these men can be read as an attempt to discredit the women visionaries and the authority they claimed. Ironically, post-Kantian characterisations of mysticism are more accurate to female than to male mystics; though the reasons for this are far from congenial either to contemporary feminists or to the female mystics in question.

Modern philosophers, concerned with the issues of rationality and epistemology which are central to the Enlightenment project, and considering mysticism in terms of intense experiences, are deeply concerned with questions of truth and evidence. Should accounts of mystical experiences be believed? Do they count as evidence for the existence of God? Can mystical experience be put into words? To what extent is a mystical experience determined by the social and cultural context of the mystic, and to what extent does it transcend it? Could there be a mystical core of religion – an inward, personal experience that people in all religions have in common, though it is then overlaid with culture-specific beliefs and practices (Katz 1978)?

When we put these philosophical concerns side by side with the writings of the mystics, one of the most glaring first impressions is that they have very little to do with one another. The concerns which the mystics addressed are not the questions which contemporary philosophers are asking. The mystics of the western Christian tradition lived in a thought world where God's existence was taken for granted. For the most part, the fact that there were religions other than Christianity was either ignored, or, as in the case of Muslims and Jews, increasingly seen as threatening. Although many mystical writers were deeply interested in language and its uses, their interest bears little resemblance to modern philosophical concerns about the alleged ineffability of mystical experience, and has far more to do with exploring resources of language to convey what they wanted to express about the rich diversity of God. All these themes deserve full exploration, some of which will occur in the following chapters, while others must wait for another occasion. The point is that it is plain that the preoccupations of most modern philosophical interpreters of mysticism were not the preoccupations of the mystics themselves; and often the philosophers do not even seem to notice. Standard approaches to mystical writings and to the lives of the mystics have imposed on them categories which fit into the systems of modern philosophical thinking, but removed them from the concerns of justice and liberation.

Sometimes it is even argued that such concerns could not properly belong to the mystics. Spirituality, it is held, is private. It has to do with the inner, subjective relation of the soul to God. Social justice, by contrast, is necessarily public, seeking to bring about at political and structural levels conditions which will foster the dignity of each individual and the welfare of the community. The spiritual and the social are therefore opposites: concentration on one means to that extent letting go of the other. Thus it is argued by John Passmore (1970), for example, that Christian mysticism is fundamentally at odds with humanitarian ethics. The goal of Christian spirituality, in his view, is to love God with one's whole being. This means that insofar as human beings are to be loved and their welfare sought, they are to be loved only for God's sake rather than for their own intrinsic worth. Above all, seeking their good must never be allowed to become a distraction from the higher occupation of the loving contemplation of God.

Passmore points out that in the history of Christian spirituality, the biblical story of Mary and Martha was endlessly retold: Martha was the type of active Christian full of humanitarian concern, while Mary cultivated her inward spirit in attentiveness to God. Although in the Bible Martha is not portrayed as doing anything wrong, her choice is definitely at a lower spiritual level than the purely contemplative lifestyle of Mary, who was not 'cumbered about with much serving'. Passmore suggests that in the mystics' emphasis on detachment from all else to devote themselves solely to the love of God, there is a fundamental spiritual egotism which precludes real care for others. In the end, in Passmore's view one must choose between the first and the second of the great commandments: the love of God and the love of neighbour are finally incompatible.

Though the point is not often argued as explicitly as Passmore does, philosophical writing on mysticism usually accepts his contention that spirituality concerns itself with the love of God, and that this love is a personal, private, subjective state. Even if many would not go as far as he does and argue that it is strictly incompatible with energetic efforts for social justice, they would assume that this is not what it is primarily about; or, at the very least, that it is not the direction that philosophers who are examining mysticism should go in order to understand it. When philosophers discuss the evidential value of mystical experience, or the question of its ineffability, they are discussing subjective psychological states, and are assuming that this is what mysticism is about, at least insofar as it is philosophically interesting (Franks Davis 1989; Yandell 1993).

Given that feminists deplore a division between the personal and the political, and are justly suspicious of any philosophical discussion which purports to be neutral with regard to issues of justice, it is obvious that there will be a fundamental difference between this philosophical outlook and the view of feminists regarding what is important about mysticism. Furthermore, as soon as we turn to the mystics themselves, we can see a great variety of emphases. While their lives and teachings are far from being unambiguously congenial to feminists, nevertheless domesticating them by Procrustean philosophical assumptions does violence to them and to their complexity. Moreover, by silencing their voices a whole tradition of challenge to the values of power and competition, the hallmarks of patriarchy, has been made unavailable to women. If philosophers in their interpretation of mysticism are regularly missing or ignoring what mystics are actually saying, it is time for feminists to ask what is going on, and why. How is it that people who are normally exceptionally careful thinkers and scholars are, in this one area, failing to study the primary sources before making pronouncements upon their nature? From a feminist perspective, suspicion is bound to arise because of the centuries of philosophical and theological patriarchy to which we have been subjected. It is time to look and see whether some other interpretation of Christian mysticism is required, which arises out of a perspective other than theological patriarchy, with all the sexism, racism and homophobia with which that patriarchal interpretation is implicated.

II A GENEALOGY OF MYSTICISM

What I am suggesting (and the evidence for the suggestion lies in the succeeding chapters) is that the idea of 'mysticism' is a social construction, and that it has been constructed in different ways at different times. Although for reasons which will emerge in later chapters medieval mystics and ecclesiastics did not work with a concept of 'mysticism', they did have strong views about who should count as a mystic, views which changed over the course of time. Furthermore, those changes were linked to changes in patterns of authority and gender relations, as we shall see. The current philosophical construction of mysticism is therefore only one in a series of social constructions of mysticism; and, like the others, is implicitly bound up with issues of authority and gender.

The idea of the social construction of reality was first popularised for English readers in a book of that title by Peter Berger and Thomas Luckmann published in 1966. Put simply, the claim that a certain aspect of reality – in this case mysticism – is socially constructed is the claim that the social context of the people who determine what shall count as mysticism is intertwined with the definition they give. Knowledge is not 'raw' or 'pure', but reflects the interests of the knower. Since those who have had the power to define who counts as a mystic have usually been privileged males, often with high standing within the ecclesiastical hierarchy, it is inevitable that the ideas of mysticism reflect that perspective. Furthermore, those who had the power to define knowledge have not remained the same: in the medieval era powerful monks and abbots gave way to bishops; gradually the authority of the church gave way to the authority of kings and secular princes; in modern society philosophers and theologians in universities are characterised as 'the ones who know'. In accordance with the concept of the social construction of reality, it would follow that the idea of who counts as a mystic would therefore have gone through alterations that would not be unrelated to these changes in power and authority. Since feminists are all too aware of the multiple

ways in which women have been oppressed, a feminist deconstruction of these changes in the understanding of mysticism and
spirituality can have the dual function of exposing the patriarchal
definitions for what they are, and at the same time reviving the
'dangerous memory' of those women and men whose lives and
writings had to be kept within bounds lest they be a threat to the
interests of those in power.

This idea has been taken much further by postmodernist
philosophers, particularly Michel Foucault, in what he has called
an 'archaeology' and a 'genealogy' of knowledge, which he
explored in his early and his later writings respectively (1972;
1980). An archaeology of knowledge is an investigation of how
discourse, in this case discourse about mysticism, has been
produced, and how relations of power, domination and oppression have been involved in that production. Foucault believed
that any form of defined knowledge has an ideological function.
Accordingly, what counts as knowledge in any given society will
be bound up with the regimes of authority and power in that
society: the interests of power will exert a regulatory influence
over 'truth' and its production. As he described it in an interview,

I have tried ... to show that in a discourse ... there were rules of
formation for objects (which are not the rules of utilisation for words),
rules of formation for concepts (which are not the laws of syntax), rules
of formation for theories (which are neither deductive nor rhetorical
rules). These are rules put into operation through a discursive practice
at a given moment that explain why a certain thing is seen (or omitted);
why it is envisaged under such an aspect and analysed at such a level;
why such a word is employed with such a meaning and in such a
sentence. (1989: 52)

The archaeological method, however, gives a greater prominence
to strictly discursive factors than Foucault later thought appropriate. In his later work, where he used what he described as the
'genealogical method', he emphasised more fully the 'symbiotic
relationship' between discursive and non-discursive factors: in
other words, all forms of knowledge both reflect and constitute
power relations. A particular regime of power will regulate what
is to count as knowledge, but in turn that knowledge sustains and
constitutes the social reality which it describes. Foucault himself

has applied this method to great effect in several areas of study, notably to the ideas of sexuality (1978; 1985; 1986), of madness (1967) and of punishment (1977). In each case he has shown how the tactical convenience of structures of power in society has been served by changes in the concepts; and how the interests of those in authority have been upheld by these seemingly innocuous developments of thought.

Foucault believed that the idea that people freed from external coercion could produce neutral, objective 'truths' (an idea beloved of modern philosophers) is deeply misguided. In his view, 'power and knowledge directly imply one another ... there is no power relation without the correlative constitution of a field of knowledge, nor any knowledge that does not presuppose and constitute at the same time power relations' (1977: 27). Putting this in terms of the delimitation of mysticism, Foucault's point would be that there is no such thing as an abstract 'essence' of mysticism which could be discovered by a theologian pondering in her study or praying in a church. Rather, what counts as mysticism will reflect (and also help to constitute) the institutions of power in which it occurs. Put starkly, the church (and nowadays the university) will exert its power to determine who counts as a mystic, excluding from that category any who are threatening to its authority: in medieval times, this exclusion was effected by, for example, the Inquisition and the burning of heretics. But on the other hand, what counts as mysticism also in part constituted the church: the church was seen as that body which has within it those who have true access to the mysteries of God.

Taking Foucault's point seriously, it follows that it is not possible to develop a history of a concept like mysticism (or any other) in the sense of seeing how that concept progressively worked toward its ideal truth. History, rather, including histories of concepts, must be seen as a struggle between competing blocks of power as they struggle for domination. Accordingly, what is necessary from the point of view of scholarship is not to present a gradual unfolding, but rather to uncover the power struggles which were inherent in the emergence of particular concepts. Rather than the sort of 'History of Mysticism' which presents it as beginning in early Christianity, gradually developing through the first millennium, flowering in the thirteenth century and coming to its apex with, say, John of the Cross, it is necessary to investigate the ways in which shifts in who counts as a mystic were part of the ongoing struggles for power in the medieval church. This will inevitably not be a systematisation but rather a fragmentation, revealing the struggles between violent forces and undermining the assumed legitimacy of the conquerors.

Feminists have been quick to point out, however, that the analysis as Foucault presents it is in large measure gender-blind. He does not see the extent to which the structures of power and knowledge have operated unequally upon women and men. In his discussion of the prison, for example, he did not consider how the treatment of male and female prisoners differed; and in his *History of Sexuality*, though he did discuss the control of sexuality by a process of hysterisation of the female body, he did not carry the concept through to show how gender was a factor in the regulation of the body more generally. It is essential that in an analysis of the shifting relations of power in the genealogy of any concept, including the concept of mysticism, thorough regard be taken of the ways in which gender and power are interlocked.

Lois McNay, in her perceptive book *Foucault and Feminism* (1992), argues that while this gender blindness on Foucault's part is serious, it is a lacuna which can be filled in with feminist studies which employ a Foucauldian approach. A much more serious problem with his methodology, in her view, is that his account of the genealogy of knowledge is strongly one-sided. It is as though the individual upon whom it acted was purely passive, with no possibility of resistance or independence. As McNay puts it,

Despite Foucault's theoretical assertion that power is a diffuse, heterogeneous and productive phenomenon, his historical analyses tend to depict power as a centralised, monolithic force with an inexorable and repressive grip on its subjects. This negative definition of power arises, in part, from the fact that Foucault's examination of power is one-sided; power relations are only examined from the perspective of how they are installed in institutions and they are not considered from the point of view of those subject to power. (38)

When we consider this in relation to the struggles over who should count as a mystic, which we will be considering in the following chapters, such a one-sided approach is clearly inadequate. Women of spirit (and some men who supported them) were not merely passive victims of a powerful ecclesiastical hierarchy: they offered resistance, pushed back boundaries, forced reconsideration. Although to a large extent the thought and action available to them was defined by the church and society in which they lived, it is also true that their resistance and determination in turn helped to reshape that church and society. In his later works, *The Use of Pleasure* and *The Care of the Self*, Foucault moves to a greater recognition of the role that the individual plays in resistance and personal choice: McNay argues that in so doing he returns in part to the fundamental Enlightenment insistence on individual autonomy, though with crucial differences from the classical Kantian version. What is important for our purposes is to be alert to the ways in which, on the one hand, what was allowed to count as genuine mysticism was a product of the interrelated struggles of gender and power in the different contexts which we will investigate; and on the other hand the ways in which women and men of spirit forced reconsideration of the categories by which they were defined, and thereby in turn effected changes in the structures of power and gender which delimited them.

Feminists have already used similar methods in many areas, sometimes, though not always, drawing directly upon Foucault's example, but in each case showing how the interests of male power have worked to define the area of study in ways that have been oppressive to women. Much work has been done in the field of psychoanalytic theory, for example, re-evaluating Freudian conceptualisations and showing how Freudian theories, while purporting to offer an understanding of female psychology, are in fact used as a tool in the ideological oppression of women (Balmary 1982; Mitchell 1974). Feminist historians have overturned the myth that only men are important in the history of the world, while women waited upon them in the background: such a stance, it can now be seen, reveals more about the men who are writing the history than about the history itself (Kelly 1984; Kleinberg 1988). Feminist philosophers have deconstructed centuries-old 'philosophies of man' as well as philosophies of mind, language and reality, demonstrating with wit and scholarship that the omission of women results in a systemic skewing of understandings of human nature and language: it is not merely an oversight which could be rectified by adding a few paragraphs on women in a subsequent edition (Garry and Pearsall 1989; Nye 1988). In moral theory, the work of Carol Gilligan showing that many girls and women reach moral decisions in a different way than do boys and men has sparked considerable analysis of the assumptions and presuppositions of traditional (i.e. male) moral philosophy and philosophy of education (Gilligan 1982; Kittay and Meyers 1987). And in biblical studies and theology there has been distinguished work demonstrating how intertwined are the notions of a patriarchal God and the oppression of women, and how the methods of biblical study and doctrinal formulation have rested on assumptions that arise out of and reinforce white male domination, not only of women, but also of other races and cultures and of the earth itself (Ruether 1983; Schüssler Fiorenza 1983).

But in the philosophical study of mysticism, with its assumption that mystical experience is an essentially private, subjective matter which, as such, does not connect with issues of social justice, the men have had it largely their own way. Now, if this meant only that there was a small academic enclave which had not taken feminist scholarship into account, and insisted on defining and studying mysticism in male-dominated ways, that would be bad enough, though feminists might well decide that in a world of starving children, battered women and rising fascism we had more important things to do than to spend energy challenging it. But the situation is very much more serious. No social construction is the property of only one small group of people: rather, the nature of a social construction is that the definition imposed in the interests of a powerful group in society becomes constitutive of the society as a whole, as part of received knowledge. The assumption, therefore, that spirituality and social justice are separate, or, in more colloquial terms, that religion doesn't mix with politics, is one which, while it is accepted and reinforced by many philosophers of religion, is also far more wide-spread. And if, as I have already suggested, it is also deemed that women are 'naturally' more spiritual than men, then only a small step is necessary to confine both the 'feminine' and the 'spiritual' to a context in which they are rendered thoroughly ineffectual.

III A FEMINIST RESPONSE

It is important for feminists to notice that in the past decade there has been a strong resurgence of interest in mysticism and spirituality outside academia as well as inside, in the churches and in secular society. Devotional and New Age books, and volumes containing 'selected readings from the mystics' (such as Llewelyn 1980) which can be read for a few minutes at the beginning or end of the day, sell thousands of copies and help to keep religious publishers solvent. Retreat centres flourish; institutes of spirituality are set up; more and more of the writings of medieval mystics are available in modern translation; and theology and religious studies departments at universities are offering courses – often heavily subscribed – on mysticism and spirituality.

Now, I suggest that for a phenomenon as wide-spread and culturally significant as the current resurgence of attention to mysticism and spirituality, feminists have paid astonishingly little attention to it. Although there has been some fine work done on particular medieval mystics and themes arising from them (Beer 1992; Bynum 1982), we have not done much to evaluate the needs to which this resurgent interest in them bears witness, or how those needs arise and make themselves felt in a society characterised by consumerism, greed and racist and sexist violence. Nor have we asked many questions about whether or how spirituality, either in its popular manifestations or in its academic study, does much to meet those needs. Still less have we enquired whether involvement in spirituality might actually deflect attention from the real needs of people, offering palliatives to individuals rather than attending to the social causes of injustice. A feminist analysis of the social construction of mysticism has hardly begun.

If, for example, we look at some of the most widely sold books on prayer and spirituality, we find that the emphasis is on personal psychological well-being. Topics like anxiety, depression and loneliness are regularly addressed, along with such matters as suffering, bereavement and sexual desires, all of which are treated as essentially private issues for an individual to work through in her or his own way, guided by the insights offered by the author of the book. Prayer and spiritual exercises are advocated as bringing an increase of peace and tranquillity, and courage for the hard things in life. Thus for example Henri Nouwen, whose books (1979, 1981) have sold many thousands of copies, concentrates on woundedness, suffering and healing through solitude and silence, prayer and meditation. Gerard Hughes, in his enormously popular *God of Surprises* (1985), guides his readers through meditations on their own self-worth, and seeks to help people to deal with crippling guilt and enable them to make life-affirming decisions. Even Matthew Fox, in his many popular books on creation-centred spirituality (e.g. 1983; 1988), emphasises personal well-being and the blessings of sexuality and growth, but beyond assurances that this approach will be good for women and the earth, he has little specific to say about structural or political injustice or the ways in which spirituality or mysticism might have a bearing on it. Perhaps most striking of all are the writings of M. Scott Peck, especially *The Road Less Travelled* (1978) which in the *New York Times Review of Books* in August 1993, was still the top of the paperback list after 508 weeks, and has spawned shoals of study and support groups. The book begins: 'Life is difficult.' Its theme is how to meet that difficulty through personal discipline, healing, love and trust, characterised as 'spiritual growth' in 'traditional values'.

Now, it is certainly no part of a feminist agenda to minimise the importance of personal psychological well-being, healthy sexuality or creative decision-making. But several things need attention. First, the immense success of such devotional and spiritual self-help books, measured in numbers of sales, shows how urgent is the felt need for psycho-spiritual well-being, for inner resources to cope with the distresses of life. Second, while at least some of these books may indeed be helpful for the inner strengthening of people, this does not address the question of where the stresses of life originate, or whether there are unjust structures in society which generate the oppression and anxiety for which help is sought. Except insofar as the psycho-spiritual well-being of an individual has an impact on her society (and this should not be minimised) there is little indication that mysticism and spirituality have anything to do with politics and social justice. Instead, they provide a private religious way of coping with life, whatever the external circumstances.

From a feminist perspective, this is deeply worrying. To the extent that prayer and meditation and books on spirituality actually help to cope with the distresses of life that arise out of unjust social conditions, without challenging those conditions themselves, to that extent they act as a sedative which distracts attention from the need to dismantle the structures that perpetuate the misery. If books and practices of spirituality help to calm jangled nerves and release anxieties and renew courage to re-enter the world as it is, then whatever the good intention of the authors and practitioners (and these are usually not in doubt) what is actually happening is that the structures of injustice are being reinforced. The social and political policies that make for starving children, battered women and the evils of rising facism are still there unchallenged as people learn through prayer to find the tranquillity to live with corrupt political and social structures instead of channelling their distress and anger and anxiety into energy for constructive change.

In this connection it is important to pay attention to the way in which the writings of medieval Christian mystics have been domesticated for a privatised spirituality. Take almost any book of short readings from the mystics, such as those in the *Enfolded in Love* series (Llewelyn 1980ff) and it is obvious that the predominant themes are ones like love of God, trust in God, humility, submission to God's will, dependence on providence and cultivation of inner peace and tranquillity. Women who are aware of how regularly such themes of trust and humility and submission have been used to keep women 'in their place' in church and society will immediately find their suspicions raised. It is clear that while a person who uses these readings as a basis for daily meditation may well find herself calmed and encouraged, it is unlikely that they will provoke her to think hard about the social causes of her stress, let alone about the ways in which the structures of capitalist society which produce the stresses she feels also threaten the survival of our sisters and brothers in economically deprived countries, and undermine the life-sustaining capacities of the earth. As Margaret Miles has pointed out, it was one thing for people to meditate trustingly on exhortations to submit to divine providence in the fourteenth century when the plague might come at any moment and no one knew how to avoid it; it is quite another thing to take those texts as blueprints for consolation and inactivity in the late twentieth century when the very survival of the planet depends on informed and concerted effort (1988: 176).

In summary, with some notable exceptions (such as Puls 1987) books of popular spirituality treat prayer and spiritual exercises as strictly private, having to do with the relationship between the individual and the transcendent. For all their differences in style and intention from philosophical explorations of mysticism and spirituality, they share the initial assumptions of the privacy and subjectivity of religious experience, including mystical experience. By this privatisation of spirituality, the relation between it and social justice cannot be addressed. The net result, whatever the intention of the authors and compilers, is the reinforcement of the societal status quo, as intellectual and religious energy is poured into an exploration of private religiosity rather than into social and political action for change. And this in turn has the effect not only of turning the attention of those seeking deepened spirituality away from issues of justice, but also of leaving the efforts for justice to those who have abandoned concern with spirituality, seeing it as having nothing to offer in the work for structural change.

It is, however, one thing for feminists to recognise that there is considerable need for analysis of the social construction of mysticism as it is reflected both in popular spirituality and in philosophical accounts of mysticism; it is quite another to provide such an analysis. We can quite easily come to suspect that the agenda with which philosophers have studied the lives and writings of medieval mystics is not an agenda which the mystics themselves would have shared. We can recognise, as well, that one of the primary effects of the current social construction of mysticism has been to turn to its personal psychological dimensions, deflecting attention away from its political and social dynamic.

But this in itself leaves most of the work still to be done. In the first place, it is necessary to look in detail at the various agendas of philosophers involved in the study of mysticism to see what it is that they find important. If these questions are not the ones to which the classical mystics of the Christian tradition would have addressed themselves, why is it that philosophers should do so? Are there significant reasons why these concerns have become paramount? The fact that philosophers are asking questions about mysticism which the mystics themselves were not asking is not necessarily nefarious: there can be perfectly good reasons for a change of emphasis. But the fact that otherwise meticulously scholarly philosophers often do not seem even to recognise how different their concerns are from the concerns of the subjects of their study raises the suspicion that the reasons for the change of emphasis may have something to do with issues of authority and power – a suspicion which we shall find to be strengthened by investigation of the genealogy of the social construction of mysticism in the succeeding chapters.

Once we look at philosophical concerns about mysticism from this perspective, it also becomes easier to identify some areas that philosophers do *not* investigate, questions that they choose *not* to ask. Again, it is appropriate to investigate with some initial scepticism whether the lack of interest in certain areas is entirely innocent, or whether it serves ultimately oppressive ends.

One of the effects of a deconstruction of the preoccupations and avoidances of philosophers studying mysticism (reflected, as I have suggested, in popular spiritual writings) reopens the possibility of considering the lives and writings of the mystics from a different perspective, which tries to refocus on the concerns vital to the mystics themselves which have been suppressed by their would-be interpreters. Not the least of these concerns is for political and social justice, including gender justice. Yet a large dose of scepticism is necessary here as well. It is manifestly not the case that the tradition of Christian spirituality is one which uniformly nurtures wholeness and justice, let alone sexual egalitarianism! There is racism and classism, sexism and homophobia, as deep in the hearts of many of the paradigm mystics of western Christianity as it is deep in the heart of the Christian church itself. And yet, while oppression runs deep, it is also true that from within the mystical tradition, especially (but not only) from some of the women mystics, came creative and courageous efforts at pushing back the boundaries of thought and action so that liberation could be achieved. None of them were unambiguous: often we find the tensions within a single individual, as strength and integrity struggles with deeply internalised misogyny and suspicion of the body and sexuality.

It is instructive, therefore, to explore what they found to be important, and to what extent they have offered liberating perspectives and resources for working for justice, whose dangerous memories should be reclaimed, even while their oppressiveness should be exposed. This does not mean that medieval mystics should be treated simply as a mine from which we quarry resources for our own projects: they deserve more respect than that. Nor can we treat any of them, no matter how insightful, as though they were late-twentieth-century feminists, or write them off if they 'failed' to be. They were women and men of their own times and contexts, which were very different from our own; and if we wish to recover their memories it is necessary to take those contexts seriously.

As I have already indicated, and as will become clearer in the chapters that follow, the understanding of what spirituality is, and who counts as the real mystic, went through many vicissitudes before it came to its present post-Kantian construction. To trace the story, I offer a (very incomplete) series of sketches, starting with the understanding of spirituality in the early church and Christian Platonism, proceeding to the idea of the mystical meaning of scripture and some strands of 'mystical theology'. I then discuss the rise and suppression of visionary women, and the radical dissent of women and men of spirit who 'spoke truth to power'. Finally I consider the ways in which mysticism has become 'depoliticised' in modern thinking and seen in terms of private, subjective experience only, whose main characteristic is ineffability. In each case, the changing social constructions reveal differences in gender relations, the multifarious ways in which women's spirituality has been defined, controlled and dominated by men of power: the series as a whole can be read as the technologies of patriarchy. If my sketches point the direction accurately, then one conclusion is that spirituality and mystical experience have come to be acknowledged as part of *women's* religiosity in direct proportion to the perceived decline of mysticism in public and political importance.

The immediately following chapters, therefore, are intended to demonstrate my claim that the idea of mysticism and who counts as a mystic is a social construction. There is no one thing in the history of Christianity that can be defined as the 'essence' of mysticism, or 'what mysticism is really about'. The idea has gone through many changes, of which the sketches I shall present are illustrations but far from exhaustive.

If this is anywhere near correct, then most current philosophical discussion of mysticism starts from a position that bears little relation to historical accuracy. It is necessary to ignore a great deal of history if one wishes to hold, in the manner of William James and many philosophers after him, that mysticism is essentially about intense ineffable subjective experiences. This is not because mysticism is essentially about something *else*, but rather because there has been a constantly shifting social and historical construction of mysticism. Consequently, much philosophical consideration of whether or not mystical experience can indicate a mystical core of religion, say, or can provide a new way of looking at issues of theodicy or can count as evidence for the existence of God, begs the question, *which* mystical experience; and why opt for that one in the light of many other available candidates?

This leads to a further consideration. Any social construction, and in particular any *shift* in social construction, reveals power relations. In the shifting understanding of who counts as a mystic that we shall explore in the succeeding chapters, we shall observe that one of the key issues is the struggle for authority, and in particular the assertion of male ecclesiastical authority over women visionaries and any other challengers to it. But this prompts the question of what power relations *current* social constructions might contain, and who benefits from them. When current philosophers and theologians opt for a particular understanding of mysticism this is also, intentionally or not, to opt for a particular social construction of mysticism which inevitably contains and conceals issues of power and authority. In our efforts at liberatory understanding, ought we not to seek to bring these, also, to consciousness – to ask, quite simply, who benefits and who loses from the conception of mysticism (and any other theological construct) that we adopt today?

CHAPTER 2

Mystics, martyrs and honorary males

> We women, sexed according to our gender, lack a God to
> share, a word to share and to become. Defined as the
> often dark, even occult mother-substance of the word of
> men, we are in need of our *subject*, our *substantive*, our *word*,
> our *predicates*, our elementary sentence, our basic rhythm,
> our morphological identity, our generic incarnation, our
> genealogy. (Irigaray 1993: 71)

The thesis that the concept of mysticism is a social construction
runs contrary to modern assumptions of an essence of mysticism.
It is therefore useful to investigate several alternative constructions and the ways in which they changed in relation to power
and gender: to use the terms of Michel Foucault, what is required
is the development of a genealogy of mysticism. Accordingly,
what I intend to show in this and the following chapters is that the
meanings of the terms 'mysticism' and 'spirituality' have undergone major changes within early and medieval usages, and that
these changes were gender-related. Once we become clear that
even in the medieval period there has been a series of social
constructions of mysticism, we are less likely to fall into the trap of
supposing that the modern conception can be taken as anything
else.

I THE MYSTERY RELIGIONS AND THE 'MYSTICAL ONES'

For reasons that will become clear, it is useful to begin with the
term 'mysticism' and its cognates. The related ideas of 'spirit' and
'spirituality' will soon emerge in connection with them. The noun

form 'mysticism' is a fairly modern word, its first known use occurring in France in the seventeenth century, and spreading from there to other European vernaculars (de Certaux 1964). Adjectival forms like 'mystical' are far more ancient, however, as also were designations of people (and sometimes things) as 'mystics' or 'mystical ones'; and it is instructive to investigate this usage.

The word derives from ancient Greek. The mystics or mystical ones (hoι μυστικοί′) were those who had devoted themselves to the mystery religions and had been initiated into their secret rituals. The term μυστικοσ′ in turn derives from the verb μύς′, which means 'I close my eyes'. It came to refer to those who also closed their mouths, that is, those who kept silence and did not reveal the secrets of their initiation and the rituals through which the initiation was accomplished. According to Louis Bouyer *et al.*, it was not an esoteric doctrine that was secret, nor was there at this stage any question of a specialised means to religious knowledge not available to normal human perception; what was secret was simply the ritual itself which must not be divulged to the uninitiated (1981; 1968: 1, 405). How successful this was can be judged from the fact that at least for some of the mystery cults, among them the important Eleusinian religion, modern scholarship has been unable to determine with certainty what the initiation ritual actually was, even though it is known that there were a great many recruits and that the festival endured at Eleusis for centuries (Godwin 1981: 9). Scholars believe that the ceremonies of this cult, which centred on Demeter and Persephone, seem to have offered a *mystical* insight into the cycles of production and reproduction overseen by Demeter, processes that guaranteed the continuity of human existence (du Bois 1988: 55). Already we can ask: does 'mystical' here refer to ancient secret rituals, or is it used in the modern sense of a private experience or state of consciousness?

Be that as it may, even at this early stage gender was an important factor in ways that would be significant for the development of Christian mysticism. Some of the cults, among them the Eleusinian, were open to people of both sexes. Others, however, notably Mithraism, were for men only. Is it significant

that it was Mithraism which underwent a major revival in the
Roman Empire during the early centuries of Christianity, when
the shape of Christian mysticism and spirituality was in formation? The extent of the influence of Mithraism and other mystery
religions upon Christian mysticism is a subject of great scholarly
debate which I do not propose to enter (for a summary, see
McGinn 1991: 41); but it is clear that there were early precedents
for male privilege and female exclusion.

Of immeasurable importance for western religious thinking
was the very ancient linkage between the female body and the
earth. In the Eleusinian mysteries this linkage focused on
Demeter, who presented corn to humankind; but the analogy is
much older and much more pervasive than one mystery religion,
even if that religion did much to perpetuate and reinforce it.
Already in Hesiod, Gaia, created first after Chaos, is described as
'Earth the broad-breasted' who gives birth to her son and lover
'starry Ouranos' and then with him to the other inhabitants of
earth and sky. The earth is for Hesiod and his fellow Greeks the
primal maternal body, the womb from which all life springs. In
Hesiod's thinking, she is prior even to the male principle,
represented first by Ouranos, and then by Kronos and Zeus, who
are her children before becoming her consorts. However, the
identification of the fertile earth with the female body did not
mean that Hesiod thought well of actual women. Pandora, the
one from whom women came, has 'a shameless and deceitful
nature' who scatters the contents of a jar of grief and suffering
over all men (Hesiod 1973: 62–3).

> From her comes all the race of womankind,
> The deadly female race and tribe of wives
> Who live with mortal men and bring them harm . . .
>
> (42)

Although the analogy between the female body and the earth is
an ancient one, it has by no means remained static. Page du Bois,
in a fascinating study, has shown how the analogy changed with
shifts in the early Greek economy. As long as it was primarily a
gathering society, the central idea that the Greeks associated with
the earth and with women was fertility, a fertility which repro-

duced of itself without need of men. With the development of agriculture, however, women's bodies, like the earth, were increasingly seen as a field or furrow to be ploughed, and sown with the male seed. Then, as fields were gradually enclosed and privately owned, it became important that women also should be enclosed lest their fertility, the product of the male seed, should be given to some other man.

Here the field has been reduced to a furrow, and the function of the female is to receive the seeds of her husband and to nurture his crop ... The transformation of the fertile earth, the naming of the woman as a furrow, is an important reinscription of the inherited paradigm, a reduction of her potential, a mastering of her fertility. She is no longer the parthenogenetic source of all nurturance, but property, marked and bounded, ordered by cultivation. (1988: 72)

Du Bois is not arguing a causal thesis; her point is that although the analogy of the female body and the earth was persistent, the meaning of that analogy and its import for actual women's lives went through significant modifications. We will have plenty of occasion to notice further playing out of the analogy in the centuries of Christian mysticism. Whether this was also how women saw themselves is simply not known. All extant accounts (with the single exception of Sappho) were written by men, and offer male perspectives on the female body. If women did manage to see things differently, they were not able to do very much about it: how women, and the earth, were seen and treated by men went through changes over which they themselves had little control.

If these were the ways in which men thought of women, ways that were symbolised and reinforced in the celebration of the mysteries, how did men meanwhile think of themselves? The dramas of Aeschylus and Euripides have long been seen to offer an important part of the answer, one that was taken up by Pythagoras and then in different ways by Plato and Aristotle. The story is not a new one; but I suggest that its impact on the gender relationships of Christian mysticism has not been sufficiently considered.

The great Greek dramatists have as a prominent theme in their writings the movement away from earth goddesses and their fertility rites to the gods and goddesses of reason: Zeus, Athena, and the rest. This corresponds to a growing self-conception of men as rational, identified with the mind, in contrast to women who were identified with the body and the earth. Furthermore, it was this male rationality which must exert control over women and the earth, not least their fertility; the male seed was now seen as essential, the woman being merely the receptacle for it. Thus for example Aeschylus in his prologue to the *Eumenides* celebrated the succession of cults at Delphi, from the fertility cults of the earth goddess to the triumph of the gods of reason; later in the same play he develops the theme of the primacy of father-right over mother-right when Orestes has murdered his mother Clytemnestra because she had killed his father Agamemnon.

> The woman you call the mother of the child
> is not the parent, just a nurse to the seed,
> the new-sown seed that grows and swells inside her.
> The *man* is the source of life – the one who mounts.
> She, like a stranger for a stranger, keeps
> the shoot alive unless god hurts the roots.
> I give you proof that all I say is true.
> The father can father forth without a mother.
> Here she stands, our living witness. Look –

and he exhibits Athena, who came forth from the forehead of Zeus, not from the womb of a woman (1953: lines 666–74). It is a far cry from the idea of woman like the fertile field bringing forth fruit parthenogenically. Reason and the principle of life are linked together and identified with maleness; the female is associated with bodiliness, the clouding of the mind, and passivity. These linkages would have a very long run in the history of Christian spirituality.

II PLATO AND THE MALE MIND

It would at first glance seem that the effect of these changes of consciousness should have been to leave mysticism to women while men were intent on being fully rational. Such a reading would be too easy, however. In fact, as we shall see, women were increasingly excluded from spirituality, and even the meaning of the term 'mystical' gradually privileged those who had access to biblical texts and interpretations – that is, men. But that is still far ahead. It came about by the identification of spirituality with reason, and reason with maleness: in classical Greece, not only the dramatists but also the philosophers were emphasising the clarity of reason, and contrasting it with female vagueness and bodiliness (Lloyd 1984).

According to Diogenes Laertius, Pythagoras was the first person to call himself a philosopher, a lover of wisdom (Robinson 1968: 62). Writing in the sixth century BC., Pythagoras took a step whose consequences would be incalculable in western philosophy: he held that the soul and the body are different and separable, the soul being immortal, while the body is subject to corruption. 'For the sake of punishment the soul is yoked to the body and buried in it as a tomb' (quoted in Robinson 1968: 58). The soul, in its quest for wisdom and immortality (which were conceptually linked) should practise asceticism, keeping itself as much as possible from the demands of the body. Pythagoras allegedly practised what he preached.

Some say that he was satisfied with honey alone, or a bit of honeycomb or bread (he did not touch wine during the day); or, for a treat, vegetables boiled or raw. Seafood he ate but rarely ... He was never observed to relieve himself, or to have intercourse, or to be drunk. He used to avoid laughter ... (62)

This asceticism, befitting a medieval monk, was clearly associated with negative attitudes toward sexuality and women, as it would be for many centuries to come.

Being asked, once, when a man ought to approach a woman, he replied, 'When you want to lose what strength you have.' (62)

Reason, life and immortality properly belonged to the minds of men. For these to flourish, the greatest possible separation from bodiliness in general and from women in particular was enjoined.

That women also might reason and love wisdom and be immortal hardly seems to have been entertained even as a conceptual possibility. In the table of opposites which Aristotle (1941 *Met.* I.5.22) ascribed to the Pythagoreans, femaleness is associated with darkness, badness and irregularity, the opposite of maleness, clarity and goodness:

limit	unlimited
odd	even
one	plurality
right	left
male	female
resting	moving
straight	curved
light	darkness
good	bad
square	oblong

The second column is the column of chaos and formlessness, while the first is the column of order and reason.

These ideas of Pythagoras had a great impact on Plato. So also, in a different way, and possibly filtered through Pythagorean categories, did the mystery religions. Plato was of course in many ways different from their practitioners; and the true knowledge which he believed was available only by the separation of the mind from the body was not necessarily the same in content as that which the mystery religions promised. However, it is clear that while the content might be different, the method, the deliberate effort toward 'closed senses' in order that the spirit might be illuminated with wisdom, is related to the techniques of the mystery religions. When the idea that the senses are useless in the pursuit of wisdom is joined together with a Pythagorean soul–body distinction, it is only a short step to the position of Plato in which the soul is the real self and has access to true (mystical) knowledge, even while it is imprisoned in the body which distracts it by focusing its attention on things knowable by the senses.

In Plato's thinking, especially in the *Phaedo* and in the *Republic*, the body serves as a prison-house of the soul or spirit, weighing it down with its needs and desires, and preventing it from reaching the heights of the Good and the True. In the famous Myth of the Cave, it is only possible to discover true reality when the prisoner has escaped the shackles of the body (the cave) so that he is no longer misled by the dance of shadows presented to his mind by his bodily senses. The spirit is intellectual, and reaches toward true reality; the body, if not exactly evil, is certainly a hindrance which must be overcome if the spirit is to find true wisdom (1961: *Rep.* VII). In the *Phaedo* Plato describes the lover of wisdom living with one foot in the grave, already separated from the body as much as it is possible to be while in this life, and looking forward to the ultimate release of death.

The term 'mystical' was not one that Plato used, perhaps in a deliberate distancing of himself from those aspects of the mystery religions, such as their ideas of the gods and goddesses and sexual relations between them, to which he was hostile (*Rep.* II.378). Yet the life of the spirit or intellect which he describes as the true path of wisdom could, with only a little stretching of the term, be called the mystical life, the life pursuing knowledge unavailable by ordinary sensory means. And since this life was held to be the life of the *spirit*, the terms 'spiritual' and mystical' now become interchangeable, though obviously they do not yet have all the connotations that they will acquire in the history of Christian mysticism.

One of these connotations – indeed, the one that came to be part of the central meaning of mysticism – was particularly furthered by Plato. This was the idea that true (mystical) knowledge was knowledge in which the knower and the known – in later usage, God and the soul – were united. In the mystery religions, one might say that the term 'mystical' referred to the *method* in which the knowledge was obtained, namely with the mouth, the eyes and the other senses closed. In Plato, this was extended to the *quality* of that knowledge. For Plato, unlike for post-Cartesians, knowledge was not something that could be acquired by a neutral stance in which the thing known was an object to the knower, who could remain detached from it. Rather, in true knowledge the mind of the knower was united to what was known. This in turn was possible because both the knower and the known were linked together in an intelligible universe, a cosmology in which rationality applied both to the principles of the universe (in Plato, the forms or ideas) and to the mind illuminated by them (Taylor 1989: 115). Accordingly, the fundamental ideas or forms, the Good, the Beautiful and the Real, are united in the One, the fundamental intelligible principle, and can be known only by a mind fit to be united with them: in Platonic terms, 'like can only be known by like'. Hence knowledge is not the act of a neutral observer, but a moral activity in which desire for union with ultimate Reality is the motivation for divesting oneself of all lesser desires.

This is portrayed incomparably in Socrates' account in the *Symposium* where he recounts how he was led by Diotima to understand the union of the loving soul with ultimate Reality. First the soul gives up bodily procreation in the interests of the pursuit of truth, then gradually leaves behind everything of the body and eventually also all learning and institutions, 'until at last he comes to know what beauty is'.

But if it were given to man to gaze on beauty's very self – unsullied, unalloyed, and freed from the mortal taint that haunts the frailer loveliness of flesh and blood – if, I say, it were given to man to see the heavenly beauty face to face, would you call *his*, she asked me, an unenviable life, whose eyes had been opened to the vision, and who had gazed upon it in true contemplation until it had become his own forever? (1961: *Symp.* 563e)

The contemplative gaze is not the detached scrutiny of a neutral observer, but the adoration and love which unites the knower with what he knows 'until it had become his own forever', no longer separable. If this is called mystical knowledge, as it would be by later Christian Platonists, then the term 'mystical' has moved from referring only to the closing of the senses to a whole moral purification, a 'mystical path' of cleansing desire and straining toward the Ultimate. It has also moved to include the contemplative act itself, the union of the knower and the known, merging together in contemplation.

One can only speculate on what Plato would have made of all the ways in which his thoughts were used and interpreted in subsequent Christian mysticism with its development of the idea of the mystical path and the union of God and the soul. It is impossible even to read Plato in a contemporary western setting without the layers upon layers of subsequent interpretation

surrounding one's consciousness and colouring one's understanding. But my object is not to get back to the historical Plato
so much as to show something of the way in which his theory of
knowledge took forward the ideas associated with mysticism and
his influence upon its subsequent development; and that, clearly,
is incalculable.

This is not a new theme; the influence of Plato upon Christian
mysticism has been widely studied and discussed (Louth 1981;
McGinn 1991). What is much less frequently noted is the extent to
which Plato's thoughts on knowledge and its acquisition are
gender-related, and how this also was taken up into the development of Christian spirituality. What I wish to do, therefore, is to
discuss some of the ambiguities in Plato's writings in relation to
gender, ambiguities that were carried over into the Christian
mystical tradition. To a large extent the identifications of women
with the earth and men with spirit, which we have already noted
in Hesiod and the Greek dramatists, were taken for granted and
carried further by Plato. Yet in some of his writings he challenged
them, and suggested quite new possibilities for the relationships
between women and men. Although to a large extent it was his
misogynism that won the day, the tensions in Plato's thinking
were not entirely lost to subsequent developments, and eventually
joined with some of the liberating strands of early Christian
thought, as we shall see.

Much of the time, Plato took for granted that the role of
women is to bear children, while the things of the mind are
reserved for men. Thus just prior to the passage from the
Symposium cited above, he began by contrasting procreancy of the
body with 'those whose procreancy is of the spirit rather than of
the flesh' (*Symp.* 209a). Those who desire the former 'turn to a
woman as the object of their love': obviously 'those' can refer
only to men. So it is *men* who turn either toward women and
procreation or to the life of the spirit, and if they choose the
latter, women are doubly excluded. Not only is this not a choice
that is open to them, but men, as they pursue it, do so in the first
instance by homoerotic bonding. A man who wishes to procreate
'of the spirit' will find a beautiful male partner with whom he will
discuss virtue and goodness.

And so the bond between them will be more binding, and their communion even more complete, than that which comes of bringing children up, because they have created something lovelier and less mortal than human seed. (209c)

In the *Phaedrus* also it is assumed throughout that lover and beloved will both be male: women do not enter the picture. Yet in each case what is presented as the best of all is when the erotic attraction between the two men is not consummated physically, but instead the physical desire is channelled toward spiritual consummation, the union of their minds. A lover of wisdom must overcome the desires of the flesh, and in so doing can actually appropriate at the level of spirit the reproductive function which in physical terms is uniquely women's. The overcoming of the (male) flesh is of a piece with the denigration of women and the assumption that women, identified wholly with the flesh, can have no part in the rational life. As Plato says in the *Symposium*, 'who would not prefer such [spiritual] fatherhood to merely human propagation?' This appropriation of reasoning to the male sex only, and the valorisation of the offspring of male intellect above the reproductive capacity of the female, was to have a very long run in western thought, very much at the expense of women (Noble 1992).

In terms of Plato, however, this was only one part of the story, and the other part stands in tension with it. If, as he held, wisdom was a matter of the soul or intellect, and the soul was separable from the body, then what bearing could the sex of the body possibly have on the capacity of the soul? In his early writings, such as the *Phaedo*, Plato represented soul and body in straightforward opposition; in later writings, however, such as the *Phaedrus*, a good deal of the conflict that a human being endures takes place within the soul itself, as the intellectual and passionate aspects struggle for mastery (1961: *Phaed.* 253d–256b). Why could this spiritual struggle not be true for women as well as for men? In the *Phaedrus* Socrates speaks only in terms of male intellect and passion and struggle; women are not mentioned. But in Book v of the *Republic* Plato confronts the gender question head on.

The *Republic* takes the familiar Platonic form of a Socratic dialogue. Initially, Socrates shares with his listeners in the *Republic* the assumption that 'there is by nature a great difference between men and women', and that their functions in the ideal state should correspond to that difference (*Rep.* v.453b). But when he comes to consider it more closely, he finds it necessary to ask in what, exactly, the difference consists. If, for instance, the difference were of no more consequence to occupational status than, say, the difference between a bald man and a hairy man, then it would be as wrong to exclude women from governing as it would be to prohibit a bald man from making shoes. In Plato's words,

if it appears that the male and the female sex have distinct qualifications for any arts or pursuits, we shall affirm that they ought to be assigned respectively to each. But if it appears that they differ only in just this respect that the female bears and the male begets, we shall say that no proof has yet been produced that the woman differs from the man for our purposes, but we shall continue to think that our guardians and their wives ought to follow the same pursuits. (454 d–e)

Plato's masculinist bias is obvious even in his language: he speaks of 'our guardians and their wives' but never of 'our guardians and their husbands' even when the very point at issue is whether women could be guardians as well as men. And there is no doubt that Plato shared to the full the misogyny of his culture: his writings, including the *Republic*, are full of disparaging remarks about women. Speaking of the education of future citizens, for example, he said,

We will not ... allow our charges, whom we expect to be good men, being men, to play the parts of women and imitate a woman young or old wrangling with her husband, defying heaven, loudly boasting, fortunate in her own conceit, or involved in misfortune and possessed by grief and lamentation – still less a woman that is sick, in love, or in labour. (III.640d)

Rather, Athenian men were deliberately to distance themselves from what they classified as womanish: 'when in our own lives some affliction comes to us ... we plume ourselves ... on our ability to remain calm and endure in the belief that this is the conduct of a man, and [not] that of a woman' (*Rep.* x.605d–e).

It is therefore hard to be persuaded that Plato's efforts toward a more liberal view of women is anything more than an intellectual exercise. But at least he did make such an exercise, which is more than other writers of his time were willing to do; and his own logic drove him to recognise that the systematic exclusion of women was irrational, even though his subsequent writings show that he was unwilling to sustain that insight. When Plato considered the question of whether women are by nature inferior to men with respect to the attributes needed for any particular occupation, whether it be medicine, soldiering or rulership of the state, he recognises that the answer can only be, as for men, that some are and some are not: 'many women ... are better than many men in many things' (v.455d). By Plato's own principles, therefore, girls and boys should receive equal education and opportunity, and should be promoted according to the aptitude and ability they show, without reference to their sex. The roles they eventually hold in the state, up to and including the highest offices, must be filled according to the same principles; and practical measures are to be taken to assist women who bear children while they are in high office, so that they do not become discouraged. Plato concludes,

Then there is no pursuit of the administrators of the state that belongs to a woman because she is a woman or to a man because he is a man. But the natural capacities are distributed alike among both creatures, and women naturally share in all pursuits and men in all ... (*Rep.* v. 455d–e)

The argument appears to be an empirical one: if you educate girls and boys similarly, you will find that they show similar ranges of aptitude and ability; and this, rather than their sex, should be the criterion for deciding upon their subsequent career. To read Plato in this way is to make him sound like a modern liberal; and (in this passage only) there is some basis for doing so. In fact, however, Plato's reasoning goes deeper. What it ultimately relies on is his radically dualistic ontology. If the philosophical life, the life of wisdom, is a life of the soul separating itself as completely as possible from the body and its desires, then the sex of that body is as irrelevant as the quantity of its hair. In just the same way that some bald men are as capable of becoming cobblers as are some hairy men, so also some girls are as capable of becoming philosophers and guardians of the state as some boys are, if through their education the girls learn to distance themselves from the demands of the flesh as much as the boys do. The life of wisdom is the opposite of the life of bodily indulgence. Education will enable women as well as men to achieve it, since sex, after all, is a physical characteristic, not a spiritual one (Spelman 1988: 19).

Plato's logic drives him to this position; but the generalised misogyny of his writings raises doubts about whether he ever really believed it. Certainly by the time he wrote the *Laws* there is not so much as a hint at the potential equality of women and men: women, like slaves, are the private property of the class of ruling men (1961: *Laws* iv.773; Okin 1979). Given the assumption that women were much more closely identified with bodiliness and sexuality than were men, it was natural to assume that while theoretically it is possible for women as well as men to separate themselves from the flesh and devote themselves to the things of the spirit, in practice the philosophical life would be much more possible for men than for women. If it is this assumption of women's identification with the body that is operative, rather than the strict logic of Plato's dualist ontology, then women are consigned once again to their reproductive function, and to the private servicing of the men who alone can serve the public realm.

In any case, it is far from obvious that modern feminists should welcome Plato's words, even at his most liberal. While obviously equal education and employment opportunities are to be advocated, Plato builds his case on an ontology of opposition to the flesh which must surely give us pause – not least in the light of the persistent identification of women with the flesh which Plato himself accepts in much of his writing. Furthermore, the equality that Plato considered was only for the elite few. As Elisabeth Spelman (1988) has shown, the whole enterprise of Plato's ideal Republic rests squarely on the backs of a large underclass of slaves, both women and men, without which the whole project could never be possible: it is thus fundamentally inconsistent with feminist principles of justice.

But the main point that I wish to emphasise is Plato's ambiguous legacy to Christian mysticism regarding gender relations. To the extent that Christianity adopted a dualistic stance, and saw reason and the contemplation of the Good/God as a function of the spiritual in opposition to the physical, to that extent mystical union with God must be a possibility for women just as much as it is for men. On the other hand, to the extent that women are identified with procreation, the flesh and the material world, they are precisely part of what has to be overcome if spiritual progress is possible. Thus to suppose that women could be spiritual is highly problematic. At the very least, it is much more difficult for women than for men, since they have their own intrinsic nature to overcome, whereas men, being already identified with mind or spirit, have a head start. Although in many respects Platonism made an uncomfortable fit with the doctrines of early Christianity, this tension in relation to gender issues was to a large extent incorporated into ideas of Christian spirituality: we shall in due course note a variety of attempts to resolve it.

The tensions were compounded, already in Plato and throughout the subsequent tradition, by the fact that in both Greek and Latin (as in many modern European languages) 'soul' is grammatically feminine. Since, however, it is the male sex which is held capable of spiritual or intellectual activity, some peculiar convolutions of thought and expression result. An instructive example occurs in the vastly influential 'myth of the charioteer' in Plato's *Phaedrus*:

Therefore it is meet and right that the soul of the philosopher alone should recover her wings, for she, so far as may be, is ever near in memory to those things a god's nearness whereunto makes him truly god. Wherefore if a man makes right use of such means of remembrance, and ever approaches to the full vision of the perfect mysteries, he and he alone becomes truly perfect. (1961: *Phaedo* 249c–d)

There is no doubt in the passage that 'the philosopher' is male:

the whole discussion of the dialogue revolves around male homosexual partnership. Yet the soul of this male philosopher is 'she', consistently in the feminine gender throughout the dialogue, as elsewhere in Greek and Latin writings, including, of course, those of early Christianity.

To argue that this is an inconsequential accident of grammar is about as convincing as to argue the same about the English 'generic man' (Moulton 1989; Spender 1985). The central implication of the feminisation of the soul was that the soul, at least in relation to true knowledge, is a passive recipient, in the way that a woman was held to be passive and a man active, paradigmatically in sexual intercourse, but also more generally. This was set out clearly by Aristotle, who as we have seen was only schematising received wisdom when he developed his own table of dualisms in the light of that of Pythagoras, setting the female together with matter, passivity and imperfection, and the male with form, activity and perfection. Aristotle says 'the woman is as it were an impotent male'; she contributes only the material substance from her menstrual blood to generation, whereas the man contributes the form and the efficient cause; that is, the active life and soul. In his view one should think of 'the female character as being a sort of natural deficiency'.

The female is, as it were, a mutilated male, and the catamenia [i.e. female secretion] are semen, only not pure; for there is only one thing they have not in them, the principle of soul. (1912: 1.728a–737a)

It is this 'principle of soul' that is the distinguishing feature of men, which they pass on in their semen, thus causing new life to develop. Women, by contrast, are passive, and supply only the matter, not the form or soul of the developing foetus.

This idea of the active male and the passive female is obvious in Greek philosophical thinking, and generally shared even where the writers differed from one another in other respects. But it does not answer the question of *why* the soul should be considered passive, feminine, even when it was the soul of a philosopher actively seeking wisdom, and philosophy was (with the exception of Plato's brief thought experiment in the *Republic*) reserved exclusively for males. To understand that, it is necessary to understand that knowledge was thought of very differently in the ancient and medieval world than it is thought of today. As Charles Taylor has shown in his book *Sources of the Self* (1989), post-Cartesian thinking is conceptualised as an active mind grasping and holding on to items of knowledge in an instrumentalist fashion. By contrast, for Plato and (in a slightly different way) for Aristotle, knowledge occurred when a purified and unified mind was illumined, grasped by the truth. There is a sense, for them, in which the vision of the truth is not so much a gaze upon something external, as a means by which the knower is connected or united to the truth, which is the cosmic order.

Taylor does not discuss the gender implications of this for Greek or modern thinkers: indeed, for a book tracing modern self-consciousness as deeply as he does, he is astonishingly gender-blind. But it is clear that if the act of knowing is, for the Greeks, better described as being grasped or illuminated by the truth than as grasping or mastering it, then it is not surprising that, given the premise that the female is passive and the male active, the soul would be feminine in gender. And obviously this will also be congenial to subsequent Christian mystics seeking 'the vision of God': such vision can only come, after all, by the grace and gift of God, by God's act. The soul must be humble, passive, female, waiting the good pleasure of her Lord. The thought and language pattern opens up a wide space for the later development of the ideas of the soul as the bride of Christ, the theme of the mystical marriage that would assume such prominence in medieval mystical writing.

But if linguistically the soul was feminine, nevertheless it was the masculine that was valorised throughout the ancient and medieval world. As we have seen, in Greek philosophy and culture it can be said that with very few qualifications reason or the life of the spirit was the preserve of males of the ruling class. Male slaves and all women, whether slave or free, were identified with the flesh and the material world. They were at best part of the infrastructure that made the life of the spirit possible for men; and at worst they were a distraction and an obstacle to the pursuit of true wisdom.

III 'SHE WILL BE CALLED MAN'

The relationship between Greek philosophical systems and early Christianity has been the subject of countless studies. Although in many respects the new wine could not be contained in the old wineskins, nevertheless with regard both to the development of mysticism generally and to gender relations within it, Christianity assimilated a good deal from its pagan forerunners, especially Platonism. Through such Christian Platonists as Justin, Origen and Augustine, Plato's thinking, mediated by Philo and Plotinus, made a huge impact on Christian spirituality, even though there were also significant divergences. I shall explore other parts of this story in subsequent sections: here, I wish to discuss only one strand of it, namely, the ways in which very early Christian spirituality took up, modified and developed understandings of gender in relation to who counts as a mystic.

Christianity had absorbed from its Jewish heritage a large measure of misogyny. Although this was no more monolithic in Judaism and Jewish Christianity than it was in Plato and Greek thinking, and although the ingredients were somewhat different, there can be no question that in the merge between Platonism and Jewish thought, the conventional wisdom bought heavily into the assumption that women are to be identified with the flesh and with the earth, while men are to be identified with reason and spirit. Philo, for instance, who did much to bring together Jewish and Hellenistic thought, and who was formative for the development of Christian theology, wrote,

The male is more complete, more dominant than the female, closer akin to causal activity, for the female is incomplete and in subjection and belongs to the category of the passive rather than the active. So too with the two ingredients which constitute our life-principle, the rational and the irrational; the rational which belongs to mind and reason and is of the masculine gender, the irrational, the province of sense, is of the feminine. Mind belongs to a genus wholly superior to sense as man is to woman. (1981: *Laws* I.xxxvii)

Here again we see the idea that man is active while woman is passive. Heterosexual intercourse was taken to be one demonstration of that; but it is a principle which Philo extends to all areas of life.

Deeply immersed as Philo was in Platonic thinking, he distanced himself sharply from Plato's idea that homoeroticism is central to philosophical pursuits and the vision of the Good. Philo's book on the Essenes, *On the Contemplative Life*, can be read as his account of an instantiation and a corrective to Plato's ideal as presented in the *Symposium*. But whereas in the *Symposium* the path toward the vision of the Good begins with the renunciation of women and involves sexual attraction between men, in Philo's account women share in the contemplative life, and male homosexuality is roundly condemned, though in terms which make it clear that Philo's view of women is as derogatory as is Plato's. Philo complains that the *Symposium*

is occupied by common, vulgar, promiscuous love, which takes away from the soul courage, that which is the most serviceable of all virtues both in war and in peace, and which engenders in it instead the female disease, and renders men men-women, though they ought rather to be carefully trained in all the practices likely to give men valour. (1981: VII)

Plato has coupled his misogyny with male homosexuality; Philo couples his misogyny with homophobia; but misogynists they are both. Given Philo's overall perspective, the inclusion of women among the contemplatives was as anomalous as philosopher queens were for Plato; but he was driven to it by the demands of historical accuracy (the Essenes had actually included women among their number) as Plato was by the demands of logical rigor. In neither case does it seem to have done much to improve their overall attitude to women. For both of them, matter, the desires of the flesh and femaleness all needed to be overcome if the spirit was to grow.

Another aspect of the development of gender theory from Pythagoras onward through the western Christian tradition was that the human being was seen as the cosmos in miniature. As in the macrocosm there were four elements of earth, air, fire and water, so too were human beings composed of these elements. But the elements were divided unequally between the sexes: men had more of the divine elements, air and fire; women were composed more by the grosser elements of earth and water (Schiebinger 1989; Ward 1990). Obviously this theory would fit somewhat uneasily with a Platonic idea that the soul was utterly different from the body and separable from it. Nevertheless, it accorded well with the view that men participated in divinity and were capable of spirituality, while women were oriented toward procreation and the earth. The changes on this theme were rung throughout medieval Christendom: we will encounter them again, for instance, in Hildegard of Bingen in the twelfth century.

In Christianity these ideas had to be squared with the belief in the Genesis account of the creation of man from the dust of the earth and of woman from a rib taken out of the man's side, and with the story of temptation and the fall into sin. Interpretations of this story were of the first importance for the development of Christian mysticism and gender relations within it. On the whole, it did not go well for women. Already in the New Testament writings, Eve was taken as a prototype for all women and Adam for all men: these incorporations became a commonplace of Christian interpretation. A letter attributed to Paul put the matter very clearly. Speaking of women in Christian congregations, he said,

Let a woman learn in silence with all submissiveness. I permit no woman to teach or to have authority over men; she is to keep silent. For Adam was formed first, then Eve; and Adam was not deceived, but the woman was deceived and became a transgressor. Yet woman will be saved through bearing children, if she continues in faith and love and holiness, with modesty. (1 Tim. 2: 12–15)

Men might aspire to the contemplation and even the teaching of divine truth; but women should be modest and humble and seek salvation through motherhood.

Many early Christian writers took up the theme, perhaps none so (in)famously as Tertullian, who wrote an exhortation to Christian women around the year AD 202. Each woman, he says, must do unceasing penance for the sin of Eve, since Eve symbolises and incorporates all women.

Figure 1 *Creation and Fall.* Note in the upper right God creating Eve from Adam's side, while Adam watches in some surprise. In the upper left Adam names the animals. In the centre Eve speaks with the serpent.

And do you not know that you are (each) an Eve? The sentence of God on this sex of yours lives in this age: the guilt must of necessity live too. *You* are the devil's gateway: *you* are the unsealer of that (forbidden) tree: *you* are the first deserter of the divine law: *you* are she who persuaded him whom the devil was not valiant to attack. *You* destroyed so easily God's image, man. On account of *your* desert – that is, death – even the Son of God had to die. And do you think about adorning yourself . . .? (MacHaffie, 1992: 27)

Neither beautiful apparel nor high spiritual aspirations would be appropriate for the sex which was so obviously sinful itself, and the source of the corruption of men. A woman – and hence, every woman – bears the responsibility for the whole wickedness of the world.

Men, on the other hand, were identified first of all with Adam, who had been corrupted by the woman (and whose culpability was therefore nothing like so great as hers who was the temptress), but also with Christ the second Adam, the bringer of salvation. There was, therefore, an enormous differential in the self-esteem possible for men and for women. Women must hold themselves in some measure guilty, responsible for evil. Men, on the other hand, while individually sinful, could also identify themselves with the Lord of creation and the bringer of redemption. Thus it became their duty and their right to dominate women and the earth, and thereby become, with Christ, mediators of salvation. 'Women shall be saved', in spite of all her wickedness, 'by her childbearing', by subjection to men and service to men, most especially sexual and reproductive service. Appropriate identification with her husband and obedience to him would constitute spiritual progress for women, not because a woman could be spiritual in herself, but rather because in her humility and his magnanimity her husband's spirituality could to some extent cover her also. For this reason also women were enjoined to keep silence in the church, and not presume to teach. The teaching role is one that could only properly be filled by spiritual people; that is, by men.

An identification of spirituality with maleness, however, raised severe problems for the Christian church. In the first place, the Christian church never said (and never wished to say) that women could not be saved. Quite the contrary: the Jesus movement and the early Christian missionary activity arguably offered one of the most radically egalitarian stances known in the ancient world, and sought the renunciation of every form of domination, whether based on sex, race or social class. Elizabeth Schüssler Fiorenza (1983) has argued that if the teachings of Jesus had been put into practice, patriarchy would have been at an end. In the earliest years of the church, women and men were equals as apostles, co-workers and missionaries.

But increasingly those elements making for enhanced dignity and autonomy for women were suppressed in the early church, and hierarchies based on sex, race and class were reasserted. The missionary activity of Paul was given prominence not accorded to the many women missionaries, some of whom he himself had recognised as co-workers; and his letters were accorded a canonical status while writings which depict the equality of women with men were ignored or suppressed and in come cases treated as heretical. Patriarchy reasserted itself, and turned the liberating gospel which Jesus had preached into a tool for its own legitimation. It was a tragic distortion; and it has characterised Christianity ever since (Fiorenza 1983; Pagels 1982).

Yet along with these strands making for oppression, Christianity has always retained strands making for the liberation of women. The teaching and practice of Jesus had included women in a way that proved too radical and dogmatic to be ignored, even if it was minimised in the redaction of the gospels. And Paul himself, for all his anti-woman statements, had pronounced the great charter of freedom and equality: in Christ 'there is neither Jew nor Greek, there is neither slave nor free, there is neither male nor female; for you are all one in Christ Jesus' (Gal. 3.28). But subsequent writers quickly spiritualised this declaration: in *Christ* all are equal, but in the real world relationships of domination and submission are necessary if proper social structures are to be preserved. Thus some writers, claiming Pauline authority, overlaid his statement of radical egalitarianism with injunctions that slaves should obey masters and wives should submit to husbands and be silent in churches. In the case of women these injunctions, as we have seen, were regularly accompanied by exhortations concerning their sinfulness and their identification with Eve who caused Adam to sin.

Elizabeth Fiorenza has pointed out that misogynist writings and proclamations do not necessarily coincide with the actual status of women in a society. They may equally well be the outpourings of men who are threatened by the presence of women, and who wish to re-establish male superiority (1983: 53). Certainly there were from the first within Christianity strong women of spirit, women whose spirituality could neither be denied nor attributed to their male partner. Those trends which sought to develop Platonic thinking and make spirituality an exclusive domain of the men of reason had to deal with the issues of submission and domination, because there were women prominent in the early church who did not fit their ideal. On the other hand, the women themselves were also wrestling with the pronouncements of their male colleagues. It was inevitable that women would to some extent internalise the denigration of their own sex and the valorisation of masculinity, though at the same time they also provided counter-examples to it. Thus we find the beginnings of a convoluted pattern which we will have cause to trace through many variations: strong women of spirit accepting and internalising male-defined boundaries and (sometimes unconsciously) pushing hard against those very boundaries while still outwardly expressing their loyalties to them.

For those who thought to conceptualise spirituality in masculine terms, the women who kept the faith in persecution and martyrdom posed a major problem. On the one hand, the whole church celebrated their steadfastness and courage, and looked to all the martyrs, male and female, as paradigms of spirituality. Yet there was no escaping the fact that some of them were indeed women. Among these, and illustrative of the ambiguities surrounding issues of gender and spirituality, were Perpetua and Felicity.

Perpetua was a young woman of high social rank, imprisoned for her faith soon after she had given birth to a son and while she was still breast-feeding him. Felicity was her servant, heavily pregnant when she was imprisoned with Perpetua. While in prison, she too gave birth. Both Perpetua and Felicity were condemned to fight with wild animals in the public arena; and both showed extraordinary courage as they were tormented and killed. There could be no doubt of their spirituality, which was portrayed as having more depth and courage by far than that of the various men who appear in the account. Indeed, the women are shown as examples and leaders to these men, rather than as subservient to them. Perpetua's father, for example, vigorously opposes her steadfastness; her husband does not figure in the account at all; and those who do respect her position, some of whom were killed with her, look to her for encouragement and support at least as much as she looks to them (Dronke 1984: 4–16). Yet, particularly in the light of their recent experiences of childbirth, no one could forget that Perpetua and Felicity were women. Indeed, when they were first brought into the arena,

the people were horrified, beholding in the one a tender girl, in the other a woman fresh from child-birth, with milk dripping from her breasts. (Musarillo, 1972: xx)

From this point on, the narrator of the account of Perpetua's death dwells on the bodily details in a manner verging on the voyeuristic, continually reinforcing awareness of her gender in a way that is not done in accounts of male martyrdoms (Miles 1989: 61).

Perpetua and Felicity are, therefore, outstanding women of spirit even while their bodies are 'an object for the male gaze', as Margaret Miles puts it. The ambiguities are compounded, however, by the fact that Perpetua herself thinks of ideal spirituality in male terms. In her diary account of her imprisonment, she writes of a dream that she had in which she dreamed that she was already being taken to the amphitheatre and being prepared for her fight. She writes,

And to me also there came goodly young men to be my attendants and supporters. And I was stripped and was changed into a man. (Musarillo, 1972: x)

It was this sex-change which, in the dream, enabled her to be victorious in the contest; and which gave her the assurance that she would be able to stand as firm in reality as she had done in the dream. 'Becoming male' was for her linked with having the courage and spiritual integrity which she feared she might lack as a woman. As her dream images make clear, Perpetua had internalised the view that spirituality is the province of males.

Yet there could be no escaping the fact that she and Felicity, and many other women martyrs and ascetics of their era, were women. In the ongoing development of theory that identified spirituality with maleness, therefore, a resolution was sought to this anomalous situation; and Perpetua's dream image was expanded to fit many other cases. Women whose spirituality was beyond question were described as honorary males.

Perpetua had not been the first to think of spiritual integrity in masculine terms. Philo of Alexandria had spoken of spiritual growth in a way suggestive of actual gender reversal:

For progress is indeed nothing else than the giving up of the female gender by changing into the male, since the female gender is material, passive, corporeal, and sense-perceptible, while the male is active, rational, incorporeal, and more akin to mind and thought. (quoted in Costelli 1991: 32)

Philo was using maleness and femaleness as categories of superiority and inferiority, not as biologically descriptive terms: in the passage cited, the readers whom he exhorts to become male would have been biologically male already. It is a prime example of the valorisation of maleness.

Though Philo's readers would have been male already, this would not have been the case for Mary, a disciple of Jesus, in a controversy portrayed in the apocryphal Gospel of Thomas. Simon did not want Mary to stay with Jesus and the other disciples, because she was a woman. Jesus' reply to him foreshadowed centuries of male writers speaking of women's spirituality as though the women were honorary males:

Simon Peter said to them [the other disciples], 'Let Mary leave us, because women are not worthy of life.' Jesus said, 'Behold, I myself shall lead her so as to make her male, that she too may become a living spirit like you males. For every woman who makes herself male will enter the kingdom of heaven.' (Robinson, 1977: 114)

Perpetua was following a high precedent when she identified her spiritual victory with becoming a man.

From that point onward, the designation of masculinity for women of spirit was frequent. It was as though there was an assumed logical progression:

> Only males, not females, are capable of spirituality.
> This particular woman is capable of spirituality.
> Therefore this woman is (really, in spirit) male.

When the second premise could not be denied, it was found to be easier to stipulate gender change even for people who were indubitably biologically female than to challenge the idea that spirituality belonged exclusively to males.

Any number of examples can be found in early Christian writing to illustrate this usage. Augustine, in his praise of early women of spirit, wrote,

For what thing might there be more glorious than those women, whom many may wonder at sooner than they may imitate? But this chiefly the glory of him in whom they do believe and they that with holy zeal in his name contend with one another are indeed according to the inward man neither male nor female; so that even in them that are women in body the manliness of their soul hides the sex of their flesh and we may scarce think of that in their bodily condition which they suffered not to appear in their deeds. (quoted in Miles 1989: 53)

We find here the same ambiguity already noted in Plato's thinking. On the one hand, the soul is bodiless, different from the flesh, and therefore categories of sex and gender do not apply: they are 'according to the inward man neither male nor female'. Yet at the same time masculinity is honorific, whereas women and womanliness are denigrated. Thus as soon as something praiseworthy is done, these same sexless souls are immediately spoken of as 'manly'. Clearly, spirituality is thought of as a domain reserved, if not for men only, then at least only for manly spirits, whatever the sex of the body. Such a way of putting it makes the inconsistencies glaring: what is important to note is that the early writers found these inconsistencies less troubling than they would have found the alternative, which would have been to think that spirituality was not defined by masculinity but was open to women *as women*, not only as honorary men.

This was unthinkable, partly because it would have required an unlinking of all the concepts regularly associated with femaleness: passivity, bodiliness and sexuality, and, above all, inferiority. None of those concepts could possibly be allied with spirituality; so it was easier to say that a woman of spirit had transcended her womanly characteristics and had become 'manly'. Thus in the patristic writers there is a continuous shuffle between the idea that there is 'according to the inward man neither male nor female' and the insistence that women of spirit are manly souls. Masculinity is simultaneously descriptive and honorific.

An essential requirement for a woman to be designated 'manly' is that she renounce her sexuality, and indeed all the needs of the body to the greatest extent possible. Male writers emphasised even more for women than for men how severely the flesh would need to be dealt with in the interests of the spirit. For women to be considered honorary males, absolute celibacy was essential, either in chaste widowhood or, preferably, in perpetual virginity. Clement of Alexandria wrote that for the one who possessed true spiritual knowledge,

his wife ... is as a sister ... as being destined to become a sister in reality after putting off the flesh, which separates and limits the knowledge of those who are spiritual by the peculiar characteristics of the sexes. For souls themselves by themselves are equal. Souls are neither male nor female when they no longer marry or are given in marriage. And is not the woman translated into a man when she becomes equal, and manly and perfect? (quoted in Miles 1989: 66)

This passage is particularly interesting because Clement requires celibacy of men equally with women. Yet women who are celibate become unfeminine, 'and manly and perfect', whereas men who are celibate do not thereby become unmasculine, let alone female. For a man to develop in spirituality, he must become even more manly, with the manliness of Christ, transcending the demands of the flesh and living by the spirit. But for a woman to develop in spirituality, she must *put off* womanliness, work *against* the grain of her gender rather than with it. And it is important to note that to whatever extent she was able to succeed in this male-defined spiritual enterprise, to that extent she also cut herself off from the community of women, becoming 'manly' and thus *other* than women rather than continuing in solidarity with them.

The fact that women were conceptually identified with the flesh while men were identified with the spirit meant that the requirement of 'mortification' (literally, putting to death) of the flesh required even greater heroism from women than it did from men. This was especially true in regard to sexuality. As we shall see repeatedly, women were considered more lustful and sexually insatiable than men; therefore when a woman renounced all sexual expression, men were filled with awe. It was this above all that enabled a woman to become like a man, because it showed the extreme mortification of her weak and corrupt flesh. Jerome, arguably one of the most misogynist of all the patristic writers, was also most preoccupied with women's sexuality, deploring it even when it was expressed within marriage (which he referred to as 'vomit'). According to him, 'women with child offer a revolting spectacle'. Yet even then it was possible for a woman to become spiritual (that is, manly):

As long as a woman is for birth and children, she is different from man as body is from soul. But when she wishes to serve Christ more than the world, then she ceases to be a woman and will be called a man. (quoted in Salisbury 1991: 26)

Similarly, Gregory of Nyssa wrote of his sister Macrina, 'It was a woman who was the subject of our discourse, if indeed you can say "a woman", for I do not know if it is appropriate to call her by a name taken from nature when she surpassed that nature' (quoted in Miles 1989: 55). A woman became altogether manly in her heroism of the mortification of the flesh. Yet there was no confusion about her biological or bodily structure: nobody thought that a holy woman had acquired male genitals. The term 'male', again, was an honorific one, serving both to describe and to valorise actual men in contrast with actual women.

Perhaps no one in early Christianity emphasised physical and especially sexual austerity as much as did the desert-dwellers, the men (and some women) who in the third and fourth centuries made a radical break with the society around them and went to seek holiness in the deserts of Egypt and Syria. Their lives and their sayings were of incalculable influence on the subsequent development of Christian mysticism, with the result that from the beginning a dominant strand of Christianity *defined* spirituality in a manner that implied gender distinctions. The flesh, the female, was what had to be overcome if the spirit was to grow.

The sayings of the desert fathers show that they imposed stringent austerities upon themselves in relation to all their bodily functions. They fasted to the point of emaciation; they went without sleep; they denied themselves any sort of bodily comfort and vied with one another for the most heroic ascetical feats. In all of this, it is not surprising that they were also preoccupied with sexuality and sexual renunciation. In many of their sayings, women are identified with sexual temptation, with demons: the female stands for the flesh and represents the devil.

An old man dwelt in a distant desert, and he had a relative who had wanted to visit him for many years. Having made enquiries about the place where he dwelt, she arose and set out on the road to the desert; meeting a camel caravan, she penetrated into the desert with it. Now she was drawn by the devil. Having arrived at the old man's door, she made herself known by signs, saying 'I am your relation', and she stayed beside him. The old man was attacked, and he sinned with her. (Ward 1975: 43)

The story continues when a fellow hermit, solicitous for the spiritual welfare of his brother, comes to persuade him to repent: he says, 'only send the woman away from here, for this has happened through the contrivance of the enemy'. By agreeing to send her away, and by increasing his austerities, the old man 'recovered his former state', and the story ends. There is no account of what happened to the woman, and no concern for her. She is identified with the demons which must be driven out.

That identification, an ominous foreshadowing of the demonising of women during the witch hunts of a much later period, repeats itself through many of the sayings of the desert fathers.

It was said of an old man that he went down to Scetis, and that he still had a son who was quite small and did not know what a woman was. Now when he became a man, the demons showed him the forms of women, and he told his father … The old man was astonished at the way the demons in the desert had shown him the forms of women … (39)

Again, the saying does not consider any possibility regarding women other than demonic ones. Even the child's mother is obliterated.

One of the most disturbing sayings is of a young desert monk who longed for a woman he remembered, and attributed the longing to demonic temptation. Eventually the woman died.

When he heard this, he took his cloak and went to open her tomb by night; he soaked the cloak in the decomposing body. Then he returned to his cell bringing this bad smell with him, and he strove against his thoughts, saying, 'Here is the desire you are seeking – you have it – be satisfied.' (40)

As before, there is no recognition of women in their own right, no compassion for the woman who died, no sympathy for the love and longing of the monk. The woman represents sexuality, and sexual desire is stirred by the demons. Overcoming the demons means vilifying women. For the desert fathers at the beginning of the Christian mystical tradition, nothing less would do. No wonder, then, that the tradition of Christian mysticism and spirituality which flowed from them was permeated with misogyny.

No wonder, either, that women who did aspire to spirituality saw great advantages in 'becoming male' or transgressing gender roles, sometimes even cross-dressing and 'passing' as men. We have already seen how Perpetua dreamed of her victory in her anticipated struggle with the wild beasts in terms of becoming a man. Some women did more than dream. Thecla, one of the women of the early missionary movement, narrowly escaped execution for her faith. Thereafter, she cut off her hair and wore men's clothing in order to avoid recapture or rape and to enable her to travel more freely in her subsequent missionary endeavours. Many other women during the patristic period dressed like men in order to escape from the world and enter male monasteries: usually such behaviour was praised by those who wrote about them (Anson 1974).

One of the most famous of the cross-dressers was Pelagia, a woman who had been a prostitute before her conversion. To show her repentance, and perhaps also to keep herself safe, she dressed in tunic and breeches, and went to live a life of contrition in a little cell on the Mount of Olives in Jerusalem. Under the name Pelagius, she became known as a (male) monk of great holiness, until (s)he died.

Then the holy fathers came with monks from several monasteries and the door of the cell was broken in. They carried out his sacred little body as if it had been gold and silver they were carrying. When the fathers began to anoint the body with myrrh, they realised that it was a woman. They wanted to keep such a wonder hidden but they could not, because of the crowds of people thronging around, who cried out with a loud voice, 'Glory to you, Lord Jesus Christ, for you have hidden away on earth such great treasures, women as well as men.' (Ward 1987: xv)

Pelagia herself perhaps had reason to try to hide her gender; and the fathers who anointed her body certainly did, since spirituality such as hers was normally reserved for men, or at least for 'honorary men'. Yet in this case the truth emerged; and it is used by the narrator as an occasion for awe and worship: the mercy of God was so great that even a woman could become holy. The preconception of the inferiority and unspiritual nature of women is what lies behind such an attitude of awe. An occasional spiritual woman who causes people to marvel is the exception that proves the rule that spirituality is a male preserve, quite beyond the aspirations of ordinary women.

It has sometimes been suggested that cross-dressing, passing as a man or being assigned 'manly' status was a release from rigid gender stereotyping and was actually liberating for women, who no longer held themselves bound by the conventions of female dress or behaviour (Ward 1987: 63). As Peter Brown has pointed out, a young women of Christian parents in the early Christian centuries would have been expected to marry and produce children, with very little personal say in the matter. For such a woman to embrace perpetual virginity (or be dedicated to it by her parents) might be an exercise of counter-cultural freedom. Unlike other women, she would not be bound to obedience to a husband, nor would she be repeatedly pregnant and giving birth. If she entered a convent, she might also gain access to literacy and to books. If she did not enter a convent, but managed to pass as a man, her freedom of movement and opportunity would be even greater, though of course she would need to maintain unceasing vigilance against discovery. The extent to which such women were asserting their freedom in a Christian alternative to the oppressive cultural pattern should not be underestimated (Brown 1988).

However, while this was true of some women, and in one sense did serve as an alternative pattern for what women could do, it is by no means the whole story. When women whose holiness was beyond question were pronounced honorary males, or when women who were engaged in a spiritual quest tried to pass as males (and sometimes succeeded), the implicit message was that 'woman' is derogatory while 'man' is valorised. Although a few women were able to break out of the cultural expectations of marriage and child-bearing, the net result was that by doing it in this way the stereotypes became even more rigid and less susceptible to challenge. Women as a sex were looked down upon by men; and women to a large extent internalised the misogyny of their culture, increasingly reinforced by the development of Christian doctrine and practice.

By the end of the patristic era, the subordination of women and the domination of men was firmly in place in Christianity, not least in Christian spirituality. The life of the spirit required freedom from the life of the flesh; and women represented the latter. As we shall see in the next chapter, spirituality was increasingly construed as openness to the spiritual or mystical meaning of scripture. And since both the education and the leisure to study scripture were largely male prerogatives, it was a foregone conclusion that this new shift in the social construction of mysticism would, like its predecessor, carry a gender imbalance in both practical and theoretical terms.

CHAPTER 3

The mystical meaning of scripture

There are words I cannot choose again . . .
Such words have no shame in them, no diffidence
before the raging stoic grandmothers:
their glint is too shallow, like a dye
that does not permeate
the fibres of actual life . . .

(Rich 1978: 66)

Some of the earliest uses of the term 'mystical' occurred, as we have seen, in connection with the initiation rites of the mystery religions of ancient Greece. The next major usage of the term is quite a different one. Early Christian writers speak often of the 'mystical meaning of scripture', a usage that continues through medieval writings and beyond. This shift in usage, from a description of what happens in an initiation rite to a description of a certain kind of reading of a sacred text, reflects, I suggest, a vast shift in what religion was perceived to be essentially about. In this chapter I propose to explore that shift, and to show that it was closely bound up with issues of gender. It will be my contention that as spirituality became increasingly the prerogative of the male, or of exceptional women who were classified as 'honorary males' as we saw in the last chapter, so also the shift to an emphasis on the mystical meaning of scripture consolidated the male appropriation of mysticism and spirituality.

I WHAT IS RELIGION ABOUT?

Modern western religions are strongly based on sacred texts. Judaism, Christianity and Islam are so anchored in normative written words that they are known as 'religions of the book'. It is difficult for people living in cultures which have been dominated by these religions even to imagine what it would be like for there to be a religion that did not in any way base itself on a text that was claimed to be in some sense 'the word of God'. We know very well, at one level, that there are many religions native to Africa and South America and to aboriginal peoples around the world that lay no claim to any sacred text; but so sure are we of the centrality of a text to a 'developed' religion that these bookless religions are automatically classified as 'primitive' (Smart 1969).

One of the results of feminist methodology in other areas of study has been to raise suspicion about what counts as progress: it may be that the division into what counts as 'primitive' and what counts as 'developed' is not an innocent one, whether in religion or anywhere else. It is worth investigating how the division, or the 'progress' came about, and in whose interests it is to classify things in this way: once again, questions of social construction emerge. My contention is that the shift from religions based on 'primitive' ritual to religions centred on texts is a shift that made it easier for a powerful male elite to control what went on in the name of religion. When those texts, which were available to only a few, were read as having within them not only their obvious literal meaning but also a hidden, mystical meaning accessible only to the purest of that inner circle, then those who were able to penetrate that meaning were powerful indeed.

The mystery religions of ancient Greece were not centred on any sacred text. The Eleusinian mysteries in particular concerned themselves with fertility, both the fertility of the fields and the procreation of children. So engaged were they in agricultural production and human reproduction that it has been suggested that the climax of the initiation rites consisted of showing the new initiates an ear of corn. Whether this was so or not cannot be known for certain because, as we saw in the previous chapter, the experience was 'mystical', that is, it was one about which the initiates kept silence. It is clear, however, that the mystical initiation was intertwined with aspects of the fertility of the earth and of human beings.

It is not surprising that this should be so. Ancient Greek society was a society in which food shortage was an ever-present possibility. Early mortality was the norm; and a high birthrate was essential if the population was not to decline. In these circumstances, both the production of food and the reproduction of children are of an obvious and immediate importance not easily grasped in modern affluent and overpopulated societies. For religion to involve fertility rites, and to include the worship of the goddess of earth and of reproduction, is only for religion to concern itself with the things that were most crucial to its adherents.

The worship of the goddess should not be too narrowly identified with fertility rites, however. As Maarten Vermaseren has shown in his study of the idea of the goddess in Asia Minor and ancient Greece, the worship of the earth as goddess arose because of her ability to create new life, plant, animal and human. But from this the goddess comes to be seen also as mother: mother of gods, mother of animals and mother of people. She receives back into herself those who die, and thus becomes queen of the dead and of the underworld. She is the one who holds the cycle of existence together, from birth to death to birth again, the present world and the world to come (Vermaseren 1977: 9).

Mystical initiation in a religion like the Eleusinian cult, therefore, would take place within a constellation of ideas of the goddess, and therefore also with particular attitudes and behaviour toward the earth and toward women and female embodiment that would show respect for their reproductive functions. In contrast to this, the philosophical systems of classical Greece were turning away from concern with procreation to a preoccupation with rationality. The shift from interest in female bodies to interest in men's minds is crystallised in Plato: as we saw in the previous chapter, he thought that procreation of offspring of the mind was far superior to mere physical reproduction and the association with women which it entailed.

Though there are vast differences between classical Platonism and the religion of ancient Israel as portrayed in the Hebrew

Bible, I suggest that it is possible to discern traces of the same shift from a religion of veneration of the goddess to a religion of rationality based, in the case of the Hebrew peoples, on a sacred text held and controlled by men. The books of the Hebrew Bible were written after the transition was well under-way, and by men who were glad to promote it. Yet it is still possible to recognise fertility cults and the worship of the goddess, even if largely as that which was being suppressed. There were still those who baked cakes for the queen of heaven, castigate them though the prophets might (Jer. 7: 17–18). The temple still had its virgins; and the goddesses of the nations surrounding Israel were not altogether forgotten (2 Kings 23). Yet from the Hebrew Bible we learn of these only by tracing a subtext under the text of the denunciation of all this 'idolatry' and the effort to uproot such 'harlotry' from Israel. The victor is Yahweh, the one and only god who, with very few exceptions, is characterised in male terms. And as the male deity conquers, so the religion becomes increasingly a religion of words, of rationality, a religion based on a sacred text the core of which is transmitted to Moses written on tablets of stone by the finger of Yahweh himself.

Perhaps the most striking gender transformation and with it the transformation of religious consciousness in the Jewish and Christian traditions is the transformation of Wisdom to Logos (Long 1992). In the Hebrew Wisdom literature, Wisdom is portrayed as a female figure, named Hochma in Hebrew and Sophia in Greek. She is spoken of in such exalted terms that male biblical commentators have been perplexed: is she a personified (female) attribute of God? Is she actually God?

The Book of the Wisdom of Solomon presents a striking portrait of Wisdom, worth quoting at length to show her characteristics.

For in her there is a spirit that is intelligent, holy, unique, manifold, subtle, mobile, clear, unpolluted, distinct, invulnerable, loving the good, keen, irresistible, beneficent, humane, steadfast, sure, free from anxiety, all-powerful, overseeing all and penetrating through all spirits that are intelligent and pure and most subtle.
For she is the breath of the power of God, and a pure emanation of the glory of the Almighty; therefore nothing defiled gains entrance into her.

For she is reflection of eternal light, a spotless mirror of the working of
God and an image of his goodness.
Though she is but one, she can do all things; and while remaining in
herself, she renews all things; in every generation she passes into holy
souls and makes them friends of God, and prophets . . .
Against wisdom evil does not prevail . . .
She reaches mightily from one end of the earth to the other and she
orders all things well. (Wisd. 7.22–8.1)

The descriptions of Wisdom in this passage are inescapably
descriptions of God: she can do all things, renew all things, and
she orders all things well from one end of the earth to the other.
So clearly is she divine that Christian biblical commentators have
frequently taken her to be a personification of divine omniscience,
treating her female gender as an accident of Hebrew and Greek
grammar in which wisdom is in the feminine (Reese 1983).
However, as Asphodel Long points out, 'the difficulty that
commentators seem to experience derives' not so much from any
insuperable problems in the text itself but 'from their preconceived notion that the Lady Wisdom and God must *not* be
identical, so some way out of the difficulty of what the text is
actually saying has to be found' (1992: 204n4).

The Book of the Wisdom of Solomon is not the only place
where discussion of Wisdom occurs. In the book of Proverbs
Wisdom speaks of the part she played in the creation of the
world, a part that again shows her as having attributes of divinity,
and that also shows her intrinsic connection with nature.

The Lord created me at the beginning of his work,
The first of his acts of old.
Ages ago I was set up, at the first, before the beginning of the earth . . .
When he established the heavens I was there, when he drew a circle on
the face of the deep.
When he made firm the skies above, when he established the fountains
of the deep,
When he assigned to the sea its limits, so that the waters might not
transgress his command, when he marked out the foundations of the earth,
Then I was beside him, like a master workman, and I was daily his
delight,
Rejoicing before him always, rejoicing in his inhabited world . . . (Prov.
8: 22–31)

It has not escaped the notice of feminist scholars that there are striking parallels between this biblical self-description of Wisdom and the goddesses of other ancient religious traditions. Wisdom is involved with nature, with production and reproduction, with birth and death and the ordering of all things. Yet she was almost completely lost to later Jewish and Christian teaching. How did this come about?

With regard to Jewish teaching, it is important to recognise that the struggle for monotheism was linked with the struggle for the centralisation of political and religious power. During the moves toward monarchy and its consolidation, it was increasingly important to frame both religious and political loyalty in terms of a covenant between God, the king and the people of Israel. This covenant was expressed in legal and moral terms, with emphasis on the duty of obedience to the commands of Yahweh. Now, although strictly speaking Yahweh might be held to be above sexuality, in practice he was regularly conceptualised as male; and his representatives on earth, the political and religious leaders, were male as well. In such a world view, female Wisdom, like the goddesses and the Queen of Heaven, might be seen as destabilising, and would need to be suppressed or reinterpreted to fit in with monotheistic thinking.

Wisdom and immortality would now come, not from observing the rhythms of the seasons and the beauty of nature, but from Yahweh alone, providing one kept to the terms of his Covenant. The terms of the Covenant, and indeed the will of God, would be interpreted by an elite body of religious functionaries. (Condren 1989: 15)

More and more, that interpretation focused on a strict separation between God and the world. Whereas religions of the goddess had seen a close connection between her and the earth, sometimes speaking of the earth as her body, or of her giving birth to the world of nature or of rivers and trees and other aspects of the earth, now we have a doctrine of creation by *fiat*, out of nothing, by the mere pronunciation of words, without the female bodiliness of giving birth. The world is created by the divine word, not by divine coupling with a sexual partner. As Mary Condren points out, creation thus became interpreted as an act of *will* rather than as an act of fertility (1989: 16). It can thus be seen as a male act, in which the female need play no part. As such, it contributed directly to the valorisation of spirit and to its identification with maleness at the expense of femaleness and the body.

In the course of the development of Christian thinking, all of this was reinforced by the transformation of the female Wisdom or Sophia into the male Logos. One can see this happening in several passages in the New Testament, notably in the writings of Paul where the male Jesus is presented as personifying and bringing to fulfilment the attributes of Wisdom. No overt comment is made on the substitution of gender: none is necessary for the text to do its work of teaching the subordination of women to their husbands (Col. 1: 13–20; 3: 18f). Perhaps the passage which had the greatest influence of all in the transformation of Sophia into Logos is the Prologue to the fourth gospel, in which the Logos is described in terms which, but for their gender, are strongly reminiscent of the Wisdom passages of the Hebrew Bible.

In the beginning was the Word [Logos], and the Word was with God, and the Word was God. He was in the beginning with God. All things were made by him, and without him was not anything made that was made. In him was life, and the life was the light of men. The light shines in the darkness, and the darkness has not overcome it ...
To all who received him, who believed in his name, he gave power to become children of God; who were born, not of blood nor of the will of the flesh nor of the will of man, but of God.
And the Word became flesh and dwelt among us ... we have beheld his glory ... (John 1: 1–14)

The message is clear: Jesus the incarnate Logos is the Wisdom of God, now firmly male. And those who are born of God are born not of female flesh or human sexuality, but by the divine will alone. Since access to God now comes only through Christ, no further place is left for female Wisdom. Religion has become a matter of the will and the word of God.

In such a context, it is only a short step from the Word to the words, the written scriptures as revelatory of God. The Hebrew Bible was already in place; and as Christianity developed it too

Figure 2   *The Temptation of Adam and Eve*. Adam points to his head,
while Eve dallies with the devil portrayed as a man rivalling Adam
for her attention.

formulated a canon of sacred texts, and became another 'religion of the book'. This book, like the Torah, became largely the possession of men: with few exceptions, women were given neither the encouragement nor the education to study it. Whereas the study of the Torah was (and still is) incumbent upon religiously observant Jewish men, and one who devoted his life to it had a high status in his community, the same was not true of women, who were discouraged from such study. The same became true in Christianity. Even though there was no formal prohibition of women studying the Bible, and indeed evidence that in the early years of the Jesus movement women may have been equal to men as missionary teachers (Fiorenza 1983), the leisure and education for the study of scripture was unequally distributed. Furthermore, women were forbidden by the scriptures to teach. Even if they circumvented that prohibition in early Christianity, very little writing from a female hand survives in the library of 'patristic' literature. Indeed, some of that patristic literature is specifically devoted to a refutation of Gnostic ideas and practices, possibly because the Gnostics' more open attitude toward women was threatening to the increasingly male-dominated power structure of what became orthodoxy (Fiorenza 1983: 270; Pagels 1982).

Thus, gradually it came about that the Wisdom of God was seen to reside in the Bible, the words of God written, studied and interpreted by men. In spite of the fact that Jesus of Nazareth may have been illiterate, the religion that saw him as the Word of God believed that it was not in nature, and certainly not in the experiences of reproduction, but in the words of a book that the voice of God can be heard. Those words of scripture, furthermore, were held to carry an outward literal sense and an inner mystical meaning available not to the masses but only to those whose inner senses are trained to receive it: in other words, to a religious elite. That elite did not include women.

II THE MYSTICAL MEANING OF SCRIPTURE

It is clear that when words and meanings of words can come to be called mystical, an enormous change in the social construction of *religion* has come about: its central concerns have shifted radically from the time of the Eleusinian mysteries. It is also clear that the idea of what counts as *mystical* has fundamentally changed. The new meaning of what counts as 'mystical' would have a very long run in the history of western Christianity as we shall see. Though it would change again in the seventeenth and eighteenth centuries, to incorporate the privatised, psychologised sense which it carries today, the focus on scripture and interpretation remained central throughout the medieval period, and in some respects is with us still.

In this section I wish to show what was meant by the idea of the mystical meaning of scripture. This will involve discussing some shifts in hermeneutical principles from medieval to modern times, particularly in relation to spirituality. It will become apparent that interpreting scripture, and commenting on its mystical meaning, became a male prerogative. Women who felt themselves called by God to teach or write were thus obliged to have recourse to some other medium than scriptural commentary: in chapter 5 I shall discuss the significance of visions as an alternative source of authority available to women. Looking further ahead, it is already possible to discern something of how the change from medieval to modern constructions of what mysticism is came about, and how gender relations were involved in that shift.

From patristic times until the Reformation, the mystical meaning of scripture was considered to be of primary importance. There were, of course, changes of nuance and emphasis during those centuries, and men who interpreted scripture did so in varying ways (Lubac 1959; Smalley 1983). For present purposes, however, I shall draw attention not to the differences, but to the continuity of presuppositions and hermeneutical principles.

According to medieval students of the Bible, and consistent with their patristic sources, the purpose of scripture could be understood only with reference to Christ. Christ is the Logos, the Word of God who brings the good news of the love of God, and thus restores humanity to God by his incarnation. This message of Christ is received through the tradition, which goes back to the apostles who had direct contact with Jesus; and it is confirmed by the Holy Spirit in the transformation of human lives and communities. It is this which is recorded in the gospels.

From this it follows that the incarnation, understood with reference to salvation, is the fundamental hermeneutical principle. Medieval students of the scripture did not start with biblical exegesis and work towards a theology; they started with the work of Christ for humanity, and used this as the key to understanding scripture. This is an immediate consequence of the understanding that the scriptures are the *words* of God which reveal the *Word* of God, the incarnate Logos. Because Jesus the incarnate Word has shown that God's intention to humanity is an intention of love and reconciliation, and because Jesus drew on the Hebrew scriptures in his teaching to make God's ways known, it follows that Jesus is both the principle and the example of how those scriptures should be interpreted. Christ used the scriptures to show 'the things concerning himself', the way in which they found their fulfilment in him and his work of reconciliation. Accordingly the scriptures are, like Christ, the Word of God, but in a secondary sense: they are the pointer to Christ who is the Word of God in the primary sense. Hence it was held that everything in scripture (indeed, every *word*, sometimes) pointed to Christ, and to the restoration of all things to God through him. Much later, Boniface, in his *Ars Grammatica* was to express it succinctly: to understand something *is* to see it in relation to Christ (Leclercq 1978: 47).

This method of interpreting the Bible in terms of its relationship to Christ goes back at least to Origen, who drew on the practices of allegorising already prevalent with Philo and Clement of Alexandria, and who in turn exercised an influence on the Latin west through the translation of Rufinus. Origen discusses exegesis in some detail in his book *On First Principles*. Just as, in his view, a human being consists of body, soul and spirit, so also the scripture has three corresponding levels of meaning: the literal, the moral, and the mystical or spiritual (1973: IV.9). Origen considers the mystical meaning to be real and important; indeed, he takes it to be the most important of all the three senses, though often it is hidden in an obscure passage, or is something that would be a 'stumbling-block' if taken literally. On the whole, the mystical meaning of scripture is the one that shows its significance in relation to Christ. Thus, for example, Origen cites Paul's discussion of the ancient Israelites' drinking of the water from the rock which Moses struck for them, an account which Paul concludes with the statement, 'And that rock was Christ' (2 Cor. 10). This procedure, by which the apostle finds the deepest meaning of the ancient Hebrew writing fulfilled in Christ, is taken as normative.

The threefold sense of scripture is often reduced by patristic writers, including Origen himself, to a twofold distinction between the literal and the mystical. The contrast between the literal and the mystical is not a contrast between objective and subjective, but rather the contrast between the old covenant and the new, the letter and the spirit, the promise and the fulfilment. It is for this reason that the mystical meaning in patristic exegesis centres on Christ, who is seen as the fulfilment of all the promises and the bringer of the new covenant. There is also often a direct correlation between the mystical meaning of scripture in its reference to Christ, and the moral drawn for progress in spirituality. For example, Origen, in his Homily XXVII on the Hebrew book of Numbers, interprets the forty-two stopping-places of the Israelites in the wilderness first in terms of the forty-two ancestors of the incarnate Christ, but then also in terms of the steps toward perfection which a Christian soul should pursue (Origen 1979: 245–269).

In Origen this fulfilment was seen, sometimes, more in terms of the Christ-Logos than in terms of the historical Jesus; and it was partly for that reason that the church took exception to his writings (Torjesen 1986). With the Cappadocian Fathers, however, influenced as they were by the strongly incarnational Christology of Irenaeus, the mystical meaning of scripture is the meaning which interprets the passage more strictly in relation to the incarnation and its redemptive significance. A famous example is Gregory of Nyssa's *Life of Moses* (1978). Gregory first recounts for his Hellenised readers the events of Moses' life as recorded in the Hebrew scriptures, and then proceeds to explain their mystical meaning: the light of the burning bush becomes Christ the radiance of the world; the manna from heaven is the

Word, Christ, who comes down from heaven and is born of a virgin; even the rod that changed to a snake before Pharaoh is 'a figure of the mystery of the Lord's incarnation' which frees those who are bound under the tyranny of the evil one.

It has been argued that the movement from the literal to the mystical sense is not a movement away from historical reality but rather a movement to a deeper understanding of its objective significance as found in Christ, and is therefore of continuing significance to Christian exegetical practice (Louth 1983). It is obvious, however, that such a move could be made and received only by those who already agreed to the presupposition that Christ indeed *was* the central objective significance of scripture: Gregory's interpretation would have left a Jewish rabbi wholly unpersuaded. Since the quest for mystical interpretations of scripture rested upon doctrinal assumptions, they would be unlikely ever to challenge those assumptions. This is obviously so in the case of the divinity of Christ, since the whole enterprise of mystical interpretation depended on finding in the words of scripture a revelation of Jesus' divinity. But it left other assumptions unchallenged as well, including gender assumptions. Two examples from Augustine illustrate the point, the first with reference to the divinity of Christ, the second with reference to gender.

In Augustine's *Expositions on the Book of Psalms* he offers a commentary on Psalm 89: 6, which reads, in the version Augustine was commenting upon, 'For who is he among the clouds who shall be compared unto thee, Lord?' Augustine was indignant at the very thought that this should be taken in no more than its straightforward sense:

Does it appear to you, brethren, a high ground of praise, that the clouds cannot be compared to their Creator? If it is taken in its literal, not its mystical meaning, is it not so: what? are the stars that are above the clouds to be compared with the Lord? what? can the sun, moon, angels, heavens, be even compared with the Lord? (1888)

He then proceeds to elucidate the mystical meaning as he sees it, in which the clouds are compared, first, to the flesh in general, which veils the brightness of the spirit (the sun); and then to the flesh of Jesus Christ in the incarnation, which veiled the heavenly brightness of his divinity from human eyes. Anyone not already convinced of the incarnation would hardly be persuaded by Augustine's interpretation. Of course this would not worry him unduly: his purpose is not so much to persuade or convince as to draw his readers to meditation and worship.

The same is true of the second example from Augustine, this one drawn from his enormously influential treatise *On the Trinity*. Augustine is considering the meaning of the phrase 'the image of God', and in particular whether women and men are the image of God, or whether it is true only of men. The biblical text he is elucidating is 1 Corinthians 11: 7–10, which reads, in part, 'For a man indeed ought not to cover his head, forasmuch as he is the image and glory of God; but the woman is the glory of man.' Taken on its own, this text would seem to imply that the 'image of God' applies to males only. But the difficulty is that such an interpretation would seem to conflict with Genesis 1: 21–8, which Augustine also cites: 'God created man: in the image of God created he him; male and female created he them: and he blessed them.' At the literal level, Augustine resolves the conflict in a way that reinforces the inferiority of women:

the woman together with her own husband is the image of God, so that the whole substance may be one image; but when she is referred separately to her quality of *help-meet*, which regards the woman herself alone, then she is not the image of God; but as regards the man alone, he is the image of God as fully and completely as when the woman too is joined with him in one. (1888: XII.7.10)

According to this interpretation, the status of women is very different from the status of men: women can be said to image God only in conjunction with their husbands, not in themselves.

But Augustine is not content to leave the matter there. He says that it is important also to interpret the words of the apostle 'figuratively and mystically, because he was speaking of covering the head of a woman, which will remain mere empty words, unless referred to some hidden sacrament'. This deeper meaning must take into account that the image of God in man is not the shape of his body or his anatomy, but his rational mind. But if rationality is a matter of the mind, not the body, then Augustine, like Plato before him, must assert that rationality can be shared by women as well as men; and he does indeed do so: women, like men, 'are there renewed after the image of God, where there is no sex ... ' that is, in the mind. But this then leaves Augustine with a problem.

Why, then, is the man on that account not bound to cover his head, because he is the image and glory of God, while the woman is bound to do so, because she is the glory of the man; as though woman were not renewed in the spirit of her mind, which spirit is renewed to the knowledge of God after the image of him who created him? (XII.7.12)

How, in other words, is Augustine to square the idea that women, like men, have a rational (sexless) mind with his assumption that women are inferior to men? His solution reverts to bodily difference between women and men, at the crux of what he offers as the mystical meaning of this passage:

But because she differs from the man in bodily sex, it was possible rightly to represent under her bodily covering that part of the reason which is diverted to the government of temporal things; so that the image of God may remain on that side of the mind of man on which it cleaves to the beholding or the consulting of the eternal reasons for things; and this, it is clear, not men only, but also women have.

Taken strictly, Augustine could be saying that both women and men must spend some of their energy and attention on 'the government of temporal things', and both sexes can also devote themselves to 'the eternal reasons for things'. But connecting the former with the female and the latter with the male is more for Augustine than a mere manner of speaking. Augustine, and much of the Christian medieval tradition with him, really did believe that women are and ought to be taken up with 'temporal things', primarily the bearing and nurturing of children. Thus, even if theoretically women are capable of 'the beholding or the consulting of the eternal reasons of things' (and Augustine here went further than many other writers were prepared to go) in practice this is a masculine activity and left to the men while women are left to serve them and bear and nurture their children. As Augustine interprets this passage, therefore, the 'mystical meaning' of scripture reinforces the inequality of gender relations.

This is given all the more weight because, like all mystical interpretations, it is taken also as a reference to Christ. It was not Jesus' physical body that was the image of God, as though God had a physical shape or form. Rather, it was Christ the divine Word who was the 'express image of God', the Logos that, in Augustine's thinking, lies at the basis of human rationality and thought (1972: XI.xxvii.2). And this in turn is the human reflection of the divine Trinity, in memory, intelligence and will, such that adequate self-knowledge leads to the knowledge of God (1888: XIV.10.12).

What this amounts to, however, in spite of Augustine's disclaimer that women, like men, can be renewed in the spirit of their minds, is that men will be able to devote themselves to the contemplative self-knowledge necessary to discern the Trinity within, while women will be otherwise engaged. Speaking of the 'renewal of the mind in the knowledge of God' which such self-knowledge involves, Augustine says,

He, then, who is day by day renewed by making progress in the knowledge of God, and in righteousness and true holiness, transfers his love from things temporal to things eternal, from things visible to things intelligible, from things carnal to things spiritual ... (1888: XIV.17.23)

But he has made it clear that for women, attention to the temporal and visible and bodily activities of reproduction and service is their moral and religious duty. It would, therefore, actually be wrong of them to 'transfer their love' away from these things. Thus right at the heart of Augustine's major doctrinal writing, and given all the authority of mystical meaning, is the reinforcement of the view that rational men, not corporeal women, are spiritually superior.

Very little writing of any sort by women survives from the first centuries of the Christian era, and that which does, like the account of Perpetua awaiting martyrdom, are accounts of their own experiences, rather than overt doctrinal instruction, let alone biblical interpretation. However, there is one fascinating fragment of writing by a woman named Egeria, written in the late fourth century, which illustrates gender differences in contemporary approach to scripture.

Egeria was probably from a convent somewhere on the Atlantic coast of Europe, possibly Spain or Gaul. Her writing is addressed to her 'beloved sisters' and is a travel journal, only parts of which are preserved, describing to them the events of a pilgrimage she undertook to the holy places of Jerusalem and the surrounding area (Wilkinson 1981). She is steeped in scripture, and makes constant reference to it as she describes the places she visits: indeed, it is because the places are mentioned in the Bible that she chooses to go and see them. Thus while her book is an account of her own experiences, it would also be a perfect opportunity for her to engage in some biblical interpretation, had she chosen to do so.

But she never does. She remains at a determinedly factual level. Here, for example, is her account of some monks showing her the sites around Mount Sinai, proceeding from a visit to the bush from which God had spoken to Moses:

> They pointed out the place where the children of Israel had their camp during the time Moses was in the Mount ... They also showed us where holy Moses ordered them to burn the calf which Aaron had made for them; and the bed of the stream from which, as you read in Exodus, holy Moses made the children of Israel drink. And they pointed out a place where a portion of Moses' spirit was given to the seventy men, and where the children of Israel had their craving for food ... And they showed us where the manna and the quails descended on the people ... (97)

It is impossible to imagine Origen or Gregory of Nyssa or Augustine writing a passage about those places and events without launching into instruction about the spiritual meanings of the scriptural accounts of those happenings. Egeria, however, leaves such interpretation strictly alone. All she says is, 'it may help you, loving sisters, the better to picture what happened in these places when you read the holy books of Moses' (98). It is the literal level, and the literal level only, with which she concerns herself.

Did she not know about mystical interpretation? Did she not approve of it? Did she feel disqualified by her gender from

offering it? The answer to the former two questions are clearly
negative: she did know about spiritual interpretation and she
speaks of an instance of it toward the end of the fragment of her
book with apparent approval. She is telling her sisters about the
observance of Lent in Jerusalem, including the bishop's teaching.

His subject is God's Law; during the forty days he goes through the whole
Bible, beginning with Genesis, and first relating the literal meaning of
each passage, then interpreting its spiritual meaning ... After five weeks'
teaching they receive the Creed, whose content he explains article by
article in the same way as he explained the Scriptures, first literally and
then spiritually. Thus all the people in these parts are able to follow the
Scriptures when they are read in church ... (144)

It is of course impossible to prove that Egeria did not enter into
some spiritual interpretation of her own in the fragments that are
now lost to us; but from the above passage, and her complete
matter-of-factness in the descriptions of her pilgrimage, what
seems most plausible is that she considered such interpretation to
be the prerogative of the bishop. As a woman, she would not
engage in it. She was unconventional enough and courageous
enough to undertake the hazardous pilgrimage to the holy places,
but she would not trespass on episcopal privilege.

   All in all, it should come as no surprise that mystical interpretations of scripture came from the pens of men, not of women, and
usually from men privileged to live in a monastery and benefit
from its educational opportunities, while at the same time being
almost completely cut off from women. It is no wonder that there
was strong impetus to seek mystical interpretations, and little to
challenge the prevalent suspicion of sexuality or the prevalent
gender assumptions.

   The idea of the mystical meaning of scripture as the essence of
its significance was developed and refined throughout the medieval period, with the 'mystical' itself being subdivided into
further categories. Thus for example in the thirteenth century
Bonaventure explained that

the depth of scripture consists in a multiplicity of mystical interpretations.
Besides the literal sense, some passages have to be interpreted in three
different manners, namely allegorically, morally, and tropologically.
There is *allegory*, when one fact points to another, by reference to which

one should believe. There is *tropology* or *morality*, when facts make us understand rules of conduct. There is *anagogy* or elevation of the mind towards the eternal felicity of the saints. (1960: Prol. 4.1)

Different thinkers subdivided the concept in different ways; but common to the writers of the late medieval hermeneutical tradition and into the Reformation we find still the Christological focus which had been to the fore in patristic writings. Martin Luther, for example, took this up in his early *Dicta super Psalterium* of 1513–15. He distinguished between two meanings of the Old Testament, the literal–historical, and the literal–prophetic meaning, by which he meant its significance concerning Christ and the church. On this basis Luther maintained that Christ is the *sensus principalis* of scripture, the one in whom it all hangs together. This Christological hermeneutical principle ties together all the senses of scripture: the literal, and the various mystical senses – allegorical, tropological and anagogical – in the central focus on Christ (McGrath 1985: 80, 122). Much as the reformers might challenge the ideas of medieval Christianity in other ways, this Christological presupposition in the interpretation of scripture was something that they reinforced rather than challenged. Given that the linkage of the male with the rational and the female with the corporeal and reproductive were in some ways parallel to the ideas of the divine Christ and his human flesh, it is easy to see why these interpretative presuppositions were congenial, and remained largely unquestioned.

Now, taking the incarnation as the fundamental hermeneutical principle is relatively plausible for the four gospels; and these were taken as the key to all scripture. But it is far from obvious in the case of other books of the canon. How could it be said that the accounts of the kings of Israel and Judah, or the cynicism of Ecclesiastes, or the meticulous details about clean and unclean beasts in Leviticus all really refer to Christ? Yet even here it was held that the incarnation gives the clue. Just as Christ was the divine Son of God, though he became truly a man for our sakes, so also all scripture was the Word of God pointing to Christ for our redemption, though it was given in human forms. Just as the human flesh both revealed and concealed the divine Son, so the words of scripture both reveal and conceal its full meaning. The eyes of the disciples had to be opened before they could recognise Jesus as the Son of God; just so must mortals be spiritually enlightened to discern Christ in all of scripture. It was the task of the leaders of the faith to show the depth of meaning of scripture: hence the examples of Gregory of Nyssa and Augustine already quoted, and the medieval practice of 'glossing' the scripture – that is, copying interpretative comments of the fathers either in the margins or interlinearly (Evans 1984, 1985). In this way their insights were preserved: in this way, also, their opinions were accorded virtually unassailable authority.

Implicit in the whole procedure of discovering the mystical meaning of scripture is a further major hermeneutical principle, namely that of the unity of the scriptures. Because of the incarnation, the Bible can be known to be unlike any other book. It is the revelation of God's salvific intentions to humankind. Accordingly, no scripture is to be taken in isolation, but each part is to be compared to every other part, with the gospels taking pride of place, because they are the primary testimony to Christ. Medieval authors were on the whole not oblivious to the fact that the books of the Bible were composed by a variety of authors writing in diverse circumstances; and to a certain extent this was recognised to be important. But far more important than the question of what the original author 'really meant' by any given passage was what the Holy Spirit, the primary Author, 'meant'. To the extent that they did concern themselves with the human author's intentions, they might follow the Alexandrians and say that although the human writer was aware only of the historical meaning, the Holy Spirit used this to convey a mystical meaning as well, though this was not part of the author's intention. Or, less likely, they would follow the Antiochenes and say that the author was indeed aware of the mystical meaning which was divinely revealed to him, but that he deliberately veiled it in the historical meaning, just as Christ deliberately took flesh in the incarnation (Smalley 1983: 6–20). But the more fundamental issue was not the human author's intentions, but the intention of God the Spirit, and this could be discussed only on the assumption and from the point of view of the incarnation. In so far as the books of the Bible are scripture, therefore, they were held to be the unified Word of God pointing spiritually to the primary Word of God who is Christ.

The physical body of Christ was affirmed to be real and important, and so also was the literal or historical sense of scripture. Indeed, it was taken as the foundation upon which the understanding of scripture rests, without which there could be no revelation, just as there could have been no incarnation without a real human body of Christ. Some medieval exegetes like Andrew of St Victor made more of this foundation than others did, but they all agreed that it was indispensable. But they agreed also that veiled by this historical sense is the inner mystical sense, and it is this which must be discerned. Should anyone get stuck on the historical sense to the exclusion of the mystical sense, that would be equivalent to recognising the humanity of Christ only, thereby missing the central point of the incarnation.

As already noted, it is obvious that this method of interpreting the scriptures would carry with it a built-in resistance to change: how could anyone presume to challenge what Augustine or Jerome or Chrysostom had declared to be the mystical meaning of a passage? Moreover, that mystical meaning would necessarily be found to be in line with what was established doctrinal orthodoxy. Modern biblical scholars might find such an approach stifling; but, within the structure of medieval Christendom with its hierarchy of ecclesiastical authority, it does not appear to have been felt as problematic. After all, it was in their best interests to take as vitally important the faithful preservation of doctrine and the suppression of heresy. And, of course, the possibility of mystical interpretation opened the door to all manner of creative thought to the faithful, while still allowing them to stay within the bounds of established orthodoxy.

In fact, it was the possibility of this creativity that caused more anxiety to dominant theological minds than the worry that orthodoxy would be a straitjacket. There was concern that putative exegesis could degenerate into sheer fantasy, with interpreters reading whatever they liked into a text and then dignifying their speculations with the term 'mystical'. It is true that medieval theologians were willing to give a much greater scope to imagination than are modern exegetes: I shall explore this further in a moment. Yet it was also felt, particularly by those who had most at stake in preserving the authority of the church, that all needed to be kept within appropriate bounds. The hermeneutical principles already discussed obviously went a long way toward ensuring this; but some felt that more was needed. Thus for example Jean Gerson, in *De sensu literali sacrai scripturae*, and in a different way Thomas Aquinas in the prologue to his commentary on the *Sentences* of Peter Lombard (both Gerson and Aquinas being urgently concerned to defend the authority of the church against the incursions of heretics and infidels) set down some further ground rules. In the first place, they held that while the spiritual sense is the essence, the literal sense is the foundation on which it is built; and any particular mystical interpretation must be established by the literal sense of the scripture as a whole. Since that literal sense is fixed by orthodoxy and maintained by the ecclesiastical hierarchy, this criterion worked to consolidate its authority even further. And lest there should be any who should protest, the second criterion was even more explicit. No interpretation is to be thought of as a private matter: it takes place within the church and is subject to the corporate exegetical judgement of the church. Thus the whole idea of the mystical was firmly tied to authoritative doctrine, and the regulations imposed by the ecclesiastical power structure. On both counts, the voices of women were effectively silenced.

Nevertheless, there were many men among those now thought of as 'mystics' whose interpretations of scripture were not merely self-serving, and who did seriously concern themselves with the transformation that Christ would work in the lives of believers. They held that since the purpose of scripture was to lead people to Christ, its effect would be to develop in them Christ's compassion for humankind; and exegesis should foster this development. The mystical meaning of scripture was not held to be of private psychological import, but rather a call to just and loving action. Augustine's *On Christian Doctrine* has been called the Magna Carta of medieval biblical interpretation (Schneiders 1987: 14). In it he said,

Whoever ... thinks that he understands the divine scriptures or any part of them so that it does not build the double love of God and of our neighbour does not understand it at all. (1958: I.xxxvi)

For the medieval exegetical tradition, this statement was normative. If Christ is at the centre of hermeneutics, then the goal of all biblical study must be the building up of love, *caritas*, which Christ restores. The mystical meaning of scripture, therefore, has a moral and social dimension, not necessarily in the sense of implying specific rules or principles of action, but in the sense that it has an application to the reader's own relationship to Christ and to the church. Bede, for instance, is reported to have said that reading the scriptures is receiving the bread of God by which 'the Lord designates the secret meanings by which the world was to be nourished into perpetual salvation' (Ward 1987: 15).

Since God's intention to humankind is revealed in Christ to be human salvation, and since all scripture points to Christ, it follows that the aim of studying scripture must be conversion, restoration of the divine image that has been fractured by sin. It is not primarily the acquisition of information that is important, not even information about God, let alone about the historical authors and their circumstances. This is a means to an end, and that end is transformation into the love of God. Thus the mystical meaning of scripture was not held to be something that could be learned while leaving everything else as it is. It was rather the means whereby one could be soaked in the love of God, so that that divine love would permeate all thought and activity. To use terms dear to the heart of Bernard of Clairvaux, it is the encounter with the love of Christ in the words of scripture that softens hearts of stone, thus restoring to dignity and freedom individually and collectively those who receive the grace of God. Echoing this, and notwithstanding all his emphasis on the importance of the scriptures, Bonaventure says at the end of his book *The Soul's Journey into God*,

> But if you wish to know how these things come about,
>> ask grace not instruction,
>> desire not understanding,
> the groaning of prayer not diligent reading,

> the Spouse not the teacher,
> God not man,
> darkness not clarity,
> not light but fire
> that totally inflames and carries us into God.
>
> (1978: VII.6)

The study of scripture is to take its readers beyond the clarity of understanding to the darkness of God, the mystery that is not a problem to be solved but the living flame of love ignited by the encounter with that love in Christ through the words of the Bible. Although the idea of the mystical meaning of scripture was an idea that profoundly entrenched the authority of the church, and that left little place for women, it was also an idea which saw the mystical as inextricably intertwined with a life of justice and love of neighbour. It would be measured, not by private psychological states, but by its impact for good on the community.

Because of this (among other reasons), medieval exegetes had a rather different understanding of the role of imagination than is found in modern biblical critics. As Augustine had said in *On Christian Doctrine*,

Whoever finds a lesson there useful to the building of charity, even though he has not said what the author may be shown to have intended in that place, has not been deceived, nor is he lying in any way. (1958: I.xxxvi)

Imaginative meditation was therefore to be encouraged, not cramped by the literal or historical sense, because it is by imaginative entry into the mystical sense of scripture that the love and grace of God can be encountered. Examples of this are to be found throughout mystical writings. Here, for instance, is the beginning of Anselm's 'Prayer to St Mary Magdalene':

> St Mary Magdalene,
> you came with springing tears
> to the spring of mercy, Christ;
> from him your burning thirst was abundantly refreshed;
> through him your sins were forgiven;
> by him your bitter sorrow was consoled.
> My dearest lady,
> well you know by your own life
> how a sinful soul can be reconciled with its creator,

> what counsel a soul in misery needs,
> what medicine will restore the sick to health ...
>
> (1973: 201)

And it is this restoration that is the object of Anselm's meditation and prayer. Subsequent scholarship might object that Anselm is illegitimately running together various Marys of scripture and tradition, and combining them with the woman at the well of the fourth gospel. This may be true, but for Anselm it would miss the point. The moral transformation effected by imaginative engagement with the mystical meaning of the text is out of comparison more important than accuracy to the precise historical or literal meaning. 'The letter killeth, but the spirit giveth life' – always provided that it does not stray outside the boundaries carefully set to preserve ecclesiastical doctrine and authority.

Accordingly, great intellectual acumen was brought to bear on the interpretation of the scriptures. Medieval biblical scholarship is characterised by stretching of the mind, creative and disciplined thinking intended to 'bring every thought into the captivity of Christ' and to love God with all one's mind. Augustine had instructed that biblical scholars should make use of all the intellectual resources available in philosophy, grammar, rhetoric and indeed all the liberal arts. In medieval schools this was taken literally: students were admitted to formal biblical study only after having completed the *quadrivium* and the *trivium*, the Seven Liberal Arts which included the study of logic and the classics, and might well take four or more years of solid study (Boyd 1975). This meant that in a situation where Bibles and other books were rare, expensive and produced by sheer hard labour of hand-copying the texts and glosses (not to mention the intricate detail of manuscript illuminations) those who did get access to them were on the whole well prepared and could be expected to take their studies seriously.

It is obvious, however, that this almost completely excluded women from the formal study of the scriptures. During the earlier medieval period, a few privileged women in convents might receive enough education to read and study the Bible, and might have access to it and to some other books, but they were not expected to study and comment on it in the same way that the monks were. In the later Middle Ages, with the development of schools and universities, the position of women became even worse. Women were not, as a rule, admitted to the pursuit of the Seven Liberal Arts, though exceptional women like Heloise might proceed far enough in private tuition to be tutored eventually by a scholar as outstanding as Abelard. But, as her example shows only too clearly, in the rare cases where women did receive education, their tutors might well see them not as serious scholars but as objects of sexual conquest. Certainly they were not expected to have anything substantive to contribute to the understanding of scripture, let alone to its mystical meaning. Even when they did have significant insights, they were likely to be trivialised by the dominant men of their own time and forgotten subsequently: who now recognises as important the thoughts of Heloise – arguably more insightful than those of Abelard, whose writings every theologian knows (Nye 1992)?

It was no accident that much of the interpretation of scripture and the quest for its mystical meaning took its origin in a monastic context, many of whose values were transferred also to the scholastics. It was in the monasteries, in the first instance, that Bibles, books and the education to study them were available. In monasteries, also, monks would be under specific vows of obedience to their superior, and thus to the ecclesiastical structure as a whole; and loyalty to its authority could be expected. The *Rule* of Benedict of Nursia, which can without exaggeration be said to be directly or indirectly formative of all subsequent western monasticism, expressly stated that the monastery was to be 'a school for God's service', a school where the monks would learn to receive and to give divine *caritas*. Inevitably, therefore, the study of scripture according to the principles I have sketched was an indispensable part of Christian formation in the monastery, and the practices of the monastery were inseparable from the developing quest for the mystical meaning of scripture. And of course monasteries were all-male environments.

Two aspects of monastic life which both expressed and gave shape to this quest were the *lectio divina* and the liturgy. The *lectio divina*, the reading of scripture, was given a large place in developing monasticism. Even when this reading was done privately, it was often done semi-audibly, forming the words of scripture with the lips and tongue; and it was done ruminatively, chewing over the sense and sound of each word and passage, and thus inscribing it upon the memory. The monks tried to learn the scriptures 'by heart', committing them to memory and being so immersed in them that thought and life flowed out of them (Leclercq 1978: 88–96). Thus, we find in Bernard of Clairvaux, one example among many others, that his writings are a catena of scriptural phrases and allusions. He thinks his thoughts in biblical language; yet though they are formed by that language, they are still very much his own. Choosing a passage at random, we find in the second Sermon on the Song of Songs the following:

How shall I, mere dust and ashes, presume that God takes an interest in me? He is entirely taken up with loving his Father, he has no need of me or of what I possess ... If it be really true, as you prophets have said, that God has determined to show mercy, to reveal himself in a more favourable light, let him establish a covenant of peace, an everlasting covenant with me by the kiss of his mouth. If he will not revoke his given word, let him empty himself, let him humble himself, let him bend to me and kiss me with the kiss of his mouth. (1977: 1.2.6)

In these few lines are at least eight quotations from the Bible, woven together to express Bernard's own intentions. The rich layers of nuance and allusion made possible by this immersion in scripture is seen as the outward manifestation of the inner encounter with Christ in prayerful attentiveness to the Word.

As such, it could be said to be sacramental, and a reflection also of the liturgy. Both of these were strongly reinforced by the development of what came to be known as the 'mystical theology', strongly influenced by the work of Dionysius the Areopagite, to whose work we shall soon turn. All these strands, the interpretation of scripture, the celebration of the sacraments and the hierarchy of the church which defined and enacted its liturgies, were increasingly the prerogative of men. Insofar as these were the central dimensions of spirituality, women were excluded.

CHAPTER 4

Mystical theology and the erotic other

It is Christianity which invests women anew with frightening prestige: fear of the other sex is one of the forms assumed by the anguish of man's uneasy conscience. The Christian is divided within himself; the separation of body and soul, of life and spirit, is complete; original sin makes of the body the enemy of the soul; all the ties of the flesh seem evil ... Evil is an absolute reality; and the flesh is sin. And of course, since woman remains always the Other, it is not held that reciprocally male and female are both flesh: the flesh that is for the Christian the hostile *Other* is precisely the woman. In her the Christian finds incarnated the temptations of the world, the flesh and the devil. (de Beauvoir 1987: 199)

The understandings of the mystical as the hidden, spiritual meaning of scripture, both revealed and concealed in its words, have parallels in other aspects of the church's practice in the medieval period which enable us to discern further shifts in the notion of the mystical. Just as Christ could be encountered in the sacred page by those able to discern its mystical meaning, so also, it was held, Christ could be encountered in the sacraments. The bread and the wine, like the words of scripture, both reveal and conceal the divine reality. The same was true of the waters of baptism: as the words of the Bible contain a mystical meaning, so the waters of baptism are, for those who discern, the mystical waters of a new birth, as the bread and wine of the eucharist are the mystical body and blood of Christ.

This indicates that the meaning of the term 'mystical' undergoes a considerable extension, for which new theological resources were needed. Not only did the words of the scriptures contain mystical meaning, but so also did the rituals and liturgy of the church. In all of these, it was held, Christ could be encountered; therefore it would make sense to hold that a common theological understanding could be applied to all. Such a theology was developed by Dionysius in about the sixth century: its culmination was called a 'mystical theology', a theology which united the idea of the mystical meaning of scripture with the liturgical practices of the church. The more closely a 'mystical theology' was linked to liturgical practices like the eucharist, however, the more it was removed from women and taken into the exclusive control of men. In this chapter I wish to look at the development of this mystical theology and its interconnections with power and gender in the medieval church. I shall look first at the patristic background to the idea of a mystical path, then at the development of mystical theology by Dionysius. This will set the stage for considering two somewhat different strands of mystical theology in the high Middle Ages: the intellectual mystical theology of Eckhart and his followers, and the more affective strand of mystical theology associated with Bernard of Clairvaux. It will become apparent that in neither case did things go well for women. Emphasis on the intellect marginalised women because they were considered to be 'misbegotten males', deficient alike in intellect and in morality. Yet when love and the will were emphasised, as in the affective strand, it was at the expense of actual bodiliness and sexuality, and therefore at the expense of actual women.

Nevertheless, it was not possible to suppress women completely. The high Middle Ages saw the emergence of a particularly female spirituality, often with a strong emphasis on the erotic. Although this was in some ways closely related to forms of affective mysticism developed by male mystical writers, it was much more related to female bodiliness, sexuality and a rejection of the dualism characteristic of male spiritual writing. Unsurprisingly, women were able to claim their own voices and their own authority on the basis of this spirituality; and equally unsurprisingly, men found such assertiveness increasingly threatening, and exerted themselves to suppress it. In this chapter and the following ones I shall show all this in more detail. These sketches toward a counter-history of Christian mysticism reveal that again and again the decision of what should count as mystical was not straightforward. Rather, the changing social construction of mysticism proceeded according to the will of the dominant males, and females had either to be excluded, or else domesticated to such an extent that they no longer posed any threat to male superiority.

I THE PATH TO GOD

As discussed in chapter 2, spirituality was seen, in early Christian times, largely in terms of the male spirit or intellect. It was the mind, 'wherein there is no sex', which was made in the image of God; and although technically this meant that women were bearers of the image of God just as much as men, in fact their status was dubious to say the least. A woman whose spirituality could not be denied might be thought of as an honorary male; this was held to be preferable to the idea that women *simply as women* could have spiritual knowledge of God.

However, even the male intellect had not escaped the effects of the fall. Because of the fall (which was often blamed on Eve and therefore on all women, as we have seen) the mind was blinded by sin, and thereby separated from God. To regain union with God, therefore, this blindness had to be overcome. The teachers of spirituality had developed a three-fold path by which the knowledge of God could be regained, so that ultimately the mind might ascend to the vision of God. The steps of this path were often called purgation, illumination and contemplation, though other terms could be substituted.

One of the earliest teachers of this three-fold path to union with God was Origen of Alexandria. Origen's whole orientation was toward union with God, understood in a way which united Christian and Platonic thought: we have already noted his emphasis on the spiritual rather than the literal meaning of scripture. Origen linked the three steps of the spiritual path to three books of the Wisdom literature of the Hebrew Bible: Proverbs, Ecclesiastes and the Song of Songs. He believed that all three of these books had been written by Solomon, the wisest of men; and he believed that when one probed beyond their literal meaning, these books mirrored the ancient Greek disciplines of ethics, physics and enoptics.

> Thus he [Solomon] first taught in Proverbs the subject of morals, setting regulations for life together, as was fitting, in concise and brief maxims. And he included the second subject, which is called the natural discipline, in Ecclesiastes, in which he discusses many natural things. And by distinguishing them as empty and vain from what is useful and necessary, he warns that vanity must be abandoned and what is useful and right must be pursued. He also handed down the subject of contemplation in ... Song of Songs, in which he urges upon the soul the love of the heavenly and the divine under the figure of the bride and the bridegroom, teaching us that we must obtain fellowship with God by the paths of loving affection and of love. (1979, Prologue)

This initially sounds simply like a practical plan, until we pursue in a little more depth what Origen actually meant by the 'morals' of the Proverbs and the 'natural discipline' of Ecclesiastes. As we might have expected, given Origen's Platonism, what he was thinking of was a dualistic split between body and mind. As Andrew Louth puts it, 'the aim of these two ways is to subdue the body to the soul and then to free the soul from the body' (1981: 60); only then is contemplation possible.

(i) Purgation

Like Plato, Origen believed that the body is an impediment to the soul; unlike Plato, he believed also in demons who can seize upon the natural impulses of the body and make them even more destructive to the project of knowledge of the divine. The way of purgation, therefore, in his view requires a strict discipline of the body and its desires, lest the Christian fall prey to the devil. This is not to say that the devil actually causes the desires themselves. 'Are we to suppose that the devil is the cause of our being hungry or thirsty?' asks Origen. If this is ridiculous, then so also is the idea that sexual desire is the devil's fault. All of these are simply the clamourings of our own oppressive physical bodies; but as soon as they are 'indulged' in a manner that is less than perfectly self-controlled, the door is opened to the devil.

It is not as though Origen thought that the body is bad in itself: it is a gift of the Creator, and as such must be good. However, it is startling to find that the body's goodness consists not in its intrinsic beauty or value, but rather because it is the perfect adversary for the soul to overcome in its quest for purity! It is a 'schoolroom', an 'educational opportunity ... whose real purpose is to teach intellects to ascend above it in their path back to the unimpeded vision of God' (McGinn 1991: 114).

Along with his view of the body as the perfect obstacle course for the soul in training, Origen bequeathed to spirituality the idea of the spiritual senses, each paralleling a physical sense. Thus for example one could 'taste' the word of God, 'smell' the divine fragrance, and feel the 'touch' of the divine presence (Origen 1979: Prol.). The physical body and its senses, however, numb the sensitivity of these spiritual senses so that they are unreceptive and unresponsive. The path of purgation or purification, therefore, involves 'withdrawing from the dull anaesthesia of common, physical sensation' (Brown 1988: 172), developing a strict discipline of the physical senses so that the 'spiritual senses' might not be numbed (Origen 1979: ii.9).

Most crucial, unsurprisingly, is sexuality. Origen says that 'just as there is said to be a fleshly love ... according to which the person who loves sows in the flesh, so also there is a spiritual love according to which the inner man when he loves, sows in the Spirit' (1979: 223). Origen here begins one of the most influential themes in the history of Christian spirituality, the language and symbolism of erotic love as a way of speaking about the relation of God and the soul, and the use of the Song of Songs as the biblical grounding for erotic mysticism. The soul becomes the bride, God the divine bridegroom. God embraces the soul, she yearns for him and for the 'kisses of his mouth', he wounds her with the wound of love. The use of erotic language allows the language of passion and desire to become a part of Christian spirituality, and to see the longed-for union with God in terms of ecstasy and even ravishing. Without this theme, dwelt upon and nuanced in countless ways in the history of Christian spirituality, that history would be unimaginably different. And as we shall see later on, it was a theme that was treated differently by women than by men.

The theme as a whole is from a feminist perspective deeply ambiguous. Already in Origen, just as the spiritual senses can come into their own only when the physical senses are severely disciplined, so also (as we might have expected by now) the love of the soul for the spiritual bridegroom makes all other love and certainly all other sexual expression highly suspect. At the beginning of his *Commentary on the Song of Songs* Origen warns that anyone not practising chastity ought not even to read the book.

For if he does not know how to listen to the names of love purely and with chaste ears, he may twist everything he has heard from the inner man to the fleshly and outer man and be turned away from the Spirit to the flesh. Then he will nourish in himself fleshly desires, and it will seem because of the divine scriptures that he is impelled and moved to the lusts of the flesh. For this reason I give warning and advice to everyone who has not yet withdrawn from the desire for corporeal nature that he completely abstain from reading this book and what is said about it. (1979 Prol.)

If the heavenly bridegroom will kiss the bride with the kisses of his mouth, and wound her with the delectable wound of love, then any other kisses are compromising and any other sexual experience is adulterous. Accordingly, we find in Origen one of the major early Christian arguments for the centuries-old emphasis on virginity. Virginity is the path, *par excellence*, of purgation, and the virgin body, in solidarity with the virgin mother of God, becomes a link between heaven and earth (Origen 1953: 1.34–9).

Thus the use of erotic imagery was at the expense of the valuation of real sexual relations. It used the language of passion, but forbade any actual physical passion in an effort to channel all desire away from the body and towards God. Human sexuality was therefore seen not as a way of knowing something of divine Eros, but as a distraction and corruption, distasteful and gross. And since it was primarily women and women's bodies that were identified throughout the centuries with passion and sexuality, women were part of the evil to be shunned or overcome by spiritual men. As Tertullian had said, women were 'the devil's gateway'. Even when baptised, they were still seductive and a threat to the chastity and hence the spirituality of men (Brown 1988: 77). Thus at whatever level the value of the erotic as symbolic of the love of God is assessed (and on any reckoning it must be very high), the price that has been paid through the centuries of Christian spirituality has been the devaluation of actual human sexuality, and a hatred and fear of women. We shall see later how even strong, passionate women of spirit were deeply affected by it.

(ii) Illumination

In Origen's thinking, furthermore, the renunciation of physical sexuality as a part of the path of purgation was closely connected to the next step, the step of illumination. In Origen's usage, as in biblical vocabulary, 'to know' could mean sexual intercourse or it could mean intellectual cognition; and at least some of the time Origen writes as though one must choose between them.

Do not think that just as the belly is made for food and food for the belly, that in the same way the body is made for intercourse. If you wish to understand the Apostle's train of reasoning, for whatever reason the body was made, then listen: it was made that it should be a temple to the Lord; that the soul, being holy and blessed, should act in it as if it were a priest serving before the Holy Spirit who dwells in you. In this manner, Adam had a body in Paradise; but in Paradise he did not 'know' Eve. (quoted in Brown 1988: 175)

In Paradise, Adam knew God. Once he began to know Eve, his knowledge of God was undermined.

In Origen's discussion, this second step was tied to the biblical book of Ecclesiastes, and had to do with the knowledge of the natural world and the cosmos, and recognition of its vanity.

Ecclesiastes ... teaches, as we have said, that everything visible and corporal is transitory and weak. And when the person who is eager for wisdom discovers that this is so, he will doubtless despise those things; and by renouncing, so to speak, the whole world, he will press on to the invisible and eternal teachings that are given to the spiritual senses in the Song of Songs through certain veiled figures of loves. (1979: Prol.)

It is clear that Origen is here appealing to the spiritual or mystical meaning of scripture, a sense which, we can now see, is directly related to purity of heart, which, in his terms, means severe discipline of the body.

Thus it follows from Origen's position (though he left it to later writers to draw out the conclusion) that not only is the mystical meaning of scripture reserved for men because of their educational and ecclesiastical opportunities, as we have already seen, but furthermore, women, being more closely linked to the flesh, would in any case be much less likely to be able to perceive its mystical meaning even if they did have the opportunity. Hence this linkage provides a (circular) justification for restricting education to men: it would be wasted on women anyway.

The renunciation of the world and its vanities are so closely linked to progress in the knowledge of God that it is not farfetched for subsequent writers to call this step 'illumination'. Origen himself always thought of the soul's journey as a journey of knowledge; and though it was a knowledge that was affective as well as intellectual, sometimes described as *amor intellectus Dei*, it should not be forgotten that the affectivity directed towards God was at the expense of any worldly love (McGinn 1991: 124). It was also essentially the prerogative of men.

(iii) Contemplation

Origen expected this process of illumination to continue after physical death. His description of it is a description which, while referring to an after-life, is also a good picture of how he thinks of spiritual progress this side of eternity.

And so the rational being, growing at each successive stage … increasing in mind and intelligence, advances as a mind already perfect to perfect knowledge, no longer hindered by its former carnal senses, but developing in intellectual power, ever approaching the pure and gazing 'face to face', if I may so speak, on the causes of things. (1973: II.xi.7)

Ultimately, that knowledge is sufficiently purified for it to proceed from illumination to contemplation, an immediate knowledge of God which is the same as union with the divine.

According to Platonic teaching, and accepted by much of the Christian spiritual tradition, like can only be known by like; only the pure in heart can see God. To know God by union with God, however, involves such a transformation that it is possible to use reflexive language. To know God is to be known by God; to be united with God is in some sense to be incorporated into divinity, to be divinised. Origen comments on how Moses' face shone when he went into the tabernacle, and continues,

According to the literal meaning, something more divine than the manifestation that happened in the tabernacle and the temple was brought into effect in the face of Moses, who consorted with the divine nature. According to the spiritual meaning, those things which are known clearly about God and which are beheld by a mind made worthy of exceeding purity, are said to be the glory of God which is seen. So the mind, purified and passing beyond everything material, so that it perfects its contemplations of God, is made divine in what it contemplates. (quoted in Louth 1981: 73)

Hence in Origen, and in much of the Christian mystical tradition, the project is to be 'made divine', to become God, or at least united with God; and this is a project of knowledge, of the intellect. To be sure, the intellect is driven by desire and transformed by love: there is no question here of a cold, calculating rationality. Nevertheless, it is reason, not the body or the emotions or the will, that is the human faculty amenable of such transformation, and of that knowledge of God which is union with God, divinisation.

The three-fold path to union with God, which came to be known as the path of contemplation or the mystical path, was taken up in various ways by subsequent writers of the patristic era, notably Gregory of Nyssa in his *The Life of Moses*. It was also prominent throughout the medieval period, as we will have occasion to note. It is beyond question that this understanding of the mystical path was productive of much sincere piety. But at what price? We have already seen how it privileges men, who start from a position of identification with mind or spirit. Even for them, part of the price of spirituality was a denial of the passions, so that there developed a distortion of both genders, and a growing alienation between them. The body had to be controlled, suppressed, mortified. Women, identified with the flesh, had similarly to be controlled, suppressed and mortified (literally, put to death). The forms which that control took will be seen more fully in subsequent chapters. First, however, it is useful to consider one of the most influential of all medieval writers, Dionysius, and his development of the mystical theology.

II DIONYSIUS AND THE HIERARCHY OF MYSTICISM

It is ironic that one of the most influential of all medieval writers is someone whose name remains unknown. This is because of a highly clever strategy which he used to identify himself as a writer of the apostolic age, in close connection with Paul the apostle of the New Testament. In Acts 17:34 there is an account of Paul preaching on the Athenian areopagus, and among his converts was someone named Dionysius: no further mention of him occurs in the biblical canon or in subsequent patristic writing. Then in the sixth century some Greek texts appeared, consisting of four books and a set of ten letters purporting to be written by this same Dionysius. Throughout the Middle Ages this identification was accepted with only occasional hesitations, and the writings were accorded almost apostolic authority: Thomas Aquinas, for instance, quotes 'Dionysius' about 1,700 times (Pelikan 1987: 21). The influence of his writings, translated into Latin first by Hilduin of Saint-Denis near Paris in the early ninth century and then by John Scotus Eriugena in 862, can hardly be overstated; though it is also true that there were major writers, Bernard of Clairvaux among them, who seem not to have known about his books, and his influence was much greater after the eleventh century than it had been before that time. It was only in the Renaissance that doubts were increasingly expressed about whether the books could really have been written by a convert of Paul; and more recently it has been shown to the satisfaction of most scholars that the authorship could not have been earlier than the fifth century.

Whereas hardly anyone now accepts that the writer was Dionysius who was converted on the areopagus in Athens, a positive identification seems impossible. Strictly speaking, all we can do is to refer to him as 'Dionysius – the whoever-he-was', as

Luther did, or simply as 'Dionysius', or 'Pseudo-Dionysius', which many contemporary writers prefer. He probably lived in the late fifth century, possibly in Syria; but even that is uncertain. What is absolutely certain, however, is the huge influence his writings had on medieval thought generally, and on the understanding of what counts as mystical in particular (Louth 1989: 1; Rorem 1993: 16).

Dionysius was preoccupied with questions of hierarchy with its implicit authority structures: in his mind it was closely connected with the mystical. He begins his book *The Ecclesiastical Hierarchy* with the words,

Most sacred of sacred sons: Our hierarchy consists of an inspired, divine, and divinely worked understanding, activity, and perfection. With the aid of the transcendent and most sacred scriptures, I must demonstrate this to those who have been initiated in the sacrament of the sacred mystagogy by our hierarchy's mysteries and traditions. (1987: 195)

For him, the mystical and the mysterious (and hence also mystagogy) are very close together: indeed, the best English translation renders either way his Greek word *mustikos*. In his usage we can see how the meaning of the term *mustikos* linked together the secret initiation rites of the ancient mystery religions with the Christian idea of the mystical meaning of scripture, and extended it also to the sacraments, to the organisation of the church, and to theology itself. What is just as striking as what Dionysius says, however, is what he passed over in silence: in none of his books does Dionysius ever once mention women. They simply have no place either in his understanding of the ecclesiastical hierarchy or in his mystical theology. It will be important to bear in mind the presence of this absence as we consider his construction of mysticism and its subsequent influence.

Dionysius emphasised the importance of secrecy regarding the divine mysteries. What he said was not to be taught to those who were uninitiated: he exhorts his reader not to forget his promise that he would never 'pass to anyone except sacred initiators of your own order the hierarch's superior sacred words' (1987: 198). When he comes to expound the *Mystical Theology* proper, he repeats the warning: 'see to it that none of this comes to the hearing of the uninformed' (136). Indeed, part of the reason why scripture contains symbols, why there is not only a literal but also a mystical meaning of scripture, according to Dionysius, is that

it is most fitting to the mysterious [i.e. mystical] passages of scripture that the sacred and hidden truth ... be concealed through the inexpressible and the sacred and be inaccessible to the *hoi polloi*. Not everyone is sacred, and, as scripture says, knowledge is not for everyone. (149)

Although Dionysius does not explicitly mention pagan mystery religions, it is easy to surmise that the practice of initiation whereby the initiated or 'mystical ones' were those who kept their mouths shut, who kept silence about what they had experienced, was not far from his mind. This is even clearer when he talks about the liturgical practices of the church. He describes in some detail the rite of baptism, which is the initiation itself, and specifies that it is not to be witnessed by any but those who are already initiated (201). Similarly with the celebration of the eucharist, anyone who is still a catechumen or a penitent, anyone who has not already been initiated, must 'leave the sacred precincts ... so that only those remain who are entitled to the vision and communion of the divine things. Some of the deacons stand on guard in the sacred place to ensure that the doors are kept closed' (210). Only then is the liturgy continued with the singing of the creed, the reading of scripture and the communion itself. Dionysius is quite clear about the reason for such secrecy and exclusion: he points out that 'it differentiates, as indeed it should, what belongs to the common crowd from the things that bind and unify a hierarchy' (204). It is a hierarchy in which there is no place for women.

The word 'hierarchy' was actually invented by Dionysius. Before his time, the word did not exist. The word *hierarch* had long been used, mainly in pagan circles, to refer to someone who led a sacred ritual: it came from two words, *heiros* which means 'sacred' and *arche* which means 'source'. By the time of Dionysius, the word *hierarch* could be applied to clergy, though it was only rarely used in that way. But when Dionysius invented the word *hierarchy*, he managed to create a concept whereby the source of the sacred was linked to a single leader, and from him, by a channel of authority, to his followers. As Paul Rorem notes, Dionysius 'used the existing term for a cultic leader to create a new word *hierarchy* and to imply that this person (the hierarch) completely dominates the system or the arrangement (the hierarchy)' (1993: 21). We are now so accustomed to the concept that we can hardly think ourselves back to a stage when it did not exist: Dionysius invented a term which has come to characterise ecclesiastical structure as we know it.

In Dionysius' thinking, hierarchy was the appropriate description not only for the structure of the church, with its bishop, priests and deacons, but also for the angelic orders. His book *The Celestial Hierarchy* was the basis for medieval angelology. Much of Dionysius' thinking regarding the angels, and indeed regarding all created things, was derived from Neoplatonism and can be encapsulated by the idea of procession and return. What this means is that while on the one hand the divine remains complete in itself, it can also be thought of as proceeding outward, like rays of the sun, thereby bringing into being all that exists. These things, however, are also drawn upward by the divine attraction and revert back again to God. The specific items in the procession form a hierarchy, a great chain of being, in which each one bears in itself the image of God to the extent possible to its position, and passes it on like a 'spotless mirror' to the being next down the chain.

If one talks then of a hierarchy, what is meant is a certain perfect arrangement, an image of the beauty of God which sacredly works out the mysteries of its own enlightenment in the orders and levels of understanding of the hierarchy, and which is likened toward its own source as much as is permitted. Indeed for every member of the hierarchy, perfection consists in this, that it is uplifted to imitate God as far as possible, and, more wonderful still, that is becomes . . . a reflection of the workings of God. (1987: 154)

This arrangement applies to the hosts of heaven, arranged in a sequence of three groups of three kinds of angelic being: Dionysius calls them thrones, cherubim, seraphim, archangels, principalities and so on. The ecclesiastical structure of bishops, priests and deacons is therefore not an arbitrary arrangement: it mirrors the heavenly structure, and is in Dionysius' view the appropriate channel for the mysteries of God.

This same tripartite hierarchical arrangement also characterises the spiritual path, only in reverse, as the soul which has fallen away from God now is drawn back in the return. Accordingly, Dionysius presses the three steps of purification, illumination (which he sometimes calls contemplation) and perfection into his system: it is a variant of the three steps which we have already seen in Origen. Also there are three sacraments: baptism, communion and the consecration of the holy ointment. And all of these are interlinked in his system:

The holy sacraments bring about purification, illumination and perfection. The deacons form the order which purifies. The priests constitute the order which gives illumination. And the hierarchs, living in conformity with God, make up the order which perfects ... Thus, our own hierarchy is blessedly and harmoniously divided into orders in accordance with divine revelation and therefore deploys the same sequence as the hierarchies of heaven. (248)

The whole arrangement is seen as deriving directly from God the Holy Trinity, and mirroring the divine likeness as far as is possible for the created order to do.

Obviously to the extent that this way of thinking is accepted, the ecclesiastical structure would be one of descending authority, with ultimate dominion vested in the bishop and a chain of command in which the laity would be expected to obey and reverence their superiors as the voice of God to them. Nor would it be possible to question such a structure, since to do so would be to question the way God had created all things. Thus while the system presented itself as a system of spirituality, a path of return to God from the falling away into sin, it was not innocent of issues of power. It was a system which vested enormous authority in the bishops and clergy. And in that whole system, women were simply absent. Although Dionysius has presented the whole structure of the celestial orders and their earthly counterparts, the whole chain of being from angels down to catechumens and penitents, women never are mentioned: there is no place specified for them in the church.

This is not to say that Dionysius would have thought that women could not be saved: such a view would have been contrary to church teaching and practice since the time of Jesus, as we have seen. But it is clear that in his writings he always thinks in terms of males only (Rorem 1993: 127n4). Given that his system is all-encompassing and a reflection of nothing less than the divine trinity, and given that his writing was taken as having almost apostolic authority throughout the medieval period, the fact that there is no place for women in this whole hierarchy of power bodes ill for women in the medieval church. There is more than one level of irony in all this. The same passage of scripture which mentions Dionysius as one of the converts of Paul on the Athenian areopagus also mentions a woman named Damaris: she too was converted. But she is never heard of again. Dionysius helps himself to the name of the male convert, and utterly ignores the female. It is characteristic of his writings as a whole.

This becomes all the more apparent when we look in more detail at what Dionysius means by mystical theology, the path of spiritual progress. Dionysius starts from the assumption of a hidden or mystical meaning of scripture which we have already examined. Perhaps typical for one who has woven an elaborate pseudonym around himself, he is very much preoccupied with the names of God as these are given in scripture, and concerns himself with how such names, which are after all words of human language, can adequately refer to the one who is above all names. At the same time, he adopted the Neoplatonist idea of procession and return: all things come from God, in a great outflowing of the divine bounty, and all things return again to God in final consummation. These two concerns are melded together in his understanding of the mystical theology. The names which are given to God in the scriptures can be understood positively as God's self-outpouring, the ways in which God can be known. Yet none of them are adequate to God's reality. Thus they must all, also, be negated, transcended. Hence the downward motion of outflowing, corresponding to the names ascribed to God in scripture, must be coupled with an upward motion of consummation, where the names are successively negated until at last all that is left is silence, a silence which, however, must be understood not as a silence of ignorance but as a silence transcending speech.

It is this negative path, albeit along the steps marked out by the names given to God in scripture, which is the mystical theology proper. What this means is that another shift has taken place in the understanding of what counts as the mystical: while it is still rooted in the concept of the hidden meaning of the Bible, it now extends to the hidden, spiritual path more generally, the path whereby the hidden meaning of words as well as sacraments is first comprehended and then transcended. It is relentlessly cognitive, as we shall see, and tightly bound up with the hierarchical authority structure of the church. On both counts, it is a male preserve.

Let us consider this spiritual path in more detail. It is set out by Dionysius in two books, *The Divine Names*, which discusses what may be called the 'positive' way, the names given to God in the Bible, and *The Mystical Theology*, which retraces the steps, negating each of the names and ending in ecstasy. In *The Divine Names* Dionysius states the problem which the two together seek to resolve:

How then can we speak of the divine names? How can we do this if the Transcendent surpasses all discourse and all knowledge, if it abides beyond the reach of mind and of being, if it encompasses and circumscribes, embraces and anticipates all things while itself eluding their grasp and escaping from any perception, imagination, opinion, name, discourse, apprehension, or understanding? (1987: 53)

Anything that could be adequately encapsulated in human language would not be worthy to be called God: in Dionysius' view God must be utterly transcendent, and therefore beyond any human capacity for conceptualisation or verbalisation.

Accordingly, the only way in which it will be possible to know or speak of God is through God's own outpouring, through creation and through the scriptures. God can be known as the Source and Cause of all things, as indicated in the biblical writings.

[God] is the Life of the living, the being of beings, it is the Source and the Cause of all life and of all being, for out of its goodness it commands all things to be and it keeps them going. We learn of all these mysteries from the divine scriptures and you will find that what the scripture writers have to say regarding the divine names refers, in revealing praises, to the beneficent processions of God. (51)

True to his usual emphasis on the importance of secrecy, Dionysius makes clear that although these mysteries are contained in scripture, they are 'wrapped in the sacred veils ... with which scripture and hierarchical traditions cover the truths of the mind with things derived from the realm of the senses' (52). This ensures that only those who have been initiated will be included in the divine knowledge. In fact, this for Dionysius is the reason why there *needs* to be a mystical or hidden meaning of scripture: it is to keep the secret things of God away from those who are unworthy to receive them. If everything were said in the literal sense, he implies, the effect would be that the pearls of knowledge of God would be cast before the uninitiated swine. Hence the mystical meaning of scripture, in Dionysius' presentation, is closely linked up with a division between those in authority, who have the ability and the right to know the secrets of God, and all others, whose part it is to receive with humility what those in authority deem appropriate to impart to them.

For those who are able to receive the mystical meaning, however, Dionysius affirms that 'we use whatever appropriate symbols we can for the things of God. With these analogies we are raised upward toward the truth of the mind's vision, a truth which is simple and one' (53). The symbols that are offered in scripture range from using physical things like fire, rock and strong tower as metaphors for God, to speaking of God as though God had a physical body with hands, eyes, ears and bowels, to much less physical metaphors like goodness, wisdom and truth as names or descriptions of God. Thus although on the one hand God is 'the Nameless One', the one who transcends all possible naming, 'yet on the other hand they give it many names', because 'as Cause of all and as transcending all, he is rightly nameless and yet has the names of everything that is' (54).

In *The Divine Names* Dionysius concentrates on the more abstract, less physical names for God: Good, Being, Life, Wisdom, Power and the like. In each case, the name is one which is presented by the scriptures to human understanding; and in each case, what is necessary is that the name is first conceptually grasped, and then transcended, negated, not in the sense that the negation cancels out what has been grasped, but rather that the mind rises above the human conceptualisation into the divine darkness which is brighter than light. The emphasis on the intellect, the understanding, is one of the most characteristic and most significant things about Dionysius. The spiritual path in Dionysius' presentation does not consist in moral purification or even in uniting with the love and compassion of God, but in a progress of the *mind* from a state of ignorance (a state shared by all who are uninitiated into the mysteries of God) to a state of knowledge, and ultimately to a state which transcends knowledge itself in an ecstasy of the mind.

Dionysius accepts the Platonic understanding that knowledge unites the knower with that which is known: knowledge is not a detached or neutral observation of an object, in the way that we have come to think of it since Descartes. Accordingly, union with God will be a union of the knowing mind: it is therefore the mind which is of utmost importance, and the greatest obstacle to union with God is not characterised as sin but as ignorance. (Indeed, sin itself can be characterised as a form of ignorance, as Plato also held; evil is described as a deprivation or falling away from good, a 'deficiency, a weakness ... mindless, unreasonable, imperfect ...' (94).) Therefore the goodness of God consists of enlightening human ignorance, rather than, for instance, rescuing human beings from demonic forces or from moral wickedness, as other writers would conceive it.

So then, the Good which is above all light is given the name 'light of the mind' ... For just as it is ignorance which scatters those in error, so it is the presence of the light of the mind which gathers and unites together those receiving illumination. It perfects them. It returns them toward the truly real. It returns them from their numerous false notions and, filling them with the one unifying light, it gathers their clashing fancies into a single, pure, coherent, and true knowledge. (76)

It is unsurprising, then, that Dionysius devotes considerable attention to the name 'Wisdom' for God. God is the one whose wisdom enlightens human understanding; yet God is also beyond anything that might be described using the human terminology of wisdom and reason. If we 'measure the divine by our human standards' the inevitable result will be that we will be 'led astray by the apparent meaning we give to divine and unspeakable reason'. Rather, we should recognise that the human mind is in a certain way an analogate of the divine.

The human mind has a capacity to think, through which it looks on conceptual things, and a unity which transcends the nature of the mind, through which it is joined to things beyond itself. And this transcendent characteristic must be given to the words we use about God. They must not be given in the human sense. We should be taken wholly out of ourselves, and become wholly of God, since it is better to belong to God rather than to ourselves. (105)

Just as our mind in its unity transcends that about which it thinks, so also God transcends everything that can be said about the divine. Human words should be used as aids to climb to the transcendent understanding of God; but they should not be taken as a substitute for that understanding.

God is the one who is the cause of all things; therefore God knows all things. But God's knowledge is of a different order than human knowledge, simply because God *is* the Cause.

God does not possess a private knowledge of himself and a separate knowledge of all the creatures in common. The universal Cause, by knowing itself, can hardly be ignorant of the things which proceed from it and of which it is the source. This, then, is how God knows all things, not by understanding things, but by understanding himself. (108)

This self-understanding is how God knows all that flows from the divine source: it is a sharp reminder of how different a word like 'understanding' is when applied to God than when applied to ourselves. Dionysius has throughout emphasised that 'we must interpret the things of God in a way that befits God' and that this will be different from the way in which the same word might befit a human being. This means that all characteristics predicated of God, all names of God, will need to be negated;

yet, as already said, this negation is a negation which does not cancel out the affirmation but rather goes beyond it. Thus Dionysius says,

> when we talk of God as being without mind and without perception, this is to be taken in the sense of what he has in superabundance and not as a defect. Hence we attribute absence of reason to him because he is above reason, we attribute lack of perfection to him because he is above and before perfection, and we posit intangible and invisible darkness of that Light which is unapproachable because it so far exceeds the visible Light. (107)

This therefore becomes the path of negation, which leads the mind step by step in its return to God in increasing illumination until the enlightenment is so dazzling that it becomes equivalent to the divine darkness, and knowing becomes the unknowing which is beyond knowledge.

This is the mystical pathway, the progress of the mind by way of negations into the hidden things of God until it plunges into what Dionysius calls the 'truly mysterious [mystical] darkness of unknowing' (137). Again, the reason for the unknowing is the transcendence of God, and the consequent inability of human language to describe God adequately. It is important to empha-sise that this is in fact the reason for the plunge into unknowing, since we might otherwise have thought that Dionysius was replacing knowledge with love, as Bonaventure would do, or even, as a proto-Kantian, denying knowledge in order to make room for faith. But Dionysius should not be read through the lens of these much later thinkers. For him, the mystical path is a path of reason, right to its end; and although in the consummation of all things reason is taken beyond itself, this does not mean that it collapses into love or faith. Just as the divine goodness, when denied on the path of negation, does not collapse into evil but rather transcends itself into superessential goodness which is beyond our knowing, and just as the divine darkness is the light of such brightness that it blinds the eyes, so also the transcendence of the human reason on the mystical path is not a collapse into ignorance or anything else, but rather is the unknowing that is beyond, but never beneath, knowing.

The fact is that the more we take flight upward, the more our words are confined to the ideas we are capable of forming; so that now as we plunge into that darkness which is beyond intellect, we shall find ourselves not simply running short of words but actually speechless and unknowing. (139)

This is what is meant by 'ecstasy': it comes from the Greek *ek-stasis*, which literally means 'standing outside oneself'. The intellect proceeds as far as it is able, step by step on the secret, mystical pathway of negation, until at last it has negated everything, including even negation itself. It can then go no farther, its state is ecstatic in the sense of standing outside itself, transcending itself, just as the negations of God's names point to the transcendent reality of God. Of course, when it reaches this point, human language has also been surpassed. But this surpassing of language must not be read in the modern sense of undergoing a psychological *experience* which is ineffable, or cannot be put into words, but rather in the patristic sense of recognising that *God* is the one who is beyond all words, all human language and constructs. Thus the final chapter of *The Mystical Theology* proceeds swiftly in a litany of negation: God is not soul or mind, God is not number or order, God is not wisdom, divinity or goodness, God is none of the things we can say. Finally,

There is no speaking of it, no name nor knowledge of it ... It is beyond assertion and denial. We make assertions and denials of what is next to it, but never of it, for it is both beyond every assertion, being the perfect and unique cause of all things, and, by virtue of its preeminently simple and absolute nature, free of every limitation, beyond every limitation; it is also beyond every denial. (141)

Silence is all that remains, the silence of the intellect in ecstasy. Later writers who took up the thought of Dionysius, like the fourteenth-century English author of *The Cloud of Unknowing*, would try to wed this intellectual ecstasy to a more affective approach, one which saw the final unknowing as a movement out of reason into love. But although it is tempting to read Dionysius in this way, it is inaccurate: love is not once mentioned in *The Mystical Theology*; neither, significantly, is Christ (Rorem 1993: 216). The union with God is a union of the mind, the intellect, even if in the end the intellect is rendered speechless and self-transcendent.

The pathway of the intellect to the summit of the divine mysteries by way of the mystical meaning of scripture is therefore parallel to the hierarchies of angels in the celestial sphere and the hierarchy of authority in the ecclesiastical domain. The sacraments are the realm of the hidden or mystical divinity just as are the words of scripture; and the bishops and clergy are their custodians. The mystical theology and the ecclesiastical hierarchy are tightly interlocked in Dionysius' thinking: it is by this interlocking that the concept of the mystical is broadened to include not only the hidden or spiritual meaning of scripture, but the whole mystery of God in church and Bible. It is not merely a mystical *meaning* but a mystical *theology*: it includes all that God has revealed, all that is held in trust by the ecclesiastical authorities who both interpret the scriptures and administer the sacraments, first excluding all who are uninitiated or unworthy. From this point forward, especially as Dionysius' influence spread after the ninth century, the idea of the mystical path which proceeded step by step through the divine mysteries until it culminated in ecstasy took an increasing grip on western Christian thinking, even when it diverged widely from the pattern which Dionysius envisaged.

It was a path on which women were faced with particular obstacles. As I have said, Dionysius himself did not mention women, and his writings seem to assume a male-only readership. Quite apart from that, however, was the fact that women would have been considered out of place in both prongs of his interlocked theory, the ecclesiastical hierarchy and the mystical pathway. It was a commonplace of medieval thinking, derived from Aristotle's biology, that women were 'misbegotten males', and were inferior both intellectually and morally. Given that assumption, and the reinforcement it received in the Pauline and patristic exhortations that women should not teach, should keep silence in the church and should be submissive to their husbands at home, it was unthinkable that any woman should enter the ranks of the clergy. If the mysteries of God were the special property of the ecclesiastical hierarchy of bishops, priests and deacons, then obviously women would not be included among those who would have access to them. The world of mystical theology that involved the administration of the sacraments or any other ecclesiastical authority would be a world without women.

But the other aspect of the mystical theology, the mystical path by way of the progress of the intellect through the names of God and then the negation of those names until the mind was transported with ecstasy in dazzling darkness, was hardly less closed to women than the ecclesiastical hierarchy. As already noted in the previous chapter, women were usually not allowed access to books or to the education necessary to appreciate them. They were not encouraged to write. Hence the scholarship involved in poring over the biblical texts and discerning their mystical meaning was not available to women. It was not for women to consider the names of God and ponder both their affirmative and their negative meaning. And it was not for women, intellectual and moral infants that they were, to presume to climb step by step along the mystical path whereby the intellect was progressively illuminated by the divine light and finally transcended itself in ecstasy. Such a path required the best of minds, minds at full stretch – the minds, therefore, of men, not of women. A mysticism of the intellect, such as Dionysius bequeathed to the medieval church, was a gendered mysticism, even though that was never spelled out in his writing, and even though there is no way of knowing whether it formed any part of his deliberate intention.

The huge influence of Dionysius in the medieval period made it inevitable that this gendered aspect of mysticism would be perpetuated. Though it is rarely noted in the histories of medieval mysticism, one of its most striking features is that until the emergence of the phenomenon of visionary women, which I will discuss in a later chapter, almost all the main figures are male. Of course, this need not all be because the mystical path itself was gendered: gender bias also played a large part in who could record their thoughts, whose records would be preserved and read and who would therefore be accorded a place in the historical records. It may be that for many a Dionysius there was a Damaris, wholly ignored in her time and forgotten in ours. Yet in my view the fault here is unlikely to lie primarily with historians' erasure of women. Once the mystical path was delimited in the way that Dionysius had done, there would not be many women who *could* walk it. The social construction of mysticism after Dionysius was a construction which precluded women from counting as mystics. Only when women developed a counter-construction could they also have a place, and then at the cost of arousing male defensiveness, as we shall see.

III ECKHART AND INTELLECTUAL MYSTICISM

Historians of medieval mysticism usually recognise that there were two main channels of thought through the Middle Ages: an intellectual mysticism strongly influenced by Dionysius, and a more affective strand, coming initially from non-Dionysian sources, but then influenced by a reading of him which incorporated a strong element of love (and of Christ) into his teaching. This division into two channels regularly comes with the warning that cross-currents flowed between them in important ways. What is not so often noticed is that neither of the channels had a place for women: both the intellectual and, more surprisingly, the affective mysticism were largely the preserve of men. I shall consider some aspects of the intellectual strand here, chiefly as represented by Eckhart who could be taken as its most important protagonist. Then in the next section I shall go on to the affective strand, before finishing the chapter with a study of female alternatives, the highly charged erotic and bodily-based mysticism which males from that time to this often found disturbing and threatening.

The Dionysian corpus was translated into Latin and commented upon in an influential way by John Scotus Eriugena in the ninth century; and although his work was at first almost ignored, it came to prominence around 1140 in Paris, especially with the work of Hugh of St Victor. Hugh himself incorporated a good deal of a mysticism of love into his interpretation of Dionysius, and thereby influenced the affective strand which I shall discuss later. But the simple fact of his work on Dionysius, together with that of Richard, his fellow Victorine, meant that the mystical theology of Dionysius became central to the thought of other major thinkers from the late twelfth century onwards.

Crucial among these was Albert the Great (*c.* 1200–80) and his pupil Thomas Aquinas. Albert lectured on *The Mystical Theology*, while Thomas took notes which are still extant. Albert stays strictly with the text of Dionysius, not incorporating into the mystical path any mention of love, as the Victorines had done. Instead, Albert emphasised the divine transcendence: the summit of the intellect's mystical path is not a leap into love but rather, as in Dionysius himself, an intellectual ecstasy, a higher form of knowledge which is unknowing. Thomas Aquinas was deeply influenced by Dionysius, both directly and as mediated to him by Albert the Great; and like Albert, he remained true to the Dionysian text, and used the work in the development of his theological system, especially (though not only) in an emphasis on negative theology and the language which it is possible to use to speak of God (Rorem 1993: 222).

The fact that two such pivotal figures as Albert and Thomas paid close attention to Dionysius and used his work extensively in their thinking is sufficient to show that his influence on high medieval thought would be immense. It would be neither possible nor desirable to trace it in detail here. What I wish to do, however, is to show a little of the way in which another student of Albert's, Meister Eckhart, developed an understanding of the spiritual life that strongly emphasises the intellect in a way similar to Dionysius. Eckhart is one of the most significant of those usually classified as medieval mystics; and although there were many other influences upon him besides Dionysius, we shall see that he has a similar stress on the intellect as Dionysius had, and one which makes very clear how women were excluded in such an understanding of the mystical path.

The claim that Eckhart's intellectual mysticism was strongly gendered in a way pejorative to women may come as a surprise to those who have thought of Eckhart in a more positive light. Sometimes, indeed, Eckhart has been claimed as a thirteenth-century feminist, largely on the grounds that he learned a great deal from women in the convents and churches and beguinages in which he preached (Fox 1980: 35). Such learning can indeed be demonstrated (Davies 1991: 51–68); but to what extent this justifies a claim for Eckhart's liberal view of women is quite another matter: certainly the mere fact that Eckhart appropriated the insights of some women (some of whom were themselves strongly male-identified) does not make him any more of a 'feminist' than all the other men who throughout history have helped themselves to women's labour, whether intellectual or physical.

More significant for an argument for Eckhart's egalitarianism is the fact that he was heavily involved in preaching to women's communities, especially the beguines, and in offering them instruction. Although this was characteristic of Dominicans of his time, who by a papal request of 1267 had become responsible for women's houses, Eckhart stands out as a teacher of women in a way that is very much to his credit. If many of the German sermons which have survived of his works were preached to women's communities, as is believed to be the case, then one thing is clear: Eckhart did not minimise the spiritual and intellectual capabilities of women. The sermons sometimes use homely examples, and a deceptively simple style; but anyone who has pondered them can see that they would not have been preached to people whom Eckhart considered either stupid or spiritually incompetent. Furthermore, the very fact that Eckhart preached in the vernacular, sometimes to lay audiences and sometimes to communities of religious women, and that in those sermons some of his most characteristic themes are articulated, shows that he did not for a moment think that holiness was a prerogative of male clerics schooled in ecclesiastical Latin and members of an ecclesiastical hierarchy. In this respect there can be no doubt of his distance from Dionysius.

It seems likely that Eckhart was criticised for preaching as he did, since the women would on the whole not have had a formal education, and there would certainly have been many within ecclesiastical officialdom who would have disapproved of any teaching which might encourage them to get above themselves. But Eckhart commented,

If we are not to teach people who have not been taught, no one will ever be taught, and no one will ever be able to teach or to write. For that is why we teach the untaught, so that they may change from uninstructed to instructed. (1981: 239)

However, Eckhart immediately goes on to cite the comment of Jesus in the gospel of Luke that 'those who are healthy do not need medicine', with the implication that he, Eckhart, is the dispensing physician and his hearers are in a needy and inferior position. Furthermore, there is no indication that Eckhart made any effort to change social boundaries. Even if he held that women and men might be *spiritual* equals, this equality did not translate into views about gender roles in society (Tobin 1986: 16). It had been a commonplace since Augustine, reinforced by Thomas Aquinas (Eckhart's fellow Dominican), that women were indeed made in the image of God, but only in terms of their spirits: this was quite compatible with holding that in social and material reality women were created to serve the needs of men, primarily in terms of reproduction.

Eckhart himself does not often talk about women, either in his sermons or in his Latin writings; but when he does, he uses the same stereotypes that were prevalent throughout patristic and medieval writing. An interesting example occurs in his sermon on Luke 10:38, which he translates (somewhat improbably) as 'Our Lord Jesus Christ went up into a little town, and was received by a virgin who was a wife.' His discussion of this verse is all in terms of spiritual receptivity and fruitfulness: one must be a virgin in order to be completely free and unimpeded by images, but one must become a wife in order to become fruitful.

'Wife' is the noblest word one can apply to the soul, much nobler than 'virgin'. That a man conceives God in himself is good, and in his conceiving he is a maiden. But that God should become fruitful in him is better; for the only gratitude for a gift is to be fruitful with the gift, and then the spirit is a wife, in its gratitude giving birth in return, when he for God gives birth again to Jesus into the heart of the Father. (1981: 178)

Eckhart continues along the same vein, linking attachment to prayer, fasting and other such religious observances to married people who are not free and therefore have no fruit, or only very little: once a year, at best, a child can be expected. But then he suggests that in spiritual terms one can be a fruitful wife and still remain a virgin, and this is the best state of all.

A virgin who is a wife is free and unpledged, without attachment; she is always equally close to God and to herself. She produces much fruit, and it is great, neither less nor more than God himself. This virgin who is a wife brings this fruit and this birth about, and every day she produces fruit, a hundred or a thousand times, yes, more than can be counted, giving birth and becoming fruitful from the noblest ground of all ... (178)

Eckhart's point here is not at all to do with gender as such; his whole concern is to make clear to his listeners the sort of spiritual freedom which is necessary for real fruitfulness. The metaphors of the virgin and the wife are introduced only to illustrate that point. But it is interesting to note that Eckhart takes for granted that such female imagery is appropriate and will make his meaning clear. He assumes that the way to talk about women is in sexualised terms, as either virgins or fruitful wives; that is, in terms of their relationship to men. When he uses male examples, he uses all sorts of characterisations and occupations – noblemen, merchants, cobblers and so on: by no means only as either bachelors or fathers. But when he (relatively infrequently) uses female examples, it is often in relation to the stereotypes of women seen in terms of sexuality and giving birth, an activity which he then appropriates in a spiritual sense also to himself and his male listeners.

Another set of gender stereotypes are reproduced in his Commentary on Exodus, when he discusses the commandment 'Thou shalt not covet.' He points out that in spiritual matters, an evil desire is already an evil fact: weaving his comments around Augustine's theme of concupiscence as evil, Eckhart equates the conception of sin with its birth. He then alludes to the story of the forbidden fruit in the Garden of Eden, and says,

But the 'woman' *who signifies sensuality*, was struck by this beauty and sweetness. She already conceived and at the same time brought forth sin by conceiving ... But make a special note that since the conception is the birth, when someone consents to the conception, as in an evil thought, the sin is already consummated, brings forth death, and hence is mortal. (1986: 109)

He then goes on to identify man with reason, to whom the command not to covet is properly made. Again, his point is not about gender as such; rather, he is trying to clarify the relationship between evil desire and actual sin, using the teaching of Augustine as a springboard. But in doing so, he matter-of-factly adopts the ubiquitous patristic and medieval identification of woman with sensuality and man with reason: it is an identification which, when he develops his mysticism of the intellect, will give it a strong gender bias. At the same time, he links sensuality with sinful desire, with original sin and with female bodiliness.

More frequently, Eckhart connects women, not with sensuality as such, but with inferior reason, and men with superior reason, though the distinction between sensuality and inferior reason is often blurred. What is very clear is that the superior reason, which in Eckhart's terminology is consistently metaphorically male, is that by virtue of which humans can be said to be the image of God; while the inferior reason, linked with sensuality, is metaphorically female. At its best this 'female' inferior reason is a servant of the 'male' superior reason; at its worst, it is that which tempts 'him' into sin. It is worth taking some trouble to examine the various occurrences of these metaphors in Eckhart's writings.

He discusses them most fully in his commentary on Genesis chapter three, the account of the fall in the Garden of Eden. Each of the three main characters of the biblical story, the serpent, Eve and Adam represent, in his view, aspects of the human soul: sensuality, the inferior reason, and the superior reason, respectively. In such an interpretation, he says,

it will also be evident how the serpent, namely the sensitive faculty, can truly and literally speak to the woman, that is, the inferior reason, and how that inferior rational faculty speaks with its superior and how this highest faculty speaks to God, as well as how God addresses all three. (1981: 108)

Although he has initially distinguished the three, however, from this point forward sensuality and the inferior reason collapse into one another, and the main distinction is between these two taken together, on the one hand, and on the other the superior reason, which is again linked to the male. Furthermore, Eckhart adopts the standard characterisation of the female as material and passive, the male as spiritual and active.

This sensitive faculty is by nature under the intellective faculty, and like a servant it is outside the genus of what is intellective through its essence, because it serves man's intellect with the phantasm without which we cannot understand ... It is the handmaid of generation ... Again, just as in the case of generation in bodily things we find two principles under the same species, namely form and matter, the active and the passive, so too our intellectual faculty is distinguished into a superior part and an inferior one ... (109)

We see in this passage an acceptance and repetition of the standard ideas about women, deriving from a combination of Aristotelian biology and patristic and medieval Christian teaching: women are classified with that which is inferior, passive and material, they are seen as servants, and thought of in terms of reproductive function.

This linkage occurs several more times, always in connection with Eckhart's distinction between the inferior and superior reason. In his 'Commentary on the Gospel of John', for instance, he discusses the phrase 'and the light shines in the darkness'. Reversing usual ideas about light and darkness in a manner echoing the writings of Dionysius, Eckhart says,

It is fitting that what is highest and finest in the realm of the intellect is as it were invisible and unknown to us and denoted by darkness ... (153)

This darkness is metaphorically male; whereas the light which shines through this darkness is the 'cloudy' knowledge derived by the senses, the female. Thus Eckhart begins to demonstrate the gendered nature of the Dionysian understanding of the pathway to the divine darkness. He continues,

You can say quite fittingly that the 'light of men' is the inferior reason signified by the woman with the veiled head. The man with the unveiled head is the image of God, the superior reason, signified through the darkness ... (153)

Eckhart uses the Pauline exhortation regarding the veiling of women again in a similar way in a sermon where he is urging his listeners to leave behind the creatureliness of the inferior reason and 'take God as he is in himself'. Here he says,

This is why males are compared to the highest powers – because they always have their head bare, while women are compared to the lower powers because their head is always covered. The highest powers are above time and place and have their origin without mediation in the being of the soul. This is why they are like men because they always stand bare. Thus their acts are eternal. (1986: 278)

The imagery in this passage is very much like that in the 'Commentary on Genesis'; but it adds the significant idea that the superior reason, the highest 'male' powers of the soul, are eternal, beyond time and place. Thus it is indicated that they are transcendent, god-like, the likeness of God in the human person. And this god-likeness is metaphorically male, while that which is not god-like in the human person is metaphorically female, and must be overcome if spiritual advance is to take place.

One last passage must suffice, again from one of the German sermons. Eckhart is discussing the verse, 'Happy is the man who dwells in wisdom' (Sir.14.22). Here we find considerable ambiguity in the gendered way he uses the imagery. First he says, 'Wisdom is a name for a mother', but immediately continues, 'The characteristic of a motherly name is passivity.' Although passivity is often linked with what is inferior, however, this passage cannot be taken in such a negative way, for Eckhart goes on, 'in God both activity and passivity must be thought. The Father is active, and the Son is passive because of his function as the one being born.' Therefore the Son is Wisdom, the mother, in whom 'the man' should dwell happily. We are still a very long way from Julian of Norwich's theology of Jesus as Mother, but there are some glimmering affinities. However, Eckhart immediately proceeds,

Now it says, 'Happy is the *man*.' I have often said that there are two powers in the soul: One is the man and one is the woman. And it says, 'Happy is the man.' The power in the soul that one calls the man is the highest power of the soul in which God shines bare; for into this power nothing enters but God, and this power is continually in God ... Therefore a person should dwell continually in this power because all things are alike in this power ... (1986: 302)

So again we have the equation of the male with the higher, god-like power and the female with the inferior power; and it is in the male-identified power, where 'God shines bare', that one should dwell.

If we consider these passages in the light of the discussion of previous chapters, we can see how much latitude has entered into the notion of a mystical interpretation of scripture, how bound up it is in Eckhart's thinking with a conception of a mystical path influenced by Dionysius' emphasis on the intellect, and how such a view becomes explicitly gendered. The patristic practice of seeking a hidden or mystical meaning in scripture in which the passage's underlying reference to Christ can be discerned has been broadened almost beyond recognition. In the passages discussed, and in many others like them in Eckhart's writings, the biblical passage he cites becomes the jumping-off point for his spiritual teaching. His interpretative method is like that of the patristic writers who looked for the mystical meaning of scripture only in the sense that what he has to say often bears little relation to any possible literal or historical interpretation. But whereas for them the goal was to discern Christ, who was held to be both concealed and revealed in every passage of the Bible, in Eckhart this Christocentric emphasis has all but disappeared. Although he does make reference to Christ (more often in terms of the Son of God than in terms of the human Jesus), he is free in his interpretation of scriptural passages to range over a wide variety of ideas, and does not restrict himself to a Christological meaning.

The intellectual emphasis of his writing and its gendered nature is already becoming clear. In Eckhart's view, the higher intellect, which is that which bears the image of God, is also the point of union with God; and he consistently identifies it in male terms. It is true that at least at the level of exposition, the gendered language is illustrative; and it could quite plausibly be argued that the passages could be restated without any reference to gender. One could retain Eckhart's idea about the superior and inferior parts or powers of the soul and their respective relations to God without those powers being connected with the male and female respectively. In contrast to other metaphors which we will examine in a later chapter, where the meaning of what is said is closely bound up with the verbal images, it might be possible to restate Eckhart's essential meaning without employing the gendered metaphors, which after all reflected the stereotypical ideas of maleness and femaleness of patristic and medieval times.

But such an ameliorative effort comes to grief when we examine Eckhart's teaching of the relation of the soul to God more closely. It then becomes apparent that Eckhart's gendered metaphors were not merely occasional throw-away remarks which could be omitted without loss, but that his mystical teaching itself, like that of Dionysius, was one which was biased against women, in spite of the fact that Eckhart spent much effort, and was probably criticised, for preaching to women as he did. Eckhart's teaching, in its emphasis on the higher intellect, was strongly opposed to any form of quasi-sensory religious experience. This meant that he was setting himself in opposition to the women's mysticism developing in the Rhineland at the time, which had a strong emphasis on visionary experience and ascetical exercises. I shall discuss this more fully in chapter 5 in connection with the suppression of visionary women; suffice it to say here that for Eckhart, genuine mysticism must involve the 'male' reason, not the 'female' sensory faculties, and that therefore visionary experiences could not be considered as spiritually significant.

Eckhart is famous for his theme of the *Vünkelîn*, or spark of the soul. From the way in which Eckhart develops the idea of this spark of the soul, we can see both parallels and contrasts with Dionysian speculative or intellectual mysticism, rather than an affective stance: Eckhart is focused upon rationality and right knowing, rather than upon love or desire. Though it would not be accurate to say that the latter have no place at all in his thinking, their role is subordinate.

As already discussed, Eckhart distinguishes between the inferior rational faculty which is conjoined to the senses, and the superior rational faculty, which is formed directly by God and which is the highest part of the soul. It is this, furthermore, which is the *imago Dei*, that which 'underlies sameness with the divine essence' (Tobin 1986: 129). Since Eckhart accepts the Platonic principle that like can only be known by like, it is this sameness which makes it possible for a human being to know God. The superior rational faculty is identified with a variety of different images that Eckhart uses in the vernacular sermons, often taking a biblical passage as a jumping-off point for an interpretation which has no obvious connection with it. He speaks of the spark of the soul, the power of the soul, the little castle or temple, the beam of light, the loftiest branch and so on. Although the idea of the superior rationality was not a new one in medieval thought, Eckhart embellished and used it in a unique way.

Medieval thinkers, especially Albert the Great and Thomas Aquinas, had accepted Dionysius' teaching that human language and concepts are inadequate to the task of describing God in positive terms. Human words can point to what God is not, but they cannot state what God is. A reason for this, already present in Dionysius and further developed by Eckhart in his *Parisian Questions* and his *Tripartite Work*, is that human language and concepts are derived from created things; but the gulf between God and created things is infinite. Being, *esse*, is God; and any being which creatures have is derived from God, not merely in the sense that God made them in the first place, but that whatever being they have at any time is of God. In themselves, Eckhart is fond of saying, they are 'pure nothing', in contrast with God who is pure being.

Creatures have no being because their being depends on God's presence. If God were to turn away from creatures for an instant, they would turn to nothing. (Eckhart 1986: 246)

Yet on the other hand they do have being, insofar as they have been granted being by God. Therefore 'the nature of a creature ... is to exist in the tension between nothingness and infinite divinity' (Tobin 1986: 64).

This tension is above all characteristic of human beings. On the one hand, people are created beings, and in that sense 'pure nothing', like all other items of creation. Yet in the case of people there is a difference from other creatures, because human beings are made in the image of God, or, to put it another way, there is that in humans which is god-like and hence akin rather to being than to nothing. This is what Eckhart designates as 'the spark in the soul', again using his characteristically gendered language:

The spark of the intellect, which is the head of the soul, is called the husband [or man] of the soul, and is none other than a tiny spark of the divine nature, a divine light, a ray and an imprint of the divine nature. (Eckhart 1979: 229)

Yet, like all other creatures, this 'spark' is directly dependent upon God; it is not something in any way independent. Indeed, insofar as it is most aptly describable as *knowing*, it is the same as God, whose being Eckhart has characterised as knowing. From this, Eckhart draws startling conclusions:

His causing me to know and my knowing are the same thing. Hence his knowing is mine, just as what the teacher teaches and what the pupil is taught are one. And because his knowing is mine and because his substance, his nature, and his being are his knowing, it follows that his being, his substance, and his nature are mine. And because his substance, his nature, and his being are mine, I am the Son of God. (1986: 328)

The spark of the soul, the *imago dei*, is that which knows God with divine knowledge, and thus participates in the divine nature or is one with God.

But not just any knowing is this oneness with God; indeed, there is a sense in which all of Eckhart's writings, and especially his sermons, are intended to draw people *towards* such knowing, such union with God, in just the way in which Dionysius' *The Mystical Theology* was meant not just as a description of a mystical path but as itself serving as that path for its readers. In the sermon just quoted, for instance, Eckhart distinguishes between inward knowing and outward knowing: it is the same distinction as the one between superior and inferior rationality which we have already considered. Outward knowing is ordinary human knowing, knowing that depends on the (female) senses and their activities. Inward knowing, however, is the (male) knowing which 'breaks through' from such external knowing into divine knowledge, which is the life of the soul. The 'break through', for Eckhart, is parallel to the 'ecstasy' of Dionysius: in neither case is it a movement from the intellect to love, but rather a break through or ecstasy of the intellect itself. Eckhart says,

In saying that knowing is something of the life of the soul, we mean the intellectual life, and in this life a person is born the Son of God and born for eternal life. This knowing is beyond time and place, beyond here and now. In this life all things are one; all things together, all and all united in all and all. (328)

The way to attain such knowing requires a turning away from all outward knowing, a state of complete detachment (*Abgeschei-denheit*). This does not mean, in Eckhart, only what it normally meant in ascetical writing, namely detachment from the pleasures of the flesh. Rather, it means turning from all false conceptions which might have been provided by the (female) inferior reason and sensuality, and coming to recognise oneself accurately, that is, as united with God. In doing so, the mind can, so to speak, become what it is. As Frank Tobin puts it in his excellent study of Eckhart, 'just as one cannot look upon God and not love him, so one cannot know one's true self and what one's true being is without detaching oneself from everything, including self, other than God' (1986: 126). It is in this sense that intellectual recognition is essential to Eckhart's spirituality: in order to be united with God, it is necessary to recognise what we are and what God is, and radically detach ourselves from all of what we are except only this true being, this higher (male) intellect, which is God. This is also why there is so little room in Eckhart's spirituality for visionary experiences: they would not bring about the recognition of divine union, and as such could only stand in its way.

It is quite clear, from all of this, that the gender implications of Eckhart's speculative mysticism are weighted against women. The inferior intellect, associated in Eckhart's metaphors with the female, is that which connects us to the world and to our own bodies and to one another. All this is to be completely left behind. We are to be sundered or detached from it, and altogether taken up into the superior intellect, that which is eternal and god-like and other than the sensory and material world. God, who is identified as active and knowing, is contrasted with the material world, which is identified as inert or passive and unknowing; and the *imago dei*, the active and rational aspect of human nature, is contrasted with the physical, un-god-like, bodily and sexual aspect. In each case, the first item of the pair is to be valued, and the second is to be devalued in comparison. The first is identified with the male and the second with the female.

It is clear, therefore, that the misogyny of Eckhart's teaching is more than metaphor-deep: the metaphors are indicative of a whole view of God, human nature and the spiritual path which keeps women in an inferior position. Speculative mysticism such as we find in Eckhart was a social construction of mysticism which accepted the Platonic ascetical idea that bodiliness and 'outward knowledge' is something which is to be transcended, something from which the one who treads the mystical path of the mind must be increasingly detached. The intellect, the 'superior rationality', is seen as somehow more god-like than the body and the senses; and it has long Platonic roots in suspicion of the body and of sexuality. It expressed itself in Eckhart and in many other strands throughout the Christian west, medieval and modern, in an exaltation of a detached intellect, fear of the body and many-layered misogyny. In spite of the fact that Eckhart's practice of teaching women was less misogynistic than the content of his theory, it is the latter which has had the abiding influence. In Hegel, in Heidegger, even in Derrida, the influence of Eckhart is still apparent. Even though they are not always aware of the gender bias of his mysticism, and even though they might repudiate it, it is so deeply intertwined with the speculative mysticism which he develops that it continues to percolate through any number of disclaimers. Speculative mysticism, a mysticism of the intellect, as it was constructed by men like Eckhart, did not make it easy to count women as mystics.

IV AFFECTIVE MYSTICISM

The uncompromisingly intellectual nature of the mystical path as developed by Dionysius, and the absence of emphasis on Christ in his thinking, was uncomfortable for many western thinkers, who modified his views even while also being influenced by them. Eckhart was one of the thinkers who accepted Dionysius' intellectualism most rigorously, and even he, as we have noted, modified it in several directions, partly through the influence of women with whom he came into contact in person or through their writings. Already with Eriugena's translation and commentary of Dionysius into Latin, there was a creative effort to combine his intellectual mysticism with the Augustinian stress on love, an effort which continued in the high Middle Ages. Before Dionysius was taken up by the Schoolmen in the twelfth century monastic writers were largely uninfluenced by him; and their spirituality was strongly affective and Augustinian. The most important of these was Bernard of Clairvaux.

The emphasis of Bernard took as central exactly what intellectual mysticism left out: an ardent love for Christ, especially Christ crucified, was at its heart. One could characterise the affective strand of mysticism from Augustine to Bernard and onward as a mysticism of the heart, as contrasted with a mysticism of the head, the strand of intellectual mysticism from Dionysius to Eckhart. To do so would be to caricature both of them: Augustine and Bernard insisted on the importance of the mind, which they agreed was the image of God in the human person, and Dionysius sometimes spoke of love (though not in *The Mystical Theology*). Nevertheless, it is a caricature with considerable truth. In the later western tradition writers such as Bonaventure, the anonymous author of *The Cloud of Unknowing*, and, much later, John of the Cross, developed creative combinations of the speculative and the affective strands. It would take us too far afield to examine the many tributaries of the channel of affective mysticism and its mergings with the speculative strands; but I wish to look at Bernard as a fundamental source.

One would expect that an affective mysticism would have more room for women than would a speculative mysticism, given the medieval assumptions about women as intellectually inferior; and to some extent that is indeed the case. But it will emerge that this is only partly true; and that the emphasis on love and will were often conjoined with an actual despising of bodiliness and sexuality, and, inevitably, of women.

Bernard of Clairvaux was born in 1090, and after he entered the monastery in his early twenties he quickly became the most dynamic leader the Cistercians had ever known. His life was an active one, as full of contradictions as his character: he advocated solitude and stability, and spent most of his time in tireless travel and political and ecclesiastical intrigue; he preached the centrality of love, and thundered forth the Second Crusade (Lerclercq 1976). While his influence was far-reaching in more than one respect, I shall focus here only on his teaching on love and its place within his understanding of Christian spirituality. According to his thinking, the whole aim of the Christian life is to come into union with God; and if this is the aim of the Christian life in general, all the more is it the aim of the Cistercian monk. The Cistercians adopted the Benedictine self-designation of a monastery as a 'school for the service of the Lord', a service that was fundamentally one of love (Benedict 1975). Thus the motto of Clairvaux, the first of Bernard's many new foundations, was *In schola Christi sumus*: the main lesson to be learned was the lesson of how to live in charity (Gilson 1955a). This notion of charity, however, is not the watered-down idea we have of it today, such that 'living in charity' means little more than living in polite harmony. Charity (*caritas*) is in its primary designation for Bernard none other than God: God is Charity. This marks him out against Dionysius, and even against Eckhart, for whom the primary designation of God is Being, and frequently also Knowledge.

If the primary designation of charity is God, its secondary designation is the gift of God, identified with the gift of the Holy Spirit and the presence of the Holy Spirit in the soul. To learn to live in charity, therefore, is to learn to live in God, by virtue of God's indwelling and transforming spirit of charity. This is the goal of the Christian life. Again, this forms a strong contrast to the speculative tradition, which, as we have seen, characterises the progress of the soul not in terms of love but in terms of increasing knowledge of God.

Bernard's writings are directed to an exploration of the dimensions of this life of love and how it can be developed. *The Steps of Humility*, for instance, is an often amusing discussion of how the individual comes to live in the truth of God's love, through the development of humility, or else descends away from truth to contempt for God and estrangement from God. His enormously influential treatise *On Loving God* has as its explicit theme the question 'why and how God is to be loved', and moves from lower stages to the point where, by God's grace, God is to be loved for God's sake alone.

When a feeling of this kind is experienced, the soul, drunk with divine love, forgetful of self, and seeming to be a broken vessel, goes completely into God, and cleaving to God becomes one spirit with him ... (1974: 1)

The parallel and the contrast with Dionysius is striking: in Bernard, too, there is a step-by-step progress, but it is a progress of humility, penitence and love, rather than a progress of the mind. And in Bernard, too, there is ecstasy, *ek stasis*, a standing outside of oneself; but it is as a broken vessel going completely into God, 'drunk with divine love', not an intellectual ecstasy that has passed into the unknowing beyond knowledge. Not that Bernard despises knowledge: even literary knowledge is important to him (Leclercq 1978). Yet of the two, love is fundamental, and most deeply engages the human psyche. It is love, he holds, which can bring about moral transformation and fulfilment, rectifying the distortions of personality which have been twisted and hurt by sin, and bringing healing in union with God who is *caritas* (Gilson 1955a).

Bernard's most sustained writing is his set of eighty-six sermons *On the Song of Songs*, a book favoured by spiritual writers since the time of Origen. True to medieval exegetical practice, Bernard explores the mystical meaning of the scripture he contemplates, and seeks in the biblical text the ways of love between God and human beings. Early in the sermons, where Bernard is about to expound upon the first verse of the Song of Songs ('Let him kiss me with the kisses of his mouth'), he addresses the monks thus:

Today the text we are going to study is the book of our own experience ... Anyone who has received this mystical kiss from the mouth of Christ at least once, seeks again that intimate experience, and eagerly looks for its frequent renewal ... (1977: III.1.1)

Significantly, the mystical is no longer confined to the meaning of scripture (though the whole exercise derives from such interpretation) nor to an intellectual progress, but is extended to *experience*. This is a major transition in the understanding of what the mystical is, a transition which was by no means even or unilinear. Bernard's emphasis on experience came long before Eckhart's rigorously intellectual mysticism that we have already examined: Eckhart knew Bernard well, but in this respect differed from him. Nor was Bernard's emphasis on experience quite what might be meant by that term today. It continued to be based on the encounter with Christ in the mystical meaning of scripture, and was strongly opposed to visions or locutions or other such sensory experiences, as we shall see in the next chapter. Nevertheless, we have in Bernard a clear recognition of the mystical as experiential: it is a shift in meaning whose resonances are with us still.

Furthermore, that experience, throughout the sermons, is, as here, modelled on the erotic: it is a mystical *kiss*. From this point forward we have in Bernard's sermons a series of meditations in which the erotic imagery of the Song of Songs becomes the basis for his understanding of union with God. He speaks in detail of the mystical meaning of the kisses of the Lord's feet, hands and mouth, the breasts of the bride and the bridegroom, the qualities of their love, and so on (and on). Bernard did not invent the idea of God as the lover and bridegroom of the soul; we have already seen how Origen used it, and there were many others who embroidered the motif in the intervening period. But in Bernard's hands erotic imagery became the guiding theme for his exploration of union with God. It was a theme that gained great prominence among both male and female writers of the high Middle Ages, though there was a pronounced gender difference in the ways they employed it, as we shall see.

Bernard dwells at length on all the possibilities of the biblical text. The phrase 'the kisses of his mouth' is taken to imply that there must be other sorts of kisses; and Bernard considers that the first kiss must be the penitent kissing the feet of Jesus, the second kiss must be the forgiven one kissing the hand of the Saviour, and only then can one hope for 'a holier intimacy'. Bernard moves from addressing his brother monks to direct address of Christ:

In the dawn you brought me proof of your love, as in my first approach to kiss your revered feet you forgave my evil ways as I lay in the dust. With the advancement of the day you gave your servant reason to rejoice when, in the kiss of the hand, you imparted the grace to live rightly. And now what remains, O good Jesus, except that suffused as I am with the fullness of your light, and while my spirit is fervent, you would graciously bestow on me the kiss of your mouth, and give me unbounded joy in your presence. (3.6)

The three kisses are here made to correspond to the three stages of the mystical path as they had been defined by Origen and Dionysius: purgation, illumination and union. Yet in Bernard's use they are very different from that of the previous writers: they are all deeply affective, progress being the result of penitence and love, not of intellectual insight. Furthermore, like Origen and Dionysius, Bernard is engaging in exegesis which seeks the mystical meaning of scripture. Apart from the fact that all the sermons are meant as a commentary on the Song of Songs, virtually every paragraph is a catena of biblical quotations woven together to convey Bernard's meaning: in the passage just quoted, for example, at least four citations from the Psalms are embedded. His immersion in scripture is if anything deeper than what we find in Dionysius, much more Augustinian in tone, and above all, much more focused on Christ and on penitent and joyful love for him.

It is this focus which the erotic imagery is meant to draw out and to foster in the hearers and readers of his sermons. It is a language of passion and desire, not a cool intellectual progress.

No sweeter names can be found to embody that sweet interflow of affections between the Word and the soul, than bridegroom and bride. Between these all things are equally shared, there are no selfish reservations, nothing that causes division. They share the same inheritance, the same table, the same home, the same marriage-bed, they are flesh of each other's flesh ... Therefore if a love relationship is the special and outstanding characteristic of the bride and groom, it is not unfitting to call the soul that loves God a bride. (2.2)

The vocabulary of erotic yearning, the hunger for the presence of the beloved and for sexual consummation, of bliss and contentment is the weft on which Bernard's sermons are woven. In Bernard, too, there is ecstasy, but it is an ecstasy not of an intellect transcending itself but of a love fulfilled. A concentration on this side of Bernard's writing could portray him as a mystic made in the image of modern romanticism.

But if the weft of his sermons is the vocabulary of erotic love, the warp is a sharp denial of the body as having any part in it. The love with which the soul is to seek God is to be purely spiritual; the desire and passion and consummation are not to be thought of as in any sense engaging actual bodiliness and sexuality. In fact, reading these sermons of Bernard (and many others in the same vein by male medieval spiritual writers), one of the most striking features is how unerotic they actually are. Although they are explicitly based on one of the most erotic love poems in the literature of the world, they manage to reduce eroticism to a sustained allegory, intellectually intricate, but hardly passionate. Here, for example, is part of Bernard's comment when he is discussing the breasts of the bride and the bridegroom: the reference in this quotation is to the latter.

These two breasts are two proofs of his native kindness: his patience in awaiting the sinner and his welcoming mercy for the penitent. This twofold sweetness of inward joy overflows from the heart of the Lord Jesus in the form of tireless expectancy and prompt forgiveness ... It is through her experience of this twofold goodness, therefore, that the bride justifies the increase of confidence that emboldened her to ask for the kiss ... (9.5)

Time after time, when Bernard begins with a theme set in an erotic key, he transposes it into a spiritual meaning which leaves out the physical and the sensual. In this passage as in countless others, it is as if Bernard had set out deliberately to de-eroticize the passage; and in a sense, that is exactly correct. Indeed, it would hardly be going too far to see his vocabulary of passionate spirituality as a substitute for actual bodily love.

Already in Origen we saw how the love of the soul for the spiritual bridegroom left no room for any other form of sexual expression: chastity was stipulated as a prerequisite for even reading Origen's book. Just the same emphasis occurs in Bernard. Any bodily passion should have been completely extinguished or at least fully controlled before so much as beginning to listen to his sermons. He warns his hearers:

This holy and contemplative discourse ... may be delivered only to well prepared ears and minds. Before the flesh has been tamed and the spirit set free by zeal for truth, before the world's glamour and entanglements have been firmly repudiated, it is a rash enterprise on any man's part to presume to study spiritual doctrines. (1.3)

The 'taming of the flesh' requires strict sexual continence. Indeed, Bernard uses the (assumed) chastity of the bride as an allegory of the chastity necessary for anyone who hopes to be the 'bride of Christ': he takes it as given that one cannot expect to experience spiritual love if one is entangled in physical passion. Those who have been thus involved and are now penitent he identified with the 'ladies-in-waiting' of the biblical book:

[they] are the ones who, once conformed to this world by shamefully prostituting themselves on the full tide of carnal lust to the princes of this world, whose law was lustful desire, are now at last filled with the shame that urges them to rid themselves of that deformity and to hasten to put on the form of the new man ... (14.5)

There is no place in Bernard's sermons for passionate bodily and sexual love which is good and wholesome and to be welcomed: there is nothing between 'shameful prostitution' and the spiritual love of Christ in which physical passion has been extinguished. As in the case of Origen, human bodiliness and sexuality is seen as a barrier to the spiritual love of God; it is not seen as an icon of that love or a channel through which it might flow. Thus whereas the *language* of Bernard's affective mysticism is a language of passion and desire, and in that sense forms a strong contrast to that of Dionysius, Eckhart and the speculative tradition, we can eventually see that the *reality* is just as hostile to bodiliness and sexuality in Bernard's affective strand as it is in the intellectual strand. This is of course entirely consistent with the ascetical fervour of Bernard and the early Cistercians. It also had sharp gender implications.

Bernard accepted the medieval commonplace that women were inferior to men, weaker in body and mind, and identified with the physical and earthly, as contrasted with the stronger male, who was identified with the spiritual. His writings use references to women as allegories for weakness and immaturity: a bishop, for instance, carries 'burdens made for men', which a weaker monk should not be expected to endure, unless 'he eventually emerges from womanhood to manhood, to mature manhood' at which time he too may 'engage in a work of corresponding dignity' (12.8; 54.2; 13.5). Furthermore, women were linked with the physical and the sensual. Commenting on what he takes to be a rebuke of the bridegroom to the bride in the Song of Songs, he says,

I believe that by women he means people who are sensual and worldly, people devoid of manliness, whose conduct lacks both fortitude and constancy, people who are entirely superficial, soft and effeminate in their lives and behaviour. (38.4)

This contrasts with 'the person who is spiritual', who enjoys 'a beauty that comes from following the ways of the Spirit rather than the ways of the flesh'. However, even such a person is still short of perfection 'by the fact of living in the body'. We have, therefore, in Bernard the standard progression from the female, linked with immersion in the physical, to the male, who, though spiritual, is still trapped in the physical body, to the perfect in heaven, freed from all physicality and made wholly spiritual. The further one moves toward heavenly perfection, the more one must leave the 'female' and its bodiliness behind.

How, then, should a woman be made perfect? What sort of spirituality is possible for her? Again, the pattern repeats itself: for a man to become spiritual he must increasingly become what he is; but for a woman to become spiritual, she must become what she is not. The affective mysticism of Bernard does no better on this score than does the speculative mysticism of Dionysius and

Eckhart. Although the spiritual, and spiritual progress, is differently characterised in these two strands, both characterisations are fundamentally opposed to bodiliness, and both of them link bodiliness with women. The spiritual path is a path for manly souls.

Bernard, in fact, was if anything even more conscious of the way in which women might act as a temptation and a snare to men: his greater emphasis on emotion and experience made him acutely aware of the sorts of emotions to which he and his monks were susceptible. His sermons contain repeated warnings against monks being with women, lest temptation and sin result. Perhaps the most striking example is one which, though not directly attributable to Bernard, comes from his *Life*, written by his friend, William of St Thierry. According to this account, Bernard's sister Humbeline came to see him and her other brothers who had gone with Bernard into the monastery of Clairvaux. When she came, Bernard, 'hating and loathing her as if she were a snare of the devil set on luring souls, refused to go out to see her'. When she protested at this treatment, another of her brothers, Andrew, who was doorkeeper of the monastery, 'rebuked her with being a parcel of dung, because of her elegant clothes'. Whereupon, William says, she repented and began to live the life of a hermit (Leclercq 1989: 121).

Jean Leclercq, who recounts this story, does so for the purpose of exonerating Bernard of misogyny, arguing that the whole episode was an invention of William of St Thierry's, and was based on the idea, prevalent in medieval thought, that a woman was 'a bag of shit' – a more literal translation of the phrase which Leclercq renders as 'parcel of dung'. Leclercq, indeed, wants to show that Bernard's view of women was on the whole favourable. He does this in part by explaining that whenever Bernard referred to the weakness or sinfulness of women, he applied his analysis to men, saying that they were 'effeminate' or insufficiently manly: it is hardly an explanation which serves as a reason to believe that Bernard thought well of women! Neither will Leclercq's emphasis on Bernard's veneration of Mary as the one who put right all the things which Eve had caused to go wrong. The image of Mary the immaculate virgin mother has been as oppressive to women who have been asked to take her as their (clearly impossible) example as has the most virulently misogynist writing.

As to the passage about woman as a 'bag of shit', it really does not matter very much whether it was said by Andrew, with or without Bernard's approval, or whether it was put into his mouth by William of St Thierry, who, after all, was almost as influential in his time as Bernard himself. The point is not so much who said it, as that this is a view of women which was prevalent among those who, like both Bernard and William, saw the spiritual path in affective terms that required leaving the body and sensuality behind. Not only were women themselves unlikely to be able to proceed far along the spiritual path (the heroic exceptions being those who became 'manly' in their endeavours) but they were also a hindrance to men. Affective mysticism, far from being more open to women than the speculative tradition, could be even more fearful and repressive of women than Dionysius or Eckhart ever were, both in theory and in practice.

The two traditions were fruitfully combined in subsequent writers such as Bonaventure and, especially, the anonymous fourteenth-century English writer of *The Cloud of Unknowing*. In each of them and many others like them, the mystical ascent to God is seen in terms of the mind and its progress, but that progress is a progress not of pure intellect, but also of love: love and knowledge enable each other. In *The Cloud*, in particular, the 'unknowing' of Dionysius is itself a term for love, and is contrasted sharply with knowledge, which, true to Dionysius' teaching, can never be adequate to the reality of God.

But no man can think of God himself. Therefore it is my wish to leave everything that I can think of and choose for my love the thing that I cannot think. Because he can certainly be loved, but not thought. He can be taken and held by love but not by thought. Therefore ... you are to smite upon that thick cloud of unknowing with a sharp dart of longing love. Do not leave that work for anything that may happen. (Anon 1981: 130)

It would take us much too far afield to trace all the combinations of this theme: some of them will emerge more fully in the following chapter, when we see how the men who were trying to combine the intellectual and the affective were threatened by a quite different kind of spirituality emerging among religious women.

V THE EROTIC OTHER

Although the women mystics of the high Middle Ages who used the erotic as their model for union with God are often lumped together with male writers like Bernard who also used erotic imagery, in fact they are strikingly different. With the women there is a direct, highly charged, passionate encounter between Christ and the writer. The sexuality is explicit, and there is no warning that it should not be taken literally. There is no intellectualising or spiritualising, no climbing up into the head, or using the erotic as an allegory hedged about with warnings. To be sure, the sexual encounter is also a spiritual one; moral and spiritual lessons are to be learned. But they are to be learned, not by allegorising what is happening, but by highly charged encounter. The usual male anchoring in the mystical meaning of scripture is often absent, since the women did not have access to the education or the ecclesiastical position which would make possible for them the years of Bible study which many of the male writers enjoyed. Here, for example, is Mechthild of Magdeburg, writing in the thirteenth century, recounting part of her mystical encounter:

Then the Most Beloved goes toward the Most Beautiful in the hidden chambers of the invisible Deity. There she finds the couch and the pleasure of Love, and God awaiting her in a superhuman fashion. This is what Our Lord says: – Stay, Lady Soul. – What is your wish, Lord? – That you should be naked. – Lord, how can this happen to me? – Lady Soul, you are so 'co-natured' in Me that nothing can be interposed between you and Me ... your noble desire and your insatiable hunger ... I shall satisfy eternally with My infinite superabundance. (Zum Brunn 1989: 59)

There is no specific reference back to scripture here; more strikingly, there is no word of caution about how this is to be read. On the contrary, there is every indication that, far from the erotic being simply an allegory for the spiritual, it is precisely through actual eroticism that lessons of God are to be learned.

The same is true of many medieval women: Gertrude the Great of Helfta, Catherine of Siena, Beatrice of Nazareth and, much later, Teresa of Avila are all obvious examples. Of course there were variations among these women which deserve to be studied in detail. For the purposes of tracing the gender relations in the social construction of mysticism, however, it is most significant to see how these women, for all their differences, nevertheless showed similarities among themselves which were in considerable contrast to the male mystical writers of either the intellectual or the affective strand or their later varying combinations. To bring this out clearly it is more useful to look in some detail at one woman writer than to pick passages out of context from many of them. I propose, therefore, to concentrate on Hadewijch of Antwerp; but I wish to be clear that although I am focusing on only this one woman, the women mystics were not monolithic and deserve to be studied individually in much more detail. Some of them will be considered more fully in the next chapter in connection with their visionary experiences.

Little is known about Hadewijch herself. She lived in the early part of the thirteenth century, probably in and around Antwerp, and is associated with the women's religious movement known as the beguines, whom we will encounter again. The beguines were women who did not join a religious order or take vows like cloistered nuns did, but rather tried to develop their own pattern of prayer, manual work and efforts of charity, especially relief of the poor and sick. Gradually they formed themselves into groups. At first they were suspected of heresy (the parallel male group, the beghards, were convicted of it); and some of them were persecuted: Hadewijch may have been one of them. Later, partly through the offices of Jacques de Vitry, they received papal authorisation, but at the price of living in common in enclosures (beguinages) and submitting to the oversight of a male religious, often a Dominican friar, who acted as confessor and adviser.

Hadewijch had somehow acquired enough education to be able to read and write, though her writings are in the vernacular Middle Dutch rather than in Latin. Her most important writings are her *Poems in Stanzas* and her *Poems in Couplets*. In addition, she wrote a series of thirty-one letters, most of which were addressed to a young beguine whom Hadewijch loved and whom she wished to instruct in spirituality. She also records a series of fourteen visions, which we will consider further in the next chapter. It has been suggested that they occurred when she was still quite young, and that they were written down at the behest of her confessor: another suggestion, which I find more plausible from the internal evidence, is that they were recorded for the instruction of young beguines (Hart 1980: 23).

However that may be, Hadewijch in her book of visions gives an account of what happened one Pentecost Sunday when she was in church at dawn for the office of matins.

With that he came in the form and clothing of a Man, as he was on the day when he gave us his body for the first time; looking like a human being and a man, wonderful, and beautiful, and with glorious face, he came to me as humbly as anyone who wholly belongs to another. Then he gave himself to me in the shape of the sacrament ... After that he came himself to me, took me entirely in his arms, and pressed me to him; and all my members felt his full felicity, in accordance with the desire of my heart and my humanity. So I was outwardly satisfied and fully transported ... but soon, after a short time, I lost that manly beauty outwardly in the sight of his form ... (281)

Hadewijch, even more than Mechthild, treats the erotic not as an allegory as Bernard did, but as an actual, though visionary, encounter. Her account of it is not meant as an account of a physical occurrence which could have been observed by other people present in the church, but neither is it meant as simply a figure of speech from which one can ring instructive changes. Rather, it is spiritual love-making. It is important that it takes place in the context of the eucharist: we shall see shortly the significance of this for Hadewijch.

Hadewijch speaks often of the goal of her longing as 'having fruition of love'. In one of her poems she writes,

> Since you, O Love, can do all with love,
> Give me, for the sake of love, the fruition
> That delights the loving soul through your highest goodness!
>
> (236)

'Fruition' is a term which, in Hadewijch's usage, has strongly passionate connotations. In the many poems in which Hadewijch appropriates the genre of courtly love, there are associations of the knight pleading with his Lady Love for consummation of his desire: the language is poignantly erotic.

> He who serves Love has a hard adventure
> Before he knows Love's mode of action,
> Before he is fully loved by her.
> He tastes her as bitter and sour;
> He cannot rest for an instant,
> So long as Love does not fetter him completely in love
> And bring him into the union of fruition.   (131)

Hadewijch is here spectacularly reversing the usual gender stereotypes: God is Lady Love, while the soul, which as has been noted is almost always feminine in medieval writing, is the male knight.

In another poem, rather than pleading for fruition, Hadewijch describes what that fruition is like: again, the language throughout the poem is unmistakably the language of sexual passion. One stanza reads,

> So for the soul things go marvellously;
> While desire pours out and pleasure drinks,
> The soul consumes what belongs to it in love
> And sinks with frenzy into Love's fruition.
> So in love the loving soul has full success,
> When Love with love fully gives her love;
> Thus is the loving soul well fed by Love alone,
> Where it enjoys sweet Love.   (244)

The images here are creatively mixed: metaphors of erotic passion are blended with metaphors of food and eating. In the light of the preoccupation with food of many women mystics of the Middle Ages, and the emphasis on feasting on the eucharist as the focus of union with Christ, this blending is highly suggestive, and very different from anything we might find in male mystical writers of the period. And the difference goes deeper than genre. Rather, the genre reveals a different perspective on what mystical union is. It is not a mysticism of reason or spirit, not even of an affective spirit, however loving and passionate that spirit might be. Rather, 'fruition' involves a union of the whole being, eating and drinking and consuming Love, having her enter one's whole self, in a union so complete and intimate that it is natural to describe it in sexual terms.

Time after time in Hadewijch we encounter this blending of metaphors of eating and of sexual passion in her writing about fruition. In another poem she writes of one from whom Love withholds herself: Hadewijch here combines the language of famished hunger with the language of acute sexual frustration.

> He who lives on love with no success
> Endures, in the madness of love,
> Suffering that can only be known
> By him who sincerely forsakes all for Love,
> And then remains unnourished by her.
> He is in woe because of Love;
> For he sorely burns
> In hope and in fear
> Incessantly renewed;
> For all his desire is
> To partake of and to enjoy
> And to have fruition of Love's nature.   (165)

Is the phrase 'to partake of and to enjoy ... Love's nature' a metaphor of hunger and eating or a metaphor of sexual desire and consummation? Surely the question is misplaced: the richness of metaphor is that it can carry more than one set of connotations at the same time. Thus here again the blended metaphor of hunger and sexual desire carries a resonance greater than would have been the case for either one of them on their own.

A more important question relates to what, exactly, these metaphors are expressing in Hadewijch's writing. The concept of fruition, and sexual encounter, is clearly a concept of union with God in direct experience. In her account of her first vision, Hadewijch tells of how, to encourage her, Christ allowed her to pluck one petal from the rose of the tree of knowledge of Love, and said,

This signifies that I will grant you myself in fruition. You shall always have knowledge of my will, and experience Love; and at the expedient time you shall feel me in fruition. So my Father did for me although I was his Son; he left me in affliction but never abandoned me; I felt him in fruition, and I served those to whom he had sent me. The heart that is found so full in the rose symbolizes the fruition of Love through feeling. (271)

Far from being intellectualised, fruition here carries an intensity of immediate experience, a feeling of the presence of God and the experience of God's love. When this is combined, as in the poetry, with metaphors of eating and sexual intimacy, both of them in different ways having associations of consummation, it is clear that 'fruition' is union with God wholly satisfying to the passionate desire for divine Love.

As we have seen, male mystics from Origen onward had also spoken of union with God as their supreme goal and the fulfilment of their desires. But it is obvious that the way in which this union is characterised is very different for women like Hadewijch than it is for male writers of the Christian tradition. In the speculative strand from Dionysius to Eckhart and beyond, there is a calm progression of knowledge as the reason moves upward from its bodily and sensory chains to the purer air of illumination and finally contemplation. In the affective strand, too, the sensory and the bodily are to be left behind: although they may serve as an allegory for heavenly love, the allegory is meant to be coupled with continence and bodily asceticism to free the spirit from bodily demands. Although there is no denial of struggle and temptation, spiritual progress has as its goal a calm serenity as the loving reason contemplates its Creator. With Hadewijch things are much more passionate. She speaks, as we have seen, of the 'madness of love', of the longing knight driven to distraction by desire. The consummation is no calmer: it is when the soul 'sinks with frenzy in Love's fruition'. Far from reaching a contemplation of pure tranquillity, Hadewijch speaks of fruition in terms that combine metaphors of ravenous devouring of food by one who has long been starving, with metaphors of intense sexual desire consummated at last in passionate love-making.

Although the various writers in the tradition are all speaking of union with God, it is clear that no monolithic philosophical concept of 'the experience of union' will be adequate to capture their variations of meaning. In Origen, as we have seen, mystical union is ultimately a union of the spirit with God, a union that is predicated on a soul–body dualism. For it to take place there must be liberation from the flesh already during this life, and ultimate completion only when death releases the spirit from the body altogether. It is this spirit or mind which constitutes the essence of the human person; and it is this mental essence which, stripped of bodily desires and sensual distractions, is at last able to know God as it is known by God. It is, indeed, like God, in that God also is spirit: like can be known by like. This dualistic understanding of human personhood, with the body and its senses and sexuality serving at best as an allegory and at worst as a hindrance to union with God is constant throughout all the male writers of the Christian tradition, as is also a sharp division between God as spirit and the material world.

Women like Hadewijch draw the lines very differently. Though many of them at varying levels affirm some kind of distinction between God and the world, and also between soul and body, this distinction often seems more perfunctory, a sort of acceptance of orthodoxy. Their thinking, and especially their experiential accounts, are much more holistic. In Hadewijch, for instance, union with God involves the mind, certainly; but it also involved the passions and emotions, the whole feeling centre of the person, including sensuality. She never explicitly denies the idea that mind or reason is the essence of a person, but she speaks of fruition in terms which would never lead a reader to suppose that she thought it was.

The gender difference emerges in another way in a comparison of their teaching on deification. As we have seen, Origen taught that the human mind, purged of the sinful desires of the flesh and illumined to recognise the things of the world as empty vanities, could be made like God, purified as God is pure. From the Platonic principle that like can be known only by like, it follows that if the soul can truly know God, it must have become God-like, deified. The soul is made divine in what it contemplates. Such deification is in Origen the ultimate goal of all spiritual progress. The speculative tradition following Origen modified this in various ways, so that in Eckhart, for instance, the spark or apex of the soul is that which actually already *is* god-like; spirituality therefore consists in 'becoming what one is', progressively eliminating any distractions and being increasingly in touch with the higher intellect.

Hadewijch also has a goal that could be labelled 'deification', but she expresses it so differently that one must ask whether lumping it together with the male traditions of western spirituality is not altogether too procrustean. The term she often uses for it is 'being made God with God': to that extent it has an Eckhartian resonance. But here is how she tells of one of her visions about her past:

I desired to have full fruition of my Beloved, and to understand and taste him to the full. I desired that his Humanity should to the fullest extent be one in fruition with my humanity, and ... I wished he might content me interiorly with his Godhead, in one spirit, and that for me he should be all that he is, without withholding anything from me ... For that is the most perfect satisfaction: to grow up in order to be God with God. (280)

Hadewijch speaks here of understanding as well as of tasting: one would look in vain in her writings for any disparagement of thought and reasoning. Nevertheless, the whole tone is vastly different from that of the speculative tradition, or even from the more affective tone of Bernard. To be God with God is not, for Hadewijch, a matter of a calm spiritual ascent, or of an encounter with the Word of God in the mystical meaning of scripture. Rather, it involves an identification with the humanity and divinity of Christ, sharing concretely in his self-sacrificing care for those who needed him, in the way that the béguine communities were putting into practice throughout northern Europe. This was the way in which Hadewijch believed that she for whom Christ had become human could with him become God.

In another vision she speaks of this more fully, this time using Love as her name for God, as she often does. God says to her,

And when you fully bring me yourself, as pure humanity in myself, through all the ways of perfect Love, you shall have fruition of me as the Love who I am. Until that day, you shall love what I, Love, am. And then you will be love, as I am Love. And you shall not live less than what I, Love, am, from that day until the death that will make you alive.

In my unity, you have received me and I have received you. Go forth, and live what I am; and return bringing me full divinity, and have fruition of me as who I am. (272)

In this passage Hadewijch shows not only what she means by becoming love with Love, but also how it takes place, and what are its consequences. She is focused on the incarnation, both in terms of the human Jesus and also in terms of the relation between humanity and divinity: her Christological emphasis is if anything even stronger than that of Bernard. In common with the male traditions, she believes that the life after death will make her fully alive; but the reason for that is not that her human body is impeding her in this life, but rather that death is the gate through which she must go, just as Jesus did, before the life of the resurrection can be hers.

For Hadewijch, therefore, the pathway of spiritual progress is held to lie, not in steadily reducing the desires and distractions of the body so as to free the mind for higher things, but in becoming 'pure humanity' in Christ 'through all the ways of perfect Love'. Hadewijch is quite clear about what that involves. It is not a matter of diminishing involvement with the cares of the world, but rather of pouring out herself as Christ poured out himself in compassion and care for the ignorant and the oppressed. If this involves also sharing in the suffering of Christ – and Hadewijch, like other medieval religious women, especially the beguines, had plenty of first-hand knowledge that this was likely to be the case – then this is not to be evaded, but rather embraced as even closer identification with his humanity.

It is by doing loving acts as Christ did loving acts that one learns to love: this is not an abstract 'theological virtue' or a detached emotion, in Hadewijch's thought (let alone an allegory), but rather a method of learning by doing. In her letters of advice to young beguines she repeatedly stresses that 'anyone who wishes to gain Love must begin with the virtues, with which God himself began, as did his saints'. In a way, this can be seen as parallel to the male tradition, with its steps of purgation and illumination, which included a moral, virtuous life as necessary for spiritual progress. But whereas in most branches of the male traditions this was seen as a means of progressive detachment from the things of the body, for Hadewijch it is a method of learning what love is: 'works with faith must precede love; then love will set them on fire' (81). It is as when a child ploddingly practises its music lessons, and gradually learns to love and to play real music, that Hadewijch speaks of practising love until one learns to love, and indeed to come to a proper appreciation of Jesus, the paradigm of love. She recounts that God promises her that it is only then, when she has learned to love Love, that 'you will be love, as I am Love' (272).

Whereas in Origen, Dionysius and Eckhart this union with God is seen as the ultimate goal in so strong a sense that it does not make sense to ask what happens next, with Hadewijch that is not the case. 'Go forth and live what I am', God says to her. In a letter, Hadewijch explains this to one of her young friends, saying that union with God does not mean cessation of the practice of love, but rather doing these acts in a way wholly united with God, who desires compassion and service to all who are in need.

But you must still labour at the works of Love, as I long did, and as his friends did and still do. For my part I am devoted to these works at any hour and still perform them at all times: to seek after nothing but Love, work nothing but Love, protect nothing but Love, and advance nothing but Love. (84)

These can be no idle words from a beguine, committed as they were to the service of the sick and distressed at a time when social services were urgently needed and in short supply, and when they were as likely as not to be persecuted for their pains.

Whereas for the male mystical tradition the mystical path led to deification, and deification meant the encounter of the mind and/or the affections with the mind of God, so that the deified person could come to think the thoughts of God, for Hadewijch 'becoming God with God' meant the encounter of the whole person with the love of God, so that the deified person could come to do the works of God. And these works were the works of love as demonstrated in the humanity of Jesus, which the beguines, like other medieval religious women (and some men, notably the Franciscans) tried to take as their pattern. There is a sense in which what Hadewijch speaks of as applying to the beginning of the spiritual path applies, in her view, equally to its end: always the emphasis is on practising the love which is shown by example in the humanity of Christ. But the position from which it is practised is different, starting with a desire to learn to love, and culminating in 'being love with Love' and thus doing the deeds of Love 'naturally' – that is, from the nature that has thus been acquired. This involves an integration of the whole person in a sense not usually much emphasised by the male traditions, as mind, passion and will are drawn together into unified action.

The contrasts with the male traditions should not be overstated. Even those like Origen and Eckhart who spoke most in terms of union of the mind with the mind of God did not usually speak of this as without love. On the contrary, it is the intellectual *love* of God which is union with God. This emphasis on love was even more pronounced in the affective strand, and in the later efforts to combine the two. Nor were the men unconcerned with charitable works, both as a prerequisite to spiritual progress and as its consequence. The Cistercians, especially, and later the Franciscans were indefatigable in their work on behalf of those around them who were in need. For her part, Hadewijch did not minimise reason. In one of her letters, she wrote,

Give reason its time, and always observe where you heed it too little and where enough. And do not let yourself be stopped by any pleasure through which your reason may be the loser. What I mean by 'your reason' is that you must keep your insight ever vigilant in the use of discernment. (103)

But as she continues, it becomes clear that 'reason' here is very different from what it is in Dionysius or Eckhart or even Bernard: it is to a considerable extent practical reason, the reason that sees to it that works of love are intelligently performed. The sentences immediately following the ones just quoted are these:

Never must any difficulty hinder you from serving people, be they insignificant of important, sick or healthy. And the sicker they are, and the fewer friends they have, the more readily must you serve them ...

Yet Hadewijch is no activist without an emphasis on contemplation. She begins one of her letters of instruction with a poem:

> Be generous and zealous for every virtue,
> But do not apply yourself to any one virtue.
> Fail not with regard to a multitude of things,
> But perform no particular work.
> Have good will and compassion for every need,
> But take nothing under your protection. (82)

When she explains these lines to her young reader, she acknowledges that they may appear to be contradictory. What she means is not that her reader is to abstain from activities of love, or only wish them well from a distance. But she is not to become possessive about them, as though they are hers alone, or her way is the only way of doing them. They must all be centred in love; and for this to be the case, she must herself be centred in love, and take the time for this to be so, and during this time not worry about those in need and 'perform no particular works that might assist them'. This is not a sudden access of callousness; rather, it is a recognition that important as the acts of love are, they must proceed out of spiritual resources, lest the springs run dry. As Hadewijch says at the close of her letter, 'you will ... have to serve much. But lack of discrimination regarding the things I have said, this I forbid you as those works were forbidden me by God's will.' One could almost read this as an early warning against feminist burn-out.

As might be expected from such an emphasis on the integration of the whole person being in love with Love, Hadewijch places considerable stress on the will. One of the most telling passages occurs in another letter, where she says,

For when the soul has nothing else but God, and when it retains no will but lives exclusively according to his will alone; and when the soul is brought to nought and with God's will wills all that he wills, and is engulfed in him, and is brought to nought – then he is exalted above the earth, and then he draws all things to him; and so the soul becomes with him all that he himself is. (90)

Whereas the tradition extending from Origen through Dionysius and Eckhart saw the mind as the essence of the human person,

Hadewijch here places herself in the strand which centres the human being in the will. But her presentation of that view is very much her own. Others had written that union with God meant that one could think the thoughts of God or know the nature of God; Hadewijch says that the person in union with God wills the will of God.

In Hadewijch's writing, this will is not a separate or separable aspect of the personality. A person in love with Love certainly wills Love's will with passionate desire. But Hadewijch never speaks in terms of an essence of a person, or isolates one aspect of the personality at the expense of others. Rather, she seeks to integrate the whole person in union with God. In a passage which shows the extent of her efforts toward integration, she writes,

When anyone seeks Love and undertakes her service, he must do all things for her glory, for during all this time he is human and needy; and he must work chivalrously in all things, be generous, serve, and show mercy, for everything fails him and leaves him in want. But when by fruition a man is united to Love, he becomes God, mighty and just. And then will, work and might have an equal part in his justice, as the Three Persons are in one God. (84)

To 'become God' is not, in Hadewijch, primarily to become all-knowing, or to be attuned to the higher intellect, or to escape from the body and its sensory needs and desires into the realm of the spirit. To 'become God' is to become 'mighty and just', strong in compassion and in work for justice. Erotic mysticism for Hadewijch is passionate, embodied mysticism; the erotic is not merely metaphorical, but rather is a focus for integration. Unlike in Bernard, there is no need to put aside the things of the body; indeed, the things of the body must emphatically not be put aside, since it is the body, not a disembodied spirit, which performs the mighty works of justice. Neither is this a spirituality for 'poor little ignorant women', women who have internalised the infantilism imposed on them by so much of the western Christian tradition. Rather, it is a spirituality for those who are 'fully grown', for strong, passionate women and men of spirit whose desire for God and longing to 'become love with Love' results in the integration of 'will, work and might' to bring about divine justice. In view of the way that medieval men spoke of women as sub-competent and sub-rational, lumped with children in their morality and rationality, and not treated as persons in their own right, Hadewijch's emphasis on being fully grown cuts straight across the infantilisation commonly placed upon medieval women.

It is not surprising that such passionate, erotic mysticism, without an emphasis on the things central to the patriarchal tradition, would be found by it to be deeply threatening. Hadewijch stressed neither the Bible, the intellect nor the ecclesiastical heirarchy; and insisted that women should be 'fully grown', not moral or intellectual infants. Furthermore, she based her authority on visions, rather than on ecclesiastical position or scholarly theological understanding, and thus placed herself in a tradition of visionary women whose understanding of what counts as mystical was at variance with that of the dominant male writers. Such subversion of male authority could not go unchecked. There is some evidence to believe that Hadewijch herself was persecuted; certainly the beguines as a whole were sharply circumscribed, and visionary women generally were increasingly suppressed from the time of the rise of clericalism in the twelfth and thirteenth centuries until the atrocities of the witch hunts in the early modern period. We will look at some aspects of that story in later chapters. First, however, I turn to another woman, Julian of Norwich, who forms an instructive parallel and contrast to Hadewijch and shows more fully how women's construction of the mystical differed from the dominant male constructions.

VI JULIAN OF NORWICH: MYSTIC OF INTEGRATION

As the Middle Ages waned, increasing numbers of women learned to read and write, in the vernacular if not in Latin. How Julian of Norwich was educated it is impossible to say. She was born in 1342, probably somewhere in East Anglia or the Midlands. Virtually everything that is known about her comes from her writings. She wrote two accounts of the same set of visions, twenty years apart, the second being much longer than the first. By comparing the two texts, it is possible to see how Julian developed in theological understanding and her spiritual teaching (Jantzen 1987). We will look again at her visions and her changing perception of herself as a woman in the next chapter. Here, I wish to focus on her theological and spiritual integration, which takes up much that was already present in medieval spirituality but develop it in a unique way.

From the outset, Julian's writing was intended for the comfort and encouragement of her 'even Christians' and for their spiritual assistance. Like Eckhart, she addressed herself not only to clerics or male or female religious, but also to a lay readership; but whereas in his case we have not only the sermons addressed to a lay audience but also more scholarly works, all we have from Julian are the two versions of her book. Furthermore, we would look as fruitlessly to Julian as to Hadewijch for any systematic exposition of a spiritual path, or steps in spiritual progress: there are none of the 'ladders of contemplation' or 'steps of ascent' which are frequent in male writing. Like other women writers, Julian chose to convey her spiritual teachings by recounting her own spiritual experiences and the insights based on them, rather than by any systematic treatise in spiritual theology.

In some ways, Julian offers a contrast to Hadewijch. Her writings breathe serenity and tranquillity; she speaks of peace and rest in God, not of frenzied desire or ecstatic madness. There is very little erotic imagery in her writings, though she speaks much of the love of God, of God who is 'all love'. Although like Hadewijch she is influenced by the courtly love tradition, Julian speaks of God as 'her courteous Lord', not as her 'Lady Love'; and she never characterises herself as a knight panting after Love and doing great exploits for her sake. None of Julian's writing is presented as poetry. Nevertheless, both Hadewijch and Julian, though very different in context, genre, style and temperament, show similarities to one another and differences from male mystical writers.

The most significant of these is that both Julian and Hadewijch emphasise the body, the physical and sensual and material; and for both of them this bodily reality is integrated into their spirituality in a way which is not true for either the speculative or the affective tradition of male spirituality. Julian's spirituality depends upon a well thought-out anthropology, which takes its starting-point from creation. Julian makes a point of stressing that 'we are double by God's creating, that is to say substantial and sensual' (1978: 294). This might be taken to signal a division between body and soul, as it would in many medieval writers; but in Julian that is not the case. Sensuality in Julian does involve bodiliness, but it also involves consciousness, the life of the senses and the mind: we are made sensual, she says, 'when our soul is breathed into our body' (286), and Jesus, in sharing our humanity, shares our sensuality. Our substance, on the other hand, is for Julian the essential part of ourselves, which she holds is directly united with God at all times, whether we are aware of it or not. There is a strong parallel here with Eckhart, who also held that the essential self was always connected with God. But whereas Eckhart defined that essential self in terms of the (male) higher intellect, Julian never does so. What she does instead is, when seen against the background of Eckhart's speculative mysticism, nothing short of astonishing.

Julian does not think of God as a remote deity, but, again similar to Eckhart, she thinks of God as the substance or essence of everything that exists. This is particularly true of ourselves. She says,

It is a great understanding to see and to know inwardly that our soul, which is created, dwells in God in substance, of which substance, through God, we are what we are. And I saw no difference between God and our substance, but, as it were, all God; and still my understanding accepted that our substance is in God, that is to say that God is God, and our substance is as creature in God. (285)

She is very near, here, to Eckhart's claims, but seems to be distancing herself from any interpretation of monism, for which he was suspect. But whereas in content her position is similar, it is focused much less abstractly than Eckhart's discussion of God as *esse* or being, and always interwoven with her understanding of human nature.

Julian goes on to say that it is substance and sensuality which form human 'doubleness': the substance is continually united with

God, while the sensuality is the locus of independence. Julian elaborates that theme of doubleness in her concept of two wills:

For in every soul which will be saved there is a godly will which never assents to sin and never will. Just as there is an animal will in the lower part which cannot do any good, so there is a godly will in the higher part, which is so good that it cannot ever will any evil, but always good. (241)

The 'godly will' can be seen as a parallel to Eckhart's apex of the soul, always united with God; but whereas he placed that apex in the intellect, for Julian it is centred in the will. This 'godly will' is a part or aspect of our substance, and it can will only what God wills. The 'animal will' which is incapable of willing what is good is an aspect of our sensuality in its fallen state. It is not to be equated with sensuality as such, and certainly not with physicality, but rather with that tendency toward evil which Julian believed was part of the sinful condition of humanity inherited from Adam.

This tendency to sin is characterised by Julian not so much as a falling away from God as a fragmentation of the human person, a split between the substance and the sensuality, so that whereas the substance wills only what is good, the sensuality is constantly lapsing into evil. 'And so in our substance we are full and in our sensuality we are lacking', she says. And then she completely subverts both the speculative tradition of Eckhart and the affective tradition of Bernard. Instead of proffering advice or exhortations about how to leave the sensuality behind and progress upwards toward the realm of spirit or substance where only the good is willed, she says, hardly pausing for breath,

and this lack God will restore and fill by the operation of mercy and grace, plentifully flowing into us from his own natural goodness. (291)

Rather than practising ascetical techniques which will free the higher self, the godly will from the sensuality, Julian looks for a reintegration of that fragmented sensuality into the substance. Spirituality does not mean leaving part of the self behind, but bringing the whole of the self, sensuality included, into the unity of the love of God in which she believes we are enfolded. It is a breath-taking reversal of Eckhart.

To accomplish the reversal, she looks to Christ, whom she sees as the remedy of the fragmentation between sensuality and substance. In taking flesh, Jesus shared human sensuality, but in such a way that, in him, it was not in conflict with substance. Put another way, Jesus' godly will and his animal will were united in constantly willing the good. This reunification of substance and sensuality in Christ is, according to Julian, the remedy for the split which we experience, as well as the prototype for our reunification and healing. She articulates the doctrine of the two natures of Christ in traditional terms of the death of Christ for human salvation:

And because of the glorious union which was thus made by God between the soul and the body, mankind had necessarily to be restored from a double death, which restoration could never be until the time when the second person of the Trinity had taken the lower part of human nature, whose highest part was united to him in its first creation. And these two parts were in Christ, the higher and the lower, which are only one soul. The higher part was always at peace with God in full joy and peace. The lower part, which is sensuality, suffered for the salvation of mankind. (287)

Traditional as this might be thus far, Julian then pushes it in the very untraditional direction of affirming that *all* people have two natures, just as Christ did, and that it is precisely because of this that the incarnation is effectual for human salvation.

And so in Christ our two natures are united, for the Trinity is comprehended in Christ, in whom our higher part is founded and rooted; and our lower part the second person has taken ... For in the same time that God had joined himself to our body in the maiden's womb, he took our soul, which is sensual, and in taking it, having enclosed us all in himself, he united it to our substance. In this union he was perfect man, for Christ, having joined in himself every man who will be saved, is perfect man. (291)

Christ reunites in himself divine substance and human sensuality, and thereby effects the healing of human fragmentation. All that the person was created to be, including the body and its sensuality, is taken up into the full spiritual life made possible by the incarnation.

Accordingly, we find in Julian's writings no comment about

ascetical practices, nothing about chastity, no cautions about sexuality or any other form of bodily need or desire. Instead, she speaks of bodily functions in a completely natural way as an illustration of the extent of divine love:

A man walks upright, and the food in his body is shut in as if in a well-made purse. When the time of his necessity comes, the purse is opened and then shut again, in most seemly fashion. And it is God who does this, as it is shown when he says that he comes down to us in our humblest needs. For he does not despise what he has made, nor does he disdain to serve us in the simplest natural functions of our body, for love of the son which he created in his own likeness. For as the body is clad in the cloth, and the flesh in the skin, and the bones in the flesh, and the heart in the trunk, so are we, soul and body, clad and enclosed in the goodness of God. (186)

The positive valuation of the body and sensuality means that, rather than being left behind or 'mortified' in spiritual progress, the body is cherished and enfolded in the love of God, and reintegrated in a spiritual whole-making. It is a vastly different perspective from the male traditions we have considered.

Julian's account of spiritual progress is directly related to this. She says that until our substance and sensuality are reunited and we are whole again, we are 'moaning and mourning', distressed at our brokenness. But how and when will they be reunited? There are three answers to this. The first is that it has happened already; 'in Christ our two natures are united', and are united because of his incarnation. The second is that it will not happen until heaven. Only then will the split within ourselves be fully healed. The third is that it can be going on gradually throughout our lives, largely by a process of our recognising that in Christ the reintegration has already taken place, and living in that growing realisation. Julian's spirituality involves this deepening awareness, gradually increasing in knowledge of God and of our own soul. In some ways this is like Eckhart, who also encourages us to 'become what we are'. Yet in Julian, rather than this involving a *detachment* from (female) sensuality and being in tune with the (male) higher reason, it requires an increasing *integration* of the sensuality and the substance, the godly will. As she puts it,

And I saw very certainly that we must necessarily be in longing and in penance until the time when we are led so deeply into God that we verily and truly know our own soul ... For until the time that it is in its full powers, we cannot be all holy; and that is when our sensuality by the power of Christ's Passion can be brought up into the substance ... (289)

Sensuality is not a barrier or a distraction from spirituality but rather is crucially involved in it.

Like Eckhart, therefore, Julian is full of the importance of self-knowledge, but her emphasis is much more homely: she stresses that we come to the recognition that we are good and beautiful and precious to God, learning to take delight in ourselves as Julian is sure that God takes delight in us.

For I saw in the same revelation that if the blessed Trinity could have created man's soul any better, any fairer, any nobler than it was created, the Trinity would not have been fully pleased with the creation of man's soul. But because it made man's soul as beautiful, as good, as precious a creature as it could make, therefore the blessed Trinity is fully pleased without end in the creation of man's soul. And it wants our hearts to be powerfully lifted above the depths of the earth and all empty sorrows, and to rejoice in it. (314)

Here is something quite different from what we find in the male traditions. Eckhart also stressed positive self-knowledge, but it was, as we have seen, knowledge of the higher intellect as the god-like apex of the soul. The affective tradition, on the other hand, would emphasise the importance of knowing oneself, not to recognise god-likeness, but to become contrite for one's sinfulness and unworthiness before God: in Bernard's *The Steps of Humility*, for instance, self-knowledge was to lead to penitence and humility. Julian does not deny the need for penitence, but her emphasis falls differently: recognising our beauty and worth will be a source of joy for us just as it is for the Trinity itself. She says that it is of great profit to us to contemplate this, because contemplation of the Trinity who delights in us 'makes the soul which so contemplates like to him who is contemplated, and unites it in rest and peace' (314). Here once again is the old Platonic theme that the knower becomes like what it knows; but it is turned to a purpose that is very much Julian's own: in taking pleasure in God who takes pleasure in us, we learn to take pleasure in ourselves.

Julian never mentions gender in this discussion. But if her reversal of the traditional theme of self-knowledge is striking, her application of it to herself as a woman, and by implication to other women, is nothing short of audacious. Women, after all, were exhorted in the Bible and throughout patristic and medieval writing to 'learn humility, in all subjection', not to learn to delight in themselves. Since it was through Eve that sin had entered into the world, and since women were still held to be the locus of temptation, especially sexual temptation, the path to holiness for women would be a path of penitence, humility, and self-renunciation. Self-knowledge would be knowledge of oneself as related to Eve, the source of temptation and a snare to men.

Julian does talk about contrition and humility, but never with the overtones of the above paragraph. She is troubled about why God permitted sin; but in all her anxious questioning about sin's nature and origin, she never once links it to women. Contrition is for sin actually committed, and not for a vague sinfulness connected with the very fact of being an embodied, sexual creature, let alone being female. Humility has to do with accepting and receiving the overwhelming love and delight of God in us, not with being ashamed of who and what we are. And surely it must be highly significant that Julian never mentions chastity or virginity. Though she herself, as an anchoress, had almost certainly taken the monastic vow of chastity, it is never raised as an issue in her book, never suggested as part of spiritual progress, in fact, never mentioned at all. In an era when it was taken as a commonplace that sexuality, especially female sexuality, was a hindrance to spiritual progress, and virginity held up to be the ideal, Julian's silence is eloquent.

Coupled with this, Julian offers other pieces of spiritual instruction unusual for women of any age and doubly unusual for her own. One of the most central of these was the admonition not to be unduly distressed by sin and failure. Julian recounts that in one of her visions, 'God brought it to mind that I should sin.' But the reason for which she was reminded of this was not to make her ashamed or fearful, but rather to reassure her of God's protection and mercy whatever happened, so that when she did sin she would not fall into despair (241). Julian agonises about sin, calling it 'the sharpest scourge with which any chosen soul can be struck, which scourge belabours man or woman', until they feel that they are 'not fit for anything but as it were to sink into hell' (244). But she develops the insight that sin and wrongdoing, though serious, are the very things which teach us most about sensitivity and compassion for ourselves and one another.

In fact, Julian develops an audacious comparison between our sins and the wounds that were inflicted on Jesus at his crucifixion. According to scripture and tradition, those wounds of Jesus, the nail prints in his hands and feet and side, became the badges of honour of the risen Christ: just so, too, the wounds of our sins will be turned into honours, so that it will be far better for us than if we had never sinned at all.

For [God] regards sin as sorrow and pains for his lovers, to whom for love he assigns no blame. The reward which we shall receive will not be small, but it will be great, glorious and honourable. And so all our shame will be turned into honour and joy. For our courteous Lord does not want his servants to despair because they fall often and grievously; for our falling does not hinder him in loving us. (245)

Again, there is no indication in Julian that this discussion is gendered, and we can only speculate about whether she might have had women particularly in mind. Whatever the case, her words carry a weight for women quite different from the shame and blame that women had been taught to assume. According to Julian, disproportionate shame or guilt is not the response God desires (even if there were those in the ecclesiastical structures who might have found it gratifying that women should bear such a weight). Although she was made to understand 'that we cannot in this life keep ourselves completely free from sin', nevertheless the remedy for that sin has already been provided.

And if we through our blindness and our wretchedness at any time fall, then let us quickly rise, knowing the sweet touch of grace, and willingly amend ourselves according to the teaching of Holy Church, as may fit the grievousness of the sin, and go on our way with God in love, and neither on the one side fall too low, inclining to despair, nor on the other side be too reckless, as though we did not care; but let us meekly recognise our weakness, knowing that we cannot stand for the twinkling of an eye except with the protection of grace, and let us reverently cling to God, trusting only in him. (281)

Thus we can see that in Julian's terms, spiritual progress involves self-knowledge, but that self-knowledge is construed differently than in the other strands of the tradition we have looked at. For her, self-knowledge also means an increasing sense of self-worth, but not one built only upon increasing identification with rationality, but rather with a realism that accepts not only bodiliness but also sinfulness without being crushed by guilt. Her words were written for *all* her 'even Christians', men as well as women; but they must have had a special resonance for women, whose sinfulness and shame was so often highlighted by ecclesiastical preaching and practice and whose self-worth was so regularly undermined. She sums up her encouraging message in a metaphor of knitting, a figure of speech which beautifully conveys her meaning:

And just as we were to be without end, so we were treasured and hidden in God, known and loved from without beginning. Therefore he wants us to know that the noblest thing which he ever made is mankind, and the fullest substance and the highest power is the blessed soul of Christ. And furthermore, he wants us to know that this beloved soul was preciously knitted to him in its making, by a knot so subtle and so mighty that it united us in God. In this uniting it is made endlessly holy. Furthermore, he wants us to know that all the souls which will be saved in heaven without end are knit in this knot, and united in this union, and made holy in this holiness. (284)

Both Hadewijch and Julian, different as they are in temperament, context and style, offer a spirituality or mysticism of integration which contrasts considerably with their male counterparts. Unlike the speculative tradition, they did not develop a spirituality centring on the mind; and unlike the male affective tradition, they did not use spiritual love as an alternative to bodily love, or see the physical as something to be overcome. Although both of them respected reason, and were no advocates of a mysticism of ignorance, they placed emphasis on love and on the will, which must be united in the growth of spiritual wholeness, based in the flesh, not in its suppression. Hadewijch used passionate and erotic language more than Julian did, but Julian was at least as emphatic about the body and its integration in spirituality. Neither woman saw spiritual development in terms of steps or stages, or used metaphors of ladders or staircases as did many male writers. Their construction of mysticism, their understanding of what spirituality is, was therefore quite different from that of their male counterparts in the tradition of western spirituality. It was, furthermore, an understanding which allowed a good deal of scope for visionary experience, on which female authority could be based; and as we shall see in the next chapter, this became a threat to male dominance in the social construction of mysticism which could not be allowed to go unchecked.

The struggle for power and authority in deciding who should count as a mystic, and the issues of gender within that struggle, are largely ignored by contemporary philosophers of religion, who frequently behave as if there is a single sort of phenomenon known as 'mystical experience' which is available for philosophical scrutiny. As is becoming evident, however, the understanding of the mystical went through major shifts within the western tradition; and those shifts were not innocent. If contemporary philosophers of religion ignore these shifts, and work on the assumption of an 'essence' of mysticism, it is unsurprising if the net result produces more obfuscation than insight. Not only are the philosophical arguments built on dubious argumentation, they are based on dubious morality as well, because an uncritical acceptance of a gender-skewed understanding of mysticism is bound to perpetuate it.

CHAPTER 5

'Cry out and write': mysticism and the struggle for authority

> Only recently have scholars begun to consider the possibility
> that there may be at least three histories in every culture –
> his, hers, and ours. (Flax 1990a: 45)

The historian Joan Kelly has described the shift of perspective that occurs when one becomes aware of the extent to which any historical tradition has been dominated and defined by men. Instead of looking only at what historians say, it becomes necessary to see with a 'doubled' vision, considering also who and what is absent from their writing and what they consider unworthy of scholarly attention: 'each eye sees a different picture' (Kelly 1984: 51). In much mainstream historical writing, women are ignored or marginalised, or else their roles have been codified in accordance with male perceptions or wishes. However, though absent from the text, women were of course present in history all along; and their perspectives and subjectivities can sometimes be retrieved from the margins, not simply to be added into the text, but to facilitate a whole shift of vision of its contents. In relation to mainstream history of philosophy, Seyla Benhabib asks, 'What would the history of ideas look like from the standpoint of its victims?' (1991: 130).

The same question can be asked of the history of mysticism. We have seen some of the ways in which mysticism and spirituality were socially constructed as a male preserve controlled by the patriarchal ecclesiastical structure. Yet it is evident that even within the church (let alone in the 'heretical' movements, which I shall look at in more detail in chapter 8) there were many women of spirit, women who in today's categories would be classified as mystics. The number of such women (or at least, the number about whom anything can be known) increased rather than declined through the medieval period. Some of them wielded great influence in their own time and subsequently: indeed, it would be only with considerable qualification that they could be called 'victims'. If it is too simple to say that only men counted as mystics, it is also too simple to say that mysticism was wholly defined by men, even though gender relations were pervasively unequal.

Yet in spite of the influence some women had, it is nevertheless true that they were circumscribed by boundaries not of their own making, and with which they had to make their peace in order to have any influence at all. When we look, for instance, at a range of women mystics in medieval Europe – women such as Bridget of Sweden, Catherine of Siena, Hildegard of Bingen, Hadewijch of Antwerp, Julian of Norwich, and Teresa of Avila, to choose only a few outstanding examples – it is striking to see how they relate to their own male-dominated and male-defined tradition. That the relationship is ambiguous should not come as any surprise.

On the one hand, the women are part of the male-defined tradition, living within it and identifying with it as women in the west have regularly lived within and identified with the interests of their dominant males. In that sense it would be incorrect to speak of them as establishing a separate women's spirituality in western Christianity. All of these women were within the church and wanted to remain there. None of them wished to be heretical. Nor is there any reason to suppose that their desire to be orthodox was only to avoid the dire consequences of being found heretical: rather, they sincerely believed the teachings of the church to be true and effective for their salvation. What they wanted was to make these teachings fully their own, and available to others.

Yet on the other hand, when we look more closely we can see these women of spirit pushing at the male-defined boundaries, challenging their definitions and preconceptions. In this respect it is indeed true to speak of a women's spirituality as an alternative to the normative tradition. The women in question did not begin, as many men did, from a study of scriptural texts and an effort to ascertain the mystical meaning of scripture: in most cases, this route was not open to them. Nor did they look primarily to their intellects or rationality as the centre of their spirituality. As we have already seen in the cases of Perpetua and Egeria, and then Hadewijch and Julian, the source of their spirituality was experiential more than intellectual, in a stronger sense than was true for most male mystics.

It was this rootedness in experience which made women mystics different from many theological writers and even many of the male mystics of their time. In this chapter I wish to look more closely at the sorts of experience women relied on, and how they used their experience as the basis of their authority. What we shall see is that although there were considerable variations in women's experiences, when a woman wrote a book she based it squarely on her own experience, often of a visionary nature. Her male contemporary, however, was much more sceptical of intense experience and relied on it much less in his writing. Furthermore, as men became increasingly threatened by the writings of female visionaries, they tried to disqualify visionary experiences as a possible source of religious authority.

But for the women, what else than their own experience was available? The usual routes of education and ecclesiastical preferment were not open to them. This is not to deny that some of the women demonstrate very solid learning indeed in their writings: the work of Hildegard of Bingen was nothing short of encyclopaedic for her time; and the nuns of Helfta, Gertrude the Great and Mechthild of Hackborne, were clearly well grounded in classical study. Yet such learning as women had, had not usually been acquired in a way that enabled them to feel educated in the traditional (that is, male-defined) sense; and often they were not comfortable to do their own writing in Latin. Hildegard used Volmar the monk as a scribe; and Catherine of Siena relied on Raymond of Capua. Hadewijch of Antwerp and Julian of Norwich wrote in the vernacular Flemish and English respectively. The fact that both of them were of the first importance in developing the vernacular was not recognised at the time, and certainly not by them. They merely thought of themselves as unlearned and not up to the standards of male scholarship: as Julian put it, 'I am a woman, ignorant, weak and frail' (1978: 135).

To discern further the lines along which mysticism was socially constructed from the eleventh to the fourteenth centuries, and how gender relations were important in that construction, it is desirable to look more closely at the ways in which the women mystics of the Christian tradition differed in their focus on experience from their male counterparts. To do this, it is necessary to examine them in context and in some detail, not merely to pick out a few prize quotations (with which, as with the Bible, one can prove almost anything). I wish, therefore, to consider the variety and nature of experiences in the lives of some women of spirit, and the way in which those experiences gave them spiritual authority. Again, this should not be seen as an exhaustive study of visionary women, but rather as a recalling of the dangerous memory of some significant women whose work has been suppressed and is only now being reclaimed.

Even while they claimed spiritual authority, however, we shall see that in a domain largely dominated and defined by males who feared and denigrated female bodiliness and sexuality, women mystics had to pay for their spirituality by fierce bodily control: control of their sexuality, and also control of such things as food and clothing, and relinquishing of physical freedom by entering into enclosures. I shall discuss this more fully in the next chapter, but it is as well to bear it in mind in an assessment of their authority as visionary women. What I wish to show in these two chapters is that whereas in large measure women accepted male-defined controls both of their writing and of their bodies, and indeed accepted and internalised their inferior and subordinate status, they also consciously and unconsciously pushed back the boundaries of male-defined spirituality. Because of these women, the modern conception of what mysticism consists in is very different from what it might have been without them, even though they and their experiences were a threat to male mystics and theorists. Indeed, it is one of the ironies of history that whereas by the end of the Middle Ages visionary women were for the most part suppressed, and were in grave danger of being executed as witches, the modern social construction of mysticism is closer to them than to the male mystics who undermined them.

I VARIETY OF VISIONS

An early and enormously influential woman mystic was Hildegard of Bingen, nicknamed 'the Sibyl of the Rhine' because of her prophetic gifts. In Hildegard the interconnections and tensions between gender and class are evident, and result in an interesting mixture of deference to men and male thought patterns, and scornfulness of them. Hildegard was born into a noble Rhineland family in 1098; and being the tenth child of her parents she was devoted by them as a tithe to the religious life, and placed under the tutelage of an anchoress named Jutta, who was attached to the Benedictine monastery of Disibodenberg on the Nahe River. In due course Hildegard became abbess of a women's community there, and, as it grew, she decided that they ought to move to Bingen, 30 kilometres down the Nahe at its confluence with the Rhine. The monks of Disiboden, who profited financially from the convent's presence, opposed the move. Hildegard wrote a fierce letter to the abbot, protesting on behalf of the nuns that

their alms do not belong to you or to your brothers ... and if you are determined to go on with your perverse proposals, raging against us, you will be like the Amalekites ... justice will destroy you. (quoted in Ward 1990: 107)

She then resorted to dual strategy. She used her aristocratic family connections to secure support for her scheme; and she took to her bed with a paralysing sickness which she said was God's punishment on the monks. She continues her account of what happened:

And when I, poor little creature, had with these words petitioned the abbot and his confreres for the freehold of the site and domains of my daughters they all granted it to me, entering the transfer in a codex.

'Poor little creature' indeed! She was a woman of enormous strength of character and extremely well connected. She was in correspondence with successive admiring popes, in touch with and adviser to some of the most influential bishops and abbots of the time, including Bernard of Clairvaux who came to esteem her highly, and linked also to the secular rulers of her time, notably Frederick Barbarossa. Yet she frequently referred to herself as 'a poor little figure of a woman', and in her rhetoric, if not in her behaviour, accepted fully her inferior status as a woman and her subservience to men. Using the gender stereotypes of her time, she complained that she lived in a 'womanish age' in which men had become effeminate – weak, sensual and lax – so that God had been obliged to make a woman 'virile' (Newman 1987: 3). But it would be wrong to suppose that her sense of inferiority as a woman was mere rhetoric: she did seriously believe it, and had to come to terms with the tension between her gender and her position of authority. Barbara Newman is right when she observes that 'no doubt, as she struggled to overcome this difference, the aristocratic ease born of rank and privilege helped her more than she realised' (1987: 35); but she still did have to struggle, and in doing so she pushed against the male-defined boundaries in her life and writing even while at another level accepting them.

Hildegard's writings fall into two categories. Some of her work is scientific and medical: in it she expounds with vast learning on the flora and fauna as well as the rocks and minerals with which she was familiar, and discusses remedies for common physical complaints, especially those related to women. I shall have more to say about this side of her work later on. The other category is her properly mystical writing. She wrote three large books: the *Scivias* ('know the ways' of the Lord), the *Book of Life's Merits*, and the *Book of Divine Works*. Each of these is based on a sequence of visions; and in each subsection of the three books she follows a roughly similar pattern. First she describes the vision that she sees, whether it be of the cosmos held in the body of God, or a magnificent building full of significant details or concentric circles of heavenly armies. In each case, Hildegard describes what she sees in sufficient detail so that one of her nuns could produce an intricate visual representation; these were used to illuminate the manuscripts of her writings. After describing what she saw, Hildegard recounts what a heavenly voice said to her in relation to the vision. Only when she has recorded these words verbatim does she proceed to offer her own interpretation of the vision, first in general and then in all its detail: the interpretation is filled with theological instruction and exhortation to the church. Hildegard enters into the visions as an active participant only very sparingly. For the most part, she records what she saw and heard and her interpretation of it in the way one might describe a scene that one witnessed but did not otherwise influence. It is almost as though she were watching a film made especially for her and out of which God spoke to her: she could watch and listen, but she could not reply or otherwise participate in the film.

Very different from this quasi-objective recording of visions are the experiences of Gertrude of Helfta, who entered into her visions herself as an active participant. Gertrude, often known as 'the Great' because of the influence of her writing, was born in 1256, probably, like Hildegard, to a noble or aristocratic family. Also like Hildegard, she was a child oblate, brought to the convent of Helfta (near modern Eisleben in north-eastern Germany) at the age of 4. Helfta, however, was a community outstanding for its learning; and, unlike most other medieval women, Gertrude received an excellent education including a thorough knowledge of Latin and of patristic and monastic writings. At the age of 25, Gertrude had a conversion experience in the form of a vision: it was to be the first of many visionary experiences. This marked a turning-point for her from largely intellectual pursuits to more strongly spiritual ones, particularly counselling those who came to her (both women and men) and offering them spiritual instruction.

Gertrude's visions begin dramatically. She writes,

I was twenty-five years old ... I was standing in the middle of the dormitory. On meeting an elder sister, according to the custom of our Order I bowed my head. As I raised it I saw standing beside me a young man. He was lovely and refined, and looked about sixteen; his appearance was such as my youth would find pleasing. (1991: 100)

The young man spoke kindly to Gertrude, comforting her and assuring her that her salvation was at hand. She longed to be with him, but, as if within the unaccountable occurrences of a dream, suddenly there was a huge hedge bristling with thorns between them. Gertrude despaired of crossing it.

While I stood hesitating because of it, both burning with desire and almost fainting, he himself seized me swiftly and effortlessly, lifted me up, and set me beside him. But then I recognised on that hand ... the glorious gems of those wounds which cancelled the debts of all.

From then on Gertrude received many more visions, which formed the basis of her spiritual growth and instruction of others. Unlike Hildegard, Gertrude took an active part in her vision. She speaks not only *of* Christ but *to* Christ in her experiences, asking questions, making requests and receiving responses. On one occasion she had a particular concern about the state of the souls of various relatives and friends who had died; and she was assured in a vision that Christ can intervene even for them. Another time, she brings her convent to God in her visions, and is shown Mary as a commander ordering angels to protect her convent from the devil, as though the angels were so many soldiers surrounding it. On still another occasion, Gertrude sees herself like a victorious warrior bringing to God a throng of souls tied to her by a golden chain like captives to a king. Though Gertrude's visions are partly for purposes of instruction, they are far more participatory than Hildegard's, which are almost purely didactic.

We have already encountered the erotic poetry of Hadewijch of Antwerp in chapter 4. However, it is important to consider Hadewijch further with respect to the relationship between her authority and her visionary experiences, and to see how she compared with other visionary women of the late Middle Ages. In this respect, the most obvious point to note about Hadewijch's visions is that they occupy a very different and smaller role in her life and spirituality than is the case for Hildegard and Gertrude. Whereas Hildegard has three large volumes describing and interpreting her visions, and Gertrude's writing is shot through with visionary experiences in a much less systematic and more personally participatory way, Hadewijch records only fourteen visions, filling only some fifty pages of a modern edition; and does not refer to them again in her other writings. They are, however, fascinating.

Hadewijch's visions are if anything even more participatory than Gertrude's, and also are much more intimately concerned with Hadewijch herself rather than with the people and events around her. In her first vision, she is led by an angel into a meadow containing trees, each of which has a name and personal significance especially for her, often of a highly commendatory sort. For example,

he led me farther to where a tall tree stood, a strong tree adorned with big, wide leaves. And then the Angel said to me: 'O powerful and strong one, you have conquered the powerful and strong God, from the origin of his Being, which was without beginning; and with him you shall wield power over eternity and in eternity!' (1980: 264)

Hadewijch is encouraged to recognise and claim her strength, and find its grounding in God. The content of all her visions revolves around Hadewijch's deep desire for union with God, 'fruition' of God, as she understands it. Her experiences in the visions are sometimes intensely erotic, as we would expect from what we have seen of her poetry. They are strongly participatory: she eats and drinks at the command of an angel, is required to make choices, is praised and admonished and given instruction, all in a far more intimate and personal way than we find in Gertrude or Hildegard. If Hildegard's visions give the impression that she sat and watched them as one might watch a film, Hadewijch describes hers as a woman would describe a drama in which she played the lead role: she saw the events from the inside.

The visions of Julian of Norwich must also be considered further. Julian's visions share some of each of the characteristics we have already observed, while being very much her own. When we look at the two accounts she wrote of her experiences, we can see how she developed both in understanding the content of her visions, and also in self-understanding, not least in relation to her authority, as a woman, to give spiritual instruction.

Unlike the other women I have described, Julian spent a large part of her adult life as an anchoress rather than in a community of women. It is not clear when she entered the anchorhold: whether before her visions or after them (Jantzen 1987: 20–5). In any case, she had been devout from her youth (about which nothing else is known), and had prayed, she says, for a 'recollection of the Passion', that is, a vision of the suffering and death of Jesus in such a way as to be a participant in events, not a detached observer. She had also prayed for a serious bodily illness – a prayer which she herself recognised as questionable:

therefore I said: Lord, you know what I want, if it be your will that I have it, and if it be not your will, good Lord, do not be displeased, for I want nothing which you do not want. (1978: 178)

She hoped that both the vision of the suffering Christ and the experience of her own bodily suffering would help to deepen in her the things she prayed for 'without any condition': contrition, loving compassion and longing with the will for God.

Julian's account of what happened next is startling.

And when I was thirty and a half years old, God sent me a bodily sickness in which I lay for three days and three nights: and on the fourth night I received all the rites of Holy Church and did not expect to live until day. (127)

Those around her expected her to die, and sent for 'the parson, my curate, to be present at my end'. The parson brought a crucifix with him, and encouraged Julian to fix her eyes on it as she expired. As she set her gaze upon it,

at this, suddenly, I saw the red blood trickling down from under the crown, all hot, flowing freely and copiously, a living stream, just as it seemed to me that it was at the time when the crown of thorns was thrust down upon his blessed head.

There follow a series of fifteen visions, with a sixteenth the following night, in all of which there is a fine counterpoint between Julian's sufferings because of her illness, and the suffering of Jesus on the cross. Although for the most part Julian remains clear about where she is (ill, in bed) and is not active in the visions as Gertrude and Hadewijch are in theirs, she participates in very lively conversations with Christ on the cross, raising questions and problems for which she expects good answers from him.

Furthermore, although she was greatly comforted and consoled by the visions and the things she understood from them, she was clear from the outset that they were not given to her only for her own private edification, but for all her 'even Christians'. When she describes the first vision of the series, she says,

In all this I was greatly moved in love towards my fellow Christians, that they might all see and know the same as I saw, for I wished it to be a comfort to them, for this vision was shown for all men. (136)

Like Hildegard, Julian's visions were for teaching others, not only for herself; but they were far less concerned with grand cosmological schemes. Rather, they were intended for the comfort and deeper spiritual understanding of individuals struggling with their own guilt and discouragement and despair, clinging to faith and hope in very difficult times. She was writing during the time of successive waves of the Black Death, one of the precipitating causes of the Peasants' Revolt and the massive social unrest of the time. It was to Christians caught in those struggles that Julian addresses the account of her visions. She writes,

Everything that I say about me I mean to apply to all my fellow Christians, for I am taught that this is what our Lord intends in this spiritual revelation. And therefore I pray you all for God's sake, and I counsel you for your own profit, that you disregard the wretch to whom it was shown, and that mightily, wisely and meekly you contemplate upon God, who out of his courteous love and his endless goodness was willing to show it generally, to the comfort of us all. For it is God's will that you accept is with great joy and delight, as Jesus has shown it to you. (191)

Contrary to expectations, Julian then got well; and probably soon after, she wrote out the account of her visions and something of her understanding of them. But this was not enough for Julian. She continued to ponder the meaning of the visions, both for herself and for her 'even Christians'. Although it is not known where she had access to books or exactly what she read, it is clear that she meditated not only on her own visions but also on the theological and spiritual resources of Christianity to work out more fully the meaning of her own experiences. As she says,

And from the time that it was revealed, I desired many times to know in what was our Lord's meaning. And fifteen years after and more, I was answered in spiritual understanding, and it was said: What, do you wish to know what was our Lord's meaning in this thing? Know it well: love was his meaning. Who reveals it to you? Love. What does he reveal to you? Love. Why does he reveal it to you? For love. Remain in this, and you will know more of the same. But you will never know different, without end. (342)

Clearly, therefore, while all these women of spirit were visionaries, they were of very different sorts; and the variety would be greatly broadened if we included others like Bridget of Sweden and Catherine of Siena, let alone Teresa of Avila. The term 'visionary women' can only be used accurately of all of them if we also keep in mind their rich diversity. Different as they all were from one another, however, they did all regard the visionary experiences as a central aspect of their spirituality and as the basis for their authority. In this they were different from most of their male contemporaries, who would be less likely to have visionary experiences, and less likely to make them the basis of their spiritual authority if they did, as we shall see in greater detail below.

II CLAIMING AUTHORITY

Why should this be so? Why would women have more visionary experiences than men, and value them more highly? And why would some men disparage visionary experience and, on occasion, also disparage the people (mostly women) who had them? One easy answer is that women are more emotionally impressionable than men (or even less emotionally stable) and were therefore more susceptible to visionary experiences, whereas men tried to bring rationality and calm into the areas of mysticism and spirituality. But such a response is nothing more than a reflection of the stereotyping of women as passionate and men as rational. There is plenty of reason to believe that a very different explanation does more justice to the situation. That explanation rests on authority and its perception by women and men in medieval society. In a society where authority was seen largely as a male preserve, women had internalised the low esteem in which they were held, exacerbated by their lack of formal education and ecclesiastical position. Any authority they claimed had to have some form of special validation.

For they did claim authority. Hildegard became an abbess; Gertrude took a position of spiritual leadership at Helfta; Hadewijch instructed young beguines; Julian took it upon herself to write for her 'even Christians'. Bridget of Sweden and Teresa of Avila founded (or reformed) convents. Many of these women castigated bishops and prelates, popes and kings about the injustices they found around them. Furthermore, they were all giving spiritual and theological instruction without being qualified to do so in terms of the formal education usually considered essential for such activity. Yet they could not expect to be taken seriously unless they had *some* basis for their authority: there had always been prohibitions against women teaching, and the restrictions actually increased in significant ways from the twelfth to the fourteenth centuries, at least in terms of alternatives open to religious women (Bynum 1982: 250).

What better basis for authority could possibly be claimed than a direct vision from God? By those who accepted it as authentic, the authority claimed by the visionary could not possibly be gainsaid; and it cut straight across all the usual channels like education and ecclesiastical position, rendering them totally unnecessary. And if a woman's visions were authenticated by someone in high position (in the case of Hildegard, for example, the pope) this would virtually guarantee her religious authority. Given all the other restrictions on women, along with the expectations of the time, it is not at all surprising that women might be more open than men to visionary experiences in the first place, make more of them when they occurred, and use them as the basis for their authority as teachers of theology and spirituality. Provided that they and others believed their visions to come from God, no stronger justification for their teaching role could possibly be required. Conversely, without such divine validation, who would bother to listen to a woman?

Indeed, the authority medieval women derived from visions might have a special twist, as Barbara Newman has shown in the case of Hildegard (1987; cf Tugwell 1984: 188). A monk, Guibert of Gemblaux, had written to Hildegard asking her about her visions and exhorting her to remain humble. In her eventual reply to his many questions, she spoke of herself again as 'a poor little figure of a woman'. This and her other formulas of humble self-description were part of a necessary self-abasement, a 'modesty formula' obligatory on medieval women writers. But, as Newman points out, these were also ideas that made it possible to compare her with Mary, the humble handmaid of God who was exalted to be the mother of Christ. If it was the very fact of Mary's humility that made her a suitable recipient of God's favour, then, it is implied, perhaps it is precisely Hildegard's lowliness as a 'poor little figure of a woman' that allows her to be exalted by the divine gift of the visions to a position of spiritual authority. Furthermore, if such lowliness is gender-related, then by a paradoxical twist women are especially privileged, at an advantage as candidates for exaltation. Of course, this would actually occur only extremely rarely; in practical terms most women's lot would not be improved at all. Nevertheless, exceptional women could claim authority and special privilege on the basis of a vision directly vouchsafed by God.

Thus at the beginning of the *Scivias*, Hildegard's first visionary book, she makes the most of the divine summons and of her own lowliness, not merely as a human being, but as of that gender of human being identified with Eve and with all the sin she brought into the world. She records that God's voice to her says,

O human, who are fragile dust of the earth and ashes of ashes! Cry out and speak of the origin of pure salvation until those people are instructed, who, though they see the inmost contents of the scriptures, do not wish to tell them or preach them, because they are lukewarm or sluggish in serving God's justice. Unlock for them the enclosure of mysteries that they, timid as they are, conceal in a hidden and fruitless field. Burst forth into a fountain of abundance and overflow with mystical knowledge, until they who now think you contemptible because of Eve's transgression are stirred up by the flood of your irrigation. For you have received your profound insight not from humans, but from the lofty and tremendous Judge on high ... (1990a: 59)

In hearing God's voice, Hildegard is finding her own; and furthermore finding herself rebuking her male counterparts. They should be the real mystics, the ones who discern the inner or mystical meaning of the scriptures; but they are 'lukewarm and sluggish in serving God's justice'. In consequence, it is Hildegard who is the mystic, the one able to 'overflow with mystical knowledge' derived directly from God. The move in the social construction of mysticism is clear: it is common ground between Hildegard and her opponents that true mystical knowledge cannot be separated from efforts for justice, it cannot be a private religious state. Therefore, since the men who are supposedly involved in seeking the mystical meaning of scripture and the mystical theology are lax in the work of justice, God intervenes directly to the lowest of the low, as had happened before when a woman was ready to bear Christ in the world.

Yet it would be going much too far to see Hildegard here as striking a blow for feminism, as some have wished to do. Although she herself found her voice and claimed her authority, she never treated this as anything other than extraordinary. She spoke by divine command, a command that would never have needed to be issued to her or any other woman if the men of the 'womanish age' – for Hildegard a term of contempt – were doing what they should be doing in the work for justice. Hildegard counts herself as a mystic only because men, who should be the mystics, are not doing their duty. Some contemporary feminists have claimed Hildegard as a role model; but it is necessary to keep in mind how strongly she herself was male-identified and part of the male-identified church, how thoroughly she despised her own sex (as we will see in more detail later), and how much her authority depended on the oppression of women in general. It would in many respects be more accurate to see Hildegard as a prototype token woman than as a twelfth-century feminist.

The case would be quite different with Gertrude the Great and the other Helfta nuns with whom she was associated. Like Hildegard, Gertrude and her friend Mechthild of Hackeborn based their authority on their visions; indeed, their convent built up a collective reputation for spiritual teaching based in part on the visionary experiences of its members. Because of this, they served as counsellors and advisers to people from far and wide, including male clergy and members of male religious orders. Caroline Bynum summarises the relationship between their visions and their authority:

> By their own account, these nuns were direct channels of God's power; they provided information about what practices Christ wished performed and about the state of souls in the afterlife. Christ himself guaranteed the efficacy of their prayers, particularly for removing souls from purgatory. The basis for their authority and for the utter serenity with which they exercised it lay in their mystical experiences. (1982: 181)

This authority was at variance with the tendencies of the time. Bynum has shown how the thirteenth century was a period of increasing clericalisation of the church, with more and more emphasis on hearing confession and on the eucharist, thus increasingly excluding women from central ecclesiastical involvement. The older double monasteries of men and women ruled by an abbess were a thing of the past; and women religious were not allowed to become mendicants as friars were, but were confined to convents.

Given this increasing circumspection of women's activity in the church, it is even more startling than it might otherwise be to see how Gertrude and her sisters took quasi-clerical roles upon themselves or else ignored them altogether. They taught and governed others, acted as counsellors and spiritual guides. They even heard confessions, if not in the strict sacramental sense, certainly in the counselling setting, all of this on the authority vested in them by their visionary experiences. On occasion this was sufficient to bypass even the eucharist and the other sacraments. In one of her visions, Christ came to Gertrude and said,

> Why are you troubled, my love? For as often as you desire it of me, I, the sovereign priest and true pontiff, will enter you and will renew in

your soul all the seven sacraments in one operation more efficaciously than any other priest or pontiff can do by seven separate acts. For I baptise you in my precious blood; I confirm you in the power of my victory; I take you for my spouse in the pledge of my love; I consecrate you in the perfection of my most holy life; I absolve you from all stain of sin in the piety of my mercy; I feed you with myself in the superfluity of my charity, and satisfy you with delights; and I penetrate your entire being like ointment by the sweetness of my spirit ... that you may grow in sanctity and aptitude for eternal life. (Bynum 1982: 202)

This bypassing of the established institutions of the church and therefore of its male representatives had the potential for a full-scale challenge both to ecclesiastical patriarchy and to the whole conceptualisation of ordained ministry.

Furthermore, Gertrude and her sisters, in contrast to Hildegard, do not disparage women and never apologise for their gender, not even with the obligatory 'modesty formula'. They do not use the typical categorisations of women as irrational, fleshly, lustful, or identified with matter; nor do they exalt men as spirit, mind, or superior to women in the likeness of God. Unusually for their time, they never find it necessary to defend the fact that they are *woman* teachers and counsellors: one will look in vain for any phrases like Hildegard's 'poor little figure of a woman' or Julian's apologetic 'though I am a woman, ignorant, weak and frail'. They are clear about what they are doing, and get on with it with confidence, even though it took them into priestly roles from which canon law would exclude them (Bynum 1982: 227).

Bynum suggests that along with the confidence inspired by the visions themselves, this greater serenity may have developed out of the fact that both Gertrude and Mechthild lived most of their lives in a convent where women's strength and spiritual competence was expected and valued. They had entered as child oblates, and had never lived in the world outside: from their very earliest years they had been surrounded by an atmosphere which was affirming of women. The convent was a large and wealthy one, linked to powerful nobility and to the top rungs of the ecclesiastical hierarchy; and its nuns would have come from the privileged upper classes. Furthermore, the convent had a tradition of learning unusual for women of the time; and books and manuscripts were prized and copied. In this atmosphere of culture, spiritual and intellectual activity were valued, and there was no question about gender being a disqualification for their pursuit. It would make sense to suppose that in such a woman-affirming atmosphere there would be less pressure to accept patriarchal restrictions and definitions, and far less internalised misogyny, so that Gertrude and Mechthild were able to assert their strength and spiritual leadership with confidence.

Ironically, however, the spirituality these women fostered contributed directly to the increasing clerical – and hence male – control of the church. The focus of much of their devotion was the eucharist. Mechthild of Magdeburg, an older contemporary of Gertrude, who entered the Helfta convent late in her life and had considerable influence on its younger members, had written of the eucharist,

> Yet I, least of all souls,
> Take him in my hand
> Eat him and drink him,
> And do with him what I will!
>
> Why then should I trouble myself
> As to what the angels experience?
>
> (1953: 48)

Although as we have seen there were occasions when Gertrude in her visions bypassed the clergy and received the sacrament directly from the hand of Christ, these were usually occasions when illness prevented her from attendance at the convent eucharist. Neither she nor her sisters minimised such attendance; in fact, their spirituality centred on it, tightly interwoven with the cult of devotion to the sacred heart of Jesus, which they did much to foster. And since the eucharist could be celebrated only by male priests, the emphasis on the eucharist and on the sacred heart in the spirituality of the strong women of Helfta weakened rather than strengthened the overall position of women in the church of that period, while increasing male clergy control.

The authority claimed by Gertrude and her sister nuns is

therefore highly ambiguous. They were confident rather than apologetic about themselves, and gave leadership in spirituality that bypassed male clergy. Sometimes they took male clergy roles frankly upon themselves, using the authority based on their visions to do so. On the other hand, however, in their emphasis on the eucharist and devotion to the sacred heart of Jesus, they were emphasising precisely those aspects of Christian belief and practice most carefully controlled by the ecclesiastical establishment and dominated by male clergy. While in some ways they can justly be seen as foremothers of contemporary Christian feminists, reconstructing traditional gender roles in even the most sacrosanct areas, strategically they played directly into the hands of a patriarchal ecclesiastical hierarchy tightening its grip on the church and causing the possibilities open to religious women to diminish. It would be unjust to call them token women – far more unjust than applying that label to Hildegard. But there is no evidence that they thought about what effect their spiritual emphasis would have on women in general; indeed there is no evidence that they would have minded that its effect would be the increase of priestly control. In any case, whatever they might have thought or intended, their own comparative freedom and assurance tended subsequently towards the restriction rather than the liberation of women.

It is harder to say with confidence of Hadewijch than of Hildegard or Gertrude that she rested her authority on her visionary experiences, though it certainly might have been the case. Since her visions – or at least the ones she recorded – probably occurred when she was still quite young, it is not unlikely that they increased her confidence. However, all her visions have to do with herself personally, and her own spiritual growth; they are not messages to anyone else. Consequently, while Hadewijch clearly felt herself summoned to deeper obedience as a result of her visions, it is less obvious either from her account of the visions themselves or from her subsequent writings that she rested authority for her spiritual leadership upon them.

Like Gertrude, and unlike Hildegard and Julian and many other medieval women, Hadewijch does not apologise for her gender, nor does she disparage or belittle women. There is less of a sense in Hadewijch that she has any *need* to justify her authority. This may be because she was more confident. In my view, however, a more plausible explanation would be that she addressed herself primarily to a young beguine whom she wished to instruct in spirituality. Although she would hardly write as she did without *any* sense of authority, it need be only a sense of the appropriateness of sharing her wisdom and experience with a woman presumably considerably her junior. She may well have derived some of her confidence, and based her authority to some extent on her visions, as the others did; but she was also in a position of seniority and leadership in relation to the young beguines, and this alone would justify her letters and poems of loving instruction to them.

One of the most interesting case studies of the relationship between visionary experiences and spiritual authority in medieval women is Julian of Norwich. Because she wrote two versions of her experiences, the second incorporating much more teaching than the first, we can see by comparing them the changes that took place in her self-understanding, not least in relation to gender and authority.

In the early Short Text, Julian is clearly worried about her status as a writer or teacher, protesting that the visions were not given to her for her private benefit, but for the comfort of all her fellow Christians. She says,

And therefore I pray you all for God's sake, and I counsel you for your own profit, that you disregard the wretched worm, the sinful creature to whom it was shown, and that mightily, wisely, lovingly and meekly you contemplate God, who out of his courteous love and his endless goodness was willing to show this vision generally, to the comfort of us all. (1978: 133)

By the time she wrote the Long Text at least fifteen years later, the self-abnegation was severely pruned, with hardly more than the expected 'modesty formula'. It is worth explicit comparison. She repeats without change the comment that the visions were intended for all her fellow Christians, and then proceeds,

And therefore I pray you all for God's sake, and I counsel you for your own profit, that you disregard the wretch to whom it was shown, and that mightily, wisely and meekly you contemplate God, who out of his courteous love and his endless goodness was willing to show it generally, to the comfort of us all. (191)

Although the passage is otherwise nearly identical, the 'worm' is gone, and so is the 'sinful creature'. They are quietly dropped, with no explanation and no substitution. Only 'wretch' remains.

As the chapter continues in the Short Text, Julian continues her justification of writing the visions. It reads as though she is acutely uncomfortable with her gender and yet feels it incumbent upon her to share what she had learned. She protests,

But God forbid that you should say or assume that I am a teacher, for that is not and never was my intention; for I am a woman, ignorant, weak and frail. But I know very well that what I am saying I have received by the revelation of him who is the sovereign teacher. But it is truly love which moves me to tell it to you, for I want God to be known and my fellow Christians to prosper, as I hope to prosper myself, by hating sin more and loving God more. But because I am a woman, ought I therefore to believe that I should not tell you of the goodness of God, when I saw at the same time that it is his will that it be known? ... Then will you forget me who am a wretch ... so that I am no hindrance to you, and you will contemplate Jesus, who is every man's teacher. (135)

The passage reads as though Julian feels caught between her gender and her religious duty, and is squirming to find a way forward: the first four sentences all begin with 'but'. Furthermore, it seems that she has internalised her inferiority as a woman. Not only is she 'ignorant, weak and frail', but she is likely to be a hindrance to her readers unless they can forget about her, and especially about her gender: in herself, she has no business being a teacher. She is only the channel through which God chooses to be revealed, the least and lowest of creatures. It is the same motif as we have already seen in Hildegard of Bingen: God chooses the humblest and the lowest, the handmaidens of the Lord. It is of course the case that many a male spiritual writer also counsels his readers to forget about him; the difference is that a male writer never does so on the grounds of *gender*.

This old familiar refrain, in itself worthy of no special notice, is made suddenly exciting by comparison with the Long Text. The whole passage simply disappears. All the internalised misogyny, all the self-doubt, all the worry about her gender as a teacher are gone. There is no more squirming. In their place is a profound spiritual reflection about the relation between experience of special revelation and making spiritual progress. It reads as follows:

I am not good because of the revelations, but only if I love God better, and inasmuch as you love God better, it is more to you than to me ... for we are all one in love, for truly it was not revealed to me that God loves me better than the humblest soul who is in a state of grace. For I am sure that there are many who never had revelations or visions, but only the common teaching of Holy Church, who love God better than I. If I pay special attention to myself, I am nothing at all; but in general I am, I hope, in the unity of love with all my fellow Christians. For it is in this unity that the life of all men consists who will be saved. (1978: 191)

From the severe self-doubt of the Short Text, Julian has moved to a position of confident exposition of the place of revelation and visions as a means to an end, though not an end in themselves; and the exposition makes no reference to gender.

This can hardly be because Julian had forgotten that she was a woman. Nor could she have forgotten that it was not considered appropriate for women to teach. Just in case she needed to be reminded, there was the example of the increasing persecution of the Lollards, which was based at least partly on the fact that they allowed women to participate in the ministry and to preach (Aston 1984; Willen 1989). The Bishop of Norwich during Julian's time, Henry Despenser, had been involved in a move which authorised the death penalty for convicted Lollards; and shortly after Julian's book was written, the fires of execution burned in the 'Lollard pit' just out of sight of Julian's cell.

In the face of this, Julian's acceptance of her role as a teacher, without disclaimer about gender, must be seen as a deliberate and courageous rejection of official ecclesiastical misogyny. It is all the more striking to remember that she wrote in the vernacular – probably the first English woman to do so – as also did the Lollards: indeed, that was another of the complaints against them. Like them, she addressed herself not to the ecclesiastical elite, but to her fellow Christians, women and men, who were not versed in Latin. She describes herself as a 'simple, unlettered creature' at the time when the visions occurred; but there is reason to believe that 'unlettered' does not mean 'illiterate' but rather 'unschooled in Latin'. She must have been aware of the danger, and of how radical was her refusal to apologise for her gender. The deliberateness is all the more obvious from the contrast with the Short Text. One can only speculate on how she did it, but somehow, in the fifteen or more years between the Short and the Long Texts, Julian lost her self-contempt and became confident of her strength and authority which she saw as divine gifts.

Perhaps, in spite of her belittling of her gender in the Short Text, Julian actually had quite a good start in self-esteem even before she had the visions. She certainly was far more psychologically robust than to fall into a swoon at the very thought of a direct experience of the passion of Christ. Where many another woman or man might have been overwhelmed by the sight of Jesus bleeding and suffering on the cross, Julian kept her wits about her and used the opportunity to ask some of the questions which had been troubling her. And when the answers were not to her satisfaction, she said so, and asked for clarification. A woman should hardly question any man, certainly not a priest, let alone God! Yet Julian did so, and gives the account of it in the Short Text, with considerable elaboration in the Long.

One of Julian's main concerns was why, if God is all-wise and all-powerful, sin had ever been allowed to enter the world. It seemed obvious to Julian that suffering is a result of sin, and if sin had been prevented, suffering would have been prevented too. When she asked about this, however, she did not get very much of an answer. She was told only that 'sin is necessary', but that 'all will be well, and every kind of thing will be well' (1978: 225). A lesser woman than Julian, had she dared to ask the question in the first place, would now have let it rest, perhaps blaming herself for her own ignorance if she felt that she still did not understand. But not Julian. She seems to have been fearful of her own audacity; yet in spite of her fear, she did not give up. Her account of what happened next is as follows:

But in this I stood, contemplating it generally, darkly and mournfully, saying in intention to our Lord with great fear: Ah, good Lord, how could all things be well, because of the great harm which has come through sin to your creatures? And here I wished, so far as I dared, for some plainer explanation through which I might be at ease about this matter. (227)

The response that Julian got certainly did not answer all her questions about sin and suffering. Rather, it set her in a train of thought and spiritual and theological investigation which she pursued for the next twenty years, and still did not feel complete when she had finished writing the Long Text. The investigation and writing were acts of a courageous woman. Perhaps it was her willingness to question, and to question even God if necessary, that helped to liberate her courage and integrity, and helped Julian find her strong, authentic voice.

Yet Julian cannot be taken without reservation as a fourteenth-century feminist, even at the time of writing the Long Text. Although she had come to a far greater acceptance of her strength and intellect by that stage of her life, and no longer needed to apologise for being a woman teacher, she was still deeply entangled with 'Holy Church' in ways which strike a modern feminist as ambiguous to say the least. From first to last, Julian displayed considerable anxiety about her loyalty to 'Holy Church', as she regularly called it. She is very careful to say repeatedly that there is nothing in her visions that is at variance with the teachings of the church; nor does she suggest anything other than that the 'common teaching of Holy Church' is sufficient for spiritual growth: special visions or experiences are not necessary. Even after she had the visions, she held that the teaching of the church was the context within which their meaning should be pondered. She says,

But in everything I believe as Holy Church preaches and teaches. For the faith of Holy Church, which I had before I had understanding, and which, as I hope by the grace of God, I intend to preserve whole and to practise, was always in my sight, and I wished and intended never to accept anything which might be contrary to it. And to this end with this intention I contemplated the revelation with all diligence, for throughout this blessed revelation I contemplated it as God intended. (192)

The last sentence is significant: *Julian*'s intention to contemplate the visions within the parameters set by the teaching of the church is conflated with *God*'s intentions for her. This means, in effect, that the teaching of the church is the truth of God. It must be accepted, not challenged.

That this is indeed Julian's position is confirmed specifically more than once in the Long Text. When Julian is faced with mysteries which she cannot understand, she rests on the teaching of the church as sufficient for her in spite of them.

God had showed the very great delight he has in all men and women who accept, firmly and wisely, the preaching and teaching of Holy Church, *for he is that Holy Church*. (235, emphasis mine)

This strong identification means that any challenge to the church would actually be challenging God; and any scepticism or disobedience to the church would be scepticism or disobedience to God.

This is not empty rhetoric for Julian: she practises what she preaches, even when she finds it difficult. One of the things which troubles her most is the church's teaching on hell and purgatory. In the visions she is deeply convinced of the love of God for all that God made, and is shown that 'there is no wrath in God'. But if this is the case, and if, as Jesus repeatedly assures her, 'all manner of thing shall be well', then how can it possibly be the case that anyone will be sent to hell? And yet this is what the church teaches, and Julian does not pretend otherwise. She writes,

Our faith is founded on God's word, and it belongs to our faith that we believe that God's word will be preserved in all things. And one article of faith is that many creatures will be damned, such as the angels who fell out of heaven because of pride, who are now devils, and many men upon earth who die out of the faith of Holy Church, that is to say those who are pagans and many who have received baptism and who live unchristian lives and so die out of God's love. All these will be eternally condemned to hell, as Holy Church teaches me to believe. (233)

If this is what the church teaches, then this is what Julian will cling to, even if it seems to go directly against what she has experienced in the visions. If there is a clash between ecclesiastical dogma and the experience of a woman, then male-defined dogma wins. Julian is clearly in considerable trouble of mind about this; but she steadily refuses to trust her own vision, and continues to insist that 'still I was not drawn by it away from any article of faith which Holy Church teaches me to believe' (234). Perhaps she should have been. Certainly her adamant refusal to question any of the male-defined dogmas from the standpoint of her own much more holistic experience is not one which most contemporary feminists could share, though it must be recognised that the power of the church now is nothing like what it was in the fourteenth century.

Julian's refusal to question the church is even more disturbing because the church of her time was badly corrupt, and Julian knew it. The papacy was divided, with pope and anti-pope in Rome and Avignon exchanging angry words, excommunications, and, eventually, full-scale military belligerence. Henry Despenser, Bishop of Norwich, led an ill-fated crusade to help Urban VI, the Roman claimant to the papacy, and extended full indulgences, release from purgatory, for all who would help in the campaign, and even for their deceased relatives. Since this campaign took place not many years after the Black Death had carried off hundreds of Norwich inhabitants, many of whom had died without the attendance of a priest and therefore without being shriven, the emotional blackmail of such offers of indulgence must have been incalculable, matched only by their complete religious inappropriateness. Add to this Henry Despenser's ostentatious militarism, his relentless persecution of the Lollards, and the firm stand taken by the English church generally and Despenser in particular against the peasants, and the decision to put down the Peasants' Revolt with ruthless violence rather than to listen to their grievances, and the church of Julian's time had a good deal to answer for. Sometimes she seems clearly aware of it. At one point she says,

Holy Church will be shaken in sorrow and anguish and tribulation in this world as men shake a cloth in the wind ... For [Christ] says: I shall completely break down in you your empty affections and your vicious pride ... (226)

This passage is all the more striking because it is the only time in all of Julian's writing that she uses vocabulary of destruction and violence. She clearly sees that the church as it was in her time was corrupt and in dire need of reformation. Yet this is also the only passage in which she mentions this need (and only in the Long Text). Apart from this one occasion she insists strictly on her loyalty to the church, with no reference to its failures and no qualifications.

Why does she do this? She cannot have been unaware of what was going on in the church, and clearly she was not undisturbed by it, or she would not have written the passage just cited. Why then should she have insisted on unquestioning loyalty quite so fiercely, and reminded herself and her readers of it quite so often? Was she frightened? She would certainly have good reason to be: the Bishop Despenser seems to have been a man who enjoyed ruthless hunting-down and destruction of any opponents and 'heretics', and Julian was definitely sailing close to the wind. But if she was frightened, would she not have played more on the 'timid, ignorant woman' angle rather than deliberately omit it from the Long Text?

In any case, it is hard to credit that Julian would be silenced by fear. Elsewhere I have suggested that perhaps Julian was making deliberate distinctions between the *teaching* of the church, to which she professed loyalty, and its actual *practice* which she found vain and arrogant (Jantzen 1987: 96). Although it is likely that that is part of the explanation, there are aspects which it leaves un-resolved: it does not explain, for instance, why she did not trust her own experience of the love of God and use it to challenge the vengeful dogma of hell and damnation.

Whatever the case, Julian's account of her visions and yet her insistence upon her loyalty to the teaching of the church shows clearly the ambiguity of a woman held in by male-defined ecclesiastical boundaries and yet compelled by her experience to push at them. Although Julian liberated herself from self-contempt based on gender, she was not able to liberate herself from strict subservience to male-defined ecclesiastical dogma. Whether that was because a heavy price would have to be paid in terms of persecution, or because her internal self-identity was so bound up with the church's teaching that she simply could not bring herself to question it cannot be known.

III BACKLASH

In contrast to the women visionaries are the writings of the male mystics of the medieval period. They tend to be much more learned, often deeply immersed in scripture and scriptural language, and increasingly through the twelfth and thirteenth centuries using scholastic method and content as well. By taking representative figures approximately contemporary with the women mystics I have discussed, it is possible to trace the development of what is at first a benign tolerance of visionary experience to a deep mistrust and condemnatory attitude toward it. Although the men in question do not specifically condemn the women visionaries, nor link their prohibitions with discussion of gender, the overall effect was that women of spirit were marginalised and 'true' mysticism was once again defined in male terms.

Bernard of Clairvaux was eight years older than Hildegard of Bingen; and when she was abbess of the convent on the Rhine, he was abbot of Clairvaux. Hildegard wrote to him, asking in her most humble manner for his validation of her visions.

I am very concerned about this vision which opens before me in spirit as a mystery ... I am wretched and more than wretched in my existence as a woman ... Gentle father, you are so secure, answer me in your goodness, me, your unworthy servant girl, who from childhood has never, not even for one single hour, lived in security ... (1987: 271)

Bernard sent her a very brief and restrained reply, allowing that she has indeed received a gift from God, but stressing above all that she must be humble. The visionary experience that she had asked him about is not specifically mentioned, whereas the grace of God and its essential link to humility is emphasised (1953: 459). As Jean Leclercq comments, 'She had asked him to judge. He replied with a brief bit of generally applicable advice, something which could have been written to anyone' (1989: 62).

Shortly thereafter, Pope Eugene III examined Hildegard

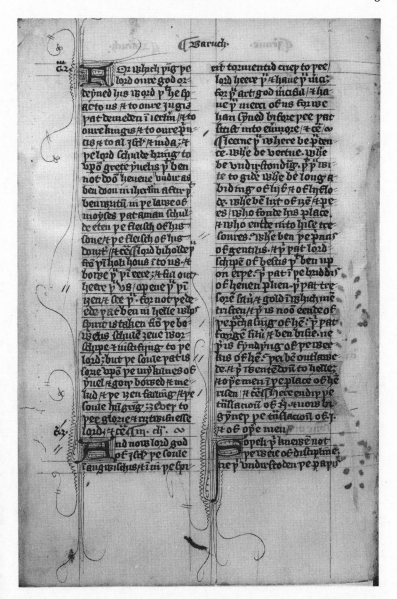

Figure 3   Lollard Bible. The Early Version, in English, translated during the time of Julian of Norwich.

himself, reading her *Scivias* and having it read aloud in Trier when Bernard was present. The pope decided that Hildegard's visions were authentic; and from that time Bernard's stance toward her became much less reserved. From this incident it appears that in the mid-twelfth century there was an openness to the occurrence of genuine visionary experience on the part of the ecclesiastical hierarchy, but that its authority to pronounce upon the validity of such experience must be scrupulously maintained. As long as Hildegard was willing to bow to the judgement of the pope and his representatives, they could affirm her visions without undue threat.

Nevertheless, Bernard himself, like most male writers of the twelfth century, would not put the accent on visions, though there can be no doubt that experience of a very different kind is central to his spirituality. The experience that is essential to Bernard has union with God as its goal, not as an abstract concept but as a felt reality. However, this is very different from the emphasis on visionary experience which we find in Hildegard; furthermore, Bernard never considered such visionary experience to be a possible basis of mystical or spiritual authority.

It is true that Bernard does speak frequently about visions of God, as well as of hearing God's voice (1977: II, 31–3). He cites prophets of the Hebrew Bible such as Jacob, Moses and Isaiah who saw God face to face, and mentions Paul who was 'rapt into Paradise, heard words that he could not explain, and saw his Lord Jesus Christ', though Bernard says that even in such cases their experience of God was not 'as he is but only in the form he thought fitting to assume' (II, 31.2.4). The unqualified experience of God is reserved for life after death, and is spoken of by such terms as Paradise, union with God, and the Beatific Vision – all to some extent metaphors for a reality which can be pointed to but not fully experienced in this life.

Far more important to Bernard than these external, quasi-sensory experiences of visual images or spoken words 'is another form of divine contemplation, very different from the former because it takes place in the interior, when God is pleased to visit the soul that seeks him'. This is the deeply felt sense of the presence of God, 'not in bodily form but by inward infusion', of which Bernard says,

It is beyond question that the vision is all the more delightful the more inward it is, and not external. It is the Word, who penetrates without sound; who is effective though not pronounced, who wins the affections without striking on the ears. His face, though without form, is the source of form, it does not dazzle the eyes of the body but gladdens the watchful heart; its pleasure is in the gift of love and not in the colour of the lover. (II, 31.3.6)

Nor are these experiences always the same; they are varied according to the needs of the recipient. Sometimes the divine Word comes 'like a physician with oil and ointments' healing hurts and correcting distortions; sometimes 'he joins up as a traveller ... on the road', and by his presence makes hardship or drudgery easier to bear; perhaps he arrives like 'a magnificent and powerful king', bringing courage in time of stress or temptation. In each case the divine Word comes with love and helpfulness; but in each case, although there is an awareness of the divine presence, it would be stretching Bernard's meaning too far to suppose that there was an actual visionary experience. The one who truly yearns for God will find that 'his heart's desire will be given to him, even while still a pilgrim on earth, though not in its fullness and only for a time, a short time' (II, 32.1.2). The awareness fades, and though it may return again from time to time, for the most part this life must be lived by faith, not by continuous direct experience of God.

It is important to note how Bernard describes the one who comes: God is the 'divine Word'. Furthermore, in each of the ways the Word comes, as physician, traveller on the road, king, and so on, the picture is drawn from one or another of the representations of Christ in the gospels. What is happening here is that Bernard is speaking of encountering Christ by penetrating to the mystical meaning of scripture. He is finding the divine Word in the words of the book, seeing Christ as the deepest meaning of the Bible, and in meditating on that meaning, encountering Christ in his own soul. Bernard is quite clear that experiences of this sort, encounters with Christ through the mystical meaning of scripture, are to be sought and 'ardently desired'. By contrast, visionary experiences of the sort that Hildegard and other women mystics had were not to be sought. These could at best be 'corporeal images', and thus could never really represent God, whose reality must be spiritual (II, 3.1.1). Although Bernard does not actually condemn visionary experiences, and at least after Hildegard's visions were ratified by the pope he was willing to support her, it is clear that in his view experiences such as hers are very much second-rate. Intentionally or not, Bernard reinforces the gender division in the western mystical tradition: the *real* mystical experience will be largely a male prerogative.

Eckhart, who was a younger contemporary of Hadewijch, took the matter considerably further. His whole spirituality was, as we have seen, focused on the (male) higher intellect. With regard to visionary experiences Eckhart's attitude was uncompromisingly negative. He reserved his most scathing language for those who claimed or wished to have such experiences.

Some people want to see God with their own eyes, as they see a cow, and they want to love God as they love a cow. You love a cow for her milk and her cheese and your own profit. That is what all those men do who love God for outward wealth or inward consolation – and they do not truly love God, they love their own profit. (1979: 127)

Eckhart did not single out women for this rebuke; but it is not hard to see that his scalding language could be used to reject any woman's pretension to spiritual authority on the basis of visionary experience. There is no room in his thinking for visionary experience based on higher motivation than personal profit, or for claiming of authority because of it: in his view all that can be said is that this would make the vision of God equivalent in value to the vision of a cow.

Indeed, Eckhart says that 'whoever seeks God by a special way gets the way and misses God' (II, 117). He does not seem to notice that for many women there was little option in terms of study of scripture or other educational opportunities. What he does say, in his typically dramatic manner, is that if a man thinks he will get more of God by meditation, by devotion, by ecstasies, or by special infusion of grace than by the fireside or in the stable – that is nothing but taking God, wrapping a cloak around his head, and shoving him under the bench.

The same, of course, would be true of any who sought visions. Once again, whether by intention or design, the spirituality typical of women was being marginalised in western mysticism, with the effect that it came more fully under men's control and definition.

Jan van Ruusbroec, a Fleming born in 1293, is widely regarded as one of the most important of all the fourteenth-century mystics. He was strongly influenced by Hadewijch; and it might therefore be expected that he would be more sympathetic to visionary experience. This, however, is not the case. In his major work, *The Spiritual Espousals*, he describes the various stages a person may go through in spiritual progress. One such stage is a condition of great enthusiasm, where the individual is filled with jubilation and love. In Ruusbroec's view, this is a particularly dangerous state. To the individual in such high spirits may come dreams, visions and voices; but as likely as not these experiences come straight from the devil. Ruusbroec warns that 'they should be relied on only insofar as they are in accord with Holy Scripture and with truth, and no more than that', otherwise the person may be deceived (1985: 88).

This much might be uncontentious; but he soon resumes the theme, likening such experiences to honeydew, a 'false sweetness' which occurs during periods of heat and contaminates growing fruit.

In the same way, some persons can be deprived of their external senses by means of a certain kind of light which is produced by the devil and which surrounds and envelops them. They sometimes have various kinds of images shown to them, both false ones and true ones, or they hear different kinds of locutions ... Whoever makes much of this receives a great amount of it and in this way becomes easily contaminated. (89; cf. 137)

According to Ruusbroec, even the true images are from the devil. Visions are to be entirely mistrusted: one should certainly not 'make much of them', as the women did who used them as the grounding for their spiritual authority. Again, Ruusbroec never explicitly mentions women visionaries; but again, the implication for the gendered construction of mysticism is clear.

A frightening note is injected into all of this is a passage from another of Ruusbroec's writings, *A Mirror of Eternal Blessedness*. His discussion is organised around saying what will happen to people who receive the sacrament in accordance with how pure of heart they are. Some people receive the sacrament unworthily, being in a state of sin; and they will have to suffer purgatory because of it. But by far the worst case is that of false mystics, those who claim that they are in direct relationship with God and consequently are not bound by the rules of the church. Ruusbroec is not talking specifically about visionaries, but rather about those who 'say they live in a formless way above all forms'; but it would not be a long extension to apply his words to anyone who claimed authority on the basis of mystical experience.

This is the greatest error and the most perverse and foolish heresy that has ever been heard. No one should give the blessed Sacrament to such persons, neither during their lifetime nor at the time of their death, nor should they be given a Christian burial. Rather, they should rightly be burned at the stake, for in God's eyes they are damned and belong in the pit of hell, far beneath all the devils. (231)

These were not empty words. All across Europe the fires were being lit that devoured 'heretics', a large proportion of them women. And in the succeeding centuries those fires would become the huge conflagration of the witch burnings.

Having visionary experiences, and claiming authority on the basis of them, became increasingly hazardous, especially for women. There were of course also men who had visionary experiences: Francis of Assisi, for example, and Richard Rolle. Interestingly, they were men who were also most accused of being 'feminine' in their dress, behaviour and activity: Richard Rolle, for example, clothed himself in his sister's cast-offs, and Francis of Assisi tended lepers, by tradition a woman's job. Neither of them placed much emphasis on formal education, nor did they undertake either the mystical exposition of scripture or the speculative mysticism of Eckhart and Ruusbroec (Watson 1991).

Although there were these exceptions, however, as the thirteenth century turned into the fourteenth many of the most influential male mystics rejected with increasing sharpness the validity, let alone the authority, of visionary experiences and of those who had them. The anonymous author of *The Cloud of Unknowing*, written in England in the late fourteenth century, had scathing denunciations for those who sought mystical experiences, whether visionary or of any other kind. He may actually have had Rolle in mind when he wrote,

When they read or hear read or spoken how men should lift up their hearts to God, they look up to the stars as though they would reach above the moon, and cock their ears as though they could hear angels sing out of heaven. In their fantastic imagination they would pierce the planets or make a hole in the firmament to look through it. They would fashion a God according to their own fancy, and dress him in rich clothes, and set him on a throne . . . And so it is their habit to sit with their mouths open as though they were catching flies . . . (Anon 1981: 231)

His sarcastic lampoon of visionaries is relentless and without sympathy: they are 'like sheep with the brain disease'; they 'hold their heads on one side as though a worm were in their ears'; they squeak and splutter and waggle their heads and smile continuously 'as though they were girlish gossips or amateur jugglers unsure of their balance' (223).

The stridency of his condemnation, coupled with the sexism never far beneath the surface and showing itself occasionally as in the comment on the 'girlish gossips', gives some indication of the extent to which authority was being reclaimed from visionaries, mostly though not exclusively women, and is a foretaste of what was to come. The author of *The Cloud* repeatedly links visionaries with heretics, and is quite sure that they will all 'go stark staring mad to the devil' (222), a devil with only one nostril which he will willingly turn upwards so that it is possible to see 'up it into his brain' which is 'nothing else than the fire of hell' (227). It is the same constellation of ideas that was being used in standard descriptions of heretics, and was soon to re-emerge in the infamous *Malleus Maleficarum* and the destruction of thousands of women as witches. I am of course not saying that the author of *The Cloud* was responsible for the witch craze or that he would have approved of what happened. But his condemnation of visionaries and his lumping them together with heretics links up a set of ideas that consolidates a new social construction of who counts as a mystic, a construction that once again gives women very little place. These ideas would be ready to hand for those who sought spiritual justification for the atrocities that were to follow.

CHAPTER 6

The visions of virgins: spirituality and sexual control

> Whether woman should have been made in the first
> production of things?   (Thomas Aquinas 1945: 1.92.3).

During the later Middle Ages, the ecclesiastical authorities increased their preoccupation with the extermination of heresy, and
the ever-present danger to women mystics of being classified as
heretics or witches continued to grow. Even for those women
whose authority and Christian piety was unquestioned, however,
their esteem was often bought at the very high price of rigorous
bodily control. In this chapter, therefore, I wish to look at the issue
of control and how that shaped the developing construction of
mysticism, before turning in the next chapter to those who were
excluded from its ranks in the eyes of the orthodox. The treatment
cannot be precisely chronological: the understanding of spiritual
authority and bodily control went hand in hand, and overlapped
with ever-increasing precision with the searching out of heresy and
witchcraft.

It was a commonplace of the Middle Ages that women were
more lustful, more prone to physical weakness, more tied to their
bodies in every way than were men. For a woman to be spiritual,
therefore, required heroics beyond what would be necessary for a
man. Already among the desert-dwellers the austerities of the
women were such as to cause the men to marvel, though men
also practised austerities which by today's standards are
awesome. Throughout the medieval period, it was assumed that
those who sought spirituality would mortify the desires of the
flesh, especially with regard to sexuality; but the demands of

vigilance and mortification were higher for women than for men, because of the ease with which woman's flesh, especially her insatiable sexual desire, would betray her.

I have already discussed the way in which the understanding of the mystical was linked to the mind or spirit rather than the body; and hence its gendered nature, because men were more naturally linked with the mind whereas women were linked to the flesh. In this chapter I wish to look at the opposite side of the equation: if the mind was to be purified and raised up to mystical vision, what was to happen to the body? In particular, what must happen to the bodies of women if, contrary to all their linkage with the flesh, women were to become spiritual? This consideration will take us back to early Christian centuries for the roots of the ideas which dominated the bodily control of women throughout the medieval period and which culminated in the witch craze of the early modern era.

I wish to begin, however, with Thomas Aquinas, whose teaching both reflected current thought and perpetuated it throughout the later middle ages and beyond. Aquinas, in his discussion of the likeness between God and human beings, said,

Since man is said to be the image of God by reason of his intellectual nature, he is the most perfectly like God according as his intellectual nature can most imitate God. Now the intellectual nature imitates God chiefly in this, that God understands and loves himself. Therefore the image of God may be considered in man ... inasmuch as man possesses a natural aptitude for understanding and loving God; and this aptitude consists in the very nature of the mind, which is common to all men (1945: 1.93.4).

Aquinas is here echoing the familiar theme that it is in the mind that man must resemble God; and the exercise of this god-like mind is the chief end of men.

But what about women? Aquinas can hardly deny that according to scripture, both male and female were created in the image of God and thus, in his terms, with an intellectual nature: we have already seen in chapter 2 how Augustine struggled with the same problem, and in fact Aquinas takes a position very similar to that of Augustine. He says, 'The image of God, in its principle signification, namely the intellectual nature, is found both in man and in woman', and again, a little farther on, 'the image of God belongs to both sexes, since it is in the mind, wherein there is no distinction of sexes' (93.4). But, as we would suspect, this cannot possibly be the whole story for Aquinas, given that he accepts without question the Aristotelian description that 'the female is a misbegotten male', and the further medieval commonplace that woman is 'an occasion of sin to man' (92.1), causing man to fall into sexual passion and thus fail to fulfil his intellectual and spiritual nature.

Furthermore, Aquinas is even clearer than was Augustine that whereas 'man is ... ordered to a still nobler work in life, and that is intellectual operation', women are created solely for the purpose of enabling men to procreate. 'We are told that woman was made to be a help to man', he says, 'But she was not fitted to help man except in generation, because another man would have proved a more effective help in anything else' (98.2). Therefore although in theory both women and men bear the image of God – the intellectual nature – in fact this is true only in a formal sense. In practice, men do the thinking while women get pregnant and bear the children. So Aquinas concludes by effectively reversing his earlier statement that the image of God is in the mind 'wherein there is no distinction of sexes':

But in a secondary sense the image of God is found in man, and not in woman, for man is the beginning and end of woman, just as God is the beginning and end of every creature ... 'For man is not of woman, but woman is of man; and man was not created for woman, but woman for man.' (92.4)

This is by now an old familiar refrain, taken over in all essential respects from Augustine eight centuries before. The time-lapse, and the almost verbatim repetition of Augustine without any need to elaborate or defend the views, makes clear how thoroughly these misogynist ideas permeated the religious thinking of the medieval church. And given such views, it is hardly surprising that throughout that time, spiritual enlightenment and the mystical path should be seen as primarily a masculine enterprise: if women could be considered spiritual, they must be exceptional indeed, as we have seen, and must have a special basis for their authority. They must also do special things to their bodies. Even for men, physical heroics were necessary for spiritual enlightenment: how much more would this be the case for women, who were much more closely bound to the flesh?

I PHYSICAL ENCLOSURE

From the earliest years of the Christian era, women as well as men had been a part of the Jesus movement. When in due course one of the means of expression of a devoted Christian life was a move to the eastern deserts, many women left the cities to live a life of austerity and renunciation. Though much more is written about the desert fathers than about their female counterparts, it is clear that ascetic women formed a large part of the desert population (King 1984). Their austerities were as intense as those of their brethren; indeed, sometimes, as we saw in the case of Pelagia (see p. 57), they wore men's clothing and passed as men until they died, in no way behind the men in the stringency of their asceticism.

In due course the men and women of the desert were gathered together into monasteries, as the church sought to take control of the individualism which they saw as characteristic of those who lived in the desert. Pachomius, for instance, developed large communities of women as well as men, with as many as 1,000 monks or nuns in each, and gave them a rule and pattern of life that would bring order into their diversity (Bouyer *et al.* 1968; Lawrence 1984). In his rule, as in that of Basil and later of Cassian and Benedict, the emphasis was less on austerity than on obedience, a curbing of the independent instinct in an effort to bring strong-minded men and women intent on devoting their lives to holiness under ecclesiastical control.

To this extent, the move to physical enclosure in monasteries applied to men and women alike: both men and women who pursued an individualistic route to holiness could be a threat to the control of the church. But as Joyce Salisbury (1991) has shown, independent women posed a further threat to ecclesiastical power. Women were thought to be weak, identified with the flesh, and properly subservient to men: their sexual passivity was only one aspect of the passivity which ought to be characteristic of the lives of women. Yet women who practised the austerities of the desert, including its rigid chastity, were seen as accruing power over their sexuality, and indeed over traditional gender roles. They thus posed in their own bodies a contradiction between the female gender which was defined as passive, and the life of active ascetical holiness. Since the proper ordering of the world was seen as requiring a power relationship between men and women in which women were subservient, the independence of undeniably holy women formed a considerable threat to the whole world view of the early Christian church. Accordingly, patristic writers spent considerable energy arguing for the control of holy women by the church, and stipulating the forms which such control would take. By the time of the Council of Elvira, in about 306, legislation was being passed requiring widows and virgins to wear clothing by which they could be easily identified, and to take public vows. Throughout Europe, the emphasis was on bringing women who sought to live a life of holiness into strict monastic enclosure, not allowing them to live independent lives which threatened anarchy to the church and to the whole ordering of the world. This is not to say that no independent women remained: indeed, there is a hagiographical tradition of the lives of ascetic women who claimed independence on the grounds of their vows of chastity. They were, however, in the minority, and the threat they posed to the church is without doubt part of the reason for the marginalisation of their *Vitae*, though the manuscripts continued to be recopied and circulated for centuries.

For the most part, women who were determined not to marry and who wished to enter a life dedicated to God had little option other than to become nuns. In practice, even this was largely restricted to women of the high aristocracy in the early Middle Ages; other women were expected to marry and bear children. Although there were a considerable number of convents in early medieval Europe, and this was 'almost the only specialized religious role available to women' during this period, it is also the case that before the turn of the thirteenth century there were far more monks than nuns, nor could most ordinary women hope to enter a convent at all (Bynum 1987a: 121). On the other hand, some of those women who did enter the religious life became very powerful indeed: one need only think of Hilda of Whitby in seventh-century England, abbess of a large double monastery, and presider over the Synod of Whitby which brought together the Celtic and Roman branches of the church of her time.

As the medieval period progressed, there was considerable change in the pattern of women's enclosure. The large double monasteries with powerful abbesses ceased to exist; on the other hand, far more convents were founded, and the proportion of females to males in religious orders increased dramatically. Once again, part of the reason for this seems to have been male fear of female bodiliness and sexuality, and the threat which this posed to male celibacy.

In the early twelfth century, wandering preachers such as Robert of Arbrissel began to call for reform of the church, inveighing against its lack of poverty and failure to live by the standards of the gospel. Robert and others like him were charismatic preachers and striking in their embrace of poverty, wearing rags and going barefoot, and living on fruits or berries in the woods or the produce of simple gardens. Women as well as men flocked to them, revering not only their preaching but also the asceticism of their lives, and joined with them in calling for the reform of the church and of traditional monasteries and religious communities. Robert, however, seems to have been uncomfortable with his large female following, though he recognised a calling to care for the needs of religious women. He founded for them as well as for his male followers the community of Fontevrault, a 'double order' of monks and nuns living in separate convents but under the rule of a single abbess, the first of whom was Petronilla. What makes his foundation stand out from previous double monasteries, however, is the fact that, whereas men had the choice to continue to follow him in a mendicant lifestyle, women who were religiously serious were expected to remain in the physical enclosure: it was held indecent of them to traipse around the countryside following a preacher, vows of chastity notwithstanding. Indeed, some of those within the ecclesiastical establishment who wished to bring discredit on Robert accused him of 'undue intimacies' with his women followers: it was the type of accusation all too likely to be levelled at any preacher or reformer who was suspect in the eyes of the ecclesiastical authorities, and says more about what they considered damaging or threatening than about Robert's actual behaviour (Lambert 1992).

In the twelfth century there was an enormous increase in the number of women's houses, as well as a rise of heretical movements such as the Cathars and the Waldensians, both of which attracted large numbers of women followers: we shall explore these in more detail in the next chapter. Women were more mobile, more independent, more able to assert their desire for a religious life, though once again the opportunities were largely restricted to well-born women and the extent of their freedom should not be overstated. But while there were more religious houses for women, it remained the case that if women wanted to enter religious life it was essential that they be thus physically enclosed: indeed the religious life for women became virtually identified with their strict enclosure, while for men there were increasing possiblities of sanctity in other forms of life: the knight as well as the priest was seen as having a vocation.

Perhaps the clearest illustration of the contrast between women and men is the case of Clare of Assisi in the thirteenth century. Francis of Assisi had won from Pope Innocent III the right for his small band to live a life of poverty, and to preach penitence, not remaining in a monastery but ministering to the lepers, the sick and the despised of society. Clare, a young woman from a wealthy home, was attracted to Francis and his work; and in spite of her parents' opposition she was determined to join his order. On the night of Palm Sunday of 1212, she fled with her cousin from her parents' home to the Portiuncula where Francis received them. He cut off their hair, and gave them brown habits like his own to wear. But far from allowing them to remain with the brothers or to become part of the mendicant band, Francis then took them, much against Clare's will, to a Benedictine convent. Even so radical a man as Francis did not see his way clear to allow women to be unenclosed. Clare insisted that she had not left her home to become a Benedictine nun but to become a follower of Francis and of Christ in evangelical poverty; but the best Francis would do for her and the women who quickly joined her was to install them in the rebuilt church of San Damiano, where they became the Order of the Poor Clares (Englebert 1950). At first, apparently, the women worked alongside the Friars Minor, ministering to the lepers, the destitute and the sick, and returning at night to their segregated residence (de Vitry 1969: 71). But although that may well have been what Clare intended all along, it was not to last.

Francis seems to have been uncertain what to do about the women. Near the end of her life, Clare wrote a 'Testament' to leave to the women of her order, in which she describes how she went to him, promising him obedience in just the way a man who wished to join his band would do. Accordingly, if he decreed that the women were to live in enclosure, there was nothing for it but to obey him. Yet enclosure was not what they had intended, and he knew it.

But when the Blessed Francis saw that, although we were physically weak and frail, we did not shirk deprivation, poverty, hard work, distress, or the shame or contempt of the world – rather, as he and his brothers saw for themselves, we considered [all such trials] as great delights after the example of the saints and their brothers – he rejoiced greatly in the Lord. And moved by compassion for us, he promised always, both through himself and through his Order, the same loving care and special solicitude for us as for his own brothers. (Francis and Clare 1982: 228)

That care and solicitude, however, was not exercised to allow them to join the brothers in the mendicant lifestyle and evangelical poverty which they had believed to be their vocation. Rather, it expressed itself in the brothers bringing to the Poor Clares the proceeds of their begging and taking the oversight of the women's physical and spiritual well-being, an oversight which required their strict physical enclosure. Once again, the threat of independent women was too great to be tolerated; and, once again, women were required to be submissive to the ruling of men.

To be fair, it is not clear how strongly Clare resisted. By looking at the Rules developed for the community, and in particular their statements on enclosure, it is possible to see that whereas Clare was dissatisifed until strict poverty was made to be a part of it, the same was not true with regard to enclosure; and certainly by the time she developed her own Rule, she was as insistent on the necessity of strict enclosure as Francis could ever have been. It was not, however, immediately possible for her to develop her own Rule, since the Fourth Lateran Council of 1215 had forbidden the establishment of any new religious communities for women: any community therefore had to follow some existing Rule. When this proved unacceptable for the Franciscan sisters, first Hugolino di Segni, Cardinal Archbishop of Ostia and Velletri, and then Pope Innocent IV wrote 'a Rule for the Poor Ladies'. Hugolino's Rule said this about enclosure:

[The sisters] must live enclosed throughout their lifetime, and after they have entered in the enclosure of this Order, taking the regular habit, the permission or faculty to go out may no longer be given to them, unless to plant or build that same Order. (212n6)

The prescription is virtually identical with that for nuns of any Benedictine or Cistercian convent, even though the Rule for the male members of the respective orders is quite different from that for the Friars Minor.

The same is true with the Rule of Pope Innocent IV. He repeats the essence of Hugolino's prescription, but adds to the possible exceptions such things as 'the reforming of some monastery, or for the sake of governing, or correction, or to avoid some grave expense, through the permission of the Minister General of the Order of Friars Minor ...' (212). The pope, therefore, relaxed the rule of enclosure very slightly, but made any excursions subject to the permission of the (male) minister-general or his deputy. Clare herself, in her own Rule, relaxed the conditions even more, saying simply that after a woman has been accepted as a full member of the community, 'she may not go outside the monastery except for some useful, reasonable, evident and approved purpose' (212). It is perfectly clear, however, that such purposes would never include the life of mendicancy that the Brothers followed; and furthermore, that the 'approval' would have to come, ultimately, from the minister-general or his deputy:

Poor Clares were as thoroughly enclosed as their sisters in the long-established orders.

Was Clare simply bowing to the inevitable, though she herself would have wished it otherwise? Attractive as such a suggestion might be, the evidence is not in its favour. As already indicated, neither of the two earlier Rules placed as much emphasis on poverty as Clare desired, and thus finally she wrote her own Rule, which was ratified by the pope shortly before her death. This sequence of events is important, because it shows that Clare was quite capable of insistence concerning something about which she felt strongly, that is, poverty. Since she showed no such dissatisfaction regarding enclosure, even though in every other respect she insisted on following closely the pattern of the Friars Minor which, especially in regard to poverty, was quite different from that of the established orders, it must be assumed that she was resigned to the idea that a mendicant life was not fitting for women.

The result was that whereas the spirituality of men could be shown in their wanderings, and in the years to come this would make a huge impact on what was to count as spirituality in European countries, the spirituality of women was still deemed to require strict physical enclosure. Religious women were in physical subjection to men: it was only with male permission that a sister could leave her enclosure even temporarily. Any woman who would not abide by such a rule of enclosure would not count as spiritual. The bodies of women were too dangerous to be allowed out of the control of men: if they would not be married and in subjection to their husbands, then they must be enclosed, and in subjection to male ecclesiastics.

To what extent the Poor Clares had internalised such attitudes in their own times and were content with their physical enclosure and subjection, and to what extent they chafed against it, wanting to be more like their brothers in religion, is a matter of speculation: what is clear is that for them the price of spirituality was enclosure, and that this price was gender-specific. Furthermore, it is clear that at least part of the reason for this was the male fear of female sexuality (or of their own sexuality projected on to women). According to Celano, who wrote the first life of Francis,

Francis himself was fearful of the dangers which might result if friars were to have contact with women, even for purposes of spiritual direction. He desisted from going too often to visit the Poor Clares (in spite of his promise to Clare that he would always care for them), with the warning that one could not be too careful about chastity; and he is said to have observed that 'It is the Lord who has preserved us from taking wives, but who knows whether it is not the devil who has sent us sisters' (quoted in Bolton 1973; cf. Englebert 1950: 145). It seems, at the very least, a less than respectful attitude towards those who were as intent on a life of evangelical holiness as he himself was, and is quite at variance with the popular portrayal of Francis as the radical mystic who welcomed the earth, his body, and all things as from the hand of a good God (Boff 1985).

The same mistrust of female bodiliness, with the same insistence on enclosure, can be seen again in the history of the beguines, except that in their case far more drastic measures were taken to make the point. In northern Europe, one of the forms of religious life for women in the thirteenth century was for women to live in small groups in family houses or in houses bought by pooling their resources. These women, who became known as beguines, did not take irreversible vows, but lived simply by the work of their hands, embracing poverty and chastity and seeking to serve the sick and destitute of their towns. They did not have a founder in the way that other religious communities did, and they did not have a specific rule of life or come directly under ecclesiastical authority. In spite of this, or possibly because of it, great numbers of women in the Rhineland and northern Europe were attracted to the beguines; it has been estimated that in the mid-fourteenth century as many as 15 per cent of the adult female population of Cologne were beguines, and there were also considerable numbers in other urban centres, especially in northern Flanders, France and Germany (Southern 1970a: 240).

The status of beguines, however, was ambiguous. Like their male counterparts, the beghards, they tried to live simply and with great piety, helping people in distress and supporting themselves with their own efforts. They paid special attention to the life of Christ as portrayed in the gospels, and saw themselves

as following his pattern of teaching and healing and caring for the
outcasts of society. But because they were not part of a regular
order, they were looked upon with suspicion by both the secular
clergy and the members of religious orders, sometimes accused of
hypocritical virtue and at other times, on equally slender grounds,
of sexual immorality (Lambert 1992: 181). Part of the problem, in
the eyes of the ecclesiastical authorities, was that they were not
bound by a Rule, they were not a female offshoot of any of the
male orders, nor were they directly subservient to any man,
whether bishop, priest, or abbot (Bolton 1973: 79). Indeed, the
Fourth Lateran Council of 1215, in its prohibition of any new
religious orders, in effect made it impossible for them to be
formally constituted, with the net result that they fell between all
the stools and became a threat to ecclesiastical orderliness.
Furthermore, the piety of the beguines was such as to lead many
of them to value and pursue the mystical life as the basis for their
works of compassion. Some of their early members, who served
as role models for younger generations of women, were women
like Mary of Oignies, Christina of St Trond, and Margaret of
Ypres, all of whom were widely known and revered for their
miraculous exploits and the mystical phenomena held to be
associated with them (Bolton 1978). This meant, however, that the
mystical way was slipping out of institutional control, no longer
confined within enclosed orders of monks and nuns. To make
matters worse, some beguines, notably Hadewijch of Antwerp
and later Marguerite Porete, wrote in the vernacular. If this were
allowed to continue, then not only would mysticism be available
to pious women not strictly controlled by a religious order, but it
would actually extend to women and men outside ecclesiastical
authority altogether.

One of the ways of seeking to regain control was to consider
such women as heretics, possibly linking them with what became
known as the 'heresy of the free spirit', a 'heresy' which arguably
existed more in the minds of those jealous for ecclesiastical order
than in reality. They could also be accused of being witches. In
either case, they could be dealt with harshly, the authorities
demanding either repentance or the death penalty, and sometimes both: the beguine Marguerite Porete, was burned at the

stake in Paris in 1310. We will look more closely at these ways of dealing with them in the next chapter.

Not everyone, however, advocated such extreme measures. There were men who were deeply impressed by the beguines, recognising the value of their piety and practical good works, and ready to characterise them as women of great strength and sanctity. Nevertheless, their irregular status, living without the jurisdiction of a recognised religious order, without a rule and without special enclosures, was seen as unusual at best: 'women's more informal arrangements for giving religious significance to ordinary life seemed odd and dangerous to male sensibilities' (Bynum 1987: 24). Thus for example Matthew Paris, an English chronicler, spoke of the beguines in tones that indicate some puzzlement, recognising their piety but yet bemused by their unusual status:

[These women] have adopted a religious profession, though it is a light one. They call themselves 'religious' and they take a private vow of continence and simplicity of life, though they do not follow the rule of any saint, nor are they, as yet, confined within a cloister. (quoted in Southern 1970a: 319)

The response of the men who set out to champion the beguines is one all too familiar in the history of male championing of women: their protection, or at least their toleration, and in particular their exoneration from the accusation of heresy, was granted on condition that the women submitted themselves to male-defined regulations. Typical is the work of Jacques de Vitry, a man who, as Brenda Bolton puts it, saw women's communities as 'being significant and potentially useful to the church', but whose 'enthusiasm ... was tempered by the possible dangers of their extraregular status. He seems to have wished them to be completely incorporated into the ecclesiastical structure so that their obedience could be ensured' (1973: 82). Jacques de Vitry was born about 1165, perhaps in Rheims, and from 1211 to 1216 he was a regular canon of St Nicholas of Oignies in the diocese of Liège, before becoming Bishop of Acre for more than a decade. During his time in Liège he was much influenced by the beguine Mary of Oignies, whose life he wrote in terms which recalled the austerities and holiness of the desert fathers, and which was clearly intended to advance their position and protect them from hostility and accusations of heresy or immorality. On his way to taking up his bishopric at Acre, he went to see the pope with the special purpose of seeking ecclesiastical recognition for the beguines; but while he was on his way Pope Innocent III, from whom he might have hoped for official approval, died and was replaced by Pope Honorius III. From this new pope all that could be obtained was oral permission and encouragement for the women to live together in religious communities: it seems that he did not take much serious interest, but gave a nod of the papal head.

From this point on, the beguines tended to develop more formal arrangements, grouping themselves into enclosures, and placing themselves under the direction of a (male) confessor, often a member of one of the mendicant orders. It was the price of survival. Women who sought to live independently pious lives, not under obedience to men, were too vulnerable to accusations of heresy and even witchcraft. By the beginning of the fifteenth century, all béguines lived in convents.

Yet even living in enclosed groups, and under male protection, the beguines faced recurring efforts at suppression: they were seen as illicit groupings of dangerous women with pretensions to the mystical life (Leff 1967: 22). The Council of Vienne (1311–12), for example, singled them out for explicit censure:

> We have been told that certain women commonly called beguines, afflicted by a kind of madness, discuss the Holy Trinity and the divine essence, and express opinions on matters of faith and doctrine contrary to the catholic faith, deceiving many simple people. Since these women promise no obedience to anyone and do not renounce their property or profess an approved Rule, they are certainly not 'religious', although they wear a habit and are associated with such religious orders as they find congenial ... We have therefore decided and decreed with the approval of the Council that their way of life is to be permanently forbidden and altogether excluded from the Church of God. (Southern 1970a: 330)

At the same time, however, it was impossible to deny either the piety of their spirituality or the compassionate practices for which they were noted; and these the church could hardly forbid. Therefore the Council continued its decree in words which could be taken as virtually the opposite to the ones just cited:

In saying this we by no means intend to forbid any faithful woman from living as the Lord shall inspire them, provided they wish to live a life of penance and to serve God in humility, even if they have taken no vow of chastity, but live chastely together in their lodgings.

Obviously a decree which appears to contradict itself is one which would be interpreted according to the will of the individual concerned; and when that individual happened in 1318 to be the hostile Archbishop of Cologne, the result was his demand that all beguine associations in the city should be dissolved, and the women in them should be absorbed into regular convents; by 1421 Pope Martin V ordered that any remaining groups should be searched out and destroyed.

It is clear, therefore, that the very piety and informality which attracted women to join the loose organisation of beguines devoted to spirituality and works of compassion were also the things that were perceived as the greatest threat: the mystical life could not be left in the hands of women, and certainly not women outside of rigorous male ecclesiastical control. As we shall see in the next chapter, the threat and then the reality of persecution of women of spirit grew in the later Middle Ages and into the early modern period, as men, both clergy and lay, struggled for control over who should count as a mystic.

II CONTROL OF FOOD

Strict enclosure as the price of women's spirituality being considered authentic was a price imposed largely by ecclesiastical men. However, the strict emphasis on food and its control in women's spirituality as a means and a guarantee of its authenticity was an emphasis which was self-imposed by women at least as much as it was required by men. Caroline Walker Bynum (1987a) has shown the importance attached to food, fasting and feasting by medieval women, and the ways in which female spirituality differed from male spirituality with regard to food. Her findings illustrate yet another example of the way in which gender differences were significant in determining who should count as a mystic.

As Bynum points out, preoccupation with food and fasting was not restricted to women. Pious men, too, practised fasting and abstinence, were fed from the breasts of the Virgin Mary, and longed for the body and blood of Christ in the eucharist. Indeed, from the time of early Christianity, fasting had been seen as a means of curbing sexual desire for both men and women, as well as a practical way to make sure that one had food available to give to those in need. The mothers and fathers of the desert took fasting to heroic lengths, practising austerities which today seem bizarre, not to say impossible. Similarly, the feast of the eucharist was always important in Christianity as a communal meal of the church and as the prefiguration of its unity with the saints in heaven; and both women and men in the Middle Ages found it increasingly a focus of their devotion.

Nevertheless, as Bynum shows, there is a distinct gender difference in the emphasis on food, fasting and the eucharist, which becomes clear in the period from the twelfth to the fifteenth centuries. Whereas men who entered monasteries or who wrote about the spiritual life were more preoccupied with the renunciation of wealth and power as a means of holiness, women (who usually did not have wealth or power to renounce in any case) were much more likely to give a large place to food (or its absence) in their spirituality. A disproportionate number of women saints of the period practised fasting with such severity that scholars who have traced the motif in their lives and writings speak in terms of 'holy anorexia', with, sometimes, a doubt about whether the severity should be seen as 'holy' or as an obsessive-compulsive disorder of the personality (Bell 1985; Vanderyecken and Van Deth 1993). There are many hagiographical accounts of women in which their sanctity is demonstrated by the fact that they were able to go without food altogether. One such is the *Life of Alpaïs* written by a late-twelfth-century Cistercian, in which the Blessed Virgin Mary says to Alpaïs,

because, dear sister, you bore long starvation in humility and patience, in hunger and thirst, without any murmuring, I grant you now to be fattened with an angelic and spiritual food. And as long as you are in this little body, corporeal food and drink will not be necessary for the sustaining of your body, nor will you hunger for bread or any other food ... because after you have once tasted the celestial bread and drunk of the living fountain you will remain fattened for eternity. (Bynum 1987a: 73)

Nevertheless, the (male) writer found it necessary to guard against possible misrepresentation: he went on to say,

But in order that the tumult of gossip be quieted, since some said she had a devil – she who neither ate nor drank – two or three times a week she was accustomed to accept some morsel. And she would roll it around for a time in her mouth ... and then spit it back whole ... And I give this on my own testimony since I received in my own hand a little bit of masticated fish she spit out ... Thus, rejoicing as if possessed, she frequently vomited from too much food, as if her drunkenness and inebriation were increased by anything beyond a tiny bit ... And this was ... how God underlined her merits and virtues with miracles.

The writer's interpretation of this behaviour as evidence of extraordinary holiness is hardly the one that would occur to a modern reader; and it is necessary to consider what assumptions made that conclusion obvious for medieval readers of her life.

In the first place, there was the assumption, already noted, that women were particularly associated with the flesh. But secondly, there was the further connection between refusal of all ordinary food and being fed solely on the eucharist, the body of Christ. Now, putting these two ideas together, it becomes clear that if a woman fasted to such an extent that her body could be said to be fed only by the eucharist, then her body was no longer to be seen as an ordinary human body, but was rather a body like Christ's: fed on the body of God, it became divine. From this set of associations, furthermore, one can see the logic of the miraculous exudings said to come from women who fasted: they did not excrete ordinary faeces nor did they menstruate, but they might give forth extraordinary breast milk or oil or sweet saliva that could be used to heal those who were ill in body or mind. Their bodies had become so united with the body of Christ by their feasting on the eucharist to the exclusion of everything else that they were able to be his presence in the world. And if the fasting

Figure 4   *Eucharistic Christ and Charity*. This is thought to portray
a vision of Gertrude of Helfta: the blood of Christ comes from his breast,
and provides eucharistic nourishment.

brought about severe suffering and even death, that was still
further indication of their unity with the one who suffered in body
for the salvation of the world.

In the case of women of sanctity, feasting, particularly eating
the body and drinking the blood of Christ in the eucharist, was
central to women's piety: indeed, fasting might well be seen not
so much as an isolated activity but as a preparation of mind and
body for the holy feast. Women who starved themselves of
ordinary food would sometimes find that eating God in the host

and drinking his blood in the wine became the occasion for visions and other paranormal phenomena associated with mystical experience. This might happen even (or especially) when for some reason they were not actually given the wafer or the chalice: Christ would then come to them directly, and feed their hunger with himself. As we saw in chapter 5, for instance, Christ came to Gertrude of Helfta on her sickbed and gave her communion of himself when she had not been able to attend the eucharist: there are numerous similar stories recounted of other pious women.

An additional twist was given by the prevalent medieval idea that breast milk was processed blood, an idea that reversed itself in eucharistic devotion in the commonplace theme that the blood from Jesus' wounded side (breast) became the nourishment (milk) of those who were born of God. Bynum tells the story of Mechthild of Magdeburg who on one occasion lamented that she was without the mass. She was given a vision in which John the Baptist came to be her celebrant.

Then the maid [Mechthild] went up to the altar with great love and widely opened soul. John the Baptist took the white lamb with the red wounds and laid it on the mouth of the maid. Thus the pure Lamb laid itself on its own image in the stall of her body and sucked her heart with its tender lips. (133)

We have here the image of eating and being eaten, nursing and being nursed: the blood of Christ is the essential spiritual sustenance, while her own blood is given, she goes on to say, for the suffering souls in purgatory.

Thus women's preoccupation with food was by no means all to do with renunciation. The everyday reality was that women on the whole were the ones who prepared food and were responsible for feeding men and children. Holy women extended this in their efforts to serve Christ by feeding others, especially those who were too poor to be able to feed themselves in the famines of the late medieval period. Sometimes these two functions coincided: women who were in conflict with their families or who felt guilt about the sources of their wealth might take the family food and give it to the poor, thus rejecting the status and security which a good supply of food brings. Unsurprisingly, this could bring the wrath of the family down upon their heads, as in the case of Christina the Astonishing, whose enraged sisters locked her up after she had given the food away. Some families, however, were more supportive or gave grudging acceptance, possibly reflecting their own ambivalence about wealth (233).

It is clear, therefore, that women's preoccupation with food was extensive, and was what in modern thinking would be considered both postive and negative – that is, it concerned itself not only with fasting to the point of starvation, but also with nourishment, both in terms of ordinary food and in terms of the spiritual food of the eucharist. Bynum points out, however, that before jumping to modern conclusions, it is necessary to look at the meaning of this behaviour on the part of women in their medieval context. How did they themselves and their contemporaries see what they were doing? What pressures focused their attention so strongly on food and its renunciation?

Women's attitudes to food were far more internalised than their attitudes with regard to the enclosure which was imposed upon them by men. Nevertheless, it would be inaccurate to say that the strict emphasis on fasting and abstinence, as well as the obsessive desire for the eucharist characteristic of many pious women, was entirely self-imposed, even though it was not ecclesiastically enforced in the same way as women's enclosure was. Male writers, including some on whom the women had to depend for protection, placed great emphasis on the importance of women fasting, as well as their nourishment in the eucharist, as we have seen in the Cistercian *Life of Aloïs* already quoted. Similarly Jacques de Vitry, the defender of the béguines, wrote of them in his *Life* of Mary of Oignies,

Some of these women dissolved with such a particular and marvelous love toward God that they languished with desire and for years had rarely been able to rise from their beds. They had no other infirmity, save that their souls were melted with desire of him, and, sweetly resting with the Lord, as they were comforted in spirit they were weakened in body ... The cheeks of one were seen to waste away, while her soul was liquified with the greatness of her love. Many had the taste of honey sensibly in their mouths because of the gift of spiritual sweetness in their hearts ... Some in receiving the bread of him who came down from heaven obtained not only refreshment in their hearts but a palpable consolation in their mouths sweeter than honey and the honeycomb ... [They] languished with such desire for the sacrament ... unless their souls were frequently refreshed by the sweetness of this food. Let the infidel heretics blush, who do not partake of this food by either faith or love. (13)

Obviously if the men on whom the women had to depend were so impressed with their fasting and their longing for the eucharist, then there was at the very least strong male reinforcement for their preoccupation with food and with fasting.

It must be said, however, that male spiritual directors and advisers also wrote in a different vein, urging the women for whom they wrote to be moderate in their fasts and abstentions. Even Jacques de Vitry warned his readers that what was required of them was to wonder at, but not to emulate, the eating behaviour of the women about whom he had written: it was a common refrain among men writing about holy women. Sometimes they went further: Francis of Assisi, for instance, required of Clare that she discontinue her practice of severe Lenten fasting; and Henry Suso wrote to Elsbet Stagel,

Dear daughter ... discontinue these excessive austerities which are unsuitable to your sex and unnecessary for your disposition ... The good Jesus did not say, 'Take up my cross', but 'Let every man [*mensch*] take up his cross.' Consequently you should aim, not at imitating the austerities of the ancient fathers or of your spiritual father, but at crucifying your bad habits without detriment to your health. (85)

Whether or not Suso was threatened by the fact that his spiritual daughter was able to emulate his own austerities must remain speculation; but it is at least clear that he did not impose on women the austerities which the women sought to take upon themselves.

This means, though, that we are left with the question of why it was that women were so concerned with food and fasting. Modern thinkers who have concerned themselves with eating disorders frequently concentrate on issues of control; and indeed, as Bynum points out, there were multiple ways in which women were able to exercise control through their identification with food. Most obviously, they were able to exert control over their own bodies. Medieval women were well aware of the correlation between body weight and menstruation, for example, and women who feared sexuality, or who (for very understandable reasons, given the customs of the times) feared being pushed into a marriage and successive childbirths over which they had no other control, might choose to reject food and with it reject their own sexuality and marriageability: we will see this in the case of Catherine of Siena below. Besides this, however, they were able to exert control over their circumstances. They were able, sometimes, to manipulate men – fathers, husbands, or priests over whom they had no other means of control – by their food practices, whether by making themselves unmarriageable, by giving away the resources of the family and redirecting energies to religious purposes, or by criticising religious authorities.

This last point needs further explanation. Holy women, who went without ordinary food and feasted on the eucharist, were held to be able to recognise any immorality in the priest who consecrated it. Thus, for example, Margaret of Cortona saw that a priest was unchaste because in her eyes his hands turned black when he touched the consecrated wafer. Women were therefore able to expose the corruption of male priests. They were also able, as already indicated, to do without male priests altogether, and to take upon themselves clerical roles, finding in their own identification with the suffering Christ an alternative prophetic stance over against the authority of ecclesiastical office. Obviously such a stance could be deeply threatening to the men of power; and pious women were always at risk of being burnt as heretics or witches rather than being venerated as saints: it was not for nothing that male spiritual directors cautioned the women for whom they cared to exercise prudence and moderation. Yet on the other hand it was precisely *because* of their fasting and becoming one with Christ in the food of the eucharist that their spirituality could be taken seriously.

The control of food in the spirituality of medieval women is therefore deeply ambiguous. On the one hand, it represents positive values on the part of the women. Because women were identified with the flesh, they could see themselves (and be seen by men) as uniquely participating in the humanity – the flesh – of

Christ; and by feasting on the eucharist and suffering the pains of fasting they can be seen not so much as denying their own flesh but as merging it with the flesh of Christ in an *imitatio Christi* which was, in their eyes, salvation not only for themselves but for the world. The bodily suffering of their fasting, frequently accompanied by other self-inflicted pain such as flagellation, can be seen as a positive identification with the agony of Jesus in his bodiliness. They thereby gave themselves, with him, for the redemption of the world. Because women were identified both with bodiliness and with food, such identification with the humanity of Christ, broken in the agony and the joy of the eucharist, could appear natural and appropriate to them.

Thus Bynum argues that whereas modern eyes might see the severe fasting and chosen suffering of medieval women as an effort to escape their bodies (and in some respects it could be exactly that) we must also recognise that for them it was a positive bodiliness. It should therefore not be understood so much as misogyny, whether imposed by a male-dominated society or internalised by the women themselves, but rather as a way in which women celebrated the religious possibilities of their bodiliness. Bynum writes,

Medieval women are not best understood as creatures constrained and impelled by society's notions of the female as inferior. Women's piety was not, fundamentally, internalized dualism or misogyny ... In their symbols women expanded the suffering, giving self they were ascribed by their culture, becoming ever more wonderfully and horribly the body on the cross. They became that body not as a flight from but as a continuation of the self. And ... that body was also God. (295)

Bynum's argument is meticulously documented and carefully developed; and I am heavily and gratefully reliant upon it. Yet it seems to me that even if Bynum is right – perhaps, indeed, *especially* if she is right – there is a sense in which what she has presented shows an even more horrifying misogyny than a simple dislike of women or disdain for female bodiliness. The misogyny consists precisely in the constellation of ideas which makes the symbolism around women and food appear natural: the identification of women with bodiliness, the identification of bodiliness with suffering, and the identification of suffering with the means of salvation. In a universe in which these ideas appear normal, it may well be the case that the behaviour of religious women in extreme fasting, food control, and identification with the macerated Christ in the eucharist is natural or even positive: this may have been one of the most creative ways of dealing with the male-defined world in which they lived. And it would indeed be the case that the ones most closely identified with Christ – those who suffered most, and gave that suffering for the salvation of others – would be the ones who would count as the true mystics. But as the case of Catherine of Siena shows, the world in which these are the criteria for women's spirituality is a world that feminists must find terrifying.

III CATHERINE OF SIENA

There is no doubt that by modern standards Catherine of Siena would be classified as suffering from anorexia nervosa. But an individual's food behaviour, whatever else it is, is clearly linked to the perceptions and symbolism of food in the culture generally; and to understand Catherine's self-starvation it is necessary to see it in the context which I have already outlined above. What I shall do, therefore, is look at some aspects of Catherine's life and teaching as a case study of the gendered nature of the relationship between food practice and the question of who should count as a mystic in fourteenth-century Italy.

Catherine Benincasa was born in 1347, the stronger of twins. Her mother Lapa, who had previously born twenty-two children (of whom more than half seem to have died in infancy) decided to nurse Catherine herself, while putting her weaker twin sister, Giovanna, to a wet-nurse. The result was that Catherine became her mother's favourite, while Giovanna soon died. However, a year later Lapa fell pregnant again and bore her last child, who was called Giovanna after Catherine's deceased twin. It is difficult to resist the speculation that the strong attachment Catherine felt to her younger sister was acutely tinged with survival guilt.

Nevertheless, Catherine seems to have been a happy and outgoing child. Her precocious religiosity was not unusual for girls in fourteenth-century Siena. Though it was carried to extremes with a group of playmates who tied ropes into knots and flagellated themselves, this might still be seen as nothing more than childish imitation of adult practice in the aftermath of a plague which had recently devastated Siena and the surrounding area (Bell 1985). Catherine's father was in the cloth-dyeing business; and an elder sister, Bonaventura, made a strategic marriage to a man who was in the same occupation. By all accounts, financial considerations and material wealth were paramount in the family's attitudes.

In due course, it was considered time that Catherine, now about twelve years of age, be prepared for marriage. At first she resisted her mother's urges to make herself attractive, seeing this as worldly; but Bonaventura persuaded her that beautifying herself would not give God displeasure. Accordingly, Catherine went along with the plan, until two events took place in quick succession. First Bonaventura died in childbirth. Shortly afterwards, Giovanna, the little sister to whom Catherine was closely bound, also died. If survival guilt was present in Catherine's awareness of the death of her twin in infancy, it was acute now. Catherine blamed herself, believing that it was her willingness to indulge in the worldliness of self-beautification which had caused God to punish the family. Things were made worse by the fact that the family seem to have planned to marry Catherine to Bonaventura's widower, a man who could help the family make money, but was unattractive, dissolute, and much older than Catherine. Catherine rebelled. She determined to have nothing more to do with marriage: she would become the bride of Christ.

Things were not so easy, however. Young women in the fourteenth century were under the control of their families, especially their father and elder brothers; and in Catherine's case they were determined that she should get over her 'nonsense' and prepare for marriage. Catherine's mother supported them; and became the focus for the family conflict. What could Catherine do? With so much of life out of her control, she exerted herself over the one thing left to her: her own body. She refused food, cut off her hair, deliberately scalded herself in hot baths when she was taken on vacation, and set about the self-conquest which ended in her starvation in her early thirties.

Her family, however, did not give in easily. Raymond of Capua, Catherine's disciple and earliest biographer, places in their mouths the following response:

Vilest girl, you cut off your hair, but do you think perhaps that you are not going to do as we wish? Despite your not wanting it, your hair will grow back and even if your heart should break, you will be forced to take a husband; you will have no peace until you have done our will. (quoted in Bell 1985: 41)

Even if these were not their words, they represent Catherine's perceptions of what was going on: a conflict of wills that was strongly gender-related. From this point, Catherine was made to be a servant of the family, sewing, washing, and cooking; but in the end, her father was the one who could stand it no longer, and gave in to her wishes.

By this time, however, her self-conquest which may have started as a method of controlling her family had taken on a life of its own. She took a vow of silence which she maintained for three years (though she was still living at home, in a room in her father's house); she flagellated herself heavily three times a day with an iron chain; she imposed upon herself severe sleep deprivation – Raymond of Capua says that she reduced her sleep to 30 minutes in 48 hours! – and, above all, she ate only raw vegetables and a little bread. Eventually she took the mantle of the Sisters of Penance, a Dominican tertiary order most of whose members were widows: it was an unusual choice for a young woman, but it was one which allowed her to give herself to the service of others while avoiding enclosure.

Multi-faceted preoccupation with food became a major focus for her life. At the same time as she was drastically reducing her own food consumption, she endeavoured to overcome her nausea at the filth and disease of the people she was trying to serve. Her biographers tell of incidents in which she drank the pus of putrefying sores, telling Raymond, 'Never in my life have I tasted any food or drink sweeter or more exquisite.' Like the women discussed in the previous section, her efforts to control her own food were directly related to her efforts to serve others, and especially to her feasting on the eucharist. The night after the incident in which she drank pus occurred, she had a vision in which Christ said to her,

Previously you had renounced all that the body takes pleasure in ... But yesterday the intensity of your ardent love for me overcame even the instinctive reflexes of our body itself: you forced yourself to swallow without a qualm a drink from which nature recoiled in disgust ... As you then went far beyond what mere human nature could ever have achieved, so I today shall give you a drink that transcends in perfection any that human nature can provide. (Bynum 1987a: 172)

Christ then gave her his own wounded side, from which she drank his blood. From that point on, her hunger was only for the eucharist, and she became quite unable to eat ordinary food. Whenever she tried, she found herself unable to digest anything she had swallowed, and would put twigs or fennel down her throat to make herself vomit.

Raymond saw these events as causally related: in his view, it was because of her vision of Christ, given to her in reward for her service to the sick, that she was unable to eat.

After the vision just described, and especially whenever she received Holy Communion, a very torrent of heavenly graces and consolations flooded her soul. These were so abundant that their efforts brimmed over upon her body also, checking the flow of its vital juices, and so altering the action of her stomach that it could no longer assimilate food. Indeed, the taking of food became to her not merely unnecessary but actually impossible, except to the accompaniment of great bodily suffering. If food was ever forced down her throat, intense pain followed, no digestion took place, and all that had been violently forced down was violently forced back again. (168)

During all this time, Catherine slept less and less, was increasingly restless, and gave herself to the service of the poor and the sick.

There were those, however, who suspected that other interpretations could be placed upon her fasting. A letter of Catherine's in response to one she had received from a male religious in Florence shows that he had suggested that her fasting might be only a frailness of bodily function, or, even worse, a demonic delusion. Rather than denying that this might be the case, Catherine replies,

You wrote to me saying in particular that I should pray God that I might eat. And I say to you, my Father, and I say it to you in the sight of God, that in every possible way I could I always forced myself once or twice a day to take food; and I prayed continually and I pray to God and will pray, that he will grace me in this matter of eating so that I may live like other creatures, if this is his will ... As to myself, I do not know what other remedy to try, other than that I beg you that you beseech that highest eternal Truth to grant me the grace of allowing me to take food, if this be more for his honor and for the health of my soul, and if it pleases him ... (quoted in Bell 1985: 22)

But there is more than one way in which this letter can be interpreted. On the one hand, its recipient would hardly have room to object to her overt humility and willingness to eat if only God would make it possible. Yet the frequent qualifications ('if this is his will', 'if this be more for his honor', 'if it pleases him') allow Catherine herself to take quite a different view of the matter: for all her protestations that her inability to eat is an infirmity which she has prayed that God should remove, she may still have seen it as a mark of God's favour. As Caroline Bynum observes, 'it was exactly her considered and mature under-standing of it *as* an infirmity (rather than a voluntary practice or a delusion of the devil) that allowed her to retain the behaviour without any effort to alter it' (1987a: 169). And given the identification of infirmity with the sufferings of Christ for the world, any such infirmity could be seen by Catherine and those around her as a way of offering herself for the salvation of humanity.

Metaphors of food, food images and discussions of food are prevalent in Catherine's book, *The Dialogue*. One of the passages most revealing of Catherine's attitude about her own eating behaviour comes in her account of St Agnes, a woman who had established a convent, gathered eighteen young women to join her, and then found herself unable to give them food, 'with nothing but greens to eat', Catherine comments that unless one has become perfect, the human body cannot live only on greens; but that God's perfect providence can enable even this. Catherine recounts God saying to her in explanation of this,

As for any human body to which a similar thing would happen, I would make it so amenable to those greens or anything else that it would fare better on that little bit of greens, or sometimes even without any food, than it had done before on bread and all the other things that are given for human life. And you know that this is so because you have experienced it yourself. (Catherine of Siena 1980: 315)

Indeed she had; but the fact that she here sees it as a direct enablement of God shows that her willingness to look upon it as an infirmity must be understood in the light of seeing any infirmity as a gift from God, a participation in the suffering of Christ, rather than as something which one should dread or seek to overcome.

As Catherine's reputation for sanctity grew, a small band of disciples clustered around her, whom she taught, and to whom she dictated her *Dialogue*. One of her great concerns was the state of the church of her time. In 1376 she had gone to Avignon to persuade the pope, Gregory XI, to return to Rome. Two years later he died, and the Great Schism broke out, with Urban VI in Rome vying for authority with Clement VII in Avignon. This time, it seemed that Catherine could do nothing to heal the breach. Given her personal history, it is perhaps unsurprising that she should try once again that device which had served her so well: total fasting. This time she went without water as well as food; and within a few months she was dead.

Catherine's life is a disturbing illustration of the gender-related construction of mysticism in her time. As is obvious from the discussion in the previous section of Bynum's research into the food behaviour of medieval religious women, Catherine in many respects fitted the pattern. She sought to control her own body and her family circumstances through control of food; she gave herself to the service of others both in her own fasting and in providing food for them; and she was devoted to the eucharistic feast, drinking the blood of Christ and identifying with his suffering and death for the salvation of the world. All of these things contributed to her reputation for holiness and her eventual sanctification as a doctor of the church. Would the same things have been seen as marks of holiness in the case of a man? The question hardly makes sense. Catherine's food behaviour is so clearly gender-related that it is not possible to think of a man engaging in the sort of things characteristic of Catherine, let alone being thought holy because of it.

It is instructive to ask why not. Why is it that fasting to the point of starvation, and obsession with participating in the suffering of Christ in order to save the world, is something which is characteristic of women but not of men? As soon as the question is asked, the answer emerges: women are identified as the ones who, in their flesh, are to serve the spirit. As Bynum says, women are linked with the humanity of Christ, who suffered to save the world, and therefore in their suffering flesh they find their true holiness. Men, on the other hand, are linked with spirit, with the divinity of Christ, with that which the flesh is made to serve. Therefore the whole constellation of symbols and behaviour manifested in Catherine, from her rejection of food for herself, to her drinking of the pus of a suffering woman, to her serving Christ through suffering, to her attempt to control the movements of the pope by her prayers and fasting, became in her case a constellation that pointed to holiness; but it is a holiness predicated on a deeply suspect cultural understanding of gender. Though Bynum asserts that it is not accurate to see women's piety as 'internalized dualism or misogyny' (1987a: 295) because they saw themselves as spirit as well as flesh and tried to assimilate their bodies to the broken wafer of the eucharist and the bleeding body on the cross in order that body and soul together should be saved, nevertheless it is clear that it is precisely *because* of the cultural identification of women with the flesh, and with the functions of serving and suffering, that such possibilities of piety ever get a purchase. The example of Catherine shows the extent to which gender issues were paramount, gender issues which were not neutral cultural symbols, but were based in a view of women as inferior, properly serving men, whether in marriage, in feeding, or in acts of piety on their behalf. Catherine herself repeatedly associated women with weakness, sensuality and the flesh and saw men as stronger and in more positive terms: so convinced of this was she that she assumed that it would be necessary for her to wear men's clothes until a vision of Christ tells her that this is unnecessary. The reason he gives is that women's inferiority makes them the suitable vessel for his message (407n6). It is a theme we have encountered before.

In fourteenth-century Italy, and indeed elsewhere in medieval Europe, women could be counted holy. But their holiness was bought at a price which no man would ever be expected to pay: acceptance of the gender stereotypes which made the identification of women with food, the flesh, and suffering service seem natural. Once again, the question of who could count as a mystic was answered in a way which, though it did not exclude women, made sure that the women who were included conformed to the needs of men for nurture and for service. The identification of women with the flesh, and with the suffering humanity of Christ, meant that the religious symbolism which went most deeply into the psyche was a symbolism which placed women to men in the role of the suffering servant.

IV SEXUAL CONTROL: VIRGINITY AND HOLISM

Pervasive as the suspicion of the body was in Christendom, it has often been noted how uncongenial a doctrine it is in relation to other central Christian teachings, most particularly the doctrines of creation and incarnation. If, as medieval Christians believed, God created the physical universe and found it good, and then proceeded to create Adam and Eve and found them, in their embodied partnership, very good, then why should there be such a suspicion of the physical world, the body and sexuality? The medieval response, of course, was along the lines that had been set out by Augustine: all of this goodness had been fatally distorted by sin, which manifested itself most particularly in sexual desire. And since women's sexual desire was seen as much greater than men's (indeed many men feared it was insatiable), while their attractiveness to men was held to be virtually irresistible, women were seen, like Eve, to be the occasion of men's downfall. For men to make spiritual progress, away from all the sinful fleshly pursuits to which women tempted them, they should therefore avoid the presence of women altogether if possible.

Even as an ideal, this could really only be held by monks; and the Christian church, even in its monastic branches, always also upheld marriage and condemned as heretical those sects which preached against it. Yet for all this, there was a double standard of spirituality, and only those who were celibate – preferably virgins – were felt to be eligible for the heights of spirituality, since only they had been uncontaminated by sexual expression. This could be as true for women as for men: Hildegard of Bingen, for instance, had much to say about the desirability of virginity as the best way of salvation (1990a: 207); and many male writers had much to say in praise of virgin women, at least in an ideal form, if not so frequently about actual women they knew.

Nevertheless, there are places where the strain of coupling this negative doctrine with the biblical account of creation is clearly visible; and in some cases, notably in Julian of Norwich, it gains the upper hand. While the tension appears in the writing of men as well as women, it is in women that we find most clearly the struggle towards holism, even while they also retain a strict doctrinal stance of dualism. In their greater appreciation of the physical universe and its beauty, in their franker acceptance of bodiliness and sexuality (even while also praising virginity) and in their choice of metaphors and themes that reinforce integration rather than separation of body and soul, these women, even while fixed in their time and ecclesiastical structure, developed a strand of spirituality whose principle of integration is a significant alternative to the dualist thinking which rendered spirituality in effect a male prerogative.

The doctrine of the incarnation also pointed towards a greater appreciation of the physical. If the Word became flesh, then the flesh cannot be negatively valued. Nevertheless, the doctrine of incarnation was so hedged about with the teachings regarding Jesus' virgin birth, and hence the absence of all taint of original sin (derived from the sexuality involved in conception) and his own virginity, that the significance of divine embodiment for a more positive valuation of the body could easily be overlooked. Still, those women and men who pondered the doctrine did sometimes feel its tension with a spirituality that was hostile towards the flesh. And as we have seen, women were particularly concerned to ponder the flesh and blood made nourishment for the church in the sacrament of the eucharist.

Yet they could not go too far. If there was one theme more than any other central to the definition of who should count as a mystic, sexuality was that theme. Contemporary feminist writers would be delighted to find examples of medieval women who formed a total contrast to the oppressive male-defined stand; but it would be unrealistic to expect the search for them to be successful. After all, such women would quickly be silenced and made invisible: they would not count as mystics where men were doing the counting. The women of whom we can expect to have any knowledge are women who were still within their own structures, and identified themselves strongly with the thought forms of those structures, oppressive though they were; we cannot make them say everything that a twentieth-century feminist might like to hear. Yet neither should they be written off altogether. Even while they worked within the structures of their time, they also developed strands of life and thought that form alternatives to those structures, forming a spirituality that valued women, and that enabled integration of soul and body in holistic being towards God. In this section I wish to show by means of case studies of two very different women, Hildegard of Bingen and Julian of Norwich, how they approached the issue of virginity and sexual control in an age where such control was deemed central to the question of who should count as a mystic.

We have already seen how Hildegard spoke of herself as a 'poor little figure of a woman', and in general showed contempt for her sex. Yet there is much in Hildegard's writing that shows that this contempt was not unqualified, or even congruent with her most deeply held theological ideas. It is worth exploring this tension in Hildegard in some detail, because her work is a striking example of the ways in which a women of spirit might accept and even promote sexual control, while at the same time push back the boundaries of misogyny.

For Hildegard as for most of her contemporaries, a human person is a microcosm of the macrocosm, a world in miniature, and participates in the four elements and their qualities. In one of her visions in the *Book of Divine Works* she sees a human being in the centre of the world, which in turn is resting in the womb of God (1987: 23). Just as, in the *Scivias*, she had taught that 'the

Figure 5 *Hildegard receiving her visions*. Divine light from heaven pours into Hildegard's mind, while her assistant, Richardis von Stade (who probably illuminated the manuscripts) stands behind her. The monk Volmar sits in a separate room ready to transcribe her visions into Latin.

visible and temporal is a manifestation of the invisible and eternal' (1990a: 95), so also the human is a manifestation of the whole cosmos. This much, in her time, was common, though Hildegard's visionary portrayal of it is striking. However, Hildegard also departed from this conventional wisdom in startling ways. For example, it was standardly held that whereas all humans participate in the four elements, men participate more fully in the warmer elements and women in the colder: Alberic of London had stated that 'scientists call these two elements [fire and air] masculine, but water and earth feminine. For the former lie above, the latter below; the former are active, the latter passive' (quoted in Newman 1987: 128). But Hildegard rejected this cosmic projection of the missionary position: in her view it was *man* who was associated with earth, since Adam had been made from the dust of the ground; whereas woman is more of an airy temperament, and thus more open to spiritual stirrings and perception as well as more sensitive to her physical environment, even though it is also true that woman is 'weak and fragile and a vessel for man' (1990b: 77).

For Hildegard, the theory that human beings are the created microcosm of the macrocosm, and made in the image of God, had physiological as well as theological consequences, and both are explored in her writings. She wrote medical and herbal treatises which, while rooted in their time so far as diagnoses and prescribed remedies are concerned, show considerable knowledge and concern for women's general and especially reproductive health. She writes about difficulties with menstruation, pregancy and childbirth, barrenness and the problem of either unwanted or unrequited love (for both men and women). Yet for all her sympathetic writing about women's gynaecological problems, she was also highly negative toward sexuality, retaining the standard Augustinian ideas regarding fallen sexuality, concupiscence and original sin, and seeing virginity as the highest possible value.

Hildegard's theological account of the creation of humanity begins by dwelling on God's pleasure and delight.

When God looked upon the human countenance, God was exceedingly pleased. For had not God created humanity according to the divine image and likeness? Human beings were to announce all God's wondrous works by means of their tongues that were endowed with reason. For humanity is God's complete work. (1987: 22)

We have already seen the contortions of writers like Augustine and Aquinas in their consideration of whether women as well as men were made in the image of God. Hildegard agrees with them about the importance of reason as the crown and seal of the divine image. She also agrees about God creating woman to be a helper for man, but she puts it in a way that carries rather different possibilities than Augustine had envisaged.

But the human species still needed a support that was a match for it. So God gave the first man a helper in the form of a woman, who was man's mirror image, and in her the whole human race was present in a latent way. God did this with manifold creative power, just as God had produced in great power the first man.

Because woman was man's mirror image, the two could not be separated as Augustine sometimes suggested; each was completely dependent upon the other.

Man and woman are in this way so involved with each other that one of them is the work of the other. Without woman, man could not be called man; without man, woman could not be named woman. Thus woman is the work of man, while man is a sight full of consolation for woman. Neither of them could henceforth live without the other.

Hildegard does not accept the idea that man could be the image of God without woman, as Augustine had said. Each needs the other.

Hildegard accepts the general identification of man with reason and divinity, and woman with body; but she makes a special point of seeing this in the light of the incarnation, in terms already familiar to us from the discussion of food control above.

Man is in this connection an indication of the Godhead while woman is an indication of the humanity of God's son. (122)

By combining the doctrine of creation with the doctrine of incarnation, Hildegard gives an important place to women in the created order. Adam is the one who indicates divinity, but Eve, in whom 'the whole human race was present in a latent way', is the one who fully represents humanity, partly as the mother of all living, and specifically as prefiguring Mary from whom the human Jesus would be born. Thus, as Barbara Newman points out, Hildegard exalts the female above the male, making her rather than him the representative human being and the one through whom salvation would come, even while retaining the traditional formula that identified man with the soul and woman with the body (1987: 93).

One might expect, from this identification of bodiliness with the humanity of Christ, that Hildegard would have a much more positive view of women's bodies and sexuality than was often found in the Augustinian tradition. To some extent this is true. Woman is the one who gives birth to God; and every child she bears is a child that bears God's image. Yet sexuality was involved in their making, and about this Hildegard is ambivalent. She sees sexuality in the Garden of Eden before the fall into sin in a very positive way, with love and mutuality between Adam and Eve, and no sense of female subordination. Moreover, contrary to Augustine and other patristic writers, love-making was pleasurable; it was not merely a cool and rational act of depositing semen into a vaginal receptacle. Hildegard writes,

When God created Adam, Adam experienced a sense of great love in the sleep that God instilled in him. And God gave a form to that love of the man, and so woman is the man's love. And as soon as woman was formed God gave man the power of creating, that through his love – which is woman – he might procreate children. When Adam gazed at Eve, he was entirely filled with wisdom, for he saw in her the mother of the children to come. And when she gazed at Adam, it was as if she were gazing into heaven, or as the human soul strives upwards, longing for heavenly things – for her hope was fixed in him. And so there will be and must be one and the same love in man and woman, and no other.

The man's love, compared with the woman's, is a heat of ardour like a fire on blazing mountains, which can hardly be put out, whilst hers is a wood-fire that is easily quenched; but the woman's love, compared with the man's, is like a sweet warmth proceeding from the sun, which brings forth fruits ... (Dronke 1984: 176)

There is no doubt that this love is mutual, and mutually satisfying; yet Hildegard does not escape the view that passion is suspect. She held, therefore, that before the fall there was pleasure in sexual expression, but there was no lust. The man and the woman would lie together, side by side,

and they would gently perspire as if sleeping. Then the woman would become pregnant with the man's perspiration, and, while they lay thus sweetly asleep, she would give birth painlessly from her side ... in the same way that God brought Eve forth from Adam, and that the Church was born from the side of Christ. (Newman 1987: 111)

This was also the way Christ had been born of Mary, 'from the side', so that her virginity, undisturbed by the conception of Christ, was also undisturbed by his birth. While Hildegard goes

much further than many of her male contemporaries in allowing
for the mutuality of pleasure in ideal (unfallen) sexuality, it is
obvious not only that she is still suspicious of pleasure, but also
that she still idealises virginity.

This is clear from her belief in the great changes in sexuality,
which she sees as a result of the fall. Gentleness in sexual
expression has turned into mutual passion with overtones of
violence.

But the great love that was in Adam when Eve came forth from him,
and the sweetness of the sleep with which he then slept, were turned in
his transgression into a contrary mode of sweetness. And so, because a
man still feels this great sweetness in himself, and is like a stag thirsting
for the fountain, he races swiftly to the woman and she to him – she is
like a threshing-floor pounded by his many strokes and brought to heat
when the grains are threshed inside her. (Dronke 1984: 176)

One can only speculate about how a nun, cloistered from an
early age, came to have this conception of love-making. Be that
as it may, Hildegard still recognises the mutuality and pleasure
of both the man and the woman; indeed, she believed that if
the deep mutual love was lacking on either side the resulting
child would be weak in character (177). At other times,
however, Hildegard wrote about sexuality in a much more
negative way, seeing the effect of the fall as bitterness and lust,
as if sexual desire itself would not occur if Adam and Eve had
not sinned.

When man transgressed God's command, he was changed both in body
and mind. For the purity of his blood was turned into another mode, so
that, instead of purity, he now ejects the spume of semen. If man had
remained in paradise, he would have stayed in an immutable and
perfect state. But all these things, after his transgression, were turned
into another and bitter mode. For man's blood, burning in ardour and
heat of lust, ejects a spume from itself that we call semen, as a pot
placed on a fire brings up foam from the water because of the flame's
heat. (Dronke 1984: 176)

Women, after the fall, wish in their turn to resist men's sexual
advances. Hildegard goes against the grain of the received
opinion of the time that women were more lustful than men, and
says that unless a woman has already 'been touched by a man'

she would normally refuse him, 'for desire in her is not as strong and burning as in a man, who is as strong as a lion in his desire for the deed of begetting. He, therefore, has the strength of the desire and the deed ... and she is then occupied with the procreation of her offspring until she brings them into the world' (Hildegard 1990a: 178). While there is a wry accuracy about this passage, it is not altogether consistent with her comments already cited about mutuality and pleasure, and shows the unresolved tension in her thinking.

Sometimes she seems to believe that even the devil has a hand, not only in the lust and passion of intercourse, but even in the resulting conception of a child, sharing that event with God the Creator.

For human conception begins with the pleasure that the serpent breathed into the first human being in the fruit, because at that time the man's blood is agitated by pleasure. This blood ejaculates a cool foam into the woman, which is coagulated by the warmth of the mother's flesh and distended into a bloody form; and the foam, retained in that warmth, later grows from the mother's dry nourishment to the dimensions of a small human shape; until the Creator's handwriting, which formed mankind, fills the whole breadth of the human shape – just as a potter fashions his chosen vessel. (Newman 1987: 134)

As Newman points out, Hildegard shifts the ancient taboos about menstrual blood to semen. It is semen that is venomous and infected by the serpent, and it only loses its poisonous quality when it is influenced by the wholesome effects of the womb (135). Accordingly, Hildegard rejects the popular idea that menstruating women should not attend church. In the *Scivias*, the divine voice says to Hildegard,

I do not remit this time of pain for women, because I gave it to Eve when she conceived sin in the taste of the fruit; but therefore the woman should be cherished at this time with a great and healing tenderness ... she should not, however, restrain herself from going into my temple, but faith allows her to enter in the service of humility for her salvation. (Hildegard 1990a: 83)

It is fascinating that this is directly juxtaposed with a prohibition against men who have been wounded in battle from attending church. As Newman observes, 'the message is clear: a man who has shed blood in warfare is unclean, like the fratricidal Cain; but a woman shedding her own blood is not. Even though Eve's wound is a punishment for sin, it is nonetheless God-given and therefore sacred' (1987: 119). From a modern perspective it is hardly possible even to calculate how great a reversal of the norm Hildegard's stance represents.

It is clear that in Hildegard's mind the fall into sin in the Garden of Eden is a major factor in how human relations, particularly sexual relations, are to be understood. In this she was no different from other medieval theologians, male and female; and she like the rest of them thought that the Genesis account was historically literal. However, once again Hildegard offered her own interpretation of it; and once again it was more sympathetic to women than was the norm.

That norm was a tendency to blame Eve much more than Adam for original sin. Eve, it was held, was sensual, and was thus all too easily tempted by the serpent's offer of forbidden fruit. Her curiosity, her sight and smell and taste were all aroused, and she became the 'devil's gateway' in a way that the rational Adam on his own would never have done. One version of this, put forward by Ambrose, Bishop of Milan and mentor of Augustine, was that Eve was doubly responsible for sin, first in eating the forbidden fruit, and then in making 'her husband a partaker of the evil of which she was conscious'. He continues,

The eyes of their mind were opened and they realized the shame of being naked. For that reason, when the woman ate of the tree of knowledge of good and evil she certainly sinned and realized that she had sinned. On realizing this, she should not have invited her husband to share in her sin. By enticing him and giving him what she herself had tasted she did not nullify her sin; rather, she repeated it. (quoted in Miles 1989: 90)

Eve, like all women, is prone to evil: her creation is good only because she is necessary for human reproduction which Adam could not accomplish on his own. She is, however, a snare to men. Just as Adam 'fell by his wife's fault and not because of his own', so also women continue to be the main source of human temptation, though she remains necessary to men because she is 'esteemed to be more adaptable to domestic ministrations', including sexual services to her husband and bearing and raising his children. But it must never be forgotten, according to Ambrose, that 'the initial violation and deceit was due to the woman ... we can discern the sex which was liable first to do wrong ... The woman is responsible for the man's error and not vice versa.' Variations on this theme became standard medieval wisdom in their theology of original sin and the initial and continuing responsibility of women for human wickedness.

Hildegard takes a radically different approach, at least some of the time, though it must be said that often she also sounds like Ambrose. When she is pursuing her own line of thinking, Hildegard shows much less interest in the psychology of Eve and Adam than many previous writers had done. She does not spend time analysing what their individual motives were, or by what process the devil was able to be effective in tempting them. Rather, Hildegard's preoccupation is with the *cosmic* drama. The real protagonists are God and Satan, not Eve and Adam, though of course they have important parts to play. As she portrays it, Satan had a huge grudge against Eve, an envy of her ability to bear children. He therefore poisoned Eve with a venomous vomit: the pictorial illustration of Hildegard's vision of the event shows Satan's tongue spewing an evil substance over Eve and thus infecting her with foul and stinking corruption. Eve then passed the poison on to Adam, not in any deliberate or seductive way, but in the way that a contagious disease is involuntarily passed from one person to another; and thus all humanity became infected (Hildegard 1990a: 71). As Barbara Newman remarks, Hildegard's Eve 'is more sinned against than sinning, not so much tempted as victimized outright, and, if any misogynism comes into play, it is Satan's' (1987: 112). From Hildegard's perspective, those who wish to blame and despise women for sin should be aware that they are choosing the devil rather than God as their role model: it was Satan, not God, who first showered woman with contempt.

Hildegard's sympathy for women is obvious: clearly she is pushing far beyond the norms of male theological discourse of her time. Yet there are also strands in her work which run in the opposite direction, and which show her own deeply internalised misogyny and fear of sexuality. Although as we have seen she could write of human passion and erotic intimacy in positive ways, she could also write of it as originating from the devil and to be avoided if at all possible. Any sort of sexuality outside of marriage is altogether evil; and even within marriage, intercourse not intended for procreation is a 'diabolical act' (1990a: 82). Hildegard does not even treat marriage as one of the sacraments, as it was usually treated in medieval theology, but rather chooses to discuss it as one of the results of the fall.

Her treatment of homosexuality makes her gender attitudes even plainer. It will have been observed that even where Hildegard writes sympathetically of sexual expression, she is relentlessly heterosexual. In her view, homosexuality is a perversion that is utterly demonic; and Hildegard's castigation of it, while fully in line with much thinking of her time, shows once again the pervasive misogyny of the culture. The reason male homosexuality is so evil in her view is that it requires one of the partners to act the part of a woman: for a man so to debase himself is perverted indeed. She writes,

A man who sins with another man as if with a woman sins bitterly against God and against the union with which God united male and female ... God united man and woman, thus joining the strong to the weak, that each might sustain the other. But these perverted adulterers change their virile strength into perverse weakness, rejecting the proper male and female roles, and in their wickedness they shamefully follow Satan. (1990a: 279)

No self-respecting man would want to be 'womanish': for Hildegard the term itself is filled with contempt. And on the other hand, for a woman to take a male role upon herself, as Hildegard supposes of female homosexuality, is utter presumption.

And a woman who takes up devilish ways and plays a male role in coupling with another woman is most vile in my [i.e. God's] sight, and so is she who submits herself to such a one in this evil deed. For they should have been ashamed of their passion, and instead they impudently usurped a right that was not theirs. And, having put themselves into alien ways, they are to me transformed and contemptible.

Hildegard was not the first and by no means the last to make allies of misogyny and homophobia; her manner of doing so illustrates her view of the relative status of the sexes.

For all Hildegard's sympathetic writing for married women undergoing problems of menstruation, conception, or childbirth, it is clear that from first to last she sees virginity as the way of true spirituality. Early in the *Scivias*, after treating the various topics to do with human procreation under a general consideration of the fall and original sin, she launches into praise for virginity, recounting the voice of God saying to her,

Virginity was made by me, for my son was born of a virgin. And therefore virginity is the most beautiful fruit of all the fruits of the valleys, and the greatest of all the persons in the palace of the unfailing King ... Virginity unspotted from the beginning is nobler than widowhood oppressed under the yoke of a husband, even though widowhood, after the grief of the loss of a husband, would imitate virginity. (85)

In Hildegard's visions, Mary, the second Eve, is able to overcome the sin of the first Eve by remaining a virgin, and thereby producing a virgin Son. In turn, the church who is the Bride of Christ is also virgin; and its central figures are the virgin clergy, monks, and nuns.

There is no doubt that for Hildegard, as for many others of her time, the path of spiritual perfection required virginity. In the *Ordo Virtutum*, Hildegard's vision of the triumphant ranks of heaven, the class of virgins takes its place with the apostles, prophets and martyrs singing the songs of the blessed, whereas a lament breaks out over the vast multitudes of those who did not 'flee from lust' (1990a: 528). In another paean of praise for virginity, Hildegard assimilates the virginity of Mary with that of her virgin son, and again with that of women who retain their virginity for love of him, and contrasts this with 'shameful filth':

O Virginity, which by the ardent enkindling produced the greatest fruit, which shone in the star of the sea and fights the savage darts of the Devil and despises all shameful filth, rejoice in celestial harmony and hope for the company of angels. How? The Holy Spirit makes music in the tabernacle of Virginity; for she always thinks of how to embrace Christ in full devotion. She burns for love of him and forgets the human frailties, which burn with carnal desire; she is joined to the One

Husband Whom sin never touched, without any lust of the flesh, but flowering perpetually with him in the joy of the regal marriage. (440)

This theme of the spiritual virgin being the bride of Christ was, of course, a common one in medieval spirituality, with its origins in patristic interpretation of the Song of Songs, and endless variations through the writings of men like Bernard of Clairvaux and William of St Thierry. In another passage she writes in somewhat the same vein (again in the voice of God):

But she who desires My Son and wants to keep her virginity for his love is greatly ornamented in his nuptial chamber, for she sets at naught the burning she endures for the sake of his love, but perseveres in chastity, choosing not to be consumed by the fire of ardent lust; and in her spiritual marriage she despises [the idea of] a fleshly husband, and renounces the thought of one to strive with her whole desire after my Son. O dearest seeds, O flowers sweeter and more exquisite than any perfumes, whose soft fragility rises like the dawn to betrothal with my Son, loving him dearly with chaste love; she is his bride and he is her bridegroom, for this race of virgins loves him dearly and is to be adorned in the Heavenly Kingdom with glorious ornaments. (178)

In the women mystics of the succeeding centuries, this theme would develop into a highly eroticised mysticism; but although the language is there in Hildegard, it does not breathe with the sexual passion which we have seen in Hadewijch.

Hildegard is quite clear that the path of virginity is a difficult one, particularly (though not only) for women. She hears the voice of God saying,

O sweetest flowers! My angels marvel at your struggle, for you escape from death, so as not to be polluted by the poisonous mud of the world; you have a carnal body, but you tread it under foot, and so you will be glorious in their company since you will appear unpolluted in their likeness. (85)

The suffering required by chastity, like the suffering of fasting, was an identification with the suffering of Christ. Indeed, it could be seen as an even more immediate identification than fasting, because Christ himself had maintained virginity, as also had his mother. And as women were particularly identified with the humanity of Christ, so their virginity was once again an identification with his bodiliness. The fact that suffering was involved only made the linkage clearer.

Thus Hildegard never doubted that the path of true spirituality was the path of virginity. Even though others also would be saved, to count as a mystic one must count as a virgin. This was, of course, true for men as well as for women; and in Hildegard's writing there is a good deal addressed specifically to men: warnings against masturbation, advice about the prevention of wet dreams, and the like. It would not be fair to say that for a woman to count as a mystic she must be a virgin, whereas a man need not be: the same requirement would apply to both sexes. Even more than in the case of food, the sexual control required for spirituality was not necessarily overtly misogynist, either in terms of male contempt for women or in terms of women's internalised self-contempt; though there was plenty of both. Men no less than women were required to maintain chastity in the monastic life; and the monastic life was seen as the prime *locus* for the flourishing of spirituality. Indeed, as we saw in the previous section, there was if anything more male preoccupation with chastity and sexuality than female: women were more preoccupied with issues of food and fasting. Hildegard, in her insistent writing about virginity, is typical of spiritual writings of her time, but probably more in line with male writers than with female. Whereas physical enclosure could be made to apply to women in a way that need not apply to men, and food control was more a preoccupation of women than of men, it could be argued that in terms of sexual control women and men were treated equally.

Yet when we look more deeply at the attitudes surrounding this emphasis on virginity, it becomes clear that, like the attitudes regarding food, there is a deep misogyny within it. The reason that spirituality was held to require sexual control was because of the understanding that bodiliness, particularly sexuality, was opposed to the life of the spirit. Accordingly, although both men and women, to pursue the life of the spirit, must practise chastity, for men this can be seen in terms of sloughing off their 'female-ness', their sexual expression, and becoming in some sense their true selves; whereas for women something far more radical is happening. Since women are *defined* in terms of bodiliness and sexuality, for a woman to embrace virginity is for a woman to live, in a much stronger sense than a man who does the same thing, contrary to her nature. Although writers like Hildegard see that men as well as women will find virginity difficult, it is clear that its difficulty for women is far more radical than it is for men: radical in the sense that it cuts to the root of their being. Women who are virgins are in a sense a contradiction in terms: yet a contradiction that is absolutely required if women are to be counted spiritual.

As Barbara Newman points out (1987), there is much in Hildegard's writing that is as dualist as anything the Christian Platonists could have wished. Spiritual progress is made only when the soul sets itself against the desires of the body, and especially sexuality, and gradually frees itself from the body's demands. Indeed, Hildegard's more sympathetic writing about women's sexuality and gynaecological concerns, the writings that have a less dualistic ring, can be seen precisely as a description of how things are in a state of *fallenness*, of the interconnection of body and soul in sin and corruption, which can be remedied only by the virgin Son of the virgin mother whose grace must be sought and whose example must be followed.

We have already seen that Julian of Norwich, two and a half centuries later, offers a startling contrast to the views of bodiliness and sexual control which Hildegard articulated, and a sharp challenge to the idea that chastity is essential for spirituality. To recognise how radical her position was, however, it is necessary to see it in terms of her whole understanding of the material world and its relation to the spiritual. One of the most famous of passages from her *Revelations*, often quoted completely out of context, occurs in the description of her first vision:

And in this [God] showed me something small, no bigger than a hazelnut, lying in the palm of my hand, as it seemed to me, and it was as round as a ball. I looked at it with the eye of my understanding and thought: What can this be? I was amazed that it could last, for I thought that because of its littleness it would suddenly have fallen into nothing. And I was answered in my understanding: it lasts and always will, because God loves it, and thus everything has being through the love of God. (1978: 183)

For this passage alone, Julian has deservedly been awarded the title of 'mother of ecofeminism': the round world, seemingly lying in the palm of her hand, whose wonder she cherishes, is in modern times identified with the round world whose photograph from outer space reveals both its beauty and its fragility. Yet Julian's own preoccupations are somewhat different. She immediately moves on from the reflection on the earth as cherished by God to herself, her own substance, in relation to God.

In this little thing I saw three properties. The first is that God made it, the second is that God loves it, the third is that God preserves it. But what is that to me? It is that God is the Creator and the protector and the lover. For until I am substantially united to him, I can never have perfect rest or true happiness . . .

It would be too hasty, however, to read this passage as though Julian thought of herself as including her body and its sexuality in this 'substantial union' with God. Julian is still a part of the church dominated by dualist ideas of the distinction between soul and body, flesh and spirit: she understands death as 'the departure of the spirit' (178) and speaks of the soul as 'joined to our body' for a time (291). Yet, although to that extent she retained the doctrines prevalent in her time, she also pushed hard against them, in ways strikingly dissimilar to what we have seen of Hildegard, and also to those of male writers like Walter Hilton or the anonymous author of *The Cloud of Unknowing* who were roughly Julian's contemporaries.

Julian is strongly focused on the body. Her writings, springing as they do from a sequence of visions of Christ's passion, describe in loving detail his physical sufferings, 'the fair skin ... deeply broken into the tender flesh through the vicious blows delivered all over the lovely body' (199), the hot blood from his head where the thorns pierce him, the effect of the drying wind in which 'his nose shrivelled and dried up, as I saw; and the sweet body turned brown and black, completely changed and transformed from his naturally beautiful, fresh and vivid complexion into a shrivelled image of death' (207). No male medieval writer, not even Francis of Assisi, ever focused so lovingly or in anything like such detail on the physical body of Jesus on the cross.

At the same time, Julian was acutely aware of her own body while she received the visions, lying, as she supposed, on her deathbed. She describes how death seemed to creep steadily nearer, as first the lower parts of her body and then the upper part recede from her control, her breath is short, and her eyes begin to fail (180). She speaks of the fluctuations of pain and its cessation, corresponding to spiritual desolation and consolation in similar flux (310). Her comments about her physical state are made in a matter-of-fact way, to further the exposition of her insight: she takes it as a matter of course (in a way that would be unthinkable for Hildegard) that her spiritual experience is also bodily experience. It is only in the light of the much more negative valuation of the body in much medieval spiritual writing that it becomes clear how radical Julian is in this regard.

Given her awareness of Jesus' body, and of her own in her visionary experience, her account of spirituality will need to take bodiliness into account in a way quite unusual for medieval spiritual writers. As we saw in chapter 4, Julian does not speak of spiritual growth as a mastery of the flesh, or even as transcending the flesh. Rather, she speaks in terms of the unification of substance and sensuality. Our 'substance' is the core of our being, created by God, and wholly good.

And from this great richness and this high nobility, commensurate powers come into our soul, whilst it is joined to our body, in which joining we are made sensual. And so in our substance we are full and in our sensuality we are lacking, and this lack God will restore and fill by the operation of mercy and grace, plentifully flowing into us from his own natural goodness. (291)

Accordingly, Julian's teaching concerning spiritual progress has everything to do with receiving and trusting the faithful love of God, and nothing to do with standard themes of distrust of the body and especially sexuality. Although she explicitly states that the purpose of her book is to advise her readers, and give them comfort and strength in their spiritual journey (191) she nowhere mentions any sort of mortification of the flesh. Neither fasting nor celibacy, well-worn themes both, as we have seen, get so much as a mention.

For Julian, the question of who should count as a mystic is much further removed from issues of sexual control than was the case for Hildegard, let alone for the tradition of male-defined spirituality that lay between them. Though she was still a woman of her time, and one should not underestimate the extent to which she too accepted the male-defined boundaries, she pushed back at them harder than most women dared. Julian, however, was sailing very near the wind: as we shall see in the next chapter, people with views not so different from hers might easily be accused of heresy or witchcraft. To their story we must now turn.

CHAPTER 7

Heretics and witches

> Justice, force. – It is just that what is just be followed, it is necessary that what is strongest be followed. Justice without force is impotent. And so, since it was not possible to make the just strong, the strong have been made just.
>
> (Pascal 1966: 58)

One of the fascinating aspects of the development of what should count as mysticism in the fourteenth century and beyond into the period of the Reformation and the Counter-reformation was that there was an increasing emphasis on distinguishing true mysticism from its false counterfeits. We saw in chapter 5 how men like Ruusbroec and the author of *The Cloud of Unknowing* distinguished true contemplation from that which they considered to be false and therefore dangerous. This development provided new avenues for understanding the social construction of mysticism: it became possible to ask not only what the mystical is but also, significantly, what it is not. And as we have seen in previous chapters, that question might better be phrased in terms of *who* should count as a mystic and *who should not*: gender divisions, especially, were of major importance.

Contemporary philosophers of religion who have considered mysticism have not usually paid much attention to actual mystics and the differences between them, let alone developed a gender analysis to help account for who was and who was not considered to be a genuine mystic. With a few exceptions, philosophers have tended to lump mystics into a monolithic group of men and women who had highly intense psychological experiences of God. As we have already seen, however, such a lumping together does an enormous injustice to the diversity in medieval Christian mysticism, and to the issues of gender and power which are implicated in that diversity. The distortion which results from ignoring these issues is so serious that it is questionable whether contemporary philosophical analysis of mysticism, which purports to be discussing the 'experiences' of mystics of the Christian tradition, is really doing so, or is fashioning an imaginary 'mysticism' for itself out of whole cloth, a construct amenable to the analysis then made of it, but bearing little resemblance to any actual people or concerns of the Christian mystical tradition.

If this is true of mysticism in general, it is all the more true that philosophers have ignored the occurrence of what was deemed, in the later Middle Ages, to be false mysticism: heresy, witchcraft and other aberrations. Vast energy was spent trying to extirpate these noxious weeds from the garden of the church: energy that could take the form of positive teaching and preaching, of inquisition and heresy hunts, or in its most extreme forms (which were not at all rare) of punishment and execution. Within the medieval period itself the question of who or what could count as genuinely mystical and what was counterfeit was a pressing issue, and it is to be expected that consideration of the ways in which the distinctions were drawn will give considerable insight into the developing social construction of mysticism.

Yet philosophers have paid virtually no attention to this. Insofar as the question of genuine versus counterfeit experience arises at all in modern philosophical writing, it arises in terms of what sorts of causes have brought about the experiential phenomena. For example, there has been controversy, especially following the experiments of Aldous Huxley with mescaline, about whether or not drug-induced experiences count as genuinely mystical (Huxley 1977; Zaehner 1957). It is clear, however, that any discussion couched in such terms has already presupposed that the crux of mysticism is intense subjective experience. The only question is whether the cause of that experience is important in determining whether it counts as the real thing. But as has already become obvious in the preceding chapters, this is much too narrow a view of what mysticism is and how mysticism has been understood through the changing centuries of the

Christian tradition. This becomes even clearer when we look at the issues of power and gender in relation to heresy and witchcraft and the effort to eliminate those who were categorised in these terms as false mystics, not because of the phenomenology of their experience in any simple sense, but rather because of a whole constellation of thought and practice that had more to do with structures of authority and struggles for integrity than it had with individual psychological states.

This chapter, therefore, will concern itself with heretics and witches, people who did *not* count as mystics. They were women and men who claimed to have direct experience of God, just as true mystics did, but who in fact were deemed by the church to be false. History shows that heretics were, speaking broadly, groups of people who spoke against what they saw as corruption and error in the church and its doctrine and practice, often basing their claims on revelation or on the experience of God. Yet the ecclesiastical authorities declared that their teaching went contrary to true doctrine, and that their experience was demonic delusion. It would be an overstatement with more than a grain of truth to say that heretics were mystics who failed.

Witches, on the other hand, were not so much those who claimed to have supernatural experiences as those who were deemed by accusers and investigators to be having such encounters. However, the encounters were not with God, but with the devil. In the later Middle Ages, and increasingly until the sixteenth century and even beyond, large numbers of women and some men were executed for the crime of witchcraft. One of the key characteristics of witchcraft was held to be direct experience, often of a sexual nature, of the devil or his representative. No analysis of what mysticism is and thus of the social construction of mysticism can be adequate if it does not take into account the gendered nature of the intense persecution that developed as those in authority tried to set boundaries around what should count as true mystical experience and how it should be controlled. A philosophical account of what mysticism is which is blind to the power struggles involved, and which proceeds as though there is some universal that can be labelled 'mystical experience' without further ado, is simply naive.

Before we turn directly to these questions, there are two general points that need to be made. The first is that there has already been a considerable shift in what counts as mystical (and who counts as a mystic) in order for the categories of truth and falsity to get much purchase. As I explained in the discussion of the mystical meaning of scripture, the imagination had a large role to play in the discovery of such meaning; and as long as the various interpretations were compatible with ecclesiastical dogma and authority, more than one such meaning could be attributed to any passage. Although mystical interpretations were not to contradict the literal meaning of the text, and were not to overstep doctrinal boundaries, the question, 'But is it *true?*' would not normally be the right question to ask of a proffered mystical interpretation of scripture.

To some extent the same would also be the case for visionary experiences. When a woman like Hildegard of Bingen had visions, her great concern, of course, would be to discern the truth of those visions. But this should be construed, not as an effort to decide whether the vision was true as contrasted with being false or delusory, but rather with an effort to discern what its *meaning* might be, how it should be correctly interpreted. However, as we saw at the end of chapter 5, male mystical writers were increasingly asking the former question as well: not simply 'what might this vision mean?' but also 'might this vision be false, or even have a demonic source?'

This leads to the second point. The increasing emphasis on the question of truth or falsity went along with an increasing preoccupation with the demonic. To a large extent it was taken as given that religious experiences had a supernatural source. They were not just natural if idiosyncratic events, or a product of a somewhat unbalanced mind, as we might think of many such claims today. Accordingly, if a religious experience, a vision, or an alleged insight into scripture or Christian doctrine was deemed to be false, it was also deemed to be demonic in origin. This, however, was not restricted to the idea that the subjective states of the putative mystic were brought about in her or him by the devil rather than by God. That might sometimes be a part of it; but the issue was far greater than individual psychological states, which might or might not be involved. True mysticism increasingly distinguished itself from false in a whole variety of ways, and saw the devil within the false, far beyond the boundaries of the psyches of individuals. Thus, for example, as the church was the mystical body of Christ, so the devil was deemed also to have a mystical body, namely the heretics. As the church was the mystical bride of Christ, so the witches engaged in foul marital pacts and sexual orgies with the devil. And as the church was obliged to fight for Christ against the wickedness of Satan, so it was required to seek to reclaim all who were in his grip. Where this was impossible, however (and in most cases this could be expected to be the case, given the strength of the enemy) it would be the duty of church and state to exterminate all who were infected by the Satanic plague and thus to purify society from its contamination. The conflagration of heretics and then of witches was the predictable result.

I HERETICS

Heresy is an invention of the Middle Ages. From about the eleventh century, churchmen increasingly worried about heresy, and in 1179 the Third Lateran Council issued a strong decree against the various forms which it believed it could discern. From that point forward, the inquisitors were kept busy hunting heretics and seeking to purge the church of them. But as R. I. Moore (1987) has argued, it can be shown that the heresy-hunters were finding what they were looking for, not so much because it had been there all along, as because they were themselves creating it by their definitions and their tactics.

Of course, there is another sense in which heresy had existed just as long as the church. The early church defined itself, in both doctrine and practice, against what it saw as erroneous and called heretical. The doctrine of the humanity and divinity of Christ, for example, was hammered out at the First Council of Nicea in 325, with the church choosing to follow the teaching of Athanasius and to reject that of Arius: the former was then seen as the true faith and the latter as heresy. Long before that, early fathers such as Irenaeus had written against the Gnostics; and even in the

Pauline writings of the New Testament there are references to
heretics and heretical teaching.

Nevertheless, during the early Middle Ages the church had not
occupied itself with hunting heretics. While it was acknowledged
that there were those who did not hold to the true faith, it was not
on the whole thought necessary to search them out and require
their conversion or extermination: in the frequently cited biblical
phrase, the wheat and the tares were to be allowed to grow
together until the final harvest of the judgement of God (Lambert
1992). In the eleventh and twelfth centuries, however, things
changed dramatically.

Part of the reason for the change was increasing popular
disillusionment with the church, following the decline of zeal for
the reforms that had been put into motion by Pope Gregory VII
and his immediate successors. People felt that they had been
betrayed, that the church was corrupt and hypocritical, with too
many of its leaders living ostentatiously while the poor were
despised. Some went further, and began to think that the aims of
the church in the regulation of all aspects of faith and life, even
supposing that they were to be properly carried out, were
tyrannical and inappropriate to a body whose first characteristic
ought to be compassion. Wandering preachers of great asceticism
like Robert of Arbrissel and Henry of Lausanne drew crowds
after them, persuaded by their calls for radical reform of the
church. Groups of lay people began to gather together to study
the Bible for themselves and to worship together: as they
continued, the conclusions they drew and the forms which their
worship took could be deemed threatening by the local ecclesiastical authorities. It is significant, also, that in some of the groups
about whom most is known, such as the Cathars and the (very
different) Waldensians, women were able to share leadership with
men in a way that was unthinkable in the church at the time; and
clearly this greater egalitarianism in gender attracted women to
the movements and at the same time was part of the reason for
the vigorous disapproval, denunciation, and finally persecution of
them by the church.

It is therefore true that the later Middle Ages saw a burgeoning
of heretical movements, if by that is meant organised movements

calling for the reform and spiritual renewal of the church, and in the meantime setting themselves up as a locus of faith and practice for their adherents. Nor is it surprising that when, instead of reform, the church mounted an inquisition to root them out they became more radical, sometimes seeing themselves as opposed to the church altogether and claiming direct access to God through their own study of the scriptures and their own spiritual experiences without having to go through the prescribed channels of ecclesiastical authority.

One of the most extreme groups, which developed in the twelfth and thirteenth centuries to a position of some strength in parts of southern France and northern Italy, were known as the Cathars. Like many other movements, the Cathars called for reform of the church, seeing it as having abandoned the teaching and practice of the simplicity and poverty of Christ and the apostles. While this appeal for renewal and rejection of the corruption of the church was common to many movements, however, the Cathars intertwined it with a doctrinal system of considerable complexity. In its strongest form, their teaching looked for a rigorist morality that was based on a sharp dualism of mind and body. The body, like all the rest of the material world, had been created by Lucifer, the enemy of God; and the path of spirituality was to distance oneself as much as possible from the demands of the body by a stringent asceticism. Sexuality was seen as a direct result of the fall into sin, not, at first, of human beings, but of the angels who followed Satan in his revolt against God. These angels, in consequence of this rebellion, found that part of their punishment was that they had become embodied, and, what was worse, their bodies were sexually differentiated: in the myth which recounts this event the angels weep when they discover their sexuality (Lambert 1992: 107). The Cathars rejected any form of sexual contact, and indeed any form of physical touch, however innocent, between men and women. They also proscribed eating any food that was related to the coition of animals; hence not only meat, but also milk, eggs and cheese were forbidden, making their diet similar to that of a modern vegan, though for very different reasons.

Clearly such rigour could not be sustained by large groups of people for the whole of their lives; consequently the Cathars divided their adherents into two groups, the adepts, or 'perfect', and the ordinary believers and sympathisers. The 'perfect' were the ones who had received an initiation rite known as the 'consolamentum', in which it was believed that the candidate's sins were forgiven, the consequences of the fall (including its sexual consequences) were removed, and the soul was no longer in the power of Satan. From that moment onwards, however, the candidate had to observe without lapse the strict code of abstinence. Any breach had dire consequences, not only for the individual, but for anyone else to whom that individual had in the meanwhile administered the 'consolamentum', since it was held that a fall on the part of one of the 'perfect' entailed the fall, also, of all whom she or he had perfected. Since many of the looser adherents and sympathisers of Catharism waited until their deathbed to receive the 'consolamentum', the possibility of its posthumous negation because of the subsequent fall from grace of the one who had administered it would be a cause of considerable anxiety. On the other hand, the attractions of the life of austerity were considerable. Apart from the companionship and the sense of escape from the power of Satan, there was also the public respect and esteem of the adherents for the 'perfect', and their important social role of religious instruction, including the power to administer the 'consolamentum'.

Large numbers of women were drawn toward the life of the 'perfect', and were accorded far more respect and esteem than would have been the case for women in the church and society generally. They were seen, like the men, to possess the Spirit; and they were accorded greater status than was available to women in any position in Catholicism, including even that of the abbesses of convents. These women sometimes stayed within their normal family structure, though renouncing any form of sexual activity within it; but sometimes they grouped themselves into small houses or communities which then became an esteemed centre for the sect as well as a place of strength and support for its inmates. In the Europe of the time, when women were often treated with contempt as nothing more than the chattels of their fathers or husbands, it is not surprising that the Cathar alternative would have considerable attraction for them. Although the strict dualism and rejection of sexuality was demanding, it was after all not so different from the asceticism and disdain for the flesh which was part of orthodox teaching and practice, and could in fact be seen as a logical extension of it. As we have seen, the orthodox, too, thought of spiritual progress as increased distancing of oneself from the demands of the flesh; and although they did not carry the teaching to the point of overt condemnation of the flesh as evil, and held that the material world was created by God, not by Lucifer, nevertheless there was sufficient affinity, especially when it came to ascetic practice rather than the precise formulation of doctrine, to persuade many that the Cathars were only putting into practice what the church was meant to preach (Bynum 1987a: 251; Lambert 1992: 105).

The church, however, hardly saw it like that. With the success of the Cathars in areas of Italy and the Languedoc, whole areas of the country had an alternative ecclesiastical structure, with the 'perfect' taking the traditional place of bishops and clergy, and an increasingly prominent hierarchy. However, the focus of much of the church's attack was not on this threatening counter-structure, or even on the specific teaching, but rather on their views of sexuality: it sometimes appears that orthodox writers are working out their own fantasies by projecting them on to the heretical group. An interesting example is the response of Bernard of Clairvaux to Everinus of Steinfeld. In 1143 Everinus had written a letter to Bernard, telling him of some heretics who had recently been discovered at Cologne: some of them had been willing to recant, but others, having been

admonished and found unwilling to repent, they were seized by the people, being incited by overmuch zeal, and put into the fire and burnt; and (what is most wonderful) they entered to the stake, and bare the torment of the fire, not only with patience, but with joy and gladness. In this case, O Holy Father, were I present with you, I should be glad to have your answer, how these members of the devil could with such courage and constancy persist in their heresy, as is scarcely to be found in the most religious in the faith of Christ. (Peters 1980: 91)

The heresy of which Everinus accuses them is in the first place their claim to being the true Christians, 'because they alone follow the steps of Christ, and continue in the imitation of the true apostolic life, not seeking the things of this world . . .', whereas they find the church corrupt and hypocritical in its claims. Furthermore, he cites their radical dualism, their rejection of any food which is related to copulation, and their rejection of marriage.

Bernard, in his response, virtually ignores all aspects other than sexuality. In Sermon 65 of his series on the Song of Songs, Bernard uses as his text the biblical writer's phrase, 'bring us the little foxes who spoil the vine', as a platform from which to preach against the heretics. His preaching shows his willingness to lump together the Cathars of Cologne with any other heretics he has ever heard of, seeing them as instructed by the ancient heretics spoken of in the Pauline writings of scripture. He objects to their secrecy, and to their crafty appearance of orthodoxy:

What you see is a man frequenting the church, honouring the clergy, offering his gifts, making his confession, receiving the sacraments. What can be more orthodox. As far as his life and his conduct is concerned he harms no one, distresses no one, does not set himself above anyone. His face is pale from fasting, he does not eat the bread of idleness, he supports himself with the labour of his hands. (Bernard 1979: III.65)

Yet, in spite of the fact that both his doctrine and his practice seems to be above reproach, Bernard is convinced that he has indeed found 'a fox'. The real reason soon emerges:

Women have left their husbands, and husbands their wives, to join these people. Clerks and priests, young and old, have left their people and their churches, and are to be found there among weavers and their women. Is this not great havoc? Is this not the work of foxes?

This abandonment of traditional class and gender roles is too much. Proper ecclesiastical authority will not be maintained if people like this, women and weavers, should be considered to have true spirituality. They must, therefore, be rejected, cast out of the church. Though Bernard does not say that they should be killed, he nowhere expresses concern that in the case of the Cathars of Cologne this was indeed what happened; nor does he respond to Everinus' question about how 'members of the devil' could show such courage in the face of torture and death. His largest concern was for social and sexual propriety.

Bernard's response, however, is nothing like as extreme as that of other heresy-hunters. Catholic writers tended to assume that Cathars, like any other deviant group, were also (or especially) sexually perverse, indulging in incestuous orgies and ritual slaughter of the children produced as a result of their illicit intercourse. The theory behind it was that if these people said that they were free from the flesh, then presumably they would also hold that the flesh could do what it liked without sin: any self-gratification was therefore permissible. Although such teaching was regularly attributed to the Cathars, there is virtually no evidence to support the contention (and such evidence as there is, was elicited under torture). In fact, it is much more plausible to hold that the Cathars, with their severe strictures on the flesh, practised at least as rigorous a sexual morality as did good Catholics; the whole sequence of accusations was a fantasy foisted on to them by their detractors (Cohn 1976: 54; Lambert 1992: 110).

It would be neither the first time nor the last. Norman Cohn, in his book *Europe's Inner Demons* (1976), shows how accusations of orgies, incest, infanticide and cannibalism first made against early Christians were in the Middle Ages made against a whole variety of groups who were seen as a threat to the church, starting with the heretical groups like Cathars and Waldensians, but also applied to Jews and finally to witches. The reality behind these fantasies must be sought at least as much in the psyches of their promulgators as in the beliefs and practices of the groups concerned, as we shall see repeatedly in the following pages.

One of the early medieval sources for the accusations was the writing of a Byzantine, Michael Constantine Psellos, who in about 1050 wrote a Greek dialogue entitled *On the Operation of the Demons*, in which he included a description of the Bogomils, an eastern sect who influenced the early Cathars. Because similar claims were so often repeated against other groups, it is worth quoting him at length.

In the evening, when the candles are lit, at the time when we celebrate the redemptive Passion of Our Lord, they bring together, in a house appointed for the purpose, young girls whom they have initiated into their rites. Then they extinguish the candles, so that the light shall not

be witness to their abominable deeds, and throw themselves lasci-
viously on the girls; each one on whomever first falls into his hands, no
matter whether she be his sister, his daughter, or his mother. For they
think that they are doing something that greatly pleases the demons by
transgressing God's laws, which forbid marriage between blood relatives. When this rite has been completed, each goes home; and after
waiting nine months, until the time has come for the unnatural
children of such unnatural seed to be born, they come together again
at the same place. Then, on the third day after the birth, they tear the
miserable babies from their mothers' arms. They cut the tender flesh
all over with sharp knives and catch the stream of blood in basins.
They throw the babies, still breathing and gasping, on to the fire, to be
burned to ashes. After which they mix the ashes with the blood in the
basins and so make an abominable drink, with which they secretly
pollute their food and drink; like those who mix poison with hippocras
or other sweet drinks. Finally they partake together of these foodstuffs;
and not they alone but others also, who know nothing of their hidden
proceedings. (Cohn 1976: 19)

The whole story was to be recounted with minor variations
against a whole variety of groups in western Europe throughout
the later Middle Ages. One writer after another believed themselves to 'know' what heretics did, and frequently the inquisitors
who questioned accused persons did not rest until they had
elicited, often with the aid of excruciating torture, confessions of
just such activities. That the accused often withdrew their confession once the torture ceased was not deemed sufficient reason to
question its veracity. After all, even the papal bull *Vox in Rama*,
issued by Gregory IX in 1233, had pronounced that these were
the sorts of things which happened among heretics: and in doing
this he was only taking the same line as was common among
medieval theologians. Heresy was regarded as something unchanging; therefore it was possible for theologians to know prior
to investigation what any particular sect must be like by the
simple expedient of consulting passages from patristic writers
(Lerner 1972: 5). Thus for example the decree of the Fourth
Lateran Council of 1215 stated,

We excommunicate and anathematise every heresy that raises itself
against the holy, orthodox, and Catholic faith ... condemning all
heretics under whatever names they may be known, for while they have

different faces, they are nevertheless bound to each other by their tails, since in all of them vanity is a common element. Those condemned, being handed over to secular rulers or their bailiffs, let them be abandoned, to be punished with due justice ... (Peters 1980: 175)

The task of inquisitors was therefore not to discover whether any particular description of the activities of the heretics was true, but rather to elicit confessions. If an accused person confessed, they might be imprisoned and their goods confiscated; but if they did not confess, this was not taken as evidence of innocence but of obduracy, and they might be burned alive. Not all inquisitors behaved in such a high-handed manner, nor were all of them as obsessed with the sexual fantasies projected on to the deviant groups. But enough of them were so obsessed as to send hundreds, probably thousands, of women and men to the stake, and many more to prison and other punishment.

In the case of the Cathars, the stringent dualism and the rejection of marriage were pegs on which suspicions of sexual licence could be hung, however improbably. In the case of the Waldensians there was even less excuse. The Waldensians were founded by Valdes, a businessman of Lyons, who in about 1175 decided to give up his money and try to live by simple gospel precepts, much as the Franciscans were to do a few generations later. He soon acquired a considerable following in France and the Rhineland as well as in northern Italy, in much the same area as the Cathars were prominent. Like them, he sought for ecclesiastical reform and a return to the gospel ideals of simplicity and poverty; but unlike them, he did not advocate dualism, nor was there any general rejection of marriage and procreation, though individual preachers might elect to live a celibate life. A great emphasis of Valdes and his followers was on the study of the Bible and the fathers, which they sought to obtain and make available in the vernacular so that their study was not restricted to monks and clergy educated in Latin. As a result of that study, some of them came to believe that various of the rites and forms of the church were unnecessary, among them the veneration of relics and prayers for the dead. On the other hand, they thought that other things were enjoined upon them, such as simplicity of life, preaching, and the refusal to kill, whether judicially or in warfare; they also refused to take oaths because the gospel says plainly, 'swear not at all'. Their lives and beliefs were sincere and influential, and from a modern perspective one wonders what the church should have found to object to (Lambert 1992: 62).

But object it did. In the first place, Valdes and his followers claimed the right to preach and teach, a right which the church refused to grant them, seeing this as the proper preserve of the clergy. The Canons of the Fourth Lateran Council, already cited above, were in part aimed directly at the Waldensians:

But since some, under the 'appearance of godliness, but denying the power thereof', as the apostle says, arrogate to themselves the authority to preach ... all those prohibited or not sent, who, without the authority of the Apostolic See or of the Catholic bishop of the locality, shall presume to usurp the office of preaching either publicly or privately, shall be excommunicated and unless they amend, and the sooner the better, they shall be visited with a further suitable penalty. (Peters 1980: 175)

The 'suitable penalty' might be imprisonment, torture, or death at the stake. Furthermore, the Council proscribed individual study of scripture, considering that this was a matter much too difficult and with too many risks for ordinary lay persons. 'The secret mysteries of the faith ought not ... to be explained to all men in all places ... For such is the depth of divine scripture, that not only the simple and illiterate but even the prudent and learned are not fully sufficient to try to understand it' (Lambert 1992: 73). Part of the problem in the eyes of the church was that the study of scripture among the Waldensians was not restricted to lay men. Women also were studying the scriptures and preaching among the Waldensians: like the Cathars in this respect, the movement treated women as equal with men and held that they too could preach and teach; and it can hardly be doubted that the respect with which women were treated by the Waldensians increased its attractiveness to them. But this meant that women, as well as lay men of all classes, could develop in spirituality: who would count as a mystic would be out of the control of the ecclesiastical authorities. This the authorities could not tolerate.

Sharp persecution of the Waldensians ensued. Large-scale campaigns against them were mounted in the thirteenth and fourteenth centuries, and they were severely hunted and persecuted by the Inquisition, with large numbers of them burnt at the stake. No punishment was too severe. So influential a churchman and theologian as Thomas Aquinas wrote as follows regarding the question of the treatment of heretics:

On their own side there is the sin, whereby they deserve not only to be separated from the church by excommunication, but also to be severed from the world by death. For it is a much graver matter to corrupt the faith which quickens the soul than to forge money, which supports temporal life. Wherefore if forgers of money and other evildoers are forthwith condemned by the secular authority, much more reason is there for heretics, as soon as they are convicted of heresy, to be not only excommunicated but even put to death. (1945: II.ii.11,3)

Though Aquinas had other heretics besides the Waldensians in mind, his words were applied to them in severe campaigns of persecution which sought to exterminate them from the face of the earth.

All the usual fantasies of sexual orgies, incest, child-killing and cannibalism were projected on to them by their inquisitors; and all the usual methods of torture were employed to get them to confess to these preconceived sins (Lambert 1992: 147). Not all churchmen believed these tales, but a great many of them did, and in the popular mind the Waldensians, like all other heretics, were equated with libertinism of the worst order. They were held to drink the excrement of toads, worship Lucifer, roast babies, and kiss the backside of a goat or a black cat, the representative of Satan, besides indulging in sexual orgies in the dark: Norman Cohn includes in his book (1976) a plate from a manuscript *Contra sectam Valdensium* written by one Johannis Tinctoris which portrays 'Waldensians adoring the Devil in the form of a he-goat'. As in similar cases, there is no evidence that these practices existed anywhere other than in the minds of the accusers. But the regularity with which such filthy and cruel practices were associated with those who sought a deeper spirituality and showed some independence from the teaching of the church raises deep questions about the way in which sexual fantasies were conjoined

Figure 6 *Waldensian Heretics.* Men and women gather together to kiss the backside of Satan in the form of a goat, while devils fly through the air.

with issues of gender and power in the authorities' bid to keep control of who should count as a mystic.

The Cathars and the Waldensians were not the only ones to face persecution during the later Middle Ages. Another group who are of great interest for our purposes are the 'Free Spirits', held by the ecclesiastical authorities of the time to be a large and well-organised group of heretics, complete with antinomianism and worship of the devil. Even in modern times, so important a scholar of medieval heretics as Gordon Leff saw them as a sect which indulged in 'lechery, hypocrisy and megalomania' (1967: 330). Other historians, however, have shown their heresy, let alone their immorality, to have been almost entirely an invention of their persecutors, cut out of whole cloth with the instruments of torture according to a pattern of preconceived ideas (Lerner 1972).

Those preconceived ideas are revealed most clearly in a document, *Ad nostrum*, issued from the Council of Vienne which met in 1311. R.E. Lerner refers to this document as 'the birth certificate of the heresy of the Free Spirit', and remarks,

Technically speaking, heresy is defined by the pope and the decree referred explicitly to heretics who spoke of their 'spirit of liberty'. But, as if it were in the theatre of the absurd, there is a birth certificate without it being fully clear whether there was any child ... We must regard *Ad nostrum* less as an accurate description of a flourishing heresy than as a document of enormous import in persecutions to come. (83)

Those to whom the heresy was attributed by the document itself were 'an abominable sect of malignant men known as Beghards and faithless women known as beguines in the Kingdom of Germany', and it was the beghards and beguines who bore the brunt of the persecutions, though it is far from evident that they held to the errors of which they were accused, let alone the lewd behaviour with which they were associated.

What, then, were the errors of which these alleged heretics were accused? *Ad nostrum* listed eight false beliefs. First and most important was the belief that it is possible to gain perfection in this life to such a degree that the individual is incapable of sin, and consequently has no further need of divine grace. Secondly, this entails that a person in this state can do as he or she wishes, since the body is wholly subordinate to reason – this, of course, would be the rationalisation for all the wicked behaviour attributed to heretics. Third, such a person need no longer be bound by the laws of the church, or subject to ecclesiastical obedience. From these three beliefs, the other five, including beliefs justifying sexual license and lack of reverence for the sacraments were held to follow. Accordingly, the decree held that such people were a menace to the church and should be exterminated, through repentance if possible, and if not, then by execution.

But if, as already suggested, there was no sect which held to these beliefs or practised the foul deeds with which they were associated, what put such ideas into the heads of the men gathered at the Council of Vienne? In the absence of clear documentary evidence, this question cannot be answered with certainty, but several possibilities suggest themselves. One is that Albertus Magnus, writing several decades earlier, had ascribed these beliefs to a quite different group of people; and that those who drew up *Ad nostrum* were appropriating his work and, without any evidence that it fitted, applying it to a quite different situation (Lerner 1972: 83). Another fascinating possibility is that they took the list of tenets from the extracts of a book by a beguine, Marguerite Porete, who was burned at the stake in 1310 on the basis of her writings: some of the tenets, at least, correspond to items for which she was condemned.

The trial and death of Marguerite Porete is a telling example of the effort of ecclesiastical authorities to control who should count as a mystic. Marguerite was a woman from Hainaut, almost certainly a beguine. Between 1285 and 1295, Marguerite wrote a book entitled *The Mirror of Simple Souls who are Annihilated and who only Remain in the Will and Desire for God* (Petroff 1986). This book did not meet with the approval of her Bishop or his allies, not least because in it she forthrightly accused the church of hypocrisy, and spoke in the name of 'free souls', simple folk whose Christianity was genuine and who could guide the church back into the way of truth. She was brought to trial, and eventually sent to Paris to be tried by the Dominican Inquisitor, William Humbert. William, however, had other things on his mind, not least the infamous affair of the Knights Templars, in which he was heavily involved. Finally, after Marguerite had already been in prison for more than a year, William sent a list of articles which he had extracted from her book to theologians at the University of Paris, who, not having seen them in context, declared them heretical; and Marguerite was burned at the stake (Dronke 1984: 217).

Marguerite speaks of seven stages which the soul may pass through in its growth toward perfect union with God: the seventh stage is the completion of that union, and is reserved for heaven. All seven of them are dependent entirely on the grace of God; they are not of the individual's own making. The first stages have to do with keeping the commandments and performing works of mercy: the teaching traditionally associated with 'purgation'. When she comes to the fifth step, Marguerite says that the soul, having completely renounced its own will and made a gift of it to God, now rests completely within the will of God.

This gift makes perfection in the soul and thus transforms it into the nature of Love which delights it with replenished peace, and satiates it with divine nourishment. And therefore it no longer need protect itself against Nature's war, because its will is nakedly laid in the place from which it was once taken, there where by right it ought to be. (Petroff 1986: 297)

Like many other medieval mystics, Marguerite is here speaking in dramatic form of the way in which, if a soul is completely united with the will of God, it can will only what God wills: it is, therefore, as perfect as it can be upon this earth, since it by definition desires only those things which God desires. She continues,

Now it sees itself from its self, and knows divine goodness, and this knowledge of divine goodness makes it re-see itself; and these two sights root out of it will and desire and good works, and thus the soul is completely at rest, and come into possession of free being which forces the soul away from all things by means of excellent nobility.

When these comments are read in the context of the chapter as a whole, it is clear that Marguerite is speaking of spiritual growth toward union with God, each stage effected by divine grace and wholly dependent upon it. Taken out of context, however, as they were by William, they could indeed look as though she was saying that human beings can reach such great perfection that they are no longer capable of sin. And this is precisely the first article of *Ad nostrum*.

The second article, which said that such a person could therefore freely do whatever their body desired, could similarly be found in Marguerite's work. As quoted above, she says that a person so united with the will of God 'no longer need protect itself against Nature's war'. And in another passage, she writes of the soul which is wholly caught up in the love of God taking leave of the virtues.

> Virtues, I take leave of you for evermore:
> I'll have a freer heart for that – more joyful, too.
> Your service is too unremitting – indeed I know.
> For a time I set my heart on you – inseverably,
> you know that to you I was surrendered totally;
> so I used to be your slave – now I am free . . .
> Yet since it is so, I am unconcerned: I am severed from you,
> for which I thank God on high – the day is good to me . . .
> I have quit your tyrannies; now I am at peace (Dronke 1984: 222)

Only by taking the passages out of context, however, could they even begin to be interpreted as leading to the idea that a person could thereupon begin to lead a life of wickedness and license. Taken in context, it is obvious that Marguerite is saying that a soul completely united with God will, for that very reason, do the things which the love and will of God prompts, because the will of God has now become one with the will of the soul. Not only is it absurd to attribute to Marguerite the teaching that a perfect soul could sinfully indulge the body with impunity; what she actually taught was that such a soul would do everything it could to help people who were in need.

Yet if this soul, who is set so high, could help her neighbours, she would help them in their need with all her power . . . If such souls possessed anything, and they knew that others might have greater need of it than they, such souls would never keep it back, even if they were certain that bread and corn and other sustenance would never grow again on the earth. (225)

Such teaching bears no resemblance to the idea that 'heretics' believed that they were beyond the law and therefore practised orgiastic and cannibalistic rites. Certainly Marguerite herself, though condemned as a heretic, was never herself charged with any immoral behaviour: presumably it was obvious that such charges would not stick.

The same discrepancy with the meaning of Marguerite's teaching is true of the third article of *Ad nostrum*, namely the charge that heretics taught that a person who had reached perfection need no longer be subject to the laws of the church. So far as Marguerite's writing goes, this would only be true in the sense already indicated, that a person united with the will of God would already be doing the things indicated by that divine will, and would therefore not need to be additionally compelled by any external law, whether of the church or any other body. But obviously this is not what the compilers of *Ad nostrum* meant, nor is it what they attributed to heretics. What they thought was that heretics held themselves altogether above the law, and did whatever they pleased no matter how outrageous, blasphemous or obscene.

Why would such ideas be attributed to Marguerite, when reading her book shows immediately how preposterous such an attribution is? The first response might be that this is just the sort of thing that can happen when statements are taken out of context; and in one sense that response is correct. But it would be much too generous to the inquisitors, and to the subsequent compilers of *Ad nostrum*, to say that they had made a regrettable but innocent mistake of scholarship. It is quite clear from the account of Marguerite's trial and execution that it was her criticism of the church, and her assertion that simple 'free' spirits who are obedient to God have a right (even a duty) to speak publicly against its spiritual corruption and to show it a better way, that earned her the contempt and wrath of the ecclesiastical authorities. If this was what her mysticism prompted her to do, then she should not count as a mystic, and articles from her book should be declared heretical. Neither should any who were of like mind. Therefore the articles of *Ad nostrum* were projected on to considerable numbers of people, many of them beguines, who like Marguerite were by their lives or their teachings or both a threat to the authority of the church because they looked for greater spiritual purity. And as Elizabeth Petroff observes, 'Marguerite Porete quite consistently (though not exclusively) addresses her book to women; her public execution must also have been a direct message to women in particular as well as to heretical or fringe groups in general' (1986: 282).

Whether or not the articles of *Ad nostrum* were culled from the accusations against Marguerite Porete, they bear a striking resemblance to them; and they were certainly used to try and to condemn many women and men who by the thought processes of the inquisitors were lumped together into what became known as the heresy of the free spirit. Beguines and beghards were at special risk; indeed in some ways beghards had the harder time of it, because as we saw in the previous chapter, beguines who were willing to live in enclosures under the authority of male clerics were eventually acceptable to the church. Torture, or the threat of torture, elicited 'confessions' of all the things the inquisitors were looking for. The remarkable uniformity of content of many of these confessions from different areas of Europe is evidence not for a widespread 'heresy of the free spirit' but rather for the fact that *Ad nostrum* had become 'a club with which to threaten one's enemies' used as a checklist for the inquisitors' efforts (Lerner 1972: 156).

This is not to say that there were not many people who might be thought of as 'free spirits': women and men who were dissatisfied with the spiritual corruption of the church, and developed a mysticism and spirituality for themselves which sought greater purity of heart and life and which taught the possibility of union with God. Late medieval nominalism, which taught the incomprehensibility of God, also led to the idea common to many mystics especially of the affective strand that God can be known not by the mind, but by love alone; and that this is therefore available as much to the simple as to the learned and erudite. Furthermore, the insecurity of the times, increased by economic disasters, wars and plagues, led many to seek religious security, and to seek it in ways that commended themselves more than did the corruption which they observed in the church. There were therefore many like-minded women and

men who could be called free spirits. But there was no over-
arching organisation such as ecclesiastics feared, and such evidence as there is for immoral activities is largely based on
confessions elicited by torture or other dubious means. Yet many,
a disproportionate number of them women, were tried and
convicted of heresy. Their criticism of the church and their search
for a better way could not be tolerated: they could not be allowed
to count as mystics.

There is considerable irony in all this. Marguerite Porete's
book *The Mirror of Simple Souls*, its authorship forgotten, was
widely circulated in the fourteenth and fifteenth centuries, and
was translated into Latin and Middle English. It was taken as a
book of deep and important mysticism, and received much
favourable attention; it was, for instance, republished in
England by the Downside Benedictines who clearly would not
have done so had they considered its contents to be heretical.
Correct attribution was not made until 1965, when Romana
Guarnieri, an Italian historian, discovered a new manuscript in
Old French which identified the author as Marguerite Porete.
Nevertheless, its author had been burned at the stake as a
heretic for what she had written in that book; and if Lerner is
right in the suggestion expounded above that articles from it
were also used as the basis for *Ad nostrum*, then this book, which
became an important source of mystical teaching for devout
men and women for centuries, was also used as the basis for
condemning other devout men and women as heretics. It is as
clear a confirmation as could possibly be found of my thesis
that who counts as a mystic rests just as much on issues of
power and gender as it does on an individual's experiences or
beliefs. Modern interpreters who lose sight of this are as likely
to create 'mysticism' out of their own presuppositions as the
inquisitors who used *Ad nostrum* were likely to create 'heretics'
after their own fancies.

II WITCHES

The gendered nature of who should count as a mystic is revealed
even more clearly in the case of the witch hunts of early modern

Europe and its sequel in seventeenth-century New England. Although it is true that men could be witches as well as women, and that some men were executed for the crime, it is clear that the vast majority of those who were tried and executed were women. It is also clear that very frequently part of the accusation against them, indeed part of the understanding of what it was to be a witch, included sexual deviance. This was often alleged to take the form of copulating with the devil, or else of committing crimes against male sexuality, such as making men impotent. Even more shocking things were said.

And what, then, is to be thought of those witches who in this way sometimes collect male organs in great numbers, as many as twenty or thirty members together, and put them in a bird's nest, or shut them up in a box, where they move themselves like living members, and eat oats and corn, as has been seen by many and is a matter of common report? (Kramer and Sprenger 1986: 268)

The authors of *Malleus Maleficarum*, who pose this question, answer that this is the work of the devil, and people who see such things are deluded; but this only means that the witches are collaborating with the devil to produce such obscene delusions in the minds of those whom they wish to affect. The writers continue,

For a certain man tells us that, when he had lost his member, he approached a known witch to ask her to restore it to him. She told the afflicted man to climb a certain tree, and that he might take which he liked out of a nest in which there were several members. And when he tried to take a big one, the witch said: You must not take that one; adding, because it belonged to a parish priest.

Although the authors say that things of this sort 'are caused by devils through an illusion', it is clear that they believe that, but for the illusory nature of the penises which the man saw in the nest, the rest of the story is credible.

Who were these authors, and why should anyone pay attention to them? They were fifteenth-century Dominicans, Heinrich Kramer and James Sprenger, commissioned in 1484 by a special bull, *Summis desiderantes affectibus*, promulgated by Pope Innocent VIII, whereby they are designated inquisitors in northern

Germany and the Rhineland. Together they wrote a large book, *Malleus Maleficarum* (The Hammer of Witches), in which they expounded the demonic origin and nature of witchcraft, the susceptibility of women to the devil to do his horrific works, and the remedies for curing witchcraft and methods of destroying it, including the methods of torture that may be used if a person accused of witchcraft denies the accusation. The book is simultaneously credulous and scholarly. The authors clearly accept that there are many witches and that they do all manner of evil things, ranging from raising up storms and tempests or causing illness to human beings and animals, to changing men into the shape of beasts or, as we have already seen, causing them to be impotent or even stealing their penises. One of the most serious accusations is against 'witches who are midwives'. These women are said to prevent conception or to cause miscarriages, or, if these methods fail, 'then they either devour the child or offer it to the devil'. Yet on the other hand the authors show enormous erudition, quoting frequently from a range of patristic and medieval theologians, and in particular relying on the work of Thomas Aquinas, their fellow Dominican. It would not be far-fetched to describe the book as a cross between a scholastic work and a pornographic magazine. Certainly in its time it was of great importance: by 1520 it had been through thirteen editions on the continent, and there were many more after that. Nor is it without significance that it was one of the first books to be printed on the newly invented printing presses, thereby gaining a much wider circulation than could have been expected with the old method of hand-copying.

Influential as it was, however, it would not be true to say that *Malleus Maleficarum* created witches in the way that *Ad nostrum* created the heresy of the free spirit. The belief in witchcraft goes back much further than the fifteenth century; indeed from the earliest times of the Christian era people had from time to time been accused and sometimes convicted of it. Nevertheless, these accusations were occasional and seemingly haphazard; and from the tenth century to the beginning of the fourteenth there are very few accounts of trials on charges of witchcraft. Then, quite rapidly, all that changed. Thousands of people, mostly women, were accused. On the continent, they could be tortured until they confessed; and if they were found guilty, they were burned at the stake. In England official torture was not permitted (though there were substitutes); and a convicted witch was hanged rather than burned, burning being reserved for the crime of treason. The *Malleus Maleficarum* was less influential in England than on the continent, and the primary learned books discussing witchcraft came somewhat later in England: no less a personage than James I wrote *The Daemonology* in 1597, in which he argued for the existence of witches and advocated their extermination. In both Catholic and Protestant countries there was a veritable witch craze, a passion for discovering and exterminating witches. It reached its peak in the sixteenth and early seventeenth centuries, and then slowly declined. One of the last outbreaks was in Salem, Massachusetts, in the late seventeenth century; by that time there were few trials taking place in England or on the continent. The last Act of Parliament in England whereby witchcraft was a statutory offence was repealed in 1736 (Thomas 1971).

What was the cause of the sudden surge of persecutions for witchcraft? Two explanations have been advanced. On the one hand, scholars like Keith Thomas suggest that the main reason for the increase of accusations of witchcraft brought against women was a result of deepening popular unrest and disquiet. On the other hand, Norman Cohn has pointed out the effects of changes in legal procedures whereby it became easier to make accusations. A brief consideration of each of these shows that they are not incompatible, but that even taking them both together, they lead to further important questions. (It is of course also necessary to remember that the witch hunts ranged over several centuries and across the varying cultures of Europe, so that generalisations must be made with caution.)

With regard to witch persecutions in England, it is clear that accusations were usually made by people who believed that they had been harmed by the 'witch': they might accuse her of causing illness, injury or death, of causing madness, of harming their livestock or their crops, or of disrupting their daily lives or the means by which they made a living, for instance by preventing milk from being churned into butter. Belief in magic and witchcraft was common, and it was commonly held to involve evil powers, but there was not in England the same focus on Satanism or on sexual orgies with the devil that there was on the continent. On occasion in England witch-hunting was led by someone appointed to the task, as was the case with Matthew Hopkins in 1644–5 who also, uncharacteristically for England, used torture at least to the extent of prolonged sleep deprivation and the water ordeal (Bartlett 1986). On the whole, however, in England accusations emanated from the local population, and could not be said to have been led by the influential of society to anything like the same extent as is plausible for parts of the continent. The tensions and conflicts occurring during the turbulent period of the Tudors and Stuarts and culminating in the Civil War affected local populations in significant ways. Not only was there religious unrest as the country swung back and forth between Catholic and Protestant rulers, but also there was a massive shift in economics as the population, which had declined severely because of the plague, now surged forward, causing greater demand for food and other commodities. Wage-labour became increasingly prominent; and although this period was still pre-industrial, it can be seen as a transition period between older forms of society and the emergence of capitalism. Also there were more poor people than ever before. In the Elizabethan era, Poor Laws were established which placed responsibility for the poor on to their local communities. It can hardly be coincidental that the available records show that those accused of witchcraft tended to be poorer than their accusers (Thomas 1971: 669).

On the other hand, as Norman Cohn points out, changes in judicial procedure did make these accusations much more likely. The older judicial procedure, which was in force throughout Europe for most of the medieval period, involved the idea of the talion: this was a procedure whereby an accuser who failed to convince a judge of the validity of his or her case would suffer the penalty which the accused would have suffered if found guilty. As Cohn points out, the intention behind this was 'to discourage malicious or frivolous accusations', but it is not surprising that it would deter many people from making accusations which they feared they might not be able to substantiate to the satisfaction of the judge, particularly if they were accusing someone more powerful or learned than themselves. Once this law was abolished, as it was in most countries in the period just before the witch hunt (or in its very early stages), it is obvious that more people would feel able to come forward with accusations than would have done so under the earlier legal system. Though this in itself would hardly cause a witch hunt, it would facilitate the accusation process (Cohn 1976: 161).

Norman Cohn argues that, at least on the continent, the witch hunt was essentially led from the top, instigated by authorities who were sure in their own minds that women were forming themselves into organised groups in league with the devil, to the detriment and destruction of church and society. In Cohn's words,

Left to themselves, peasants would never have created mass witch hunts – these occurred only where and when the authorities had become convinced of the reality of the sabbat and of nocturnal flights to the sabbat. And this conviction depended on, and in turn was sustained by, the inquisitorial type of procedure, including the use of torture. (252)

As the Inquisition was developed to rid the true church of heretics, so now its powers were extended to deal with the even greater danger of women in league with the devil. Witches were perceived to be the mirror image of true mystics: as true mystics experienced God, so these women experienced communion with the devil; and as genuinely holy people could work miracles by the power of God, so the witches could work malice by the powers of hell. The engagement of ecclesiastical authority with who should count as a mystic, and its gendered nature, could hardly be clearer.

The significant feature that emerges is that, while the emphasis on Satan worship and the involvement of the Inquisition was far greater on the continent than it was in England, in both cases by far the most frequently accused and convicted were women. Brian Levack has produced statistics which show that in most European regions those prosecuted for witchcraft were at least 75 per cent female, and in some regions more than 90 per cent (1987: 124). Why was witchcraft so strongly correlated with gender, whether the persecutions were led from above or from a more popular level of society?

Part of the reason is already clear from what we have seen of the way in which gender was constructed in the church and society. Churchmen had long taught that women were simultaneously oversexed and rationally and morally inferior to men. They were therefore 'naturally' less spiritual than men, and were the ones who would most easily succumb to the devil's allurements, particularly sexual allurements, even though they were also often reported to confess that sex with the devil was painful and his semen icy cold. (The problem of how a devil, who was after all not a physical being, could produce semen and beget children was solved by Kramer and Sprenger by saying – with the backing of Thomas Aquinas – that the devil received the semen by being a succubus to a man, and then, transforming himself into an incubus, transmitted it to a woman (1986: 81).) The church, having sown the wind in its teaching about women, was now reaping the whirlwind.

These misogynist teachings, however, were not new, and neither was popular belief in sorcery and magic; yet until this time full-scale witch hunts had not broken out. Furthermore, as Levack points out, the image of the witch forming a sexual liaison with the devil who then gave her the power to work harm was a much more important image to the educated classes who led the witch hunts than it was to the common people who brought forward accusations. In those cases, Levack suggests, it was women's roles as cooks, healers and midwives, roles which were strongly gender-related, which made them especially vulnerable. As cooks, they were able to identify and gather herbs, and to turn them into potions, unguents, or even poisons. As healers, also, they would have knowledge of herbs, and could develop potions and ointments out of natural ingredients. It would be completely unsurprising if when these were applied they were accompanied by magical rituals or prayers: indeed, the line between what would count as Christian prayer and what would be seen as superstitious might well be drawn only after the suspicion of witchcraft had already arisen in any particular case. As midwives, women performed an important but risky role in society: as

Levack says, 'in an age when as many as one-fifth of all children died either at birth or during the first few months of life, and when infanticide was by no means a rare occurrence, the charge that a midwife had killed a child by sorcery was both functional and plausible, and it offered the bereaved parents a means of revenge' (1987: 127). Add to this the belief of the inquisitors that witches wanted to procure babies for sacrifice to the devil and as a feast for their sabbath meal, and the notion that midwives were witches gained an additional dimension of plausibility.

Yet while all of these things are true, they can hardly be the whole story. They were true, after all, long before the witch hunt: from time immemorial women have been cooks, healers and midwives, just as from time immemorial women have been considered mentally and morally inferior to men. There must, therefore, be some additional reason why this set of conditions should erupt into a witch hunt of massive proportions. As we have seen, Cohn believes that the crucial added ingredient was the development of the inquisitorial procedure and the adoption of beliefs about the witches' sabbath and nocturnal flying; and perhaps this was all the trigger that was necessary. But the work of feminist scholar Marianne Hester (1992) suggests another possibility, at least in the case of witch persecutions in England (where the conditions specified by Cohn were in any case much less to the fore).

Hester suggests that in the developing capitalist economy, there were new tensions in male–female relationships; and that these tensions should not be ignored when we consider the gendered nature of witch persecutions. In one respect, this is not a new suggestion: as long ago as 1973 Ehrenreich and English had argued that one of the chief reasons for the persecution of women as witches was the rise of the medical profession, with male physicians seeking to take to themselves the traditional role of healer and later midwife, which had hitherto belonged to women. However, although their view has in some quarters become received feminist wisdom, closer consideration shows it to be implausible as it stands. Either the category of healer or midwife is too broad to be of use (in the sense that virtually *all* medieval and early modern women would as a matter of course

Figure 7 *Hildegard's Vision of the Cosmos*. The universe is the body of God (note God's head and feet above and below the sphere); while humanity is represented as the microcosm of the macrocosm. Hildegard sits in the bottom left, recording the vision.

and expectation have such skills) or, if the category is more narrowly defined, it becomes impossible to ascertain what proportion of accused women actually fall within it (Karlson 1987: 141). Furthermore, it is clear that some of the greatest *opposition* to the persecution of witches in England came from the medical profession: William Harvey, physician to both James I and Charles I and member of the Royal College of Physicians, is the most prominent case in point. Harvey rejected the idea that women could be witches on the grounds that women were essentially passive, whereas to be a witch a woman would have to be active, contrary to her nature.

Hester's suggestion is more nuanced. She points out that in the changing economic climate, women and men frequently found themselves in competition, though women were in a weaker position than men. This was especially true amongst traders and artisans, which was precisely the group in which there were a large number of accusations of witchcraft.

Evidence of women's work suggests that there was a struggle between the sexes around making a living, which also had the overall effect of ensuring that men rather than women obtained the better positions in, and thus overall control of, the new capitalist economic structure. (1992: 140)

In various ways, in particular in relation to the important developing textile and brewing industries, women were 'squeezed out' of areas of production. There was a marginalising of women in the increasingly competitive economy that was to continue into the modern capitalist and industrialist period.

In such an economic climate, it is important to notice again what sort of women were most likely to be accused. The chief victims, at least in England, tended to be poor women, a disproportionate number of them widows or single women. These women would be the ones who would either be a drain on the resources of those who were involved in the developing economy, or else if they were actively trying to support themselves, they would be in competition with men in the economic structures. Thus men acted to protect their own interests: in the seventeenth century, for example, brewing became restricted to those designated 'Common Brewers', who, unsurprisingly, were male. Thus women, especially but not only single women and widows, were either the most vulnerable group in the population or the ones in most direct competition with men, or (frequently) both. Hester argues that in this economic context, persecution of women of these groups as witches acted as an important, gender-specific, method of social control.

Hester's suggestions gain plausibility from her observations of what it was that brought the period of witch trials to a close. Historians have attributed the decline of the witch hunts to a variety of factors, including the weakening power of the clergy in both Protestant and Catholic countries after the Reformation (Trevor-Roper 1967: 97) and the rise of rationalism and the scientific method (Thomas 1971: 681). While these facts may indeed have played a part, there is an additional dimension which is of enormous importance, both in terms of the decline of the witch hunts, and, more generally, in terms of gender relations in the subsequent construction of mysticism. That dimension is the fact that during the seventeenth century, changes in gender ideology were taking place which would affect the social control of women without any need to have recourse to witch persecutions (Hester 1992: 156).

We have already noted that William Harvey argued against the belief in witchcraft. The reasons for his rejection of the idea may well have included greater scientific understanding; but they were also part of a changing view of women. In Harvey's thinking, women were by nature inferior, potentially defective. He thought that women were particularly prone to 'hysteria' or 'dysfunctional womb', and that women who suffered in these ways might think themselves to be witches and even exhibit some strange phenomena. Like Reginald Scot before him, Harvey believed that women who thought they saw demons were mentally ill, and that their illness was directly related to their biological femaleness: Scot had argued that the reason so many of the witches were *old* women was because the post-menopausal state shut up in her body the ill humours which in a younger woman escaped with each monthly period. These humours then might make her imagine that she saw demons, or have sexual fantasies about them, but the reality lay with her biology (Laqueur 1990: 144).

The increasing attention to the biology of women, characteristic of Harvey and Scot, went along with a much stronger emphasis on men as active and women as passive. This was by no means a new idea in western thinking: as we saw in an earlier chapter, its roots go back at least as far as Aristotle. But during the witch hunt, some aspects of it had receded. For a woman to be a witch, she must be seen as active, capable of entering into a devious and passionate relationship with the devil, and able to be a threat to people around her, and, in the eyes of the inquisitors, so great a danger to the church that no method of torture and extermination was too extreme. But with the seventeenth century, the passivity of women was reasserted. She was seen, once again, as being the passive vessel in procreation: indeed the Puritan preachers in England taught that coition was only 'natural' when the man lay on top of the woman, because this was the symbol of masculine domination and showed him to be the 'tiller of the soil' (Flandrin 1979: 162). Furthermore, as men increasingly took over from women areas of the pre-industrial economy like weaving and brewing, it was in their interests that women should be seen as weak, unable to cope with competitive public life, and therefore restricted to home and child-rearing, incapable of reasoning or moral decision-making. This, however, meant that women could not simultaneously be seen as active and cunning participants in organised diabolical sabbats and malicious witchcraft. Accordingly, men like Scot and Harvey argued against the belief that women were witches, and helped to bring the persecutions to a close, but did so on the basis of the new gender construction resting on the infantilisation of women which they themselves did much to create.

At the same time, the developing scientific rationalism which is usually cited as an important factor in the demise of witch persecutions was itself connected with new gender constructions. Philosophers developing the new approach to the world, sometimes known as the 'mechanical philosophy', defined this approach in strongly masculine terms. One of the most important of the new philosophers in England was Francis Bacon, who lived from 1561 to 1626, the later period of the witch hunt. Bacon categorised philosophy as masculine, a philosophy whose task was to penetrate the secrets of Nature, which was of course always described in female terms. As Londa Schiebinger explains, 'masculine' for Bacon is a term of praise, while 'feminine' or especially 'effeminate' is an insult: that which is female is passive, weak, and waiting, whereas 'masculine philosophy was to be active, virile, and generative' (1989: 137). Nature, like women, is mysterious, aloof, and whimsical, and most progress can be made if the male scientist approaches her as he should approach a woman: not with violence, but with patience and gallantry. Nevertheless it is clear that he will become the master. 'Let us establish a chaste and lawful marriage between Mind and Nature', Bacon wrote; 'Nature betrays her secrets more fully when in the grip and under the pressure of art than when in enjoyment of her natural liberty' (Lloyd 1984: 11).

Bacon, of course, was English; and the patterns on the continent were somewhat different. Indeed, Bacon himself not only characterised his philosophy as masculine, but deliberately and insultingly contrasted it to continental philosophy, which he considered to be 'effeminate' (Schiebinger 1989: 138). Yet although there were differences in area and time-scale, by the middle of the seventeenth century scientific philosophy, everywhere thought of in male terms, was flourishing in many parts of Europe, and the witch hunts were drawing to a close.

Thus to say that it was the rise of science by itself which discredited belief in witches is too simple. The combination of new economic patterns, new religious structures, and the new 'masculine' science all worked together to develop a new variety of the social control of women, based on her passivity and inferiority. It can hardly be insignificant that the witch hunts ceased just when they were no longer necessary as a means of asserting male dominance.

Once the idea of men as active and rational, and women as passive and non-rational, was firmly re-established, this in itself was sufficient to effect social control, and removed the need for the prosecutions of women as witches. The institution of marriage and the family became ever more central to society in its patterns of production and consumption; and men ruled over their wives with the same divine right as was held to pertain to kings. Women were kept firmly in the private domain, outside of the public, competitive world of economics and politics: Lawrence Stone shows how their status and legal rights declined in England during the sixteenth century (1979: 136). Though popular belief in magic and superstition did not disappear, it was no longer necessary to use accusations of witchcraft to keep women in their place.

CHAPTER 8

The language of ineffability

Silence itself – the things one declines to say, or is forbidden
to name, the discretion that is required between different
speakers – is less the absolute limit of discourse, the other
side from which it is separated by a strict boundary, than an
element that functions alongside the things said, with them
and in relation to them within over-all strategies. There is
no binary division to be made between what one says and
what one does not say; we must try to determine the
different ways of not saying such things, how those who can
and those who cannot speak of them are distributed, which
type of discourse is authorised, or which form of discretion
is required in either case.   (Foucault 1981: 27)

The preceding chapters have been intended to show how the
concept of the mystical changed during the patristic and medieval
period, and to show that those changes were implicated with
issues of power and gender. This means that contemporary
philosophers of religion cannot legitimately assume that there is
one thing that is 'mystical experience', or indeed that any discussion of mysticism and religious experience can avoid taking a
stand on the issues of power and gender, since to be silent about
them means colluding with the ways in which they have operated
and with the triumph of the dominant. I shall discuss this further
in the final chapter. Before doing so, however, I wish to give
specific attention to one aspect of the construction of mysticism
which looms large in most contemporary discussions of it, namely
the question of language and ineffability. Study of this issue
crystallises the way in which what counted as mystical within the
history of Christianity was closely related to gender issues, since

linguistic style and imagery can be shown to vary considerably between male and female writers in every era: I shall give some examples below. Furthermore, it shows how modern philosophers of religion are themselves involved in a social construction of mysticism which distorts insight both into historical mystics and into contemporary concerns.

Throughout the changing constructions of mysticism in the Middle Ages, the wealth of linguistic resource in metaphor, image and genre was outstanding. The richness of language and vividness of imagery across differences of genre, context and personality is clearly intended by its users to enable the readers to enter into their writings both intelligently and imaginatively as spiritual instruction which guides and evokes as well as describes experience. Careful reading of their writings is intended not only to provide information, but to provide an entry into longing for God and experience of God: it was not for nothing that spiritual reading – the meditative reading of the great writers of the spiritual life – had long been considered an essential part of prayer and the formation of character.

In the light of such vividness and wealth of expression in mystical writings, it comes as something of a shock to remember that when contemporary philosophers discuss mysticism they regularly take ineffability – the impossibility of verbal articulation – as a primary characteristic of the mystical. William James cites ineffability as the first and most important characteristic of mystical experience, saying that 'the incommunicableness of the transport is the keynote of all mysticism' (1960: 367). Similarly Walter Terence Stace (1961), discussing types of mystics as introvertive and extrovertive, selects ineffability as the hallmark for each of the two categories of what he deems as genuine mystical experience. Later writers, notably Steven Katz (1978) and Renford Bambrough (1978), accept that ineffability is central to mystical experience, even though they have serious reservations about the implications which James and Stace had sought to draw from this characteristic. Although all these writers put the claims of ineffability together with claims about what constitutes mystical experience, to reinforce an account about which we should by now be dubious, their concurrence that such experience is ineffable must be taken seriously.

On what grounds do they take this view? The acquaintance we have acquired through this study of the writings of some medieval mystics would be unlikely to lead to the idea that ineffability is the key that will unlock for us an understanding of their lives and writings. On the contrary, they come across as skilled in linguistic usage, and not in one genre only but in many. Patristic writers like Origen and Gregory of Nyssa used the biblical text as a well from which to draw mystical meaning in buckets full of allusions and quotations. Hildegard of Bingen not only wrote out her visions in language full of imagery, but actually had them portrayed in paintings which illuminated her manuscripts. Bernard of Clairvaux's sermons *On the Song of Songs* combined classical style with hundreds of phrases taken directly from the Bible. Women like Hadewijch and Gertrude used metaphor, and frequently showed great daring in their use of erotic language.

Furthermore, one has to read quite a long way into their works, in which they do not complain of any particular trouble in expressing themselves, before one comes upon occasional remarks which could perhaps be used to support a thesis of ineffability. Julian, for example, says that 'I may not and cannot show the spiritual visions as plainly and fully as I should wish' (1978: 102), but she says this in the context of a long and clear exposition of her message to her 'even Christians'. Much later, John of the Cross emphasises silence, the silence of 'my house being now all stilled' as a significant quality of the dark night of tryst with his beloved (1973: 711). But he conveys much meaning with that image; it is certainly not obvious that it is meant as a claim of ineffability. Indeed, unless one already had a preconceived notion about the ineffability of mystical experience, it is doubtful that these remarks would be construed as indicative of it.

I suggest, therefore, that it is necessary to look again at the claim of the ineffability of mystical experiences, to see exactly why this claim is being made. It will be my argument that when mystical writers of the Middle Ages protest about the inadequacy of language, they mean something very different from what recent philosophers of religion attribute to them. The former are seeking to convey something of what they find of the beauty and wonder of God; while the latter are trying to support a particular understanding of mysticism within post-Enlightenment categories of epistemology and philosophy of language. The mystics did not share these categories; and in fact they are called into question on the one hand by a study of mystical literature, as we have seen, and on the other by the deconstruction proposed by postmodernist thinkers.

This in turn leads us to put the issues the other way around. What were the ways in which the mystical writers used language? What forms of epistemology and theology were implicit in their metaphors and images? To what extent did women and men use language differently, and what happened to the metaphors and genres which women developed? In the sections of this chapter, I shall examine first the language some male mystical writers used to talk about God. Then I shall turn to some of the uses of language by some female writers, and show that they developed ways of speaking and thinking about God which offered creative insights for spirituality; but that they were largely suppressed, along with the women visionaries. A final section will be devoted to an analysis of the modern philosophical discussion of the use of language by mystical writers, showing that, as with mysticism more generally, contemporary philosophers preoccupy themselves with a social construction of mysticism quite different from what we find in the classics of Christian mystical writing, and with virtually no consciousness of the struggles of power and gender embedded in that discourse.

I THE INEFFABILITY OF GOD

None were as aware as the male mystical writers of the Middle Ages that 'the Divine cannot be named'; none were as confident that the nameless one has many names. Whether we look at Augustine or Dionysius, Bernard or Eckhart, Bonaventure or John of the Cross, all took it for granted that the names of God do depict some aspect of divine reality; and simultaneously that all carry their negation within themselves and cannot be understood as literal. With such an understanding of language, they were free to explore the resonances of the names of God without worrying that they were thereby diminishing God. As we have seen, the names of God which they chose to examine for their mystical meaning were often ones derived from the biblical text in which they were immersed.

We have already seen how the tension between the affirmative value of metaphors about God and their inherent self-negation was explored for the tradition of Christian spirituality by the fifth-century writer known to us as Dionysius. It is worth looking at his writing again, briefly, with the theme of ineffability specifically in mind. In his book *The Divine Names* he lists the many names that scripture gives to God the nameless one: life, light, truth, ancient of days, Lord, 'sun, star, and fire, water, wind, and dew, cloud, archetypal stone, and rock, that he is all, that he is no thing' (1987: 56). Though all of these and many more have value, indeed revelatory impact, it is stressed by Dionysius that none are adequate or even proper if they are not also seen as inherently self-negating. God, he holds, is beyond any formulation or expression that could be conceived or devised by a finite mind, and even when the source of the concept is divine revelation, human capacity cannot contain the superlative wonder of God.

Indeed the inscrutable One is out of the reach of every rational process. Nor can any words come up to the inexpressible Good, this One, this Source of all unity, this supra-existent Being. Mind beyond mind, word beyond speech, it is gathered up by no discourse, by no intuition, by no name. (49)

While the names of God are held by Dionysius to be of enormous significance, they are fatally misunderstood, in his view, if their self-negation is not taken into account.

Accordingly, already in *The Divine Names* and more emphatically in its sequel *The Mystical Theology* Dionysius proceeds by systematic negation of the previous affirmations about God.

The Cause of all is above all and is not inexistent, lifeless, speechless, mindless. It is not a material body ... Nor is it a spirit, in the sense in which we understand that term. It is not sonship or fatherhood and it is nothing known to us or to any other being ... It is beyond assertion ... It is also beyond every denial. (140)

And with that the treatise ends, passing over into silence. It is the silence of the *ek-static* intellect, the intellect 'standing outside of itself', transcending itself in its insight into what God is/not. Here indeed is ineffability; but the ineffability is of *God* and of God's unspeakable wonder. It is important to be clear about this, because the ineffability of *God* should not be confused with the alleged ineffability of *subjective experiences* with which contemporary philosophers are preoccupied.

As different as were Augustine and Dionysius, on this matter they were agreed. Augustine also showed an awareness of the inadequacy of human language to contain God; and his expression of this entered western Christianity through his enormously influential treatise *On Christian Doctrine*.

Have we spoken or announced anything worthy of God? Rather I feel that I have done nothing but wish to speak: if I have spoken, I have not said what I wished to say. Whence do I know this, except because God is ineffable? If what I said were ineffable, it would not be said. And for this reason God should not be said to be ineffable, for when this is said, something is said. And a contradiction in terms is created, since if that is ineffable which cannot be spoken, then that is not ineffable which can be called ineffable. This contradiction is to be passed over in silence rather than resolved verbally. For God, although nothing worthy may be spoken of him, has accepted the tribute of the human voice and wished us to take joy in praising him with our words. (1958: I.6)

Once again, the emphasis here is on *God* who is beyond words; not on a quality of subjective human experience. As in the case of Dionysius, Augustine's aim in pointing to divine ineffability is to connect a doctrinal position with an invitation to worship. But whereas Dionysius' emphasis was to point out the idolatrous consequences of fixation on any names of God, and thereby to encourage the intellectual ascent which would bring about the *ek-stasis* of the intellect, Augustine's tone is rather one of encouragement in the creative use of language on the grounds that such verbal tributes are received by God as praise.

From both Dionysius and Augustine comes the clear teaching that the language of finite and sinful human beings cannot encapsulate the Creator, who therefore remains ineffable, unspeakable by mortal tongue. It is this recognition which is intended to bring their reader to a point of silence: not the silence of frustration at being unable to express a subjective experience, nor the silence of a *quod erat demonstrandum*, but the silence of recognition that God is beyond human expression. Ineffability, for these authors, is a way of indicating the transcendence of God; but that transcendence must also be understood, for them, as inexhaustible fecundity, the very opposite of frustrated speechlessness.

This is why, in their different ways, both Augustine and Dionysius take the doctrine of ineffability as the counterpart to considerable latitude in experimentation with language. In Augustine's terms, whatever will draw to wonder and worship, or, in Dionysius' terms, whatever will enable the mind to climb the steps toward intellectual ecstasy, is legitimate language to use. None of it can be taken as unproblematical or literal description of God: as Dionysius pointed out, neither spirit nor son nor father nor anything else we might say could encapsulate the divine essence. But if the words that are used lead the mind onward into the divine darkness, then they themselves become the steps of the spiritual ascent. Accordingly, a proper grasp of divine ineffability is an invitation to experiment with language, to stretch it to its limits so that its very articulacy may lead beyond itself to the silence of God.

We can see in these writers the development in spiritual terms of the focus on words and language as central to religion which I discussed in chapter 3. Here, words themselves become the vehicle of ascent, just as they are also held to be the vehicle of divine self-revelation: indeed, in true Neo-platonic fashion, the way up and the way down are the same. As God is made available to humankind through the Word incarnate and through the words of scripture, so humans ascend to God through the words which reveal and conceal the divine mystery. The doctrine of divine ineffability, therefore, is a counterpart to the doctrine of divine revelation. And it can hardly be over-emphasised that as these writers use it, and as it becomes part of the western Christian tradition, that doctrine is a doctrine about God, not a statement about a quality of human experience.

Particularly within the speculative mystical tradition, there continued to be writers intrigued by the relation between finite human language and the infinite transcendence of God. There was a recognition that, while all sorts of verbal expression was essential at a penultimate level, ultimately nothing could be adequate; hence there was interest in the relationship between the penultimate and the ultimate. I suggest that it is this interest which lies behind some of the medieval theories of religious language. To take only one well-known example: Thomas Aquinas' 'doctrine of analogy' is often nowadays taken as a formal doctrine of predication, specifying exactly how language can and cannot be used of God. It might be more illuminating, however, to consider his remarks first of all as an exploration of *method*: how can language best be used to open windows to that which is beyond conceptual grasp? Thinking along these lines would make it possible to treat the use of analogy more like a *literary skill* rather than as a theological dogma. Skilfully used, analogy, like the paradoxes of Dionysius or the metaphors of Augustine, could enable the reader to enter into the subtleties and nuanced interplay of meaning, and thereby enable the mental ascent into the silence of the divine mystery.

Be that as it may in the case of Aquinas, it is clear that some such procedure was at work in his fellow Dominican, Meister Eckhart, in his appropriation of the work of Dionysius for his spirituality centred in the (male) higher intellect. Eckhart demonstrates great care in his comments about the uses and limitations of language in relation to the fecund ineffability of God, and, like Dionysius but in a much more popular mode, deliberately used dialectic and paradox to lead beyond speech to the silence of transcendence. In his *Commentary on the Book of Exodus* Eckhart reflects on the phrase 'Almighty is his name', making specific reference to Thomas Aquinas and with the apophatic teaching of Dionysius and the Jewish philosopher Moses Maimonides much to the fore. Drawing this together with the reflections of Augustine and his own extensive deliberations on language about God, Eckhart says,

The superior is not deprived of the inferior's perfections, but precontains them all in a more excellent way. Therefore the 'Name that is above every name' is not unnameable but 'omninameable,' so that Augustine … says, 'Everything can be said of God, but nothing can be worthily said. No gap is greater than this: to seek a fitting name and not to find it; to look for a way of speaking *and to find all of them*. (1986: 54)

In this tradition, then, the ineffability of God, the inadequacy of every name, leads not to speechlessness but to 'omninameability': the invitation to stretch and pull language beyond all boundaries. 'To look for a way of speaking' does not result in finding *no* such way but in finding *'all of them'*, an embarrassment of riches, none of them ultimate, all of them penultimately provocative. Eckhart's practice as a vernacular preacher made full use of this principle, as we have seen: time after time he proposed the most outrageous paradoxes to lead his listeners to the moment of recognition. Recent admirers of Eckhart have on occasion likened this use of paradox to Buddhist koans, where the hearer is also meant to achieve insight through the shock of the paradox. The parallel is attractive, but it should not be forgotten how deeply saturated in the Christian Platonist speculative tradition Eckhart was, and how fully his account of language is all of a piece with his understanding of the nature of God and of divine self-giving in the great chain of being.

In the affective tradition, and in the later interweaving of the two strands, the exuberance of language is if anything even greater. Here there is not so much insistence about the need to deny as well as affirm everything that is said; and there is also a freer interplay of language. Though the contrast should not be overstated, the intention is not so much to lead the *intellect* forward step by step to its own self-transcendent as to motivate the *heart* to love and worship. Spiritual development is seen more in terms of the increase of purity of heart, letting not only their minds but their hearts and lives be stretched in the love of God and neighbour. Thus Bernard of Clairvaux writes,

When from the generous bounty of [a person's] good will he strives to reach out to all his neighbours, loving each of them as himself … indeed he has made himself vast. His heart is filled with a love that embraces everybody … Then the width, height, and beauty of your soul will be the width, height and beauty of heaven itself. (1977: 27.11)

This is the aim of spiritual instruction: not a focus on the ascent of the mind (and certainly not an encouragement to 'mystical experiences' in the way that a modern philosopher of religion would speak of them) but to 'become vast', so that the beauty of one's love will reflect the beauty of heaven. All the resources of affective language can be called into play to draw listeners and readers to this love.

Several times in his writings Bernard addresses the question of why and how God should be loved: why the union of love should be sought. In his book *On Loving God* he explains that we start by loving ourselves, for our own sake. When we begin to seek God, we do so still for our own sake, for that which God does for us now and promises to do hereafter: we may seek God because of fear of hell or hope of heaven, because of need for help and healing for ourselves or for those we love, or even for the spiritual insights or consolations which we may receive. Bernard continues,

When he is forced by his own needs, he starts to worship and draw close to God, through meditation, reading, prayer and obeying God. He gradually becomes acquainted with God in this way, and discovers the delight of God. Once he has experienced how wonderful the Lord is ... he loves God, not from selfish motives, but for God's sake. (1974: 118)

As Bernard expresses it, loving God for God's sake, longing for union with God, in one sense does not admit of further justification as though it were a means to some other end.

Yet there is another sense in which Bernard does indeed seek to give a justification, by explaining how it is that such love for God does constitute an end. By meditating on God and God's ways, he says, comes the discovery of 'the *delight* of God', the experiential knowledge of 'how wonderful the Lord is'. This theme of the delightfulness of God, God's supreme wonder and desirability, is a major theme in the affective tradition as exemplified by Bernard. God is the altogether lovely one, the one of immeasurable glory, whose beauty attracts those who begin to perceive it, and whose wonder is irresistible to those whose hearts begin to respond. Bernard becomes lyrical about the attracting beauty of God as seen by the one who seeks God in love:

His eyes will see the king in his beauty going before him into the beautiful places of the desert, to the flowering roses and the lilies of the valley, to gardens where delights abound and streams run from the fountains, where storerooms are filled with delightful things and the odours of perfume, till last of all he makes his way to the privacy of the bedchamber. (1977: 32.9)

We have already considered Bernard's use of erotic imagery: this passage adds to that consideration the recognition that the abundance of metaphor and erotic imagery in Bernard finds its place not least in his message of the delight of God, God's attraction, the drawing power of the divine beauty.

This attraction was a prominent theme throughout the later western mystical tradition: we need think only of such writings as Dante's *Divine Comedy*, for instance, in which the attractiveness of the love of God first through Beatrice and then in itself draws Dante through all the realms of hell and purgatory into paradise. It is not necessary for my present purpose to examine all the ways in which this theme was developed: the point is simply that it was this divine attractiveness and the love and desire which it evoked which was seen as the basis and justification of linguistic exuberance. To take only one example from a somewhat later era, John of the Cross, whose prose writings are on the whole notable for their austerity, nevertheless nearly trips over himself when it comes to describing the beauty and attraction of God. Speaking of his longing, he prays,

that I may be so transformed in your beauty that we may be alike in beauty, and both behold ourselves in your beauty ... hence, I shall see you in your beauty, and you shall see me in your beauty, and I shall see myself in you in your beauty, and you will see yourself in me in your beauty; that I may resemble you in your beauty, and you resemble me in your beauty, and my beauty be your beauty and your beauty be my beauty; wherefore I shall be you in your beauty and you will be me in your beauty, because your very beauty will be my beauty; and therefore we shall behold each other in your beauty. (1973: 547)

The rather breathless tone of this passage reveals through repetition of the word 'beauty', which occurs no fewer than seventeen times, the way in which John of the Cross utilised language both to express and to evoke awareness of divine attraction. Although he held fully to the doctrine that God was ultimately beyond all human language, and in that sense ineffable, he viewed that doctrine, not as a reason to keep silent, but as a licence to use language to draw his readers to the divine fecundity.

Whereas in the speculative tradition the use of language emphasised how all words needed to be negated in the ascent of the intellect up the great chain of being, the affective tradition rooted their confidence in language more explicitly in divine revelation in general, and particularly in the incarnation. If the Word became flesh, if the divine became human, then God became one who used and is expressed in human language. The incarnation thus becomes a validation of language, and allows for confidence and experimentation in human expression. At the same time, the incarnation is the measure of the truth and adequacy of human expression, and sets the standard for critical appraisal of every instance of it, showing the partiality of any words about God, and their potentiality for falsehood and distortion. Here again, we can see that in the male mystical tradition, the use of language was all of a piece with the doctrine of scripture and incarnation as well as of the sacraments. As Jesus both revealed and concealed divinity, so also the words of the scriptures both reveal and conceal the mystery of God, making it necessary to discern the mystical meaning beneath the literal. In the same way, human language both reveals and conceals the divine truth; and the body and blood of Christ is both revealed and concealed in the bread and wine of the eucharist.

It should be abundantly clear from all this that the uses of language and the claims of ineffability in the various strands of the medieval mystical tradition are very different from what contemporary philosophers of religion impute to it in their characterisation of 'mystical experience' as fundamentally ineffable. In a later section of this chapter it will be necessary to ask what is going on in contemporary philosophy which allows such blatant misrepresentation to go undetected, and indeed gives it credibility. I shall suggest that a vital clue is to be found in the other theme that has been running through the preceding chapters, namely the gendered nature of the construction of mysticism. The use of language, and the stress on the ineffability of God, is not immune from such gendering. Indeed, given that it is interwoven with the emphasis on words and the Word, the mystical meaning of scripture, and the understanding of the sacraments, it is inevitable that as those were developed in such a way that women were excluded, so also women would find themselves out of step with the theologies of language underlying much male mystical writing. And it is likewise predictable that as women increasingly found their own voices from the twelfth and thirteenth centuries onward, their use of language would be considerably different from that which the men had developed. Before turning to contemporary philosophical preoccupation with the ineffability of mystical experience, therefore, I wish to sample a few of these differences in women's mystical writings.

II GOD OUR LADY LOVE AND JESUS OUR MOTHER

The recognition on the part of the male mystical tradition that all words applied to God were ultimately inadequate applied also to words like 'son' and 'father', as Dionysius explicitly affirmed. In spite of this, however, and although the characterisation of God could very occasionally be stretched to include female attributes, these were not normally the ones present to consciousness. God is 'Father, Almighty Lord is he'. The masculine is taken as normative throughout the medieval period, and female connotations are suppressed as unworthy of God. Since it was in the higher reason or spirit that the *imago dei* was to be found, the link between God and maleness, and the valorisation of maleness, was given religious legitimation, as also was the denigration of women, who were created to help and serve men.

Though we might wish it were otherwise, it is necessary to recognise that women mystics of the medieval period largely accepted this characterisation. Only rarely did women writers break out of the linguistic conventions which reflected the normativity of maleness, just as they only rarely challenged the assumptions of male superiority in general. Apart from some possible exceptions in those identified with heretical movements, religious women were deeply identified with the patriarchal thought patterns of their times, in which the dominance of males and the lesser nature of women were taken for granted at every level by women as well as by men. If we expect a full-scale challenge to this in women's use of language we shall be disappointed.

Nevertheless, the fact that women in such a climate of thought found the courage and the resources of imagination to develop female imagery at all, and to reconceptualise God from female experience, shows a strong need to push back the boundaries of thought and language to include women in an honoured place. And the fact that these female ways of thinking about God have been largely suppressed in the modern period shows again how gender struggles have consistently formed a part of the changing construction of mysticism.

One of the most fascinating motifs of the Middle Ages in which female language is used for God can be found in the writings of the thirteenth-century religious *Minnesingers*, poets of courtly love. We have already looked at Hadewijch of Antwerp's use of erotic imagery; it is worthwhile to consider again her gendered linguistic usage. Hadewijch and the other *Minnesingers* drew their central imagery from the ideas of late medieval courtly love, in which a knight pledged himself to a – usually inaccessible – lady, and went on arduous adventures to prove his devotion to her. The gentle lady was almost invariably already married, so the knight's devotion required chastity; nevertheless, in his worship of his lady love, faithlessness to her was the worst of all possible moral failures.

There is much written about the secular literary tradition inspired by chivalry and courtly love, which was complex and multi-faceted. It was encouraged by Eleanor of Aquitaine in the twelfth century, to whom troubadour poets wrote their lyrics of happiness and despair; and it found expression in such compositions as *Launcelot* and *Le Roman de la Rose*. It is no great surprise that a literary genre as popular as this should also have found religious expression. What is startling, however, is the way in which women mystical writers used it. In their hands, the genders of the lady love and the adoring and obedient knight remain what they were in the secular courtly love literature. The effect of this, however, is that when it is applied to the relation of God and the

soul, the traditional gendering undergoes a complete reversal:
God is female, the Lady Love, while the soul becomes male, the
ardent knight.

This reversal is facilitated by the fact that in the vernacular
German and Dutch which were the native languages of the
women mystical writers who saw themselves as troubadours for
God, 'love' is a feminine noun and thus requires feminine
pronouns. Thus Hadewijch writes of devotion to God:

> Whoever spares nothing for sublime Love's sake
> Is wise in all his work.
> Love is noble maiden and queen;
> When she gives anyone loftiness of mind,
> He fulfils her every wish
> And does his utmost with strength and forethought,
> So that Love acknowledges his work . . .
>
> But in this it appears she is Love and lady,
> That she is mother of the virtues:
> She is fertile, and she alone bears the fidelity
> From which all you who love are endowed with power.
>
> (1980: 131)

In most medieval writing, the soul is seen as female and passive,
open to the penetration of God who is characterised in terms of
maleness and activity. However, if the reversal Hadewijch introduced were to take hold, so that the soul were seen instead as the
male knight venturing all for his Beloved, and God as the female
analogue of the ideal Lady Love, the scope for theological
reconstruction would be virtually limitless.

Hadewijch explores some of the possibilities. Just as in courtly
love the Lady would at first encourage her knight and then
withdraw, so it seems to Hadewijch that God behaves, alternating
consolation with desolation, divine presence with divine absence.

> Sometimes afire and sometimes cold,
> Sometimes cautious and sometimes reckless,
> Love is full of fickleness.
> Love summons us all
> To pay our great debt
> For her rich power,
> Which she invites us to share.

Sometimes gracious and sometimes fierce,
Sometimes aloof and sometimes close by:
For him who understands this in fidelity to Love
It is a matter for jubilation:
How Love knocks down
And seizes
At one stroke.

Sometimes stooping low and sometimes mounting high,
Sometimes hidden and sometimes revealed:
Before Love cherishes anyone,
He suffers many adventures
Ere he arrives
Where he tastes
The nature of Love

(140)

On the one hand, we have here many of the standard themes which run throughout western medieval mysticism: the sense of both the revelation and the hiddenness of God, the pain and the delight of divine encounter, the necessity of risking all for the spiritual quest. Yet although the themes are not new, they are presented in the radical new form of God the Lady Beloved who is Herself Love.

Again, the troubadours of God found the courtly love metaphor helpful in expressing their bewilderment at the fluctuation of spiritual experience. Many earlier mystical writers had expressed their confusion at how they felt the comfort and delight of the presence of God and then, for no apparent reason, God seemed to withdraw and remain absent. If God is imaged in terms of the Lady Love of courtly romance, however, then this is to be expected. This does not make it easy, and Hadewijch frequently complains bitterly at the absence of Love.

Sweet as Love's nature is,
Where can she come by the strange hatred
With which she continually pursues me
And transpierces the depths of my heart with storm?
I wander in darkness without clarity,
Without liberating consolation, and in strange fear.

(229)

In courtly love, however, the favours of the Lady were notoriously few and unpredictable: that was taken to be the nature of the case, and while it might be painful, it was not something for which the knight need reproach himself. What was absolutely vital, however, was that the knight should do nothing unworthy of his Lady, that he remain faithful to her and refuse to settle for substitutes. Thus Hadewijch, having complained of the bitter torment of the withdrawal and absence of Love, proceeds in a set of striking metaphors:

> But although I have no fish,
> I do not want any frog;
> Or any elderberries either,
> Instead of a bunch of grapes:
> Although I have no love,
> I do not want anything else,
> Whether Love is gracious to me or hostile.

> (335)

For those versed in religious writing, 'fish' and 'grapes' are obvious allusions to Christ and the eucharist; 'frog' and 'elderberry' are deceptive and bitter substitutes to be rejected with revulsion. While the ideas are not new in themselves, a whole new perspective is developed by seeing them as the gifts of divine Love, the Lady who is free to withhold herself or be graciously present.

Another of the significant aspects of the courtly love theme is the emphasis on obedience and courageous acts of mercy and justice. These are what Love requires, as any gentle lady would require of her knight. In the secular literature of courtly love, it was assumed that the knight would do great things for his lady, partly in gratitude for her favour, and partly in hopes of pleasing her again. Similarly, the *Minnesingers* make it clear that the religious life has in it much more of charity and steady obedience than of comfort, and that this is only to be expected. Lovely as are the moments when God's presence is felt, the main business of the lover is to perform the acts designated by the Beloved's charity and justice, thereby being her ambassador and faithful representative. Mechthild of Magdeburg, one of the earliest women to use this genre, wrote,

You must be very active
And free of all things:
You must deliver the captives
And force those who are free.
You must comfort the sick
And yet have nothing for yourself.
You must drink the water of suffering
And light the fire of Love with the good of the virtues.
Thus you live in the true desert.

(Zum Brunn 1989: 60)

The desert, of course, had its own long history of allusion in scripture and tradition, as the place of aridity and temptation, of the bush that burned but was not consumed, and of the visitation of the divine love.

For all the fruitfulness of the female imagery of God as Love in the *Minnesingers*, however, it would not be accurate to represent even the most radical of them as conceptualising God in consistently female terms. For them, too, ultimately the male is normative, and hence God must be thought of as male rather than as female. This is so in spite of the fancy grammatical footwork required to keep track of the pronouns in some of the writing: Love or the Beloved is 'she' but God, who *is* this Love, is still 'he'. A passage from one of Hadewijch's letters illustrates the difficulties by going backwards and forwards from 'the Beloved' (female, she) to 'God' (male, he) while yet intending to convey that the Beloved *is* God. What her reader must do, she says, is

by ardent striving to grow up a loved one in the Beloved in every respect: to work with his hands; to walk with his feet; to hear with his ears where the voice of the Godhead never ceases to speak through the mouth of the Beloved, in all truth of counsel, of justice, of sweet sweetness, of consolation for everyone according to each person's need, and of caution against sin; to appear like the Beloved, unadorned and without beauty, live for no one else but for the Beloved in love alone, live in him as the loved one in the Beloved, with the same way of acting, with one spirit, and with one heart; and in another to taste the unheard-of sweetness he merited by his sufferings. (1980: 118)

In that passage the awkwardness is apparent when we remember that 'Beloved' is grammatically feminine in the original. In many other passages of the *Minnesingers* the problem is eliminated by abandoning female forms altogether and reverting completely to male vocabulary. Mechthild of Magdeburg, for example, has many passages of dialogue between divine love (feminine) and the soul, though unlike some of the other women troubadours, in Mechthild's writing the soul always also remains a lady, and not, as in Hadewijch, a male knight. But when Mechthild writes of the consummation of this love, she uses frankly heterosexual erotic imagery. In chapter 4 I quoted her account of the encounter between Lady Soul and her Deity in which he desired her to be naked. She then breaks into verse:

> Lord, now I am a naked soul,
> And You, in Yourself, a richly adorned God.
> The communion between us
> Is life eternal, stripped of death.
> Now there is blessed silence
> According to their mutual will:
> He gives Himself to her, and she to Him.

> (Zum Brunn 1989: 60)

The language of God as female, as Lady Love, has here been abandoned altogether.

It should be observed that in the courtly love tradition the idealisation of women by the troubadours who offered them their devotion was not unproblematic, either in terms of the exceptional women thus idealised or in terms of the effect on the many ordinary women who were not. This was no less true of its use within the spiritual writings of women. Indeed, in some respects there are parallels with the oppressiveness of the idealisation of Mary as the virgin mother: it is an impossible ideal that nevertheless seemed to justify contempt for real women and domination of them because they did not meet this 'perfect' standard. Yet for all the ambiguity of the religious use of the language of courtly love, it did at least offer the religious imagination female images of God. We need only think of how difficult many in the churches still find it to think of God as 'she' as well as 'he' to recognise how thoroughly those female metaphors and images of God were suppressed, leaving the Christian imagination for several centuries firmly possessed only of male images for God: Lord, King, and above all Father.

There had been alternatives to the idea of God as Father in medieval spiritual writing: a strand of thought developed in which God was also spoken of as Mother. The source of these metaphors is found in biblical writings, and was thus available to those who sought the mystical meaning of scripture or who, like Dionysius, sought out the names of God in the Bible (though significantly this is not one that he mentioned). Isaiah, for instance, speaking of God's care for her people, puts into God's voice the words,

> Can a mother forget her sucking child,
> that she should have no compassion for the son of her
> womb?
> Even these may forget,
> yet I will not forget you.

> (Isaiah 49: 15)

Maternal imagery for God goes back to Genesis, where the Spirit of God hovers over 'the face of the deep' like a hen brooding over her chicks, an image taken up explicitly in Jesus' lament over Jerusalem: 'How often would I have gathered your children together as a hen gathers her brood under her wings, and you would not' (Matt.23: 37). And throughout the Hebrew Bible there is a recognition of the Spirit as female, the *shekinah* presence, a recognition continued especially in the Wisdom literature we considered in chapter 3, where, in Greek, Wisdom is *Sophia* and in Hebrew *Hochma*. It was only in the Latin west that the Holy Spirit became masculine as the *Spiritus Sanctus*.

In spite of the dominance of Latin in the west, some medieval writers took up maternal imagery in their theology. The church was invariably female, the 'Holy Mother Church', haven for souls. Monastic writing, particularly Cistercian, saw the role of the abbot in maternal terms, romanticising the aspects of maternal tenderness and nurturing (Bynum 1982: 110). Some writers were prepared to go further than this, meditating after the manner of seeking the mystical meaning of the maternal names and images of God in the scriptures. Anselm of Bec, in the twelfth century, wrote a 'Prayer to St Paul' which shows the fruitfulness of such meditation:

And you, Jesus, are you not also a mother?
Are you not the mother who, like a hen,
gathers her chickens under her wings?
Truly, Lord, you are a mother;
for both they who are in labour
and they who are brought forth
are accepted by you.
You have died more than they, that they may labour to
    bear.
For if you had not been in labour,
you could not have borne death;
and if you had not died, you would not have brought forth.
For, longing to bear sons into life,
you tasted of death
and by dying you begot them ...
And you, my soul, dead in yourself,
run under the wings of Jesus your mother
and lament your griefs under his feathers.
Ask that your wounds may be healed
and that, comforted, you may live again ...
Mother, know your dead son [Anselm],
both by the sign of your cross and the voice of his
    confession.
Warm your chicken, give life to your dead man,
justify your sinner.
Let your terrified one be consoled by you;
and in your whole and unceasing grace
let him be refashioned by you.

(1973: 153–6)

Anselm's imagery of divine motherhood is not everything that modern feminists might wish, burdened as it is with sentimental stereotypes of the sacrificial mother suffering pain and death in labour for her child, and being unfailingly gentle and nurturing; but at least there is here a sustained alternative to the dominant theme of the male God Father.

Some of these sentimental stereotypes were overcome by women spiritual writers who used maternal imagery for God. Gertrude the Great of Helfta, for example, used both paternal and maternal metaphors to refer to God; and whereas paternal metaphors are sometimes tender, maternal metaphors can express not only tenderness but also much tougher testing. In one

passage, she compares God to a mother who has her well-clothed
elder daughter sit near her at her feet, but the smaller child who
is naked she takes on her lap, wraps her own clothes around it,
and warms and cradles it in her arms (1989a: 445). On another
occasion, God speaks of herself as a mother teaching her daughter
to do needlework: although at first the mother holds and guides
her daughter's hand, eventually the daughter is skilled enough to
do it by herself (236). However, Gertrude also speaks of a mother
as stern, testing the child and sometimes disciplining it: a mother
is not necessarily always tender and comforting. On one occasion
she even, rather disconcertingly, speaks of Christ as a mother who
puts on terrifying masks to frighten the young child back into her
arms.

An interesting feature of the way in which Gertrude and other
women spiritual writers use imagery is that it does not necessarily
come from the Bible. Their writing arises out of their own visionary
experience; and consequently the language they use of God is not
rooted in the study of the mystical meaning of scripture, as we find
in male writers. This means that they have a far wider range of
possibilities, especially for female imagery; and they use it to the
full, especially as they discover the possibilities in using maternal
imagery for God. On the other hand, they also use a wide range of
male imagery; and quite unselfconsciously pass from one to
another, crossing traditional gender lines for God and for themselves. Thus for instance both Gertrude and her friend Mechthild
of Hackeborn use both mothering and fathering images for God;
and as Caroline Bynum points out, in their writings 'fathers feed
and console, as do mothers; mothers teach, as do fathers: the full
range of such images applies both to God and to self. God is
mother, emperor and pope; Mary is mother and queen; Mechthild
herself is a prince leading an army, a preacher, a conduit for grace,
a parent to her [spiritual] children' (1982: 226). Most of this
imagery was suppressed in the late medieval and early modern
period, so that the richness of language which these women used as
a matter of course was no longer available to Christian women and
men through most of the modern period. In the light of what we
have already seen, it is stretching credulity to suppose that this
suppression was accidental.

Some women writers retained the same emphasis that we find in Anselm on the labour pains of Christ the mother, continuing the notion of maternal sacrifice: Marguerite of Oingt (died 1310) drew a parallel between the sacrifice of Mother Jesus and the sacrifice Marguerite herself had made for Christ:

My sweet Lord, I gave up for you my father and mother and my brothers and all the wealth of the world ... For are you not my mother and more than my mother? The mother who bore me laboured in delivering me for one day or one night but you, my sweet and lovely Lord, laboured for me for more than thirty years. Oh, my sweet and lovely Lord, with what love you laboured for me and bore me through your whole life. But when the time approached for you to be delivered, your labour pains were so great that your holy sweat was like great drops of blood that came out from your body and fell on the earth ... Ah! Sweet Lord Jesus Christ, who ever saw a mother suffer such a birth! For when the hour of your delivery came you were placed on the hard bed of the cross ... and your nerves and all your veins were broken. And truly it is no surprise that your veins burst when in one day you gave birth to the whole world. (Bynum 1982: 153)

The imagery of Jesus as mother giving birth on the cross was sometimes altered to the imagery of Mary giving birth to Jesus; and this in turn became the basis for reflection about spirituality expressed in terms of 'giving birth to God in the soul'. We find such imagery in Eckhart, for example, and other male writers. But perhaps the most sustained meditation on this theme comes once again from Hadewijch, who in her poem 'Allegory of Love's Growth' speaks of the conception of Love in the soul, and then the growth of Love through the nine-month period of gestation, until finally the soul gives birth to Love (God). Each month has a different characteristic: faithful fear, joyful suffering, sweetness, confidence, justice, wisdom, and so on. Finally the day arrives when she can say,

Now is born full-grown this Child
Who was chosen by humility,
And carried to term nine months.
And each month has four weeks,
And each calls for preparation and adornment
Before the great high day,
So that Love can be born perfect ...

One could look long and hard in male spiritual writers without finding a comparable passage.

No one, however, male or female, made so thorough a theology out of the theme of God as Mother as did Julian of Norwich in the fourteenth century. For other writers, maternal imagery had been at best a creative sub-theme, subordinate in their writings to dominant male imagery for God. With Julian, however, the theme of God as mother was central to her theology; it is far more than merely a variant figure of speech. Furthermore, she managed to combine the themes of Jesus' sacrificial motherhood with other aspects of maternal care in a way that makes the whole less stereotyped and more in touch with what women actually experience.

Julian is clear that 'as truly as God is our Father, so truly is God our Mother' (1978: 295). She is also quietly insistent that there is at least as rich a theological understanding to be gained from the latter as from the former.

I understand three ways of contemplating motherhood in God. The first is the foundation of our nature's creation; the second is his taking of our nature, where the motherhood of grace begins; the third is the motherhood at work. (297)

Julian consistently sees the creation of the world, and particularly of human beings, as a maternal act. She does not explicitly refer to the Genesis passage where the divine Spirit broods over the chaos of the unformed world; but it is hard to believe that it was not in her mind when she wrote about the maternal creator God.

And so, in our making, God Almighty is our loving Father, and God all wisdom is our loving Mother, with the love and the goodness of the Holy Spirit, which is all one God, one Lord. (293)

As noted in a previous chapter, Julian thought of human nature as having the two aspects of substance and sensuality which must be integrated in mature spirituality. Human sensuality was what the second person of the Trinity took on in becoming flesh; therefore in Julian's view, Jesus can be seen as Mother in both aspects of creation, sensuality as well as substance: 'the second person of the Trinity is our Mother in nature in our substantial creation, in whom we are founded and rooted, and he is our Mother of mercy in taking our sensuality' (294).

This 'motherhood of grace' is carried on, in Julian's thinking, in Jesus' labour for humanity in his life and death.

We know that all our mothers bear us for pain and for death. O, what is that? But our true Mother Jesus, he alone bears us for joy and for endless life, blessed may he be. So he carries us within him in love and travail, until the full time when he wanted to suffer the sharpest thorns and cruel pains that ever were or will be, and at last he died. And when he had finished, and had borne us for bliss, still all this could not satisfy his wonderful love ... therefore he must needs nourish us, for the precious love of motherhood has made him our debtor. (298)

Julian then proceeds to meditate on the eucharist as 'Mother Jesus feeding us with himself', as a mother suckles her child; and the kind and tender protection of Jesus as a mother for her children. The shifting back and forth between masculine and feminine pronouns does not seem to concern Julian in the least.

Although Julian discusses the self-sacrifice of Jesus as Mother in ways reminiscent of Marguerite of Oignt, her meditation does not revolve solely around this, but also reflects on how Jesus' mothering works for the reintegration of humanity.

And so our Mother is working on us in various ways, in whom our parts are kept undivided; for in our Mother Christ we profit and increase, and in mercy he reforms and restores us, and by the power of his Passion, his death and his Resurrection he unites us to our substance. (294)

Furthermore, although the intentions of Mother Jesus toward his children are all good, so that they will not ultimately be allowed to come to harm, nevertheless no child learns to walk without being allowed to suffer and stumble and sometimes fall 'heavily and grievously', or grows up without sometimes becoming filthy and wretched. Thus Mother Jesus allows these woes and pains and terrors, being stern in order to be kind.

To the property of motherhood belong nature, love, wisdom and knowledge, and this is God ... The kind, loving mother who knows and sees the need of her child guards it very tenderly, as the nature and condition of motherhood will have. And always as the child grows in age and stature, she acts differently, but she does not change her love. And when it is even older, she allows it to be chastised to destroy its faults, so as to make the child receive virtues and grace ... So he is our Mother in nature by the operation of grace in the lower part, for love of the higher part. (299)

This is the 'motherhood at work', the third aspect of divine motherhood which, with the motherhood of creation and the motherhood of the passion completes Julian's theology of God as Mother: creator, redeemer, sanctifier.

Julian's teaching on God as mother is in many respects as traditional an orthodoxy as the ecclesiastical hierarchy could have hoped to find. In her hands, the metaphor was capable of being transformed into a theological pattern quite compatible with the usual constellation of ideas surrounding the metaphor of God as Father; and there is no reason to suppose that she intended anything else. If the church had retained and explored both sets of metaphors, they would have given a balance of nuance and allusion, and in particular could have served as a reminder that both are indeed intended as *metaphor*, not as literal descriptions of the gender of God. Yet, to the great impoverishment of Christianity, Julian's metaphors were suppressed to such an extent that the metaphor of God as mother was almost wholly lost while the metaphor of God as father was developed without check, so that the modern feminist challenge to its one-sidedness has caused bewilderment and outrage.

Not only was an important way of thinking about God lost in this suppression, but also an important affirmation of women: if God can be thought of as Mother and in female terms, then mothering, and femaleness, can be thought of as god-like. The *imago dei* need not be seen to reside wholly in the mind, but the gendered body, too, can be integrated into godliness. Had this line of thought been carried forward, there would have been possible a significant reclaiming of spirituality by and for women. Exactly how the suppression took place is not clear, nor is it clear to what extent it was a deliberate or even conscious suppression of female imagery: simply, Julian's work was not widely circulated in manuscript nor was it given prominence or taken up seriously for centuries after her death. There is at present more interest in

Julian than there has ever been: in the past, she remained at best marginal, and so, therefore, did the maternal imagery for God which she developed.

The metaphor of divine motherhood is of course not without ambiguities from a feminist perspective, especially because of the sentimental ideals of motherhood perpetrated especially by male writers like Bernard and Anselm, but also to some extent by women like Marguerite of Oingt and Julian, as we have seen. This could have been more readily balanced and corrected if the other female imagery for God had also been retained: metaphors of a female God the healer, God the needle-worker, God the Lady Love, and so on that were used by the women writers we have been considering. There are after all dozens of male metaphors for God in addition to the metaphor of God as father: there is God as king, as lord and master, and as warrior, to take only a few; and even metaphors like teacher, physician, master-builder, and judge which theoretically could be gender inclusive are regularly understood as implying the masculine when applied to God. All of these are taken as showing the richness of God: yet the additional richness which would have been made available by retaining the female imagery along with the male was largely lost, in a loss that can hardly be construed as innocent. As women were increasingly suppressed and the mystical was delimited in ways which excluded women in the late medieval and early modern period, female metaphors and images for God were not acceptable to those who exercised the power to define who should count as a mystic.

III THE TOOLS OF INARTICULACY

Two things have emerged very clearly from the chapter so far: first, the medieval mystical writers of the Christian tradition used language with great fecundity and versatility, and if they claimed ineffability at all, it was the ineffability of *God* that they were speaking of, not the ineffability of a subjective experience. Second, the language they used was not gender neutral: although some writers, especially but not only women, developed female imagery for God, it was increasingly suppressed as the Middle

Ages waned and the early modern period began, while male-dominated imagery was retained as standard. Both these things need to be kept in mind as we ponder the frequently made claim of contemporary philosophers of religion that mystical experience is ineffable. Since this claim seems contrary to obvious evidence, it is worth asking why it is so frequently made: why, both in terms of the arguments in support of it, and why, also, in terms of what is at stake for contemporary philosophers such that they unhesitatingly accept this claim, often without so much as looking at the evidence? Might it be the case that here is yet another social construction of mysticism? And might it be the case that it is no less innocent of issues of power and gender than other historical constructions have been?

William James' work on mysticism is commonly taken as an authoritative and well-researched basis grounding modern philosophical discussion. Unlike many subsequent writers on mysticism who accepted James' characterisation, James himself tried to present his philosophical discussion as anchored in the lives and writings of actual mystics. In *The Varieties of Religious Experience* he seems to display a breadth of acquaintance with primary sources, quoting liberally to illustrate his arguments: this was part of his avowed empiricist stance.

Unfortunately, however, the documentation is not as sound as it at first appears. A revealing clue to this is that in his citation of primary sources, relatively brief quotations are frequently made to stand on their own: James did not pay attention to the literary contexts from which they were drawn, let alone to the historical and social conditions out of which they arose. When these are considered more carefully, we often find that James' interpretations are doubtful. To give only one example among many, James cites a passage from the Islamic mystic Al-Ghazali and one from John of the Cross to show that 'the incommunicableness of the transport is the keynote of all mysticism' (1960: 391). Now, whatever the views of Al-Ghazali, it is certain that this is a very superficial reading of John of the Cross, who has a carefully nuanced philosophy of language along Thomistic lines, and who is able to move from the genre of erotic poetry to that of scholastic commentary to convey his meanings with precision.

Even with our suspicions thus aroused, however, it comes as something of a shock to discover that James did not actually spend much time reading the mystical writers himself, but rather culled almost all of his quotations from a compilation of short extracts put together by his friend and former student, R. Starbuck, without any reference to their literary or historical context (Perry 1935: II). It is therefore little wonder that when philosophers depend almost exclusively on James rather than going back to primary sources in discussion of mysticism, they are likely to find themselves mired in misrepresentation.

According to James, ineffability is the first and most clear-cut characteristic of mysticism; and he elaborates his claim by saying,

The handiest of the marks by which I classify a state of mind as mystical is negative. The subject of it immediately says that it defies expression, that no adequate report of its contents can be given in words ... In this peculiarity mystical states are more like states of feeling than like states of intellect. (1960: 367)

Thus right at the beginning, James identifies the mystical with subjective states of feeling, an identification which as we have seen begs serious questions. Furthermore, these subjective states, he says, are ineffable. They cannot be put into words, and can only be directly experienced. We will need to look carefully at the reasons why he makes this claim.

Even though James saw ineffability as the first characteristic of mystical experience, he was impressed by the striking and vivid language prominent in mystical literature. He focused particularly on the frequency of paradox and apparent self-contradiction in the metaphors used. Mystical writing is likened to musical composition, and is contrasted with conceptual speech.

In mystical literature such self-contradictory phrases as 'dazzling obscurity', 'whispering silence', 'teeming desert', are continually met with. They prove that not conceptual speech, but music rather, is the element through which we are best spoken to by mystical truth. (405)

James is willing to use the term 'mystical truth' even though it is central to his case that this 'truth' is unconceptualisable and ineffable. He allows that 'music gives us ontological messages which non-musical criticism is unable to contradict' (406), but he

does not (and indeed given his principles presumably he *could* not)
comment on what those ontological messages might be.

Imitating the mystics' use of evocative language, James writes
of the paradoxes encountered in mystical literature:

There is a *verge of the mind* which these things haunt; and whispers
therefrom mingle with the operations of our understanding, even as the
waters of the infinite ocean send their waves to break among the pebbles
that lie upon our shores. (406, my emphasis)

The implication is that the metaphors and paradoxes of mystical
writings are the best the mystics can do to render into language
the intensity of their essential ineffable and incommunicable
experiences; and although we cannot form a *conceptual* understanding of their content, the language appeals to our feelings and
emotions in such a way as to evoke resonances in us. Although
they are not conceptual, they may deepen our sensitivity, and
influence for good the attitudes with which we think.

Now, quite apart from the historically irresponsible romanticising of mystical experience in which James is here indulging,
there are major problems with his analogy between music and
'mystical truth'. These come to the fore when we look more
closely at the important Jamesian theme of the 'verge of the
mind', the fringe of consciousness which he takes to be the point
at which encounter with transcendence could take place if it can
take place at all. Understanding the sources from which James
derives this idea, so modern, and so different from what we have
seen the various protagonists of the Christian medieval mystical
tradition to have held, takes us a good deal further in seeing how
the modern conception of mysticism as ineffable is yet another
social construction.

The idea of the 'verge of the mind' arises in James because by
and large he accepts, first, the Kantian view that our normal
consciousness cannot encounter God, and second, the Romantic
idea that this impossibility can be circumvented in feeling, and in
particular in intense or unusual emotion. Thus James sees in
strange visionary or ecstatic experiences at the fringe of the
psyche the possibility of evading the strictures of normal consciousness as understood by post-Enlightenment philosophers.

According to Kant, all knowledge comes to us by experience. However, since the experience of any object is always *our* experience, rather than the pure grasp of the object, all experience must be shaped by the structure of our minds and the categories of our thinking which are as it were built into us simply in virtue of our being human, rational beings. We never get to any uninterpreted given. Anything as it is in itself, independent of our apprehension of it, is necessarily not something which we can experience. Consequently, for anything that we do experience, our subjectivity is indelibly stamped upon it. We are restricted to the phenomena. The noumenal, as Kant called the world as it is in itself, is beyond our grasp. Furthermore, according to Kant religious beliefs and metaphysical speculation arise from the misguided attempt to extend the categories of judgement that derive from our subjectivity, which can only legitimately apply to the contents of our experience, beyond the bounds of sense.

Kant did not deny the existence of God; but he did deny that we could possibly acquire any knowledge of God through theoretical reason. Nor, in his view, would reason ever be able to assess the claims of revelation, since there is literally nothing available against which to test them. Nor did Kant believe that the existence of God could be proved: indeed, Kant offered refutations of all the traditional proofs for the existence of God. Nevertheless, Kant did believe that the concept of God serves as a regulative idea for human morality.

Important as this regulative idea was for Kant's system, however, he coupled it with a rejection of the very possibility of experience of God. God is by definition not available to sense perception; Kant accepted that God in Christian teaching is pure spirit. However, we have access to no other source of knowledge besides sense perception. Supposed experience of God is therefore nothing but a projection of our own thoughts and feelings on to a spurious metaphysical plane (1929: A631–A704). It is a 'self-deception prejudicial to religion' to suppose that we are capable of any 'feeling of the immediate presence of the Supreme Being'; we simply do not have the mental equipment for such experience (1960: 162).

Furthermore, to suppose that we *could* somehow experience

God would be to misunderstand the very meaning of the term. 'God' is to be understood, not as defining an object for us, but as *ens realissimum*, that is, 'a transcendental *ideal* which serves as a basis for the complete determination that necessarily belongs to all that exists' (1929: A576). This can be employed as a method for conceptualising all reality; but it is illegitimate to move from this conceptual ideal to supposing that there really exists an individual being called 'God' who corresponds to this ideal (A580). The temptation first to think of the ideal as the most real existing object, and then to personify it by bestowing on it intelligence and self-consciousness, is one which, if not resisted, would lead us 'into an intellectual fraud whereby we attribute objective reality to an Idea that functions only as a rule' (A509). But if God cannot be thought of as an object at all, but rather as a regulative Ideal, then clearly God cannot be a being or person who can be *experienced*. The whole notion of personal experience of God is thus misguided from the beginning (Cassirer 1981: 207–217).

Now, James, like almost everyone else in the nineteenth century, accepted the Kantian idea that our knowledge is structured by categories imposed on experience by our minds. This means that James would have had to agree that human beings cannot experience God or the transcendent. Nevertheless, he held that Kant was mistaken in thinking that we could have no glimpse of a supernatural realm. Just as our senses are able to perceive material things via ordinary consciousness, so perhaps the margins of our consciousness or our subconscious minds might be the point at which 'higher spiritual agencies', if there are any, could directly touch us (James 1950: 1.62; Bird 1986: 176). It was no doubt partly for this reason that James was particularly interested in the fringes of consciousness: psychic phenomena, hallucinations, the effects of nitrous oxide and intoxication, and intense or bizarre accounts of religious experience including visions, trances, levitations, seizures, hallucinations, and the like. He was himself a religious believer, though hardly an orthodox Christian; and he believed that 'the evidence for God lies primarily in inner personal experiences' (James 1907: 109).

To the extent that James really did accept Kant's view, his position here would be untenable. It is misguided to suppose that although Kant's categories apply to all normal thinking, odd or 'fringe' consciousness could manage to escape them. It is as though James visualises our minds as plates just slightly larger than the grid of Kant's categories, so that at the extreme edges a tiny bit of our psyche manages not to be covered by them, and so can experience something of the noumenal after all. But such a picture is highly misleading. Quite apart from the fact that it ignores Kant's understanding of God not as a possible object but as a regulative ideal, it also ignores the fact that if Kant's epistemology is correct, then *all* our experiences are *necessarily* formed by the categories supplied by our own minds. This is what it is to have any sort of experience: consequently it is misguided to suppose that some – perhaps the most psychically odd – could escape such formation. The categories are after all a contribution imposed by our own mental structure; they are not foisted upon us from without. Therefore if, in Kant's terms, they form part of the very fabric of our thinking, then we cannot hope that religious or any other 'fringe' experiences can fall outside of their weft.

James was, of course, well acquainted with Kant; but he was also deeply influenced by the German Romantics who tried to offer an alternative picture. James had grown up in a household in which theological and philosophical issues were a regular part of meal-time conversation. His father, Henry James Sr, was a Swedenborgian who spent much of his time and effort lecturing and writing books expressing his rather eccentric viewpoint. William James did not find his father's religious position satisfactory for himself, but he respected it, especially the inner experience that informed it, even if not the written accounts of it which the elder James produced. A wide circle of Henry James' friends made an impact on the family, among them Emerson and Carlyle, who have been described as 'familiar divinities in the James household' with whom both father and son must settle their account (Perry 1935: 1.140). Through Emerson and Carlyle, the Jameses made deeper acquaintance with Romantic philosophy, both in the English version of Coleridge and in the German tradition of Goethe, Schelling, Schiller and others. Besides this acquaintance via his father, William James developed an intimate knowledge of Romanticism in his own right. Part of his education took place in Europe where he was a regular visitor; he was fluent in German, and widely read in German philosophical literature. Thus when James considers religious experience, and particularly mysticism, his discussion must be seen to be influenced by both the empiricist and the Romantic traditions. I suggest that while his empiricism is widely recognised, his Romanticism has been insufficiently noticed; and that it was a key ingredient in the formation of his understanding of mysticism, especially with regard to ineffability.

We can see this best by looking at the work of Friedrich Schleiermacher. He, like other Romantics, reacted against what they saw as the excessive formalism and intellectualism of the critical philosophy of Kant and his successors, and, like them, turned his attention not simply to thought but to feeling and intuition. Schleiermacher examined afresh the phenomenon of religious consciousness, thereby reopening doors which Kant thought he had slammed shut. As we saw, Kant had taught that experience of God is impossible, firstly because we can never get beyond the phenomena of experience to reality as it is in itself, and secondly because the term 'God' can in any case only stand for a regulative idea, not a possible object of experience. But if, as the Idealists had argued, the subject–object distinction can be grounded and thus transcended in an Absolute identity, and the Absolute knows itself through human consciousness, then a new examination of that consciousness, particularly of its religious dimension, is required.

Schleiermacher attempted to give such an examination. He sought to give an account of religion from within, appealing to feeling and intuition rather than to any external source, such as scripture or tradition. Scholars disagree about the extent to which Schleiermacher's account of feeling derives from acceptance of Kantian strictures and to what extent it is simply the application of Romantic concepts to religion. In either case, his account of religion and his explicit use of the vocabulary of inward experience set the stage for the modern understanding of what mysticism is and how it should be studied (Brandt 1968; Proudfoot 1985; Reardon 1985).

In his famous *Speeches on Religion to its Cultured Despisers* Schleiermacher repudiated the identification of religion with either doctrine or morality. It is rather, he says, a fundamental part of human nature, springing from the depths of the self: neither knowledge nor activity, but feeling. 'The true nature of religon is ... immediate consciousness of the Deity as he is found in ourselves and in the world' (1958: 101). Religion is 'to have life and to know life in immediate feeling, only as such an existence in the Infinite and Eternal ... it is an affection, a revelation of the Infinite in the finite, God being seen in it and it in God' (36).

It is worth asking what Schleiermacher meant by this notion of immediate feeling or consciousness. In the context of the philosophy of Idealism of his time, it need not be interpreted simply as subjectivity, as contrasted with the objective content of experience. Rather, immediate consciousness points to the stage before subject and object are differentiated. There is, Schleiermacher suggests, a primal stage of consciousness in any experience, a stage before the objective content is discriminated from the subjective participation. This consciousness cannot be consciousness *of* anything, it cannot have any specificity, because by the time the object of consciousness has been specified one has already moved away from the primal undifferentiated state. Such movement is of course necessary for thought or knowledge to take place: in this Schleiermacher agrees with Kant. But the truly religious moment is the moment before such differentiation into subject and object has taken place: this is what he means when he speaks of religion as immediate consciousness.

Because we are thinking beings, the process of objectifying begins virtually at once, and we may not even be aware of the primal religious moment. If we try to reflect on it, it vanishes; it is like turning round quickly to try to see the back of one's head. Nevertheless the primal moment can be sensed or felt, even if indirectly. It is the business of piety to rediscover this essential experience, this 'original though fleeting unity or identity of subject and object' (Reardon 1985: 35). Schleiermacher argues that it is only in one's innermost self that one can discover 'the original relation of intuition and feeling from which alone this identity and difference can be understood', and continues,

You must know how to listen to yourselves before your own consciousness. At least you must be able to reconstruct from your
consciousness your own state. What you are to notice is the rise of
your consciousness and not to reflect on something already there. Your
thought can only embrace what is sundered. Wherefore as soon as you
have made any given definite activity of your soul an object of communication or contemplation, you have already begun to separate. (1958: 41)

Because this is the case, any claim of religious belief or knowledge is secondary to this pure experience, and is nothing more
than our stammering attempt to articulate its essence. The
attempt is natural and right; but it is not right if we then become
wedded to these articulations and make them into dogmas which
must be believed, or, even worse, treat them, rather than the
spring from which they arise, as the essence of religion.

Whence do these dogmas and doctrines come that many consider to be
the essence of religion? ... They are all the result of that contemplation
of feeling, of that reflection and comparison, of which we have already
spoken. The conceptions that underlie these propositions are ...
nothing but general expressions for divine feelings. They are not
necessary for religion itself, scarcely even for communicating religion,
but reflection requires and creates them. (87)

The original feeling, the immediate consciousness, Schleiermacher holds to be essential to human nature, as we have seen, and
according to Schleiermacher this is everywhere the same; but the
way in which it is articulated varies with the language and culture
and situation of the experiencer. Hence arise the different
religions of the world. Their differences of dogma and ritual are
simply different expressions of the same essential experience,
more or less adequate according to the degree of authenticity,
balance, or corruption of its proponents, but all of them only
efforts at expressing the inexpressible pure experience (Jantzen
1990; Williams 1978).

This account of Schleiermacher's is not without grave problems. It is, for instance, far from clear that his understanding of
pure pre-interpretative experience in which subject and object
are united is a coherent one (Katz 1978; Proudfoot 1985); and if it
is not, then the idea of a pre-doctrinal core lacks the foundation
he sought to give it: in another context, this would require careful

investigation. What is important for present purposes, however, is the way in which Schleiermacher's *Speeches* both illustrate and continue the modern subjectivist meanings of the term 'mysticism'. Schleiermacher called himself a mystic, and conceived of his account of religion as essentially mystical (Brandt 1968: 95–104). In this he took up and carried forward the notion as it was used in Romanticism generally; and, although there is no reason to suppose that he ever consciously set out to redefine the term, his work had the effect of setting the parameters for subsequent thought about mysticism and religious experience. By retracing the central features of his concept of religion, therefore, we are presented with some of the key ingredients to modern understanding of mysticism, even though for Schleiermacher himself these are explicitly about the essence of religion and only by implication about mysticism. What is immediately apparent is the striking resemblance between these ingredients and William James' characterisation of mysticism, though James never refers to Schleiermacher in his discussion of it.

In the first place, religion according to Schleiermacher is, as we have already seen, essentially experiential, and at a level preceding intellectual construction. It is not therefore a question of penetrating to the objective significance of scripture or sacrament, as it was for the fathers, but rather of becoming more deeply in touch with the state of one's innermost being, finding in feeling the immediate consciousness of God. Even to call it 'God', however, already imposes interpretation on the essential experience, which is pre-rational and to which rational doctrinal accounts are therefore secondary. Thus the first characteristic of mysticism deriving from Schleiermacher's account of religion is that it consists of *pre-rational immediate consciousness* or feeling.

Secondly, this immediate consciousness is one in which there is as yet *no distinction between subject and object*. That distinction comes about only when rational considerations are applied. The mystical experience itself is therefore the experience of complete unity with the Infinite in immediate consciousness.

The third characteristic follows directly from this. Because mystical or religious experience is pre-rational, it is also pre-linguistic. As soon as it is put into words, it is objectified, and thus becomes something other than the immediate experience in which subject and object are completely unified. Accordingly, mystical experience is of its very nature *ineffable*. Although we struggle to express it, any expression is a severing of the subject–object unity, and is to that extent a falsification.

Fourthly, just as there is no object separated out in the immediacy of the experience, so also there is no subject. In this sense one could say that the subject or self is annihilated. The self or subject is completely *absorbed*, just as the object is, in the complete unification of immediate experience. The self is lost in the Infinite, merged with it in a unity preceding discursive thought.

Because of the sort of beings we are, however, Schleiermacher holds that we cannot sustain this state of immediate consciousness, but pass over quickly to reflection upon it, thereby severing the unity of subject and object. Thus the experience itself is *transient*, and gives way to the objectifying activity of the intellect. Furthermore, Schleiermacher held that this experience or immediate consciousness is not something we create. We are *passive* in relation to it. It is in some sense a given of our innermost being; we can discover it, but we cannot create it. Our part is to try to strip away the layers of intellectual sophistication or cultural presupposition which keeps us from awareness of this immediate consciousness, and to foster our receptivity to its emotional dimensions. We will then discover it within ourselves; but it is not of our own making.

In spite of the fact that the experience is pre-rational and ineffable, however, Schleiermacher also held that it has a *noetic quality*. That is, it is not reducible to a subjective psychological state without remainder, but makes reference to objective reality beyond the individual. In the experience itself, this reality is in some sense apprehended, even though it cannot be put into words. There has been much debate about whether this aspect of Schleiermacher's thought is consistent with his other claims, since it would seem on the one hand that only what is believed to be true (and thus has a noetic dimension) could arouse religious feelings (Brandt 1968: 110–30), and yet on the other hand Schleiermacher's situating of religion in the subjectivity of immediate consciousness appears not to allow for the possibility of objective knowledge (Proudfoot 1985: 32–40).

When we see the relationship of Schleiermacher's programme to that of the Idealists, however, we can see that his account of religion in terms of immediate consciousness is not intended as mere psychologising or subjectivising of religion. Rather, it is an effort to understand Reality, conceived of as the Absolute Identity prior to the subject–object differentiation, by way of an exploration of the subjective consciousness with particular reference to its religious dimension. Accordingly, for Schleiermacher himself the noetic quality is an indispensible characteristic of mystical experience.

With Schleiermacher's younger contemporary Schelling, however, the notion of mystical consciousness was moved further toward subjective psychology. While the immediate consciousness of which Schleiermacher speaks is *pre-rational*, with Schelling mystical experience is characterised as *non-rational*. Schelling says,

Mysticism has always been distinguished in contrast with rationalism ... Only that tendency of the mind can be called mysticism, which scorns all scientific foundation or analysis and wishes to derive all true knowledge from a so-called inner Light, from an immediate revelation, from a merely ecstatic intuition or a mere emotion ... (1860: x.192)

Schelling goes on to repeat that the mystical is that which is declared 'on the basis of a merely subjective emotion' even though it is not scientifically understood.

From this it might be thought that Schelling would be opposed to mysticism as he understood it. However, the opposite is the case. He was much influenced by the sixteenth-century mystic Jacob Boehme, and explicitly aligned himself with 'the mystics and religious temperaments of all ages' who found their wisdom in direct encounter with God rather than through philosophical speculation (Gutmann 1936: xxv). He asserts, furthermore, that mystics throughout the Middle Ages had actually *achieved* the union with God, transcending subject and object distinctions which Idealist philosophy was only now coming to recognise as fundamental (1860: ii.119). Thus Schelling, in common with Romantic thinking, found the essence of mysticism in feeling, and saw it as an *experience* of union as contrasted with a process of rationality.

Before turning to a consideration of the way in which this construction of mysticism is intertwined with modern definitions of gender, it is instructive to underline how radically the word has shifted in meaning since patristic times. Instead of referring to the central, if hidden, reality of scripture or sacrament, the idea of 'mysticism' has been subjectivised beyond recognition, so that it is thought of in terms of states of consciousness or feeling. Whether or not twentieth-century writers on mysticism would subscribe to the letter of Idealist or Romantic epistemology, or are even aware of the debt which they owe to it, the spirit of subjectivisation and with it a psychologising of mysticism rests upon them.

Thus, for example, this emphasis can be discerned clearly in the early writings of Evelyn Underhill. In her book *The Mystic Way* she states that the 'Way' consists in a 'sequence of psychological states ... attested by countless mystics of every period and creed' (1929: viii). Her vastly influential book *Mysticism*, first published in 1911 and in its twelfth edition by 1930, was actually subtitled *A Study in the Nature and Development of Man's Mystical Consciousness*. In justice it should be pointed out that by the time she wrote the preface to the 1930 edition of *Mysticism* she was dissatisfied with this psychologising emphasis, and said that if she were to do it again she would among other things pay more attention to the objective 'richly living yet unchanging character of the Reality over against the mystic' (1930: viii). But she did *not* rewrite it, and the popularity of the book helped to reinforce the appeal of the psychological approach to mysticism in contemporary thought (Underhill 1943: 17). It is precisely because mysticism is now understood in terms of a private state of consciousness that the notion of its ineffability can get a purchase.

We should notice that this approach also means that mysticism now designates a difference in kind, not merely in degree. A person who has these psychological states is a mystic; a person who does not, is not. Furthermore these states are no longer necessarily particular to Christianity. In Schleiermacher, the immediate religious consciousness is essential to humanity, and these states are therefore experienced by people in all religions (this is clearly also Evelyn Underhill's view in *The Mystic Way*). This is how it becomes possible for the question to arise whether perhaps they could be induced by such things as ascetical practices, breathing techniques, or even taking drugs: such a question would not have been thinkable for the constructions of mysticism of early and medieval Christianity, and is directly parasitic on the modern subjectivised understanding.

Again, it is significant that the *Oxford English Dictionary* now concentrates largely on subjective psychology in its first definition of mysticism:

The opinions, mental tendencies, or habits of thought and feeling, characteristic of mystics; mystical doctrines or spirit; belief in the possibility of union with the Divine nature by means of ecstatic contemplation; reliance on spiritual intuition or exalted feeling as the means of acquiring knowledge of mysteries inaccessible to intellectual apprehension.

Not only does this modern definition concentrate on the psychological state of the experiencer rather than on the objective content of the experience it also gives, as we have seen, an indication of what these psychological states are like. In this respect by far the most significant change in the modern usage from that of the patristic is the shift from the intellect to the feelings: mystics are said to rely on 'spiritual intuition or exalted feelings' rather than 'intellectual apprehension'. As the early fathers used the term, discovery of the mystical meaning of scripture involved the full engagement of the intellect, though before Bernard they would not have understood the intellect to be unfeeling in the way that modern writers often do; and although this was taken up differently in the speculative than in the affective strand, and differently again by visionary women, none of them would have been content to locate the mystical in ineffable states of feeling, as we have seen. The distinction between intellectual apprehension and exalted feeling would therefore not be part of their teaching, and in mystical knowledge the two could never have been separated.

By contrast, modern subjectivist thinking about mysticism concentrates on the states of feeling to the exclusion of the intellect, sometimes going well beyond the Idealists and even the Romantics in open avowals of anti-intellectualism, sometimes simply seeking to 'transcend' reason in a merging of subject and object. Thus Margaret Smith, in her account of mysticism, says,

It is to be described ... as an attitude of mind; an innate tendency of the human soul, which seeks to transcend reason and to attain a direct experience of God ... (1980: 20)

In one sense, of course, writers like Origen and Gregory would agree, since they never intended their biblical exegesis to be stuck at what was *merely* intellectual. But in their view the intellect would only be transcended when it was at full stretch in discerning the mystical meaning of scripture; it could never be by-passed or short-circuited if direct experience of God was to take place. Even those who were most concerned to integrate feeling into their knowledge of God, like Julian and Hadewijch, would seek to do so by way of *uniting* the 'substance and sensuality', to use Julian's terms. In modern thinking, a complete reversal has taken place from the notion of speculative mysticism that the mystical is the *intellect* in *ek-stasis* to the idea that it is a state of ineffable *feeling*, and the irony is that the former is now frequently interpreted in terms of the latter in modern writings about mysticism, so that passages from Dionysius or Eckhart are made to serve as evidence for the ineffability of mystical states of consciousness.

This shift in the meaning of the term 'mysticism' and its cognates, and in particular the cluster of characteristics associated with it since the time of Schleiermacher, must be taken seriously in any philosophical study. The dimensions of Schleiermacher's thought arose, after all, out of his Romantic conception of religion as feeling, and, more basically, out of his reaction to Kantian critical philosophy. What is clear is that without necessarily being aware of their debt to Schleiermacher, many modern writers on mysticism have incorporated Enlightenment and Romantic assumptions into their thinking, and insofar as they have discussed actual mystics, have tended to interpret them according to these preconceived categories.

From the foregoing, it is obvious that one of the most glaring

examples of this is the work of William James, which we can now
see in terms of its enormous and unacknowledged debt to
Schleiermacher. This is true in spite of the fact that the precise
meanings of the terms differ slightly in James' usage, partly
because of the considerable difference between his pragmatist
philosophical stance and Schleiermacher's Romanticism.
Although James gives the appearance of deriving his data from
original sources, and no doubt believed himself to be finding
these characteristics in the quotations he culled from Starbuck's
compilation, the similarity between his account and that of
Schleiermacher makes clear the extent to which he was reading
into his sources the very things he thought he was reading out of
them.[1]

In summary, we have in Schleiermacher's account, and in the
Romantics more generally, the major ingredients of modern
conceptions of mysticism, including the annihilation or absorption
of the self, the merging into complete unity of subject and object,
the intensity of feeling, and the inadequacy of rationality or
language. These are central, for instance, to the discussion of
Walter Terence Stace (1961: 131), and provide the framework for
the analysis given by William Wainwright (1980), along with
many modern philosophers of religion, as cited in chapter 1. This
is not to say that Stace and Wainwright and the others are aware
of the Romantic background of this characterisation, nor that
Schleiermacher would approve of the way in which they apply his
ideas. Nor does it show that Schleiermacher was wrong. It does,
however, make clear the extent to which the modern conception
of mysticism, with the characteristic of ineffability as the key
ingredient, is as much a social construction as were all the
previous constructions which we have already considered. The
failure of most modern philosophers to look carefully into the
work of medieval mystics is not accidental: the whole modern
construction depends on *not* looking at the medieval evidence, for
such an examination would expose the historical inaccuracy of
the modern understanding. It would thereby undermine the

---

[1] It is disconcerting to find that Evelyn Underhill was involved in just such another
unscholarly method, instructing her friend Lucy Menzies to cull passages which would
suit her preconceived purposes (Jantzen 1993).

usefulness of 'mysticism' for modern philosophical preoccupations, like giving reasons to believe in the existence of God, or showing that there might be a mystical core of religion. For such projects to be possible, it is essential that mysticism be seen as an ineffable, private state of consciousness: evidence that those who are counted as paradigm mystics do not fit into this construction must be suppressed. I am not, of course, arguing that philosophers know perfectly well that those whom they themselves count as mystics of the Middle Ages are counter-examples to modern claims, and that the evidence is deliberately ignored or hidden. What I am suggesting, however, is that if modern philosophers of religion were to recognise the extent to which what counts as mystical has undergone a series of constructions, and that the current one is significantly different from those which went before, a great deal of modern philosophical argumentation about mysticism would have to be seriously qualified or even rejected altogether. I shall discuss this in more detail in chapter 9.

Now, it has become clear throughout the previous chapters that the varying social constructions of mysticism were never innocent of an agenda which included power and gender; and this is just as true of the modern one, unrecognised though that is by modern philosophers. It would take another book to adequately characterise the contemporary western construction of women; but some elements are immediately obvious. One is that the ancient and medieval characterisation of the female as emotional and the male as rational is with us still. The other is that as the world has increasingly been divided into the private and the public domain, women are seen as belonging to the private, the domestic, the realm of hearth and home, feeling and nurture. When these are combined in modern secularism, it has the ironic result that whereas in the medieval era the religious in general and the mystical in particular was far too important to be left to women, in the modern era mysticism and religious experience are indeed seen as available to women, but with their feminisation, they have also been marginalised. Women can be mystics only in a world where mysticism is no longer constructed as public or powerful. The final chapter will draw these threads together.

CHAPTER 9

Conclusion: mysticism and modernity

Who will claim to be just by economizing on anxiety?
(Derrida 1992: 20)

Present-day philosophers and theologians, feminists among them, regularly speak of mysticism as though that term is clearly understood: it stands for a subjective psychological state, perhaps a state of 'altered consciousness', in which an individual undergoes a private intense experience, usually of a religious nature. As we have seen in the preceding chapters, however, such an understanding of what mysticism is is relatively recent, and bears little resemblance to the self-understanding of those who are taken paradigmatically as mystics of the Christian tradition. In this concluding chapter, I wish to draw out some of the implications which follow from this finding. I shall begin with a summary of the main points to be drawn from the recognition of the ways in which mysticism has been socially constructed in the Christian west. This will be followed by a discussion of the bearing of these findings on some of the issues preoccupying philosophers of religion who think and write about mysticism. In the final section, I shall raise questions about this philosophical agenda from a feminist perspective sharpened by the recognition derived through the investigations into the lives and writings of mystics of the interconnection of issues of power and gender in the definition of mysticism. I shall suggest that this interconnection is not restricted to the single topic of mysticism, but can be generalised much more widely within the philosophy of religion and beyond it.

I REVIEW OF THE EMPIRICAL FINDINGS

The chapters of this book do not constitute anything like a complete history of 'Christian mysticism'. Indeed, there is much reason to be suspicious of the idea of such a history if it implies that there is something like an 'essence' of mysticism which can be seen to have a beginning in the biblical writings, develop in the patristic and medieval era, make progress toward its full flowering in the thirteenth and fourteenth centuries, and then send out seeds for new developments in the Protestant and Catholic Reformations. Taking a cue from the work of Michel Foucault, what I have done instead is to ask how the mystical has been understood in a variety of times and places within the Christian west. Foucault's work on madness, for example, reveals how the modern notion of madness is quite different from the ways in which madness was understood in other periods: similarly, I have shown that mysticism as it is presently understood is a modern invention, and that within the Christian tradition it has had a variety of meanings quite different from those which are ascribed to it today.

The historical chapters of this book, then, are to be understood as sketches toward a counter-history, an attempt to cast doubt upon the received opinions of what constitutes mysticism and its history. Far from having a constant meaning, we have seen how the ideas surrounding the mystical and of who counts as a mystic have undergone major changes. In the classical context in which Christian theology had its beginnings, mystics were simply those who had been initiated into the mystery religions, who had undergone a rite of initiation about which they kept silent. Far from there being anything ineffable about the experience, the point was simply that the ritual was to be kept secret, it was not to be talked about with the uninitiated. Clearly the assumption behind such an injunction to silence is that without such a rule, the ritual *might* have been talked about: the assumption, in other words, is diametrically opposite to an assumption that the ritual is 'ineffable'. From this idea of the mystics as those who kept their mouths shut came the further idea, linked with Platonic philosophy, that mystics are those whose knowledge of the divine comes with the shutting of *all* the senses: mystical knowledge is knowledge available only to the mind or spirit that is as detached as possible from bodily concerns. And thus the mystical or spiritual came to mean, in this context, that which is beyond ordinary sense perception and the normal means of human knowledge.

As these ideas were linked up with early Christian theology, they were interwoven with the understanding of the Bible as having a literal, historical sense on the one hand, and a spiritual or mystical sense on the other. The mystical meaning of scripture was not some special intense psychological experience imparted to the reader, but rather the perception of its hidden depths, its reference to Christ even in passages which in literal terms are speaking of something quite different. Similarly the sacraments, whether of baptism or of the eucharist, were to be understood not merely as literal water or bread or wine but as the mystical entry into the church by the washing away of sins, or as the mystical body and blood of Christ. And it was not held to be the case that receiving them in their mystical sense either required or effected a psychological transformation of the people concerned: indeed, the whole point of *faith* in their efficacy was that no such intense subjective experiences need take place, but that the sacraments are valid for all that. Such an understanding of the mystical is obviously far from current ideas regarding altered states of consciousness and ineffability as essential characteristics of mystical experiences, as I shall discuss in more detail below.

Once again, however, the mystical under this description was largely the domain of men. Women, on the whole, did not have the education necessary to study the text and its multiple glosses; and even in exceptional cases where they did have the requisite education and access to manuscripts, they were not considered suitable to teach or to have the authority which discernment of the mystical meaning would confer. An alternative source of authority about the mysteries of God might come by visions, a direct communication of God to the most humble creatures of divine creation. Since women were those who could be seen as most like 'the handmaiden of the Lord', they might, ironically, be most likely to be privileged with a vision of the mysteries of God.

Thus Hildegard of Bingen marks an important transition in the social construction of mysticism: whereas, as she insists, it is men who should be the mystical ones, expounding the knowledge of God by means of their insight into the mystical meaning of scripture, because of their laxity God has had to turn to herself, a woman, and give her the message to be communicated, doing so by means of visions rather than by the 'normal' method of years of prayerful study of the scriptures. In the high and late Middle Ages, numerous women visionaries claimed spiritual authority for themselves. The construction of mysticism could no longer exclude women.

What is apparent in the high Middle Ages, however, is the increasing wariness of the male ecclesiastical authorities toward (women) visionaries. Strict criteria were set down for the assessment of their claims. Many of those who today are counted as the male mystics of the medieval period, such as Eckhart, Ruusbroec, and the author of *The Cloud of Unknowing*, decried such putative direct communications from God altogether. At the very least, strict adherence to the male-defined doctrines and practices of the church was expected of any woman who claimed spiritual authority. Among the requirements were obedience to the counsel of her (male) spiritual director, strict physical enclosure and absolute chastity.

Even this, however, was not enough to guarantee that women would be counted as genuine mystics, or thought to be as likely as men to be in receipt of divine communication. As the controls were more tightly drawn, many women and men were tried and condemned as heretics, often on charges of false mysticism – another notable shift in the possibilities included in the term. False mysticism was seen as the demonic counterpart of communication with God, and was regularly characterised in terms of sexual obscenities and murderous evil. Within the prevailing misogyny of the late medieval and early modern period, this characterisation resulted in the execution of thousands of women and some men as witches. The connection of power and gender in the social construction of mysticism could hardly have been made clearer than in this condemnation and slaughter of those who were considered, as false mystics, to be sufficiently threatening to church and society to justify their extermination.

It was only with the development of the secular state, when religious experience was no longer perceived as a source of knowledge and power, that it became safe to allow women to be mystics. Thus it came about that when mysticism became constructed as private and personal, having nothing to do with politics, it was also possible to see it as compatible with a woman's role as the 'angel in the house', servicing her husband and children not only physically but spiritually as well. The decline of gender as an issue in the definition of who should count as a mystic was in direct relation to the decline in the perception of mystical experience, and religion generally, as politically powerful. At the same time, such experience came to be described as 'ineffable' – a notion that would have simply baffled many of the medieval women and men whom we standardly count as mystics and who wrote volumes about their insights and experiences. As I have demonstrated, the characterisation of mystical experience as ineffable has much more to do with the construction of modern epistemology than with what those who are counted as mystics have actually said about their experiences. Furthermore, the alleged inexpressibility of mystical experience correlates neatly with the silencing of women in the public arena of the secular world: women may be mystics, but mysticism is a private intense experience not communicable in everyday language and not of political relevance. Given what we have seen regarding the interconnection of power and gender in the social construction of mysticism in the past, it is hardly far-fetched to investigate the sort of power and gender issues that are at work in this modern construction. Feminists have every reason, both historical and current, to be suspicious of an understanding of mysticism which allows that women may be mystics, but which makes mysticism a private and ineffable psychological occurrence and which detaches it from considerations of social justice. I will return to this point toward the end of this chapter.

It is thus clear that, as Foucault showed with regard to madness, medicine, and sexuality, the social construction of the idea of mysticism is closely connected with issues of power. Those who are in control are the ones who define what shall count as genuine and what shall count as deviant. We have seen in detail in the preceding chapters how those who held power in the ecclesiastical establishment were able to determine, whether by their articulation of doctrine or by their control of the courts and the judiciary system, who should be honoured as mystics and who should be considered demonic. Any 'history of Christian mysticism', therefore, would have to be a history of power and its control in the Christian centuries, power that was beyond any doubt often used not simply to protect and preserve what was held to be true, but to oppress and undermine any who would challenge privilege and corruption.

What Foucault's work does not do, however, is recognise the gender issues involved in the wielding of power in the areas which he studies, gender issues which feminist discussions of Foucault's work have been quick to specify (Diamond and Quinby 1988; McNay 1992). Throughout the book it has become clear that the power involved in the social construction of mysticism has consistently been a gendered power. Women have been allowed (by men) to count as mystics if they were 'honorary males', if they were appropriately submissive and humble, if they supported rather than challenged the (male) ecclesiastical establishment. But when they asserted authority in their own right, when they began to write and to preach and to take an equal part with men, then they were quickly suppressed, and so were any men who sympathised with them. The suppression might take the form of preaching and writing on the inferiority of women and women's forms of religious experience; more terribly, it might extend to the trials of women and men as heretics and the burning of witches.

One caveat must be entered. Although it has been clear throughout this book that to a very large extent the definition and control of who should count as a mystic has been in the hands of powerful males intent on retaining ecclesiastical or intellectual dominance, and that they have exercised that control to their own advantage, it has also been evident that women were not simply passive victims. Even women who had strongly internalised male ideals of womanhood as passive and humble, and who accepted the authority of the ecclesiastical establishment, often pushed back the boundaries of what could be counted as genuinely mystical by the courageous integrity of their lives and writings. Women like Hildegard of Bingen or Julian of Norwich cannot be studied without recognising their strength and insight. Furthermore, it is obvious that at least in some respects that strength and insight is directly related to their gender: Julian's theology of God as mother, for example, and her insistence that her recognition of God's love shall be available to all her 'even Christians' is hardly detachable from her experiences as a woman. Although the women in the Christian tradition were in many respects bounded by male definition and authority, they still found unconventional possibilities of working within those boundaries and indeed in pushing them back in ways that remain instructive for contemporary feminists. The many women and men who were willing to stand against the ecclesiastical structures of authority that were often corrupt and self-serving, and who were defined as heretics or witches because of it, have shown even more radical ways of taking responsibility for what they would count as genuinely religious, whether or not it was approved by those with the power of the sword. It is appropriate that the dangerous memory of these women and men should be preserved in a study of who counts as a mystic, and that their lives should be included in the parameters of the question of power and gender in the Christian mystical tradition.

II PHILOSOPHICAL ISSUES

Contemporary philosophers of religion are much exercised with the question of the truth of mystical or religious experiences. They ask whether such experiences are true or false, meaning by that, whether they are experiences of some transcendent objective reality (God) or are simply self-deceptions or delusions on the part of the person who has them. They also ask the related question of whether such experiences can be used as evidence for the existence of God or the truth of religious claims. Opinions are divided. Caroline Franks Davis (1989), following Richard Swinburne (1979), uses the 'principle of credulity' to argue that in the absence of considerations which defeat the claims of those who have religious experiences, their claims should be taken as evidence for the truth of religious doctrines. That is, just as we standardly accept that a person who claims to see a tree or a flower really does see a tree or a flower unless there is serious reason to doubt the person's trustworthiness or the reliability of their senses, so also we should accept that if a person says that she has seen or otherwise experienced God, that is in itself good reason to believe that her experience is veridical unless we have serious reason to call it into doubt. On the other side, Richard Gale (1991) argues that the parallels between mystical experience and sense experience are too weak to allow for such an application of the principle of credulity, and that therefore mystical experience cannot serve as evidence for the truth of religious claims, particularly the claim that God exists. And so the debate goes on (Alston 1991).

From what I have written in the preceding chapters, it is obvious that this preoccupation was hardly one which those who are counted as mystics themselves shared. Although they were indeed concerned that their experiences should not be self-induced or, worse, of demonic origin, the basis for this concern was not a need for evidence for the existence of God. What today is essentially contested was to them completely clear. Philosophers who use the accounts of mystical writers to argue about the existence of God or the truth of the doctrines of Christianity are using these accounts in ways that would have been foreign and in some cases perhaps abhorrent to the people who wrote them.

However, as I pointed out in chapter 1, from the fact that modern philosophers ask questions different from those asked by the mystics themselves, it does not follow that modern philosophers are wrong to do so. Although the mystics were convinced of the truth of God's existence, that claim has now become problematic: why should philosophers who investigate it not use the resources which the mystics provide, even if that was not the original intention behind their writings? Of course, it would be courtesy (to put it no higher) to notice that this is a different use of the mystical writings than that which their authors intended. But in itself there is nothing particularly problematic about finding resources in a text which were not part of the author's designs. For example, it is entirely legitimate to use the Icelandic sagas as evidence that certain species of birds mentioned in the text must have been resident in Iceland at the time of the Viking era, even though giving that evidence was only incidental to the text, and not what was important to those who developed the sagas. Similarly, if the experiences of the mystics in the Christian tradition as described in the books they wrote give evidence for the existence of God, then it is legitimate for modern philosophers to recognise that evidence, even though the original writers were not making that their main point, and indeed would have been astounded that anyone should need evidence of that which they themselves thought to be obvious.

But now another problem arises, and it is this one which I am concerned to highlight. If mystical experience is indeed used as evidence for the truth of religious claims (or rejected as providing such evidence) *which* mystical experience are we talking about? Contrary to what would be assumed from reading philosophical discussions of mysticism, we have seen that what counts as mystical experience has gone through enormous variations, and that these variations have been essentially connected with issues of power and gender. Accordingly, if philosophers are going to use 'mysticism' as part of their argument, it is first necessary for them to decide what they mean by that term, and in consequence who they will count as a mystic. What regularly happens is that philosophers at this point do two incompatible things. The first is that they use an understanding of mysticism largely derived from the work of William James, which constructs mystical experience as intense private psychological states having the characteristics of ineffability, a noetic quality, transiency and passivity. We have seen how problematic such an understanding is, not least in regard to historical accuracy. And secondly, in doing so philosophers suppose themselves to be discussing the experiences of the classical mystics of Christianity, all of whom, they suppose, had experiences characterisable in roughly Jamesian terms. Where they consult primary sources at all, they select passages, often out of context, which can be construed as (and sometimes are) descriptions of intense personal experiences, and then hold these to be the central accounts of mysticism, all the rest being approximations or preliminaries to such intense states. With this sort of procedure, and with a careful selection of sources, it is possible to make 'the mystics' say anything at all: like the Bible, the corpus of early and medieval mystical writing can be used to support any interpretation whatever if short passages are taken out of their literary and historical contexts. One of the most astonishing things about current philosophy of religion is that there is *both* a fascination with mysticism *and* hardly any serious study of the primary sources, even by the philosophers using the subject as pivotal in their arguments. Given that this is so, it is not surprising that issues of power and gender go unnoticed; and feminists have been quick to point out in other areas that where such issues are unnoticed, they are reinforced.

If the argument of this book has been anywhere near correct, then one thing that stands out is that, James and his followers notwithstanding, there is no such thing as an 'essence' of mysticism, a single type of experience which is characterisable as mystical while others are excluded. The 'mystical', for those initiated into ancient mystery religions, was simply that part of their initiation ritual about which they kept their mouths shut. In the early Christian tradition, by contrast, the 'mystical' was the hidden meaning of scripture, the meaning which saw its connection to Christ rather than only its literal truth. The 'mystical' to Hildegard of Bingen referred to the hidden mysteries of God made plain to her in her visions. For none of these would the mystical refer essentially to that which was subjectively experienced, neither would a distinction between true and false mysticism find purchase in their thinking. By contrast, the inquisitors, worried as they were by the possibility of heresy, thought that there were both true and false mystics, that is, those who revered God and those who paid homage to the devil; and their work consisted of an attempt to distinguish between them. The basis of that distinction, however, is not to be sought in the subjective psychological experiences of the two groups: indeed, there is no indication that the subjective states of these two groups of people were necessarily different. Both true mystics and false ones might have visions or ecstasies or other forms of intense experiences:

Marguerite of Porete, for example, apparently was a visionary while Jan van Ruusbroec was not, yet she was burned at the stake while he became known as one of the foremost spiritual teachers of the fourteenth century. Similarly in the trial of Eckhart, the presence or absence of unusual states of consciousness was not what the inquisitors sought to determine, but rather the orthodoxy or unorthodoxy of Eckhart's life and teaching. It is only latterly that the term 'mystical' began to be applicable to 'experience' at all: in earlier times, one might speak of a 'mystical interpretation' or of the 'mystical body of Christ', but not of a 'mystical experience'. Similarly, 'the mystics' were not those who had particular states of consciousness, but those who were able to elucidate the spiritual interpretation of a passage of scripture, say, or who were faithful participants in the (mysteries of the) eucharist.

Now, if philosophers wish to ask whether certain altered states of consciousness can provide evidence for the existence of God, that may be a legitimate question, as I have already indicated. But it is necessary to be clear that this is a very *different* question from asking whether 'mystical experience' (which ones? whose?) provides such evidence, let alone whether 'mysticism' does. The point is that all these terms have long histories of social construction; they are not unproblematic terms with clear referents, nor are their variations innocent of the machinations of power. Philosophers who pick on any one construction – usually one that involves intense subjective states of consciousness – as the 'evidential data' for their discussion have not usually recognised that it *is* a construction, rather than 'what mysticism really is', let alone that that construction carries with it a weight of implications of power and gender.

Thus for example Caroline Franks Davis tries to find a common thread in religious experiences which will enable her to use them as part of a cumulative case for the truth of religious beliefs. Franks Davis is well aware that mysticism is not mono-lithic, and recognises this as a problem to be resolved in her effort to use the claims of mystics as evidence for religious doctrines: put bluntly, the claims of mystics of various religions, and even within religions, on the face of it contradict one another. However, she argues that the apparent conflict can often be reconciled, and that even where differences remain with regard to specific doctrinal claims, what the mystics making these claims have in common is more important than what divides them. For example, while it is true that a Christian mystic like Teresa of Avila might experience Jesus as the Son of God, whereas a Muslim mystic would reject this claim, and a Buddhist mystic would experience 'emptiness', all three, despite these differences, would agree that 'the mundane world of physical bodies ... is not the whole or ultimate reality' and that 'whatever *is* the ultimate reality is holy, eternal, and of supreme value' (1989: 191). These agreements on what Franks Davis calls 'relatively unramified' doctrines she sees as of very great importance in the cumulative case for a broad theism, even though she recognises that the people who make such claims are not themselves 'broad theists' but rather are people who hold to specific doctrines.

There are a variety of problems with Franks Davis' argument here. In the first place, even granting the terms of the argument, it is far from clear that her conclusion holds. After all, the more highly ramified beliefs which are in conflict with one another are often held, according to Franks Davis, on the basis of *exactly the same* mystical or religious experiences as those which produce the less ramified, compatible beliefs. If she wishes to use those experiences as evidence for the truth of the latter, how is it that they can be side-stepped (or re-interpreted) when it comes to the former?

Her strategy of response involves the even more doubtful move, familiar since Stace's book *Mysticism and Philosophy* (1961), of distinguishing between interpretation and experience. During the experience, she says, 'mystics generally admit that little interpetation is possible'. When we look closely at what they say after the fact, we find, however, that

mystics very probably have the same sort of experience, viz. freedom from all sense of time, space, personal identity, and multiplicity, which leaves them with a blissful, 'naked awareness' of perfect unity and a sense that 'this is it', the ultimate level of reality. (1989: 178)

It is only upon emerging from their experiences that mystics interpret them in accordance with their prior 'doctrinal set', and it is this, rather than the experiences themselves, which cause the apparent conflict.

The historical chapters of this book have shown, however, how problematic such a line of argument is. In the first place, Caroline Franks Davis concentrates exclusively upon intense subjective experiences, as though that is what is important about mysticism: I have already shown how such a concentration is a modern selection, having more to do with a modern philosophical agenda than with accuracy to the mystical tradition of Christianity, within which the focus on intense experiences was for long periods absent altogether. When such experiences did occur, for example among the visionary women of the thirteenth and fourteenth centuries, their status was highly contentious. Far from it being the case that intense psychological experiences were at the centre of the Christian mystical tradition, therefore, they were usually regarded as peripheral and frequently as highly suspect. I have done nothing to show that the same would be true in the case of other world religions, but I suspect that in them, too, the 'discovery' of mystical experience by western scholars has more to do with the preoccupation of post-Enlightenment philosophy than with the indigenous religious traditions themselves (Cantwell Smith 1981). For Franks Davis and other modern philosophers to take these as central to mysticism is thus simply inaccurate, at least to the Christian tradition, and since it is this tradition which most concerns them, their conclusions must be highly suspect.

Furthermore, even in those cases where Franks Davis could indeed appeal to intense experiences in the Christian mystical tradition, such as, for example, the visions of Gertrude or Hadewijch or Julian of Norwich, they would tend to cast doubt on her case rather than to assist it. As we have seen, these women, and others like them, kept their wits about them during their intense experiences, taking part in the visions not as though they were watching a film, but as full participants in a drama. Julian asked pointed questions of God about the evil and suffering in the world; Gertrude sought assurances about the fate of particular people; Hadewijch was involved in profound soul-searching. To say, as Franks Davis does, that 'mystics generally admit that little interpretation is possible *during* such an experience' simply betrays unawareness of the descriptions of the experiences given by women such as these. Of course they were not *writing down* their 'interpretations' during the time of the experiences, but that is not to say that they were having some sort of undifferentiated ecstasy, and only later invented the narrative of their experiences, cutting it out of whole cloth. The only way out of this would be to say that these women were not *really* mystics, or at least that these experiences are not paradigmatically mystical; but the preceding chapters have shown how high-handed such an approach would be. To make that sort of a move would only be to repeat in modern philosophical guise the same sorts of power/gender strategies which we have seen active in ecclesiastical dress in the medieval period. It is obviously not legitimate both to *stipulate* that only certain sorts of experience shall count as genuinely mystical, and at the same time to suppose that it is an *empirical* claim that all mystics have experiences of roughly this nature; yet this is the sort of circular reasoning which too often characterises projects of showing that mystical experiences have a common core which can serve as part of a cumulative case for religious belief. The modern enterprise of fitting mystics into a procrustean bed has many antecedents, as we have seen. It is clear that from a historical and empirical perspective such an effort is highly dubious. In the final section of this chapter I shall explore why it might be that such a move nevertheless has strong appeal for modern philosophers, even though moderate historical investigation shows it to be untenable; and shall suggest that the issues of power and gender which we saw operating in medieval definitions of who should count as a mystic are still with us, albeit in modern liberal costume.

First, however, I wish to make some further comments about the distinction between interpretation and experience, since this, also, is a modern preoccupation whose provenance is worth investigating along the same lines. The distinction became important in philosophical discussions of mysticism with the work of Stace and his vivid example of the American and the waxwork policeman.

There is a doubtless apocryphal but well-known anecdote about the American visitor in London who tried to shake hands with a waxwork policeman in the entrance of Madame Tussaud's. If such an incident ever occurred, it must have been because the visitor had a sense experience which he first wrongly interpreted as a live policeman and later interpreted correctly as a wax figure. If the sentence which I have just written is intelligible, it proves that an interpretation is distinguishable from an experience; for there could not otherwise be two interpretations of one experience ... [A]lthough it may be true that at no time was the experience free of interpretation and even that such a pure experience is psychologically impossible ... it seems a safe position to say that there is an intelligible distinction between experience and interpretation, even if it be true that we can never come upon a quite uninterpreted experience. (1961: 31)

From this 'safe position' Stace makes the application to mystical experience, arguing (in the way that Caroline Franks Davis – along with many others – appropriates) that there is an essentially uninterpreted core experience shared by mystics of many religious traditions. This experience is subsequently interpreted along their individual linguistic and doctrinal lines, thus resulting in incompatibilities. These incompatibilities, however, do not belong to the experiences themselves, but only to the layer of interpretations which comes later and is not the essential thing.

I have already pointed out some of the historical and empirical difficulties with such a position, but it is also worth looking more closely at what is involved philosophically in a distinction between interpretation and experience. As Steven Katz has pointed out, the idea that there could be 'pure' experiences, whether mystical or of any other kind, to which interpretations are applied only later, is contrary to our basic understanding of what experience is. To be fair, Stace had not said that there were 'pure' experiences; nevertheless his position requires that mystical experiences can be separated from their interpretation in such a way that in spite of the obvious conflicts in interpretation among mystics within and among religious traditions, Stace can affirm that there is a basic, core experience that is the same in all cases, underlying the variations of interpretation.

In Katz's view, this is untenable. He maintains that there are and can be no pure or unmediated experiences. For anything to be an experience, it must be experienced *by* someone, and this already implies that it is experienced from within a particular cultural and linguistic context which will to some extent shape it. In his words,

all experience is processed through, organised by, and makes itself available to us in extremely complex epistemological ways ... (1978: 26)

This is true not only of mystical experience, but of any experience at all. We cannot step out of our culture and language, or even out of the particular space we occupy, and see things as though we were universal. The importance which Katz attaches to the context of experience, such that the experience is to some extent at least constructed out of it, has resulted in his position, and that of others who agree with him, being labelled 'constructivist' (Stoeber 1992a).

Katz's position on this is one that is congenial to feminists, who have long insisted that the ideal of a neutral, objective, universal stance is a fiction which disguised male partiality. There are no views from nowhere; and there are no views from everywhere. There are only views from somewhere, and the particular place will have an inescapable effect on what can be seen. If one assumes the contrary, then what is in fact happening is that one is falsely universalising a particular perspective. Just as there is no possibility of seeing things without seeing them from somewhere, so also there is no way in which human beings can experience things without experiencing them from some prior linguistic and cultural context. The perspective from which we look makes it possible to see things which we might be unable to see from anywhere else, and also places limitations on what we can see: sitting in my study with the garden doors open means that I can watch the bluetits, but I cannot simultaneously see around the corner into the kitchen. Similarly, someone like Katz who holds a contextualist position on religious experience argues that the religious and cultural context in which one is immersed makes certain sorts of religious experiences possible and others out of the question: Julian of Norwich could have a vision of Jesus dying on the cross, but could not have had a vision of Shiva dancing. As Katz puts it,

The significance of these considerations is that the forms of consciousness which the mystic brings to experience set structured and limiting parameters on what the experience will be, i.e. on what will be experienced, and rule out in advance what is 'inexperienceable' in the particular given, concrete context. (1978: 26)

Constructivist analyses of mystical experience have the advantage of making more obvious sense of the wide diversity of experiences to be found even in the literature of Christian mysticism, let alone that of other religious traditions. Although this approach still focuses exclusively on intense subjective experiences as what is crucial to mysticism (with all the problems which we have seen to be attendant upon such a focus) it at least does more justice to the diversity of reports offered by those who did have such experiences.[1] Of course, this does not rule out the possibility of ever more ramified interpretations of these experiences: one can always add layers of interpretation to any experience. Nor does it make nonsense of the idea that even experiences that differ sharply may still have some things in common, such as, for instance, a recognition that there is more to life than the physical or material. What it does do, however, is to undermine the foundations of the argument for a mystical core of religion, a common pre-interpretative subjective essence. I have argued elsewhere (1990) that the idea of such a mystical core of religion derives in large part from Schleiermacher's attempt to circumvent Kantian strictures on religious knowledge: it has become clear from the chapters of this book that even within the Christian tradition it is completely untenable from a historical perspective.

It has also already become apparent that the modern preoccupation with ineffability as centrally characteristic of mysticism is just as problematic as the preoccupation with intense experiences, and indeed is linked to it. If the mystical is constructed in terms of initiation rites, or in terms of interpretation of scripture, then the

---

[1]   This seems to me to be obviously true in spite of what Nelson Pike (1992: appendix 2) says in his comments on Steven Katz. Although Pike himself tries to base his book on some actual mystical texts, notably those of Teresa of Avila and Jan van Ruusbroec, comments he makes such as those on the possible influence of Plotinus and Dionysius on various strands of the Christian tradition show his lack of acquaintance with standard historical scholarship on the availability of texts (and hence the possibility of their influence) in the medieval period.

idea of ineffability gets no purchase whatsoever. It is only if mysticism is thought of in terms of, say, the visionary women of the high Middle Ages, that one can ask whether they were able to put their experiences into words. And yet that seems to have been the least of their worries. The visions of Hildegard of Bingen, for instance, were as far as she was concerned given to her in order to instruct the faithful in the ways of God – a task which she believed would not have been laid upon her had the male clerics been doing their jobs properly. She writes volumes of interpretation of her visions; she does not complain about ineffability. Similarly Julian of Norwich believes that her visions were given not for herself alone, but for her 'even Christians', lay as well as cloistered. Although it required great effort on her part to under- stand the full meaning of the things she had been shown, and to write them down, that is very different from saying that the experiences themselves were ineffable. It is of course possible to find passages in which medieval writers say that God is a being who cannot be fully described, and even that their own experi- ences go beyond their ability to articulate them; but that is a far cry from the whole weight of ineffability with which modern philosophers like to invest mystical experiences, let alone from the idea that ineffability is the most fundamental characteristic of mysticism.[2]

III TRUTH FROM A FEMINIST PERSPECTIVE: WOULD THE REAL MYSTIC PLEASE STAND UP?

What I have been concerned to show throughout this book has been that there is no one thing that has counted throughout Christian history as the mystical, no one group of people who were counted as mystics, and that furthermore there were issues of power and gender at work in all the various constructions. But this still leaves a central question: which one of them, if any, is

[2] It is obvious that my conclusions here are reached via a different path than similar conclusions of Steven Katz (1992). Katz continues to assume that the selected passages which he cites show that claims of ineffability are central to mystical experience, even though these claims must not be interpreted as a simplistic rejection of language. But this assumption is itself part of the modern construction of mysticism, as we have seen.

veridical? Might it not be the case that one of these constructions, or some subset of them, is the 'real' one – the one which we ought really to count as mysticism, even if perhaps it must first be stripped of some accretions peculiar to its context? Is it *all* social construction, right down to the bottom?

Although I have said that there is no such thing as an essence of mysticism, it must be granted that that conclusion does not strictly follow from the fact that there have been shifts in its social construction: it may simply be the case that some of those constructions have been false or misguided, while others approximate more nearly to the truth. And if this is the case, then perhaps all the modern philosophical questions are legitimate after all. First we must determine *which* of the constructions of mysticism are really central, perhaps stripping it of some of its entanglements with power and gender. Then we are able to use this somewhat chastened construction as the basis from which we can ask whether it gives evidence for the existence of God, whether using this construction it might be possible to find a mystical core of religion, and so on.[3]

On the face of it, this seems like a reasonable suggestion. I think that it can be shown, however, that when we look at it more closely from a feminist perspective sharpened by an awareness of the interplay of power and gender in the construction of mysticism, it becomes clear that the same interplay is also at work in modern constructions, and in the philosophy of religion more generally, not least in this suggestion itself. I wish, therefore, to look at the possiblity of discerning such an 'essence' of mysticism in relation to two issues: first, the question of philosophical neutrality and second, the question of relativism. It will emerge that the two questions are, in the end, inseparable.

(i) *Philosophical neutrality*

We may begin by asking again, *which* construction of the available historical alternatives should be selected as representing the real 'essence' of mysticism, and on what grounds? It will clearly not do

---

[3] I am grateful to my colleague Peter Byrne for not allowing me to evade this issue.

to suggest that we should choose the one that has been most prominent or most frequent historically, since that only begs all the questions of power and gender with which we are by now familiar. Those forms of 'mysticism' which were compatible with dominant ecclesiastical perspectives were allowed to flourish, and those forms that were not compatible were suppressed: we simply cannot know what 'might have been' if things had been allowed to proceed unhindered. Accordingly, it is not at all surprising if more books and manuscripts were written and preserved which articulate a particular perspective on mysticism; but this in itself does not tell us what 'real' mysticism is, if by 'real' mysticism is meant the sort of mysticism which would occur if (*per impossibile*) there were no external pressures. We cannot get at an 'essence of mysticism' by counting.

Another possibility, then, would be to suggest that the form of mysticism which we should adopt for investigation is the modern Jamesian construction, albeit with the recognition that it *is* a construction, and that it does not fit all those who are standardly recognised as Christian mystics. The rationale for selecting this particular construction is that it would enable investigation of the issues which form a large part of the modern philosophical agenda: issues of truth, the existence of God, language, the possibility of a mystical core of religion, and so on. It is true that we could no longer pretend that all putative mystics fit this description; and therefore arguments which hitherto have been thought to rest on empirical or statistical generalisations ('all mystical experience is ineffable', 'most mystics have intense experiences which they only later articulate in terms consistent with their doctrinal beliefs') must be seen to be, at best, stipulative definitions of what shall count as mystical experience, rather than evidence based on a large and unbiased sample of the available cases. Nevertheless, it is certainly true that some people, past and present, *have* had intense experiences which they take to be of God; and claims made on the basis of such experiences may be worth philosophical investigation, even if it is doubtful that what is being investigated, in that case, is mysticism or mystical experience *per se*.

This response, however, only pushes the issue one step backwards. Justifying the selection of a particular construction of mysticism as the one that shall be investigated on the grounds that this is the one that fits in with the modern philosophical agenda must raise questions, not least for feminists, about that agenda itself. What exactly are the driving factors behind the current philosophical preoccupations with a particular construction of mysticism? One thing is clear: the driving motivation cannot be fascination with and respect for the mystics themselves, for if that were the case then philosophers of religion would pay far more attention to the primary sources, many of which are, after all, readily available in excellent modern translations. Yet as we have seen, respect for the lives and writings of the mystics themselves, evinced by careful study of them in their literary and social contexts, is conspicuously absent from much current writing on mysticism by philosophers of religion.

Given that the various social constructions of mysticism have been bound up with issues of power and gender, and given also that this is largely unrecognised by modern philosophical discussion of mysticism, it is pertinent to ask whether such issues are once again involved. Could it be the case that the Jamesian characterisation of mystical experience, adopted as normative by subsequent philosophers of religion, is not the neutral, objective description which it is usually taken to be? I do not mean, by this, that either James or subsequent philosophers deliberately and consciously adopt a construction of mysticism which suppresses women and which reinforces modern structures of power. Conspiracy theories are sometimes tempting, but in this case, at least, such a theory would be far-fetched. But what is not far-fetched is to suppose that knowledge and power are regularly interconnected, and are just as regularly gendered: indeed we have seen one example after another of this in the book; and in most of the cases we have looked at, it would have been just as true as it is today that the dominant voices were not aware of being oppressive, and were not intentionally in the service of power in their definitions and delimitations of what should count as mystical. Feminists (like anti-racists) are well aware that some of the worst and most intractable oppression can come from those who sincerely believe themselves to be well-intentioned. The protest on the part of modern philosophers that the modern construction of mysticism is neutral and objective, and unconnected with issues of power and gender, is therefore unlikely to cut much ice: at best, it reveals that where such issues *are* involved, the philosophers in question are unaware of them – and are perpetuating them by that very lack of awareness.

It would take (at least) another book to explore adequately the ingredients of power and gender in the modern understanding of mysticism. Nevertheless, it is not difficult to see some of the lines of investigation that would be necessary. The contours of modern mysticism are drawn along the lines of modern philosophy generally, contours which both postmodernism and feminism, for all their differences, have called into question (see Nicholson 1990). In the first place, the Jamesian account of mysticism depends on a focus on the individual as subject, as constructed from Descartes to Kant (see Taylor 1989). It is in this knowing subject that epistemology is founded: things can be known only by that subject, whose mind serves as the 'mirror of nature' (Rorty 1980). A consequence is that the mind as the knowing subject becomes a focus of philosophical attention. The knowledge of God, too, is knowledge known by this subject (or not at all); and is equally subject to scrutiny. Hence mysticism is constructed as a state of the putatively knowing subject; and the big question for philosophers of religion is whether that putative knowledge is veridical, or whether it is a delusion.

That big question could never be asked in its modern form, however, unless one already accepted the modern construction of the self as the knowing subject. But that construction is itself increasingly open to question. Psychoanalytical perspectives from Freud to Lacan and Irigaray have raised the spectres of what the knowing subject does not know, the vast reservoir of repressed, unconscious knowledge that subverts conscious strategies of knowing. Postmodernists write of the death of the subject, the end of totalising discourses which purport to be universal and objective and are instead the imposition of the powerful. To put it another way, if the self is constructed as the knowing subject, who is left out of this construction? Who is deemed *not* to know, and therefore not to count as a subject? Feminists have been at the forefront of this questioning, and have demonstrated the extent to which the Cartesian/Kantian 'man of reason' is indeed male. In spite of (or because of) all the efforts of the mind to transcend and master the body, the mind and body in question have not been female: women were seen as the ones who were identified with bodiliness, reproduction and production, and therefore not as philosophical subjects/minds who are capable of real, that is objective, knowledge (see Lloyd 1984; Okin 1979; Schiebinger 1989). It is interesting, to put it no higher, that Kant, who was both a lifelong enemy of mysticism and an arch-misogynist, linked what he thought of as mystical *schwärmerei* with women.

Modern philosophical consciousness is, however, also fundamentally shaped by the legacy of Romanticism, the reaction against Kantian rationality and its replacement with the exaltation of feeling. Kant had argued that since experience as we know it could only be of phenomena, never of things themselves, it is impossible for a human subject to experience God, even if God exists (which Kant affirmed only as a regulative ideal). Schleiermacher, and the religious Romantics who followed him, sought to escape the Kantian strictures by affirming that while God could not be discovered in thought, it is possible to experience God in pure preconceptual consciousness. This intense, pre-linguistic experience is available only to those who will enter into themselves and recognise their own innermost feelings. Any attempt to put the divine experience into words inevitably detracts from it; furthermore, any such effort can necessarily be made only in terms of the words and concepts available in the subject's language and culture. It is in this way that various religions and creeds are born; but the basic, pre-linguistic experience is what really counts, and it is this which is shared across the divides of language, creed and culture. Thus is born the modern idea of a mystical core of religion, ineffable and based in the intense experience of the modern knowing/feeling subject.

Schleiermacher and his fellow Romantics did not limit this subjectivity to women; on the contrary, they saw it as essential to full humanity. Nevertheless, for a multitude of reasons including legacies from Christian theology as well as the emergence of new political and economic patterns, men continued to be linked with objective reasoning, which was also seen to be the reasoning of the public workplace, while women were linked with emotion, subjectivity, and the privacy of the home. Consequently, the picture which begins to emerge (and which would need to be established in detail on another occasion) is that modern philosophical thinking fosters a conception of mysticism which is complicatedly gendered. On the one hand, it is thought of as an experience or state of the subject; however, it is also thought of as subjectivity rather than objectivity, having to do with intensity of emotion rather than with discursive thinking. Therefore women, who are deemed to be prone to such emotional intensity, are prime candidates for being counted mystics, while mysticism itself is thought of in terms of fundamentally subjective states.

Another of the features of modernity, importantly interconnected with the gendered account of reason and subjectivity, is the division already mentioned of the world into the public and the private realms, with religion increasingly in the latter. The weariness of wars of religion in the early modern period, combined with the dread of 'enthusiasm' as articulated by *inter alia* Locke, Hume, and Kant, were strong impulses to separate religion from political and economic activity and to make it a sphere of private belief and practice. This was particularly true of religious experience: the increasing subjectivisation of the self and the increasing privatisation of religion came together in the idea of religious experience as essentially a private, inner state, having nothing to do with outer, public realities. It was, instead, a strictly personal matter. It could, however, be cultivated; and could produce states of calm and tranquillity which would enable return to those public realities with less anxiety and inner turmoil. Understood in these terms, mysticism becomes domesticated, is rendered unthreatening to the public political realm.

Mysticism has, therefore, from a public point of view, become safe: anyone can be counted a mystic who chooses to be. But as already noted, women, too, are domesticated in the modern period, increasingly removed from the economic world to be the keeper of home and hearth, the 'angel in the house', and therefore also the keeper of the moral and spiritual values. Accordingly, while anyone can be counted a mystic who wants to be, in practice it is left largely to women, or else to men who for one reason or another abandon, either forever or temporarily, for the purpose, the (real, male) public world of commerce and business and warfare.

All the above comments suggesting the provenance of the modern conception of mysticism require elaboration and qualification; they can be taken as no more than very broad brush-strokes. As is the way of broad brush-strokes, they make up a caricature rather than a nuanced picture. Yet caricatures are important ways of conveying aspects of reality which may otherwise go unrecognised; and so it is with this. From even so brief a glance at the constituents of the modern construction of mysticism, it is clear that feminists have much to be concerned about. Far from being a neutral, objective account, the Jamesian account of mysticism accepted by modern philosophers of religion is an account inextricably intertwined with issues of power and gender in ways which feminists need to deconstruct. The privatised, subjectivised ineffable mysticism of William James and his followers is open to women as well as to men; but it plays directly into the hands of modern bourgeois political and gender assumptions. It keeps God (and women) safely out of politics and the public realm; it allows mysticism to flourish as a secret inner life, while those who nurture such an inner life can generally be counted on to prop up rather than to challenge the status quo of their workplaces, their gender roles, and the political systems by which they are governed, since their anxieties and angers will be allayed in the privacy of their own hearts' search for peace and tranquillity.

(ii) *Feminism and relativism*

Nevertheless, the question continues to hang over such a feminist perception of the implications of issues of power and gender in the social construction of mysticism: is the mystical, or any other concept, really social construction 'all the way down'? Might it not be the case that, while we must grant the historicising insights generated by the preceding chapters, there is nevertheless a 'true' mysticism, or at least some form of religious experience which does grant access to a transcendent reality? To deny this, after all, is just as much to fall into the hands of a Kantian model of modernity as to affirm it.

This question is a specific formulation of the more general question of the relation between feminism and postmodernism. On the one hand, it is clear that feminism has much to gain from the deconstructive methodology of postmodernist thinkers. The foregoing chapters are, in part, an application to the concept of mysticism of the techniques pioneered by Foucault (though with inadequate attention to gender) on concepts of madness, punishment, and sexuality. When we see the extent to which mysticism, like them, has been constructed in various periods, and moreover see the interweaving of the issues of power and gender in those constructions, it is obvious that feminist deconstruction is long overdue. It is time to recognise that the idea of an essence of mysticism is a patriarchal construct, and one of which women have every reason to be suspicious.

Yet on the other hand, even putting the issue in those terms already reveals a tension between the implied relativism of the various constructions, and the affirmation of a non-relative feminist standpoint from which those constructions are scrutinised and undermined. The aim of this book, after all, is not simply to catalogue a variety of constructions of mysticism, but to use that catalogue as a tool in the service of feminists and philosophers who are concerned to put things right. I have tried to reclaim some of the dangerous memory of women's spirituality in ways which I hope will nurture contemporary women and men. I have sought to warn of the ways in which men of power, whether in the churches or the universities, have appropriated the concepts of mysticism and spirituality, either by retaining their power but reserving them for male use, or by divesting them of power and thereby domesticating and feminising them. I have pointed to the danger of a privatised, inward spirituality which soothes and tranquillises and promotes an inner harmony that is content to leave the public and political world as it is. I have tried to write justice and truth.

Now, how is it possible to do these two things simultaneously: to show the relative nature of the concept of mysticism (and by implication, very much else), and yet to reject the idea that feminist concerns for justice and truth are similarly relative? Can one have it both ways? Jane Flax, writing more generally of feminist theory and postmodern practice, argues that choices must be made:

We cannot simultaneously claim (1) that the mind, the self, and knowledge are socially constituted and that what we can know depends upon our social practices and contexts and (2) that feminist theory can uncover the truth of the whole once and for all. (1990a: 48)

Applying this to the present concern, it would seem that if we accept that mysticism, like madness, sexuality, and many another concept, has been constructed in ways that are relative to historical conditions of power and gender, then we must accept that the concepts of justice and truth are also thus constructed and cannot be universalised. But if that is the case, then there is no particular reason why feminist concerns for 'justice' should be privileged in any way. These concerns, after all, presumably also originate simply from a particular context, in this case a feminist one; why should people with a non-feminist or anti-feminist perspective support them? If the relativist consequences of postmodernist deconstruction are fully grasped, they effectively subvert the justice-seeking intention of feminist theory (1990: 88). More generally, it can be argued that any commitment to morality and integrity requires an undergirding in epistemology and metaphysics, even if a chastened one: such an underpinning is not an optional extra which could be dispensed with while still retaining standards of truth and justice which are more than expressions of personal or social preference. But if this is so, then the deconstructing efforts of postmodernist thinkers like Foucault, which have served as a model and basis for this book, must be rejected.

Feminist theorists have struggled to find ways of retaining the insights of deconstructionism while rejecting its relativistic implications. Some thinkers, however, notably Richard Rorty, have argued that this is an unnecessary struggle: feminists can have a relativism without tears (1993). In Rorty's view, it all depends on what one wants. If feminists want to change the social world, and we do, then it is no good denying that social construction goes all the way down. In fact, accepting this relativism will enable us not to be too respectful of the past or of social institutions which we wish to change. On the other hand, Rorty does not believe that deconstruction can give any further help in bringing about that change, let alone in giving criteria about what sorts of changes we should work for.

The most interesting question about the utility of deconstruction for feminism is whether, once Nietzsche, Dewey, Derrida, et. al. have convinced us that there is nothing 'natural' or 'scientific' or 'objective' about any given masculinist practice or description, and that all objects (neutrinos, chairs, women, men, literary theory, feminism) are social constructs, there is any *further* assistance that deconstruction can offer in deciding which constructs to keep and which to replace, or in finding substitutes for the latter. I doubt that there is. (99)

Although it is necessary for us to make political and moral choices, there are no universal, objective truths or foundations upon which such choices can be grounded, and no criteria for evaluating them (1982).

Nevertheless, Rorty is himself committed to working for a better and more just society, in particular a society in which there is less cruelty. This, in turn, depends crucially upon being able to see an increasingly widening range of people as like ourselves, and therefore to be included among those whom we consider partners in conversation, and thus entitled to the respect and civility which conversation demands.

There is such a thing as moral progress, and ... this progress is indeed in the direction of greater human solidarity. But that solidarity is not thought of as recognition of a core self, the human essence, in all human beings. Rather, it is thought of as the ability to see more and more traditional differences (of tribe, religion, race, customs, and the like) as unimportant when compared with similarities with respect to pain and humiliation – the ability to think of people wildly different from ourselves as included in the range of 'us'. (1989: 192)

In a world increasingly shattered by groups unwilling to recognise each other's humanity, and pursuing paths of increasing cruelty, humiliation, and 'ethnic cleansing', there is no doubt that this widening of the circle of who counts as humanity is urgent. But on Rorty's own terms, what is to prevent someone with an alternative view, say one which looks for racial purity and the humiliation and eventual extermination of those who do not fit their description, from claiming this as an equally valid moral vision? In his own terms, it is the 'strong poet' and the 'revolutionary artist' who offer the metaphors which will shape our understanding of what humanity is; and it is important 'to see one's language, one's conscience, one's morality, and one's highest hopes as contingent products, as literalizations of what once were accidentally produced metaphors' (61). There is nothing objective or necessary about them, nor are there any independent criteria by which we can evaluate them: morality is simply "'our" set of practices'. But in that case, there is no *moral* reason to object to *Mein Kampf* as the product of a 'strong heroic poet'; and if the events of 1944 had turned out just slightly differently, extermination of Jews, homosexuals and other 'undesirables' might well today be 'our' set of practices – or 'our' extermination if 'we' are lesbian, gay or Jewish. If masculinist efforts produce a backlash against feminism sufficient once again to silence and subordinate women, then provided that such oppression is rooted in the 'new metaphors' of the heroic poet, there would be no basis for moral objection. I do not suggest that this is what Rorty intends; but I see nothing in his work which would allow him to escape from such eventualities (Brickford 1993).

Confronting the issue in such stark terms makes clear that feminists cannot evade the question of the compatibility of deconstructionism with truth and justice. Feminists are only too aware of how regularly the 'poets' and shapers of morality of the past have done so in ways that have oppressed women, and indeed made that oppression part of what was deemed to be the moral fabric of society. The rejection of the possiblity of women as godly or spiritual, the suppression of women visionaries, the burning of heretics and witches, and the modern construction of a domesticated and feminised mysticism all indicate that leaving the development of morality to the voices most able to make themselves heard, whether by force or by poetic seduction, is unlikely to result in a state of affairs which feminists could welcome. If that is the ultimate consequence of a deconstructionist programme, then feminists have every reason to resist it.

And yet it is by undertaking a process dependent precisely on the methodology of deconstruction that I have been able to show how power and gender have regularly been implicated in the changing conceptualisation of mysticism. Feminists can no more give up such probings of history and culture than we can abandon efforts for justice and truth. And yet the two seem, in their ultimate conclusions, finally incompatible.

But are they? It is necessary to look again, and more deeply, at what deconstructionism is, and why it is undertaken. The practice of deconstructionism is, after all, not a neutral academic exercise or a display of scholarly virtuosity, but rather an effort to show how power and knowledge have been hooked together in oppressive ways, and by that recognition make it possible to see through and resist such hook-ups where they continue. Putting it another way, it is precisely the demand of justice which calls forth the efforts of deconstruction: as Derrida insists, 'deconstruction is justice' (1992: 15). This means, however, that justice itself cannot be ultimately reducible, cannot be deconstructible. Derrida examines the apparent paradox by making a crucial distinction between law (*droit*) and justice. Law he interprets in terms of 'legality, legitimacy or legitimation': this, he points out, is always deconstructible, since it is a social construct. Justice, however, is something else. He describes it as an 'infinite "idea of justice"',

infinite because it is irreducible, irreducible because owed to the other, owed to the other, before any contract, because it has come, the other's coming as the singularity that is always other. This 'idea of justice' seems to be irreducible in its affirmative character, in its demand of gift without exchange, without circulation, without recognition or gratitude, without economic circularity, without calculation and without rules, without reason and without rationality. And so we can recognize in it, indeed, accuse, identify a madness ... . And deconstruction is mad about this kind of justice. Mad about this desire for justice. (25)

Consequently, it is precisely this urgent, 'mad' desire for justice which demands deconstruction of law, legality, legitimacy, the methods of the strong: 'deconstruction takes place in the interval that separates the undeconstructibility of justice from the deconstructibility of *droit* (authority, legitimacy, and so on)' (15). Any concept, any authority, all the methods of patriarchy and all the methods of feminism which appropriate legitimacy must be subjected to criticism and self-criticism in the name of justice which is owed to the other.

But this, of course, applies to the concept of justice too. Any idea of justice must itself be subjected, in the name of justice, to deconstruction. As an infinite and irrreducible ideal, it can never be fully grasped or articulated; in this respect Derrida's presentation of the ideal of justice has links with both a Platonic Form and with a Kantian regulative idea, and, not least, with the God of western religion, the God who is above all names and yet is named. Because the idea of justice is not fully graspable, and yet demands attention, all efforts at articulation must always be subject to critique. It is not far from the religious insistence that any images, whether conceptual or material, which can be made of God, are, if taken as the substance rather than the symbol, idols, and as such must be shattered; yet as symbols they are necessary. It is an understanding which was shared by many of those who have been counted mystics, many of those whom we have looked at in this book. In the name of justice, justice must be deconstructed: it is as Eckhart prayed, 'in the name of God, rid me of God'. And so it is no accident that the article in which Derrida struggles with deconstruction and the possiblity of justice is named 'The "Mystical Foundation of Authority" '.

Thus we are returned again to the question with which this section began: is the mystical a social construction all the way down, or is there some 'real' or 'true' mysticism against which all others can be measured and to which it might be appropriate to aspire? I have no neat answer to this question. It is no part of my agenda to belittle the women and men who have struggled for justice and truth and the liberating life of the spirit, whether in the early and medieval period or in our own society. Yet it is surely premature to latch on to any particular understanding of mysticism and label it the 'essence' when it is still so necessary to take seriously all the ways in which mysticism, and religion more generally, have been used and are still used in the interests of power. But if Derrida is correct that it is precisely the demand of justice which requires the deconstruction of legitimacy, if it is precisely the idea of God which requires the critique of every concept of God, then the deconstruction of mysticism and of contemporary spirituality is an urgent task. Perhaps, indeed, it is *the* mystical task.

References

Acts of the Christian Martyrs. 1972. Trans. H. R. Musarillo. Oxford: Clarendon.

Aeschylus. 1953. *Eumenides* in *The Oresteia*. Trans. Robert Fagles. Harmondsworth, Middlesex: Penguin.

Almond, Philip C. 1982. *Mystical Experience and Religious Doctrine: An Investigation of the Study of Mysticism in World Religions*. Berlin and New York: Mouton.

1984. *Rudolf Otto: an Introduction to his Philosophical Theology*. Chapel Hill and London: University of North Carolina Press.

Alston, William P. 1991. *Perceiving God: The Epistemology of Religious Experience*. Ithaca and London: Cornell University Press.

Anderson, Bonnie S. and Zinsser, Judith P. 1988. *A History of Their Own: Women in Europe from Prehistory to the Present*. Vols. I and II. New York and London: Harper and Row.

Ankarloo, Bengt and Henningsen, Gustav, eds. 1990. *Early Modern European Witchcraft: Centres and Peripheries*. Oxford: Clarendon.

Anonymous. *The Cloud of Unknowing*. 1981. Ed. James Walsh. Classics of Western Spirituality. New York: Paulist Press, and London: SPCK.

Anscombe, Elizabeth and Geach, Peter Thomas. 1954. *Descartes' Philosophical Writings*. London: Thomas Nelson Ltd.

Anselm. 1973. *The Prayers and Meditations of St. Anselm*. Trans. Benedicta Ward. Harmondsworth, Middlesex: Penguin.

Anson, John. 1974. 'The Female Transvestite in Early Monasticism'. *Viator*. Vol. 5.

Aristotle. 1912. *De Generatione Animalium*. Trans. Arthur Platt in *The Works of Aristotle*. Vol. v, eds. J. A. Smith and W. D. Ross. Oxford: Clarendon.

1941. *The Basic Works of Aristotle*, ed. Richard McKeon. New York: Random House.

Armstrong, D.M. 1978. *Nominalism and Realism: Universals and Scientific Realism*. 2 vols. Cambridge University Press.

Aston, Margaret. 1984. *Lollards and Reformers: Images and Literacy in Late Medieval Religion*. London: Hambledon Press.

Auclair, Marcelle. 1988. *Saint Teresa of Avila*. Petersham, Massachusetts: St Bede's Publications.

Augustine. 1888/1976. *On the Holy Trinity*. Ed. Philip Schaff. Nicene and Post-Nicene Fathers of the Christian Church. Vol. III. Grand Rapids, Michigan: Wm. B. Eerdmans.

1888/1983. *Expositions on the Book of Psalms*. Ed. Philip Schaff. Nicene and Post-Nicene Fathers of the Christian Church. Vol. VIII. Grand Rapids, Michigan: Wm. B. Eerdmans.

1958. *On Christian Doctrine*. Trans. D. W. Robertson Jr. The Library of Liberal Arts. New York: Bobbs-Merrill.

1960. *The Confessions of Saint Augustine*. Trans. John K. Ryan. New York: Doubleday.

1972. *City of God*. Trans. Henry Bettenson. Harmondsworth, Middlesex: Penguin.

1984. *Selected Writings*. Trans. Mary T. Clark, Classics of Western Spirituality. New York: Paulist Press, and London: SPCK.

Axters, Stephanus. 1954. *The Spirituality of the Old Low Countries*. London: Blackfriars Publications.

Bainton, Roland. 1950. *Here I Stand: A Life of Martin Luther*. New York: Abingdon–Cokesbury.

1963. *Studies on the Reformation*. Boston: Beacon Press, and London: Hodder and Stoughton.

Baker, Derek, ed. 1978. *Medieval Women*. Oxford: Blackwell.

Balmary, Marie. 1982. *Psychoanalysing Psychoanalysis: Freud and the Hidden Fault of the Father*. Baltimore and London: Johns Hopkins University Press.

Bamborough, Renford. 1978. 'Intuition and the Inexpressible' in Steven T. Katz, ed. *Mysticism and Philosophical Analysis*. London: Sheldon.

Barnes, Jonathan. 1979. *The Presocratic Philosophers*. Vol. 1 *Thales to Zeno*; vol. 2 *Empedocles to Democritus*. London and Boston: Routledge and Kegan Paul.

Barr, Jane. 1990. 'The Influence of Saint Jerome on Medieval Attitudes to Women' in Janet Martin Soskice, ed. *After Eve: Women, Theology and the Christian Tradition*. London: Collins.

Barrett, Michèle. 1991. *The Politics of Truth: From Marx to Foucault*. Stanford University Press.

Barth, Karl. 1957. *Church Dogmatics*. Vols. I–IV. Edinburgh: T & T Clark.

Bartlett, Robert. 1986. *Trial by Fire and Water: The Medieval Judicial Ordeal*. Oxford: Clarendon.

Beer, Frances. 1992. *Women and Mystical Experience in the Middle Ages.* Rochester, New York, and Woodbridge, Suffolk: Boydell.

Bell, Rudolph M. 1985. *Holy Anorexia.* Chicago and London: University of Chicago Press.

Benedict. 1975. *The Rule of St. Benedict.* Trans. Anthony C. Meisel and M. L. de Mastro. New York: Image Books, Doubleday.

Benhabib, Seyla. 1990. 'Epistemologies of Postmodernism: A Rejoinder to Jean-François Lyotard.' In Linda Nicholson, ed. *Feminism/ Postmodernism.* London and New York: Routledge.

— 1991. 'On Hegel, Women and Irony' in Mary Lyndon Shanley and Carole Pateman, eds., *Feminist Interpretations and Political Theory.* Cambridge: Polity.

— 1992. *Situating the Self: Gender, Community and Postmodernism in Contemporary Ethics.* Cambridge: Polity.

Berger, Peter and Luckmann, Thomas. 1966. *The Social Construction of Reality: A Treatise on the Sociology of Knowledge.* Harmondsworth: Penguin.

Bernard of Clairvaux. 1953. *Letters.* Trans. Bruno Scott James. London: Burns Oates.

— 1961. *On The Love Of God.* Oxford and London: Mowbray.

— 1974. *Treatises II (The Steps of Humility, On Loving God).* Cistercian Fathers Series 13. Kalamazoo, Michigan: Cistercian Publications.

— 1977–80. *On the Song of Songs.* Vols. I–IV. Trans. Killian Walsh, OCSO, Cistercian Fathers Series 4, 7, 31, 40. Kalamazoo, Michigan: Cistercian Publications.

Bickford, Susan. 1993. 'Why we Listen to Lunatics: Antifoundational Theories and Feminist Politics'. *Hypatia* vol. 8 no. 2.

Bird, Graham. 1986. *William James.* London and New York: Routledge.

Blamires, Alcuin, ed. 1992. *Women Defamed and Women Defended: An Anthology of Medieval Texts.* Oxford: Clarendon.

Boff, Leonardo. 1985. *Saint Francis: A Model for Human Liberation.* London: SCM.

du Bois, Page. 1988. *Sowing the Body: Psychoanalysis and Ancient Representations of Women.* University of Chicago Press.

Bolton, Brenda M. 1973. 'Mulieres Sanctae' in Derek Baker, ed. *Studies in Church History* vol. 10. Published for the Ecclesiastical History Society. Oxford: Blackwell, and New York: Barnes and Noble.

— 1978. '*Vitae Matrum*' A Further Aspect of the *Frauenfrage*' in Derek Baker, ed. *Medieval Women* . Oxford: Blackwell.

Bonaventure. 1960–1970. *The Works of Bonaventure.* 5 vols. Trans. José de Vinck. Patterson, New Jersey: St Anthony Guild.

— 1978. *The Soul's Journey into God.* Trans. Ewert Cousins. Classics of Western Spirituality. New York: Paulist, and London: SPCK.

Bordo, Susan R. 1987. *The Flight to Objectivity: Essays on Cartesianism and Culture*. Albany, New York: SUNY.

Boulding, Elise. 1992. *The Underside of History: A View of Women Through Time* Revised edition vols. I and II. Newbury Park, California, and London: Sage.

Bouyer, Louis. 1981. 'Mysticism. An Essay on the Meaning of the Word' in Richard Woods, ed.,*Understanding Mysticism*. London: Athlone.

Bouyer, Louis, Leclercq, Jean, Vandenbrouke, François and Cognet, Louis. 1968. *History of Christian Spirituality*. Vol. I *The Spirituality of the New Testament and the Fathers*; Vol. II *The Spirituality of the Middle Ages*; Vol. III *Orthodox Spirituality and Protestant and Anglican Spirituality*. London: Burns Oates, and New York: Seabury.

Bowie, Fiona, ed. 1989. *Beguine Spirituality: An Anthology* . London: SPCK.

Bowie, Fiona and Davies, Oliver, eds. 1990. *Hildegard of Bingen: An Anthology* London: SPCK.

Boyd, William. 1975. *The History of Western Education,* 11th edition revised by Edmund J. King. London: Adam & Charles Black.

Braidotti, Rosi. 1991. *Patterns of Dissonance: A Study of Women in Contemporary Philosophy*. New York: Routledge, and Cambridge: Polity.

Brandt, Richard B. 1968. *The Philosophy of Schleiermacher*. Westport, Connecticut: Greenwood.

Brennan, Gerald. 1973. *John of the Cross: His Life and Poetry*. Cambridge University Press.

Bridenthal, Renate, Koonz, Claudia, and Stuard, Susan, eds. 1987. *Becoming Visible: Women in European History*, 2nd edition. Boston: Houghton Mifflin Co.

Brooke, Christopher. 1975. *Europe in the Central Middle Ages 962–1154*. New York and London: Longman.

1991. *The Medieval Idea of Marriage*. Oxford and New York: Oxford University Press.

Brown, D. Catherine. 1987. *Pastor and Laity in the Theology of Jean Gerson*. Cambridge University Press.

Brown, Judith C. 1986. *Immodest Acts: The Life of a Lesbian Nun in Renaissance Italy*. Oxford University Press.

Brown, Peter. 1967. *Augustine of Hippo: A Biography*. London and Boston: Faber and Faber.

1981. *The Cult of the Saints: Its Rise and Function in Latin Christianity*. London: SCM.

1987. 'The Notion of Virginity in the Early Church' in Bernard McGinn, John Meyendorff and Jean Leclercq, eds. *Christian Spirituality: Origins to the Twelfth Century*. New York: Crossroad.

1988. *The Body and Society: Men, Women and Sexual Renunciation in Early Christianity*. New York: Columbia University Press.

Brown, Raphael. 1958. *The Little Flowers of St Francis*. New York: Doubleday.

Brunner, Emil. 1947. *The Mediator*. Philadelphia: Westminster.

Bruyn, Lucy de. 1979. *Woman and the Devil in Sixteenth Century Literature*. Tisbury, Wiltshire: Compton.

Burford, E.J. and Shulman, Sandra. 1992. *Of Bridles and Burnings: The Punishment of Women*. New York: St Martin's Press, and London: Robert Hale.

Burnaby, John. 1938. *Amor Dei*. London: Hodder & Stoughton.

Burrows, Ruth. 1982. *Interior Castle Explored: St Teresa's Teaching on the Life of Deep Union with God*. London: Sheed and Ward.

Butler, Cuthbert. 1967. *Western Mysticism: The Teaching of Saints Augustine, Gregory and Bernard on Contemplation and the Contemplative Life*, 3rd edition. London: Constable.

Bynum, Caroline Walker. 1982. *Jesus as Mother: Studies in the Spirituality of the High Middle Ages*. University of California Press.

1987a. *Holy Feast and Holy Fast: the Religious Significance of Food to Medieval Women*. University of California Press.

1987b. 'Religious Women in the Later Middle Ages' in Jill Raitt, ed. *Christian Spirituality: High Middle Ages and Reformation*. New York: Crossroad, and London: Routledge and Kegan Paul.

1991. *Fragmentation and Redemption: Essays on Gender and the Human Body in Medieval Religion*. New York: Zone Books.

Byrne, Peter. 1984. 'Mysticism, Identity and Realism: a Debate Reviewed'. *International Journal for Philosophy of Religion* 16.

1989. *Natural Religion and the Nature of Religion: The Legacy of Deism*. London and New York: Routledge.

Calvin, John. 1957. *Institutes of the Christian Religion*. 2 vols. Trans. by Henry Beveridge. Grand Rapids, Michigan: Wm. B. Eerdmans Publishing Company.

1975. *A Commentary upon the Book of Genesis* Trans. John King. Edinburgh: Banner of Truth.

Cantor, Norman F. 1991. *Inventing the Middle Ages: The Lives, Works and Ideas of the Great Medievalists of the Twentieth Century* . New York: Quill.

Cantwell Smith, Wilfred. 1962. *The Meaning and End of Religion*. New York: Macmillan.

1981. *Toward a World Theology*. London and New York: Macmillan.

Cassirer, Ernst. 1981. *Kant's Life and Thought*. Trans. James Haden. New Haven and London: Yale University Press.

Catherine of Siena. 1980. *The Dialogue*. Trans. and intro. Suzanne Noffke. Classics of Western Spirituality Series. New York: Paulist, and London: SPCK.

Certaux, M. de, 1964. ' "Mystique" au XVII siècle. La probleme du langage mystique' in *L'Homme devant Dieu. Mélanges Henri de Lubac*. Vol. II. Paris.

Chapp, James Gordon. 'Locke, John' in Paul Edwards, ed. 1967. *The Encyclopedia of Philosophy*. Vol. IV. London and New York: Macmillan.

Christ, Carol P. 1986. *Diving Deep and Surfacing: Women Writers on Spiritual Quest*, 2nd ed. Boston: Beacon.

 1987. *Laughter of Aphrodite: Reflections on a Journey to the Goddess*. San Francisco and London: Harper and Row.

Christ, Carol P. and Plaskow, Judith. 1979. *Womanspirit Rising: A Feminist Reader in Religion*. San Francisco and London: Harper and Row.

Christie-Murray, David. 1976. *A History of Heresy*. Oxford University Press.

Clark, Alice. 1992. *Working Life of Women in the Seventeenth Century*. New edition with an introduction by Amy Louise Erickson. London and New York: Routledge.

Clissold, Stephen. 1979. *St Teresa of Avila*. London: Sheldon.

Cloud of Unknowing, The. 1981. Ed. James Walsh. Classics of Western Spirituality. New York: Paulist, and London: SPCK.

Code, Lorraine. 1991. *What Can She Know? Feminist Theory and the Construction of Knowledge*. Ithaca and London: Cornell University Press.

Code, Lorraine, Mullett, Shiela, and Overall, Christine, eds. 1988. *Feminist Perspectives: Philosophical Essays on Method and Morals*. University of Toronto Press.

Cohn, Norman. 1976. *Europe's Inner Demons*. London: Paladin.

Condren, Mary. 1989. *The Serpent and the Goddess: Women, Religion & Power in Celtic Ireland*. San Francisco and London: Harper and Row.

Conn, Joann Wolski, ed. 1986. *Women's Spirituality: Resources for Christian Development*. Mahwah, New Jersey: Paulist.

Cornell, Drucilla. 1991. *Beyond Accommodation: Ethical Feminism, Deconstruction and the Law*. New York and London: Routledge.

 1992a. *The Philosophy of the Limit*. London and New York: Routledge.

 1992b. 'The Philosophy of the Limit: Systems Theory and Feminist Legal Reform' in Drucilla Cornell, *et al.*, eds. *Deconstruction and the Possiblity of Justice*. London and New York: Routledge.

Cornell, Drucilla, Rosenfeld, Michel, and Carlson, David Gray, eds. 1992. *Deconstruction and the Possiblity of Justice*. London and New York: Routledge.

Costelli, Elizabeth. 1991. '"I Will Make Mary Male": Pieties of the Body and Gender Transformation of Christian Women in Late Antiquity' in Julian Epstein and Kristina Straub, eds. *Body Guards: the Cultural Politics of Gender Ambiguity*. New York and London: Routledge Chapman Hall.

Cottingham, John, ed. 1992. *The Cambrdge Companion to Descartes*. Cambridge University Press.

Cousins, Ewert, trans. 1978. *Bonaventure: The Soul's Journey into God*. Classics of Western Spirituality. New York: Paulist, and London: SPCK.

Coward, Harold and Penelhum, Terence, eds. 1977. *Mystics and Scholars: Calgary Conference on Mysticism 1976*. Calgary: Canadian Corporation for Studies in Religion.

Cranston, Maurice. 1957. *John Locke: A Biography*. London and New York: Longmans, Green and Co.

Crawford, Patricia. 1993. *Women and Religion in England 1500–1720*. London and New York: Routledge.

Cugno, Alain. 1982. *St John of the Cross: The Life and Thought of a Christian Mystic*. London: Burns and Oates.

Curtayne, Alice. 1981/1929. *Saint Catherine of Siena*. Chumleigh, Devon: Augustine Publishing Co.

Daly, Mary. 1979. *Gyn/Ecology: The Metaethics of Radical Feminism*. London: Women's Press.

1984. *Pure Lust: Elemental Feminist Philosophy*. London: Women's Press.

1985. *Beyond God the Father: Towards a Philosophy of Women's Liberation*. London: Women's Press.

Davies, David Brion. 1966. *The Problem of Slavery in Western Culture*. Oxford University Press.

Davies, Oliver. 1988. *God Within: The Mystical Tradition of Northern Europe*. London: Darton, Longman and Todd.

1991. *Meister Eckhart: Mystical Theologian*. London: SPCK.

ed. 1989. *The Rhineland Mystics: An Anthology*. London: SPCK.

Davis, Caroline Franks. 1989. *The Evidential Force of Religious Experience*. Oxford: Clarendon.

De Beauvoir, Simone. 1987. *The Second Sex*. Harmondsworth: Penguin.

De Vitry, Jacques. 1969. *Lettres*. Ed. R.B.C. Huygens. Leiden: Brill.

Derrida, Jacques. 1992. 'The "Mystical Foundation of Authority"' in Drucilla Cornell, *et al.*, eds. *Deconstruction and the Possibility of Justice*. London and New York: Routledge.

Descartes. 1954. *Philosophical Writings*. Trans. and ed. Elizabeth Anscombe and Peter Thomas Geach. London: Thomas Nelson Ltd.

Diamond, Irene and Orenstein, Gloria Feman, eds. 1990. *Reweaving the Word: The Emergence of Ecofeminism*. San Francisco: Sierra Club.

Diamond, Irene and Quinby, Lee, eds. 1988. *Feminism and Foucault: Reflections on Resistance*. Boston: Northeastern University Press.

Doyle, Eric. 1980. *St Francis and the Song of Brotherhood*. London: George Allen and Unwin.

Dronke, Peter. 1984. *Women Writers of the Middle Ages*. Cambridge University Press.

Dryer, Elizabeth. 1989. *Passionate Women: Two Medieval Mystics*. New York: Paulist.

Duffy, Eamon. 1992. *The Stripping of the Altars: Traditional Religion in England 1400–1580*. New Haven and London: Yale University Press.

Dupré, Louis. 1986. 'Mysticism' in Mircea Eleade, ed. *The Encyclopedia of Religion*. New York and London: Macmillan.

Eckhart. 1979–87. *Sermons and Treatises*. Vols. I–III. Trans. M. O'C. Walshe. London: Watkins.

  1981. *The Essential Sermons, Commentaries, Treatises, and Defense*. Trans. and intro. Edmund College and Bernard McGinn. Classics of Western Spirituality Series. London: SPCK, and New York: Paulist.

  1986. *Meister Eckhart, Teacher and Preacher*. Ed. Bernard McGinn. Classics of Western Spirituality Series. London: SPCK, and New York: Paulist.

Edmee, Sister, SLG. 1975. 'Bernard and Abelard' in Benedicta Ward, ed. *The Influence of St Bernard: Anglican Essays with Introduction by Jean Leclercq*. Oxford: SLG Press.

Egeria. 1981. *Travels to the Holy Land*. Trans. John Wilkinson. Revised ed. Jerusalem: Aris & Phillips, Warminster & Ariel Publishing House.

Ehrenberg, Margaret. 1989. *Women in Prehistory*. London: British Museum Publications.

Ehrenreich, Barbara and English, Deirdre. 1973. *Witches, Midwives, and Nurses: A History of Women Healers*. New York: The Feminist Press.

  1979. *For Her Own Good: 150 Years of the Expert's Advice to Women*. New York and London: Doubleday.

Eileen Mary, Sister, SLG. 1983. *Pilgrimage and Possession: Conversion in the Writings of St John of the Cross and St Teresa*. Fairacres Publication 86. Oxford: SLG Press.

Eisenstein, Zillah. 1981. *The Radical Future of Liberal Feminism*. Boston: Northeastern University Press.

Eleade, Mircea, ed. 1986. *The Encyclopedia of Religion*. New York and London: Macmillan.

Elshatin, Jean Bethke. 1993. 'Christianity and Patriarchy: The Odd Alliance' in *Modern Theology* 9.2.

Englebert, Omer. 1950. *Saint Francis of Assisi: A Biography*. Trans. Edward Hutton. London: Burns Oates.

Epstein, Julia and Straub, Kristina, eds. 1991. *Body Guards: the Cultural Politics of Gender Ambiguity*. New York and London: Routledge Chapman Hall.

Euripides. 1953. *Iphigenia at Tauris* in *Three Plays*. Trans Philip Vellacott. Harmondsworth: Penguin.

Evans, G.R. 1984–5. *The Logic and Language of the Bible*. Vol. I *The Earlier Middle Ages*. Vol. II *The Road to Reformation*. Cambridge University Press.

Fatula, Mary Ann. 1987. *Catherine of Siena's Way*. London: Darton, Longman and Todd, and New York: Michael Glazier.

Fiero, Gloria K., Pfeffer, Wendy and Allain, Mathé, eds. 1989. *Three Medieval Views of Women*. New Haven and London: Yale University Press.

Fiorenza, Elizabeth Schüssler. 1983. *In Memory of Her: A Feminist Theological Reconstruction of Christian Origins*. London: SCM.

Fischer, Kathleen. 1988. *Women at the Well: Feminist Perspectives on Spiritual Direction*. New York: Paulist.

Flanagan, Sabina 1989. *Hildegard of Bingen: A Visionary Life*. London and New York: Routledge.

Flandrin, J. 1979. *Families in Former Times*. Cambridge University Press.

Flax, Jane. 1990a. 'Postmodernism and Gender Relations in Feminist Theory' in Linda Nicholson, ed. *Feminism/Postmodernism*. London and New York: Routledge.

1990b. *Thinking Fragments: Psychoanalysis, Feminism and Postmodernism in the Contemporary West*. University of California Press.

Foucault, Michel. 1967. *Madness and Civilisation: A History of Insanity in the Age of Reason*. London: Tavistock Publications.

1972. *The Archaeology of Knowledge and the Discourse on Language*. New York: Pantheon, and London: Tavistock.

1973. *The Order of Things: An Archaeology of the Human Sciences*. New York: Vintage.

1977. *Discipline and Punish: The Birth of the Prison*. London and New York: Penguin.

1978; 1985; 1986. *The History of Sexuality. Volume One: An Introduction; Volume Two: The Use of Pleasure; Volume Three: The Care of the Self*. London and New York: Penguin.

1980. *Power/Knowledge: Selected Interviews and Other Writings 1972–1977*. New York: Pantheon.

1989. *Foucault Live: Interviews, 1966–1984*. New York: Semiotext.

Fox, Matthew. 1980. *Breakthrough: Meister Eckhart's Creation Spirituality in New Translation*. New York: Doubleday.

ed. 1981. *Western Spirituality: Historical Root, Ecumenical Routes*. Santa Fe, New Mexico: Bear and Co.

1983. *Original Blessing*. Santa Fe, New Mexico: Bear and Co.

1988. *The Coming of the Cosmic Christ*. San Francisco and London: Harper and Row.

1991. *Creation Spirituality: Liberating Gifts for the Peoples of the Earth*. San Francisco: Harper and Row.

Fox, Robin Lane. 1986. *Pagans and Christians in the Mediterranean World from the Second Century AD to the Conversion of Constantine*. London: Penugin.

Francis and Clare. 1982. *The Complete Works*. Trans. and intro. by Regis J. Armstrong and Ignatius C. Brady. Classics of Western Spirituality Series. New York: Paulist, and London: SPCK.

Fraser, Antonia. 1989. *The Weaker Vessel: Women's Lot in Seventeenth-Century England*. London: Mandarin.

Fuhrmann, Horst. 1986. *Germany in the High Middle Ages c.1050–1200*. Cambridge University Press.

Gadol, Joan Kelly. 1984. *Women, History and Theory*. University of Chicago Press.

Gale, Richard M. 1991. *On the Nature and Existence of God*. Cambridge University Press.

Garry, Ann and Pearsall, Marilyn, eds. 1989. *Women, Knowledge and Reality: Explorations in Feminist Philosophy*. Boston and London: Unwin Hyman.

Gertrude the Great of Helfta. 1989a. *Gesandten der Gottlichen liebe*. Trans. Walter Berschin. Heidelberg: Verlag Lambert Schneider.

1989b. *Spiritual Exercises*. Trans. and intro Gertrud Jaron Lewis and Jack Lewis. Cistercian Fathers Series 49. Kalamazoo, Michigan: Cistercian Publications.

1991. *The Herald of God's Loving Kindness*. Books 1 & 2. Trans. and annotated by Alexandra Barratt. Cistercian Fathers Series 35. Kalamazoo, Michigan: Cistercian Publications.

Giles, Mary E., ed. 1982. *The Feminist Mystic: and Other Essays on Women and Spirituality*. New York: Crossroad.

Gilligan, Carol. 1982. *In a Different Voice: Psychological Theory and Women's Development*. Cambridge, MA and London: Harvard University Press.

Gilson, Etienne. 1955a. *The Mystical Theology of St Bernard*. London: Sheed and Ward.

1955b. *History of Christian Philosophy in the Middle Ages*. New York: Random House.

Ginsburg, Carlo. 1991. *Ecstasies: Deciphering the Witches' Sabbath*. London and New York: Penguin.

Glatzer, Nahum N, ed. 1971. *The Essential Philo*. New York: Schocken Books.

Godwin, Joscelyn. 1981. *Mystery Religions in the Ancient World*. London: Thames & Hudson.

Gospel of Thomas. 1977. In James M. Robinson, ed. *The Nag Hammadi Library*. Leiden: E.J. Brill.

Green, Deirdre. 1989. *Gold in the Crucible: Teresa of Avila and the Western Mystical Tradition*. Shaftesbury, Dorset: Element Books.

Greene, Theodore M and Hudson, Hoyt T. 1960. Trans. and introduction to Kant, *Religion Within the Limits of Reason Alone*. New York: Harper.

Gregory of Nyssa. 1961. *Commentary on the Canticle,* Eng. trans. Herbert Musurillo, SJ and Jean Danielou, SJ, *From Glory to Glory* . New York: Charles Scribner's Sons.

    1978. *The Life of Moses*. Ed. Abraham Malherbe & Everett Ferguson. Classics of Western Spirituality. London: SPCK, and New York: Paulist.

Gutmann, James. 1936. 'Introduction' to Schelling *Of Human Freedom*. Chicago: Open Court.

Hadewijch. 1980. *The Complete Works*. Trans. and intro. Mother Columbia Hart. Classics of Western Spirituality Series. New York: Paulist, and London: SPCK.

Haining, Peter, ed. 1974. *The Witchcraft Papers: Contemporary Records of the Witchcraft Hysteria in Essex 1560–1700*. London: Robert Hale and Co.

Haldane, Elizabeth S. 1905. *Descartes: His Life and Times*. London: John Murray.

Hall, David D, ed. 1991. *Witch-Hunting in Seventeenth Century New England: A Documentary History 1638–1692*. Boston: Northeastern University Press.

Harding, Sandra. 1986. *The Science Question in Feminism*. Ithaca and London: Cornell University Press.

    1990. 'Feminism, Science and the Anti-Enlightenment Critiques' in Linda Nicholson, ed. *Feminism/Postmodernism*. London and New York: Routledge.

Hardy, Richard P. 1987. *The Life of St John of the Cross: Search for Nothing*. London: Darton, Longman and Todd.

Harrison, Beverly Wildung. 1985. *Making the Connections: Essays in Feminist Social Ethics*. Ed. Carol S. Robb. Boston: Beacon Press.

Hart, Columba. 1980. 'Introduction' in *Hadewijch: The Complete Works*. Classics of Western Spirituality. New York: Paulist and London: SPCK.

Hellman, J.A. Wayne. 1987. 'The Spirituality of the Franciscans' in Jill

Raitt, ed. *Christian Spirituality: High Middle Ages and Reformation.* New York: Crossroad, and London: Routledge and Kegan Paul.

Herben, Jan. 1926. *Huss and his Followers.* London: Geoffrey Bles.

Heyward, I. Carter. 1982. *The Redemption of God: A Theology of Mutual Relation.* New York and London: University Press of America.

1989. *Touching our Strength: The Erotic as Power and the Love of God.* San Francisco and London: Harper and Row.

Hesiod. 1973. *Theogony* and *Works and Days* in *Hesiod and Theognis.* Trans. Dorothea Wender. London and New York: Penguin.

Hester, Marianne. 1992. *Lewd Women & Wicked Witches: A Study of the Dynamics of Male Domination.* London and New York: Routledge.

Hibbert, Christopher. 1974. *The Rise and Fall of the House of Medici.* London: Penguin.

Hick, John. 1977. 'Mystical Experience as Cognition' in Harold Coward and Terence Penelhum, eds. *Mystics and Scholars: Calgary Conference on Mysticism 1976.* Calgary: Canadian Corporation for Studies in Religion.

1989. *An Interpretation of Religion: Human Responses to the Transcendent.* London and New York: Macmillan.

Hildegard of Bingen. 1987. *Book of Divine Works with Letters and Songs.* Ed. Matthew Fox. Santa Fe, New Mexico: Bear and Co.

1990a. *Scivias* Trans. Columba Hart and Jane Bishop, Intro. Barbara J. Newman. Classics of Western Spirituality Series. New York: Paulist.

1990b. *Heilweissen: Von der Ursachen und der Behandlung von Krankheiten [Causae et Curae].* Edited by Manfred Pawlik. Freiberg: Herder Verlag.

Hill, Christopher. 1988. *A Turbulent, Seditious, and Factious People: John Bunyan and his Church.* Oxford University Press.

Hobbes, Thomas. 1985. *Leviathan: or The Matter, Form and Power of a Commonwealth Ecclesiastical and Civil* edited by C.B. MacPherson. London and New York: Penguin.

Howell, Martha C. 1986. *Women, Production and Patriarchy in Late Medieval Cities.* University of Chicago Press.

Hughes, Gerard W. 1985. *God of Surprises.* London: Darton, Longman and Todd.

Huizinga, J. 1924. *The Waning of the Middle Ages.* Harmondsworth, Middlesex: Penguin.

Hussey, Edward. 1972. *The Presocratics.* London: Duckworth.

Huxley, Aldous. 1977. *The Doors of Perception* and *Heaven and Hell.* London: Grafton Collins.

Hyman, Arthur and Walsh, James J., eds. 1973. *Philosophy in the Middle*

Ages: The Christian, Islamic, and Jewish Traditions. Indianapolis, IN: Hackett Publishing Company.

Inge, William Ralph. 1925. *Christian Mysticism*, the Bampton Lectures for 1899. Sixth edition. London: Methuen.

Irigaray, Luce. 1993. *Sexes and Genealogies*. New York and Chichester: Columbia University Press.

Jacobsen, Grethe. 1989. 'Nordic Women and the Reformation' in Sherrin Marshall, ed. *Women in Reformation and Counter-Reformation Europe: Private and Public Worlds*. Bloomington and Indianapolis: Indiana University Press.

James, William. 1907. *Pragmatism: A New Name for some Old Ways of Thinking*. London and New York: Longmans, Green and Cc.

   1950. *The Principles of Psychology*. 2 vols. New York: Dover.

   1960. *The Varieties of Religious Experience*. The Gifford Lectures of 1901–2. Glasgow: Collins.

Jantzen, Grace M. 1985. 'Luther and the Mystics' in *King's Theological Review*. Vol. VII, no. 2.

   1986a. 'Ethics and Mysticism: Friends or Foes?' in *Nedelands Theologisch Tijdschrift*. Vol. III, no. 4.

   1986b. 'Human Autonomy in the Body of God' in Alistair Kee and Eugene Long, eds. *Being and Truth: Essays in Honour of John Macquarrie*. London: SCM.

   1986c. 'The Mystical Meaning of Scripture: Medieval and Modern Presuppositions' in *King's Theological Review*. Vol. VII, no. 2.

   1987. *Julian of Norwich: Mystic and Theologian*. London: SPCK, and New York: Paulist.

   1989. 'Mysticism and Experience' in *Religious Studies*. Vol. 25.

   1990. 'Could There be a Mystical Core of Religion?' in *Religious Studies*. Vol. 26.

   1993. 'The Legacy of Evelyn Underhill' in *Feminist Theology*. Vol. II, no. 3.

Jerome. 1986. 'Letter to Marcella about her Daughter Petra' and 'Letter 22 to Eustochium: the Virgin's Profession' in Elizabeth Alvida Petroff, ed. *Medieval Women's Visionary Literature*. Oxford University Press.

John of the Cross. 1973. *The Collected Works*. Trans. Kieran Kavanaugh and Otiolio Rodrigues. Washington, D.C.: Institute of Carmelite Studies.

   1987. *Selected Writings*. Ed. Kieran Kavanaugh. Classics of Western Spirituality. New York: Paulist, and London: SPCK.

Jones, A.H.M. 1966. *The Decline of the Ancient World*. London and New York: Longman.

Jones, Rufus M. 1914. *Spiritual Reformers in the Sixteenth and Seventeenth Centuries*. London and New York: Macmillan.

1923. *Studies in Mystical Religion*. London and New York: Macmillan.

Jordan, Constance. 1990. *Renaissance Feminism: Literary Texts and Political Models*. Ithaca and London: Cornell University Press.

Julian of Norwich. 1978. *Showings*. Trans. Edmund Colledge and James Walsh. Classics of Western Spirituality. New York: Paulist, and London: SPCK.

Jüngel, Eberhard. 1983. *God as the Mystery of the World*. Edinburgh: T & T Clark.

Kant, Emmanuel. 1929. *Critique of Pure Reason*. Trans. Norman Kemp Smith. London and New York: Macmillan.

1960. *Religion Within the Limits of Reason Alone*. Trans, with and Introduction by Theodore M. Green and Hoyt T. Hudson. New York: Harper.

Karlson, Carol E. 1987. *The Devil in the Shape of a Woman: Witchcraft in Colonial New England*. New York: Random House.

Katz, Steven T., ed. 1978. *Mysticism and Philosophical Analysis*. London: Sheldon.

1992. *Mysticism and Language*. Oxford University Press.

Keller, Mara Lynn. 1990. 'The Eleusinian Mysteries: Ancient Nature Religion of Demeter and Persephone' in Irene Diamond and Gloria Orenstein, eds. *Reweaving the World: The Emergence of Ecofeminism*. San Francisco: Sierra Club.

Kelley, C.F., ed. 1954. *The Book of the Poor in Spirit by a Friend of God (Fourteenth Century): A Guide to Rhineland Mysticism*. London and New York: Longmans, Green and Co.

Kelly, Joan. 1984. *Women, History and Theory*. University of Chicago Press.

Kenny, Anthony. 1993/1968. *Descartes: A Study of his Philosophy*. Bristol: Thoemmes.

Kerr, Fergus. 1985. *Theology After Wittgenstein*. Oxford: Blackwell.

King, Margot. 1984. *The Desert Mothers: A Survey of the Feminine Anchoretical Tradition*. Saskatoon, Canada: Peregrina.

Kittay, Eva Fedor, and Meyers, Diana T., eds. 1987. *Women and Moral Theory*. Savage, Maryland: Rowman and Littlefield.

Klapisch-Zuber, Christine, ed. 1992. *A History of Women: Silences of the Middles Ages*. Cambridge, MA, and London: Harvard University Press.

Klein, Joan Larson, ed. 1992. *Daughters, Wives and Widows: Writings by Men about Women and Marriage in England 1500–1640*. Urbana and Chicago: University of Illinois Press.

Kleinberg, S. Jay. 1988. *Retrieving Women's History: Changing Perceptions of the Role of Women in Politics and Society*. Providence, RI, and Oxford: Berg Publications.

Kramer, Heinrich, and Sprenger, James. 1986/1928. *Malleus Malificarum*. Trans. Montague Summers. London: Arrow.

Labarge, Margaret Wade. 1986. *A Small Sound of the Trumpet: Women in Medieval Life*. Boston: Beacon.

Ladurie, Emmanuel Le Roy. 1978. *Montaillou: Cathars and Catholics in a French Village 1294–1324*. London: Penguin.

Lambert, Malcolm. 1992. *Medieval Heresy: Popular Movements from the Gregorian Reform to the Reformation*, 2nd edition. Oxford: Blackwell.

Laqueur, Thomas. 1990. *Making Sex: Body and Gender from the Greeks to Freud*. Cambridge, MA, and London: Harvard University Press.

Lash, Nicholas. 1988. *Easter in Ordinary: Reflections on Human Experience and the Knowledge of God*. London: SCM.

Laslett, Peter. 1992. *The World We Have Lost – Further Explored*, 3rd edition. London: Routledge.

Lawrence, C.H. 1984. *Medieval Monasticism: Forms of Religious Life in Western Europe in the Middle Ages*. London and New York: Longmans.

Leech, Kenneth. 1985. *True God: An Exploration in Spiritual Theology*. London: Sheldon.

Leclercq, Jean. 1976. *Bernard of Clairvaux and the Cistercian Spirit*. Cistercian Studies Series 16. Kalamazoo: Cistercian Publications.

1978. *The Love of Learning and the Desire for God*. London: SPCK.

1989. *Women and St Bernard of Clairvaux*. Cistercian Studies Series 104. Kalamazoo, Michigan: Cistercian Publications.

Leff, Gordon. 1967. *Heresy in the Later Middle Ages: The Relation of Heterodoxy to Dissent c1250–c1450*. 2 vols. Manchester University Press, and New York: Barnes and Noble.

Le Goff, Jacques. 1988. *Medieval Civilization 400–1500*. Oxford: Blackwell.

Lerner, Gerda. 1986. *The Creation of Patriarchy*. Oxford University Press.

Lerner, R.E. 1972. *The Heresy of the Free Spirit in the Later Middle Ages*. University of California Press.

Levack, Brian. 1987. *The Witch-Hunt in Early Modern Europe*. London and New York: Longman.

Lindbeck, George. 1984. *The Nature of Doctrine: Religion and Theology in a Post-Liberal Age*. London: SPCK.

Llewelyn, Robert, ed. 1980ff. *Enfolded in Love*. Readings with the Mystics Series. London: Darton, Longman and Todd.

Lloyd, Genevieve. 1984. *The Man of Reason: 'Male' and 'Female' in Western Philosophy*. London: Methuen.

Locke, John. 1690/1959. *An Essay Concerning Human Understanding*. Edited in two volumes by Alexander Campbell Fraser. Oxford University Press.

1690/1960. *Two Treatises of Government*. Critical edition by Peter Laslett. Cambridge University Press.

1695/1958. *The Reasonableness of Christianity*. Edited by I. T. Ramsey. Stanford University Press.

1706/1993. *Of the Conduct of the Understanding*. Intro. John Yolton. Bristol: Thoemmes Press.

Lonergan, Bernard. 1972. *Method in Theology*. London: Darton, Longman & Todd.

Long, Asphodel P. 1992. *In a Chariot Drawn by Lions: the Search for the Female in Deity*. London: Women's Press.

Louth, Andrew. 1975. 'Bernard and Affective Mysticism' in Benedicta Ward, ed. *The Influence of St Bernard: Anglican Essays with an Introduction by Jean Leclercq*. Oxford: SLG Press.

1981. *The Origins of the Christian Mystical Tradition: from Plato to Denys*. Oxford: Clarendon.

1983. *Discerning the Mystery*. Oxford: Clarendon.

1989. *Denys the Areopagite*. London: Geoffrey Chapman.

Lubac, Henri de. 1959–1964. *Exégèse Médiévale: Les quatre sens de l'Écriture*. 2 vols. Paris.

Luther, Martin. 1952. *The Table Talk of Martin Luther*. Edited and with an introduction by Thomas S. Kepler. Grand Rapids, Michigan: Baker Book House.

1958. *Lectures on Genesis (Luther's Works Volume 1)* ed. Jaroslav Pelikan. St Louis: Concordia Publishing House.

1963. *Lectures on Galatians 1535 Chapters 1–4 (Luther's Works Volume 26)* ed. Jaroslav Pelikan. St. Louis: Concordia Publishing House.

1970. *Three Treatises (To the Christian Nobility of the German Nation, The Babylonian Captivity of the Church, The Freedom of a Christian)* trans. Charles M. Jacobs. Philadelphia: Fortress Press.

McGinn, Bernard. 1983. 'Mesiter Eckhart on God as Absolute Unity' in Dominic J. O'Meara, ed. *Neoplatonism and Christian Thought*. Norfolk, Virginia: International Society for Neoplatonic Studies.

ed. 1986. *Meister Eckhart, Teacher and Preacher* Classics of Western Spirituality. New York: Paulist, and London: SPCK.

et al., eds. 1987. *Christian Spirituality: Origins to the Twelfth Century*. London: Routledge & Kegan Paul, and New York: Crossroad.

1991. *The Foundations of Mysticism: Origins to the Fifth Century*. London: SCM.

McGrath, Alistair. 1985. *Luther's Theology of the Cross: Martin Luther's Theological Breakthrough*. Oxford: Blackwell.

MacHaffie, Barbara J., ed. 1992. *Readings in her Story: Women in Christian Tradition*. Minneapolis: Augsburg Fortress.

McLaughlin, Eleanor Commo. 1974. 'Equality of Souls, Inequality of Sexes: Women in Medieval Theology' in Rosemary Ruether, ed.

Religion and Sexism: Images of Women in the Jewish and Christian Traditions. New York: Simon and Schuster,

1979. 'Women, Power and the Pursuit of Holiness in Medieval Christianity' in Rosemary Ruether and Eleanor McLaughlin, eds. *Women of Spirit: Female Leadership in the Jewish and Christian Traditions.* New York: Simon and Schuster.

McNay, Lois. 1992. *Foucault and Feminism: Power, Gender and the Self.* Cambridge: Polity.

MacPherson, C.B. 1962. *The Political Theory of Possessive Individualism: Hobbes to Locke.* Oxford: Clarendon.

Mackie, J.L. 1982. *The Miracle of Theism: Arguments For and Against the Existence of God.* Oxford: Clarendon.

Marshall, Sherrin, ed. 1989. *Women in Reformation and Counter-Reformation Europe: Private and Public Worlds.* Bloomington: Indiana University Press.

Martin, C.B. 1959. *Religious Belief.* Ithaca: Cornell University Press.

Mavrodes, George. 1978. 'Real vs Deceptive Mystical Experiences' in Steven Katz, ed., *Mysticism and Philosophical Analysis.* London: Sheldon.

Mechthild of Magdeburg. 1953. *The Revelations of Mechthild of Magdeburg (1210–1297) or The Flowing Light of the Godhead.* Trans. Lucy Menzies. London: Longmans, Green and Co.

1980. *Offenbarungen der Schwester Mechthild von Magdeburg* oder *Das Fliessende Licht der Gottheit* from the manuscript of the Einsiedeln convent. Trans. P. Gall Morel. Darmstadt: Wissenschaftliche Buchgesellschaft.

Mechthilde von Hackeborn. 1986. *Das Buch vom Strömenden Lab (Liber specialis gratise)* selected by Hans Urs von Balthasar. Einsiedeln: Johannes Verlag.

Merchant, Carolyn. 1983. *The Death of Nature: Women, Ecology and the Scientific Revolution.* San Francisco and London: Harper and Row.

Metz, Johannes B. 1980. *Faith in History and Society.* London: Burns and Oates.

Miles, Margaret R. 1988. *The Image and Practice of Holiness: a Critique of the Classic Manuals of Devotion.* London: SCM.

1989. *Carnal Knowing: Female Nakedness and Religious Meaning in the Christian West* . Boston: Beacon Press.

Mitchell, Juliet. 1974. *Psychoanalysis and Feminism: A Radical Reassessment of Freudian Psychoanalysis.* London and New York: Penguin.

Mollat, Michel. 1986. *The Poor in the Middle Ages: An Essay in Social History.* New Haven and London: Yale University Press.

Mollenkott, Virginia Ramey. 1992. *Sensuous Spirituality: Out From Fundamentalism.* New York: Crossroad.

Moore, R.I. 1987. *The Formation of a Persecuting Society: Power and Deviance in Western Europe 950–1250.* Oxford: Blackwell.

Moorman, John R. H. 1977. *Richest of Poor Men: The Spirituality of St Francis of Assisi.* London: Darton, Longman and Todd.

Moulton, Janice. 1989. 'The Myth of the Neutral "Man" ' in Ann Garry and Marilyn Pearsall, eds. *Women, Knowledge and Reality: Explorations in Feminist Philosophy.* Boston and London: Unwin Hyman.

Mud Flower Collective. 1985. *God's Fierce Whimsy: Christian Feminism and Theological Education.* New York: Pilgrim Press.

Mullett, Michael. 1980. *Radical Religious Movements in Early Modern Europe.* London and Boston: George Allen and Unwin.

Mundy, John H. 1973. *Europe in the High Middle Ages 1150–1309.* London and New York: Longman.

Murdoch, Iris. 1992. *Metaphysics as a Guide to Morals.* London: Chatto and Windus.

Murray, Margaret A. 1931. *The God of the Witches.* Oxford University Press.

Musarillo, H.R., ed. 1972. *The Acts of the Christian Martyrs.* Oxford: Clarendon.

Newman, Barbara. 1987. *Sister of Wisdom: St Hildegard's Theology of the Feminine.* University of California Press.

Nichols, John A., and Shank, Lillian Thomas, eds. 1987. *Peace Weavers: Medieval Religious Women Vol. 2.* Cistercian Studies Series 72. Kalamazoo, Michigan: Cistercian Publications.

Nicholson, Linda J. 1990. *Feminism/Postmodernism.* New York and London: Routledge.

Nicholson, Linda J. and Fraser, Nancy. 1990. 'Social Criticism without Philosophy: An Encounter between Feminism and Postmodernism' in Linda J. Nicholson, ed., *Feminism/Postmodernism.* New York and London: Routledge.

Noble, David F. 1992. *A World Without Women: The Christian Clerical Culture of Western Science.* New York: Alfred A. Knopf.

Nouwen, Henri J.M. 1979. *The Wounded Healer: Ministry in Contemporary Society.* New York: Doubleday.

1981. *The Way of the Heart.* New York: Ballantine.

Nye, Andrea. 1988. *Feminist Theory and the Philosophies of Man.* New York and London: Routledge.

1992. 'Philosophy: A Woman's Thought or a Man's Discipline? The Letters of Abelard and Heloise'. *Hypatia.* Vol. 7 no. 3.

Nygren, Anders. 1982. *Agape and Eros.* London: SPCK.

Oberman, Heiko A. 1963. *The Harvest of Medieval Theology: Gabriel Biel and Late Medieval Nominalism.* Cambridge, MA: Harvard University Press.

Ockham, William of. 1957. *Philosophical Writings*. Trans. and intro. by Philotheus Boehner. London: Thomas Nelson and Sons; and New York: Bobbs-Merrill.

1969. *Predestination, God's Foreknowledge, and Future Contingents*. Trans. and intro. by Marilyn McCord Adams and Norman Kretzmann. New York: Appleton-Century-Crofts.

O'Hear, Anthony. 1984. *Experience, Explanation and Faith: An Introduction to the Philosophy of Religion*. London and Boston: Routledge and Kegan Paul.

O'Meara, Dominic, ed. 1983. *Neoplatonism and Christian Thought*. Norfolk, VA: International Society for Neoplatonic Studies.

Okin, Susan Moller. 1979. *Women in Western Political Thought*. Princeton University Press.

Origen. 1953. *Contra Celsum*. Trans. Henry Chadwick. Cambridge University Press.

1973. *On First Principles*. Trans. G. W. Butterworth. Gloucester. MA: Peter Smith.

1979. *An Exhortation to Martyrdom, Prayer, and Selected Works*. Ed. Rowan Greer. Classics of Western Spirituality. London: SPCK and New York: Paulist.

Otto, Rudolf. 1950. *The Idea of the Holy: An Inquiry into the Non-Rational Factor in the Idea of the Divine and its Relation to the Rational*, 2nd edition. Oxford University Press.

Overall, Christine. 1988. 'Feminism, Ontology, and "Other Minds" in Lorraine Code, Sheila Mullett, and Christine Overall, eds., *Feminist Perspectives: Philosophical Essays on Method and Morals*. Toronto University Press.

Pagels, Elaine. 1982. *The Gnostic Gospels*. London: Penguin.

1988. *Adam, Eve and the Serpent*. New York: Random House.

Pantel, Pauline Schmitt, ed. 1992. *A History of Women: From Ancient Goddesses to Christian Saints*. Cambridge, MA: Harvard University Press.

Parker, T.H.L. 1975. *John Calvin*. Tring, Hertfordshire: Lion.

Pascal, Blaise. 1966. *Pensées*. Harmondsworth: Penguin.

Passmore, John. 1970. *The Perfectibility of Man*. London: Duckworth.

Pearsall, Marilyn and Garry, Ann, eds. 1989. *Women, Knowledge and Reality: Explorations in Feminist Philosophy*. Boston and London: Unwin Hyman.

Peck, M. Scott. 1978. *The Road Less Travelled: A New Psychology of Love, Traditional Values, and Spiritual Growth*. New York: Simon and Schuster.

Pelikan, Jaroslav. 1987. 'Introduction' in *Pseudo-Dionysius: The Complete Works*. Classics of Western Spirituality. London: SPCK and New York: Paulist.

Penelhum, Terence. 1977. 'Unity and Diversity in the Interpretation of Mysticism' in Harold Coward and Terence Penelhum, eds. *Mystics and Scholars: Calgary Conference on Mysticism 1976*. Calgary: Canadian Corporation for Studies in Religion.

Perry, Ralph Barton. 1935. *The Thought and Character of William James*. 2 vols. Oxford University Press.

Peters, Edward, ed. 1980. *Heresy and Authority in Medieval Europe: Documents in Translation*. University of Pennsylvania Press.

Petroff, Elizabeth Alvida, ed. 1986. *Medieval Women's Visionary Literature*. Oxford University Press.

Philo of Alexandria. 1981. *The Contemplative Life, The Giants, and Selections*. Classics of Western Spirituality. New York: Paulist, and London: SPCK.

Pike, Nelson. 1992. *Mystic Union: An Essay in the Phenomenology of Mysticism*. Ithaca and London: Cornell University Press.

Pizan, Christine de. 1990. *A Medieval Woman's Mirror of Honour: The Treasury of the City of Ladies*. New York: Bard Hall.

Plaskow, Judith. 1990. *Standing Again at Sinai: Judaism from a Feminist Perspective*. San Francisco: Harper.

Plaskow, Judith and Christ, Carol, eds. 1989. *Weaving the Visions: New Patterns in Feminist Spirituality*. New York: Harper and Row.

Plato. 1961. *The Collected Dialogues*. Ed. Edith Hamilton and Huntingdon Cairns. Princeton University Press.

Porter, Roy. 1987. *Mind-Forg'd Manacles: A History of Madness in England from the Restoration to the Regency*. London: Penguin.

Proudfoot, Wayne. 1985. *Religious Experience*. University of California Press.

Pseudo-Dionysius. 1987. *The Complete Writings*. Trans. Colm Luibheid and Paul Rorem. Classics of Western Spirituality. New York: Paulist, and London: SPCK.

Puls, Joan. 1987. *Every Bush is Burning: A Spirituality for our Time*. Geneva: World Council of Churches.

Radice, Betty, trans. 1974. *The Letters of Abelard and Heloise*. Harmonsworth: Penguin.

Rahner, Karl. 1968. *Spirit in the World*. New York: Herder and Herder.

Raitt, Jill. 1987. *Christian Spirituality: High Middle Ages and Reformation*. New York: Crossroad.

Raymond of Capua. *The Life of Catherine of Siena*. Trans. George Lamb. New York: P.J. Kennedy and Sons.

Reardon, Bernard. 1985. *Religion in the Age of Romanticism: Studies in Early Nineteenth Century Thought*. Cambridge University Press.

Reese, James. 1983. *The Book of Wisdom*. Wilmington, USA: Michael Glazier.

Rich, Adrienne. 1978. *The Dream of a Common Language. Poems 1974–1977.* London and New York: W.W. Norton.

Riches, John, ed. 1986. *The Analogy of Beauty: The Theology of Hans Urs Von Balthasar.* Edinburgh: T & T Clark.

Ritschl, Albrecht. 1887. *Theologie und Metaphysik,* 2nd edition. Bonn: Marcus.

Robinson, James M., ed. 1977. *The Nag-Hammadi Library in English.* Leiden: Brill.

Robinson, John Mansley. 1968. *An Introduction to Early Greek Philosophy.* Boston: Houghton Mifflin Co.

Roper, Lyndal. 1989. *The Holy Household: Women and Morals in Reformation Augsburg.* Oxford: Clarendon Press.

Rorem, Paul. 1993. *Pseudo-Dionysius: A Commentary on the Texts and an Introduction to their Influence.* Oxford University Press.

Rorty, Amélie Oskenberg. 1992. 'Descartes on Thinking with the Body' in John Cottingham, ed. *The Cambridge Companion to Descartes.* Cambridge University Press.

Rorty, Richard. 1980. *Philosophy and the Mirror of Nature.* Oxford: Blackwell.

1982. *The Consequences of Pragmatism.* Minneapolis: University of Minnesota Press.

1989. *Contingency, Irony and Solidarity.* Cambridge University Press.

1993. 'Feminism, Ideology and Deconstruction: A Pragmatist View'. *Hypatia.* Vol. 8 no. 2.

Rosen, Barbara, ed. 1991. *Witchcraft in England 1558–1618.* Amherst: University of Massachussets Press.

Ruether, Rosemary Radford and McLaughlin, Eleanor, eds. 1979. *Women of Spirit: Female Leadership in the Jewish and Christian Traditions.* New York: Simon and Schuster.

Ruether, Rosemary Radford, ed. 1974a. *Religion and Sexism: Images of Women in the Jewish and Christian Traditions.* New York: Simon and Schuster.

1974b. 'Misogynism and Virginal Feminism in the Fathers of the Church' in Ruether, ed. *Religion and Sexism.* New York: Simon and Schuster.

1975. *New Woman/New Earth: Sexist Ideologies and Human Liberation.* San Francisco and London: Harper and Row.

1979. 'Mothers of the Church: Ascetic Women in the Late Patristic Age' in Ruether and McLaughlin, eds. *Women of Spirit.* New York: Simon and Schuster.

1983. *Sexism and God-Talk: Towards a Feminist Theology.* London: SCM.

Runciman, Steven. 1953. *A History of the Crusades.* 3 vols. Cambridge University Press.

Russell, Jeffrey B. 1980. *A History of Witchcraft: Sorcerers, Heretics and Pagans*. London: Thames and Hudson.

1984. *Lucifer: The Devil in the Middle Ages*. Ithaca and London: Cornell University Press.

Ruusbroec, John (Ruysbroeck). 1916. *The Adornment of the Spiritual Marriage; The Sparkling Stone; The Book of Supreme Truth*. Ed. Evelyn Underhill. London: J.M. Dent.

1943. *The Seven Steps of the Ladder of Spiritual Law*. Trans. F. Sherwood Taylor. Westminster: Dacre Press.

1985. *The Spiritual Espousals and Other Works*. Trans. and intro. by James A. Wiseman. Classics of Western Spirituality. New York: Paulist.

Salisbury, Joyce E. 1991. *Church Fathers, Independent Virgins*. London and New York: Verso.

Schelling, F. 1860. *Schellings Sämmtliche Werke*. Fourteen Volumes. Ed. K.F.A. Schelling. Stuttgart and Augsburg: Cotta.

Schiebinger, Londa. 1989. *The Mind has no Sex? Women in the Origins of Modern Science*. Cambridge, MA: Harvard University Press.

Schlamm, Leon. 1991. 'Rudolph Otto and Mystical Experience'. *Religious Studies*. Vol. 27 no. 3.

Schleiermacher, Friedrich. 1958. *On Religion: Speeches to its Cultured Despisers*. New York and London: Harper.

Schneiders, Sandra. 1987. 'Scripture and Spirituality' in Bernard McGinn *et al.*, eds. *Christian Spirituality: Origins to the Twelfth Century*. New York: Crossroad.

Schouls, Peter A. 1980. *The Imposition of Method: A Study of Descartes and Locke*. Oxford: Clarendon.

Shahar, Shulamith. 1990a. *Childhood in the Middle Ages*. London and New York: Routledge.

1990b. *The Fourth Estate: A History of Women in the Middle Ages*. London and New York: Routledge.

Smalley, Beryl. 1983. *The Study of the Bible in the Middle Ages*, 3rd edition. Oxford: Blackwell.

Shanley, Mary Lyndon and Pateman, Carole, eds. 1991. *Feminist Interpretations and Political Theory*. Cambridge: Polity.

Smart, Ninian. 1965. 'Interpretation and Mystical Experience'. *Religious Studies* vol. 1 no. 1.

1969. *The Religious Experience of Man kind*. New York: Charles Scribner's Sons.

1970. *The Philosophy of Religion*. London and New York: Macmillan.

1978. 'Understanding Religious Experience' in Steven T. Katz, ed. *Mysticism and Philosophical Analysis*. London: Sheldon.

Smith, Margaret. 1981. 'The Nature and Meaning of Mysticism' in Richard Woods, ed. *Understanding Mysticism*. London: Athlone.

Soskice, Janet Martin, ed. 1990. *After Eve: Women, Theology and the Christian Tradition*. London: Marshall Pickering.

Southern, R.W. 1970a. *Western Society and the Church in the Middle Ages*. Harmondsworth: Penguin.

1970b. *Medieval Humanism and Other Studies*. New York: Harper.

Spelman, Elizabeth V. 1988. *Inessential Woman: Problems of Exclusion in Feminist Thought*. Boston: Beacon Press.

Spender, Dale. 1985. *Man Made Language*, 2nd edition. London and New York: Routledge and Kegan Paul.

Spretnak, Charlene, ed. 1982. *The Politics of Women's Spirituality: Essays on the Rise of Spiritual Power within the Feminist Movement*. New York: Doubleday.

Staal, Frits. 1975. *Exploring Mysticism*. Harmondsworth: Penguin.

Stace, Walter Terence. 1961. *Mysticism and Philosophy*. London: Macmillan.

Stoeber, Michael. 1992a. 'Constructivist Epistemologies of Mysticism: A Critique and Revision'. *Religious Studies*. Vol. 28. no. 1.

1992b. *Evil and the Mystics' God: Towards a Mystical Theodicy*. London: Macmillan.

1993. 'Introvertive Mystical Experiences: Monistic, Theistic and Theo-monistic'. *Religious Studies*. Vol. 29 no. 2.

Stone, Lawrence. 1979. *The Family, Sex and Marriage in England 1500–1800*. Abridged edition. London: Penguin.

Straub, Kristina and Epstein, Julia, eds. 1991. *Body Guards: the Cultural Politics of Gender Ambiguity*. New York and London: Routledge, Chapman Hall.

Strawson, P. F. 1966. *The Bounds of Sense: an Essay on Kant's Critique of Pure Reason*. London: Methuen.

Stuard, Susan Mosher, ed. 1976. *Women in Medieval Society*. University of Pennsylvania Press.

ed. 1987. *Women in Medieval History and Historiography*. University of Pennsylvania Press.

Summerville, Ernest H. 1972. 'Benediction' in *The Tides of Spring and Other Reflections*. Boston: Unitarian Universalist Association.

Swanson, R.N. 1989. *Church and Society in Late Medieval England*. Oxford: Blackwell.

Swinburne, Richard. 1979. *The Existence of God*. Oxford: Clarendon Press.

Tauler, Johannes. 1985. *Sermons*. Trans. Maria Shrady. Classics of Western Spirituality Series. New York: Paulist and London: SPCK.

Taylor, Charles. 1989. *Sources of the Self: the Making of the Modern Identity*. Cambridge University Press.

Teasdale, Wayne. 1985. *Essays in Mysticism: Explorations into Contemplative Experience*. Lake Worth, Florida: Sunday Publications.

Teresa of Avila. 1951. *The Letters of Saint Teresa of Jesus*. Vols. i and ii. Trans. E. Allison Peers. London: Burns Oates & Washbourne.

1976. *The Collected Works of St Teresa of Avila*. Vols. i and ii. Trans. Kieran Kavanaugh and Otiolio Rodriguez. Washington, D.C.: Institute of Carmelite Studies.

Tertullian. 1992. *On the Apparel of Women*, in Barbara J. MacHaffie, ed. *Readings in Her Story: Women in Christian Tradition*. Minneapolis: Augsburg Fortress.

Thomas Aquinas. 1945. *Basic Writings of Saint Thomas Aquinas*. Vols. i and ii, Anton C. Pegis, ed. New York: Random House.

Thomas, Keith. 1971. *Religion and the Decline of Magic*. London: Penguin.

Tobin, Frank. 1986. *Meister Eckhart: Thought and Language*. University of Pennsylvania Press.

Torjesen, K.J. 1986. *Hermeneutical Procedure and Theological Method in Origen's Exegesis*. Patristische Texte und Studien. Berlin & New York: de Gruyter.

Trevor-Roper, H.R. 1967. *The European Witch-Craze of the Sixteenth and Seventeenth Centuries*. London: Penguin.

Tuchman, Barbara W. 1978. *A Distant Mirror: The Calamitous 14th Century*. New York: Ballantine.

Tugwell, Simon. 1979. *The Way of the Preacher*. London: Darton, Longman and Todd.

1984. *Ways of Imperfection: an Exploration of Christian Spirituality* London: Darton, Longman &Todd.

Underhill, Evelyn. 1929. *The Mystic Way* . London: J M Dent & Sons.

1930. *Mysticism,* 2nd edition. London: J M Dent & Sons.

1943. *Letters*, with an introduction by Charles Williams. London: Longmans, Green & Co.

Undset, Sigrid. 1954. *Catherine of Siena*. London: Sheed and Ward.

Vanderyecken, Walter and Van Deth, Rob. 1993. 'Miraculous Maids? Self-Starvation and Fasting Girls'. *History Today* 43.

Vermaseren, Maarten J. 1977. *Cybele and Attis: the Myth and the Cult*. London: Thames & Hudson.

de Vinck, José, trans. 1960–1970. *The Works of Bonaventure*. 5 vols. Patterson, New Jersey.

Von Balthasar, Hans Urs. 1982f. *The Glory of the Lord: A Theological Aesthetics*. Vols. i–vii. Edinburgh: T & T Clark.

Wainwright, William. 1981. *Mysticism: a Study of its Nature, Cognitive Value and Moral Implications*. Brighton: Harvester.

Wakefield, Walter L. and Evans, Austin P. 1969. *Heresies of the High Middle Ages*. New York: Columbia University Press.

Ward, Benedicta, trans. 1975a. *The Sayings of the Desert Fathers: the Alphabetical Collection*. London: Mowbray

1975b. *The Wisdom of the Desert Fathers*. Fairacres Publications 48. Oxford: SLG Press.

ed. 1976. *The Influence of St Bernard: Anglican Essays with and Introduction by Jean Leclercq*. Oxford: SLG Press.

1987. *Harlots of the Desert: a Study of Repentance in Early Monastic Sources*. London: Mowbray.

1990. 'Saints and Sybils: Hildegard of Bingen to Teresa of Avila' in Janet Soskice, ed. *After Eve: Women, Theology and the Christian Tradition*. London: Marshall Pickering.

Ward, Jennifer C. 1992. *English Noblewomen in the Later Middle Ages*. London and New York: Longman.

Warner, Marina. 1983. *Joan of Arc: The Image of Female Heroism*. Harmondsworth: Penguin.

1985. *Alone of All her Sex: The Myth and the Cult of the Virgin Mary*. London: Picador.

Watson, Nicholas. 1991. *Richard Rolle and the Invention of Authority*. Cambridge Studies in Medieval Literature. Cambridge University Press.

Watts, Michael. 1978. *The Dissenters: From the Reformation to the French Revolution*. Oxford: Clarendon.

Weber, Alison. 1990. *Teresa of Avila and the Rhetoric of Femininity*. Princeton University Press.

Weisman, Richard. 1984. *Witchcraft, Magic and Religion in 17th Century Massachusetts*. Amherst: The University of Massachusetts Press.

Wiesner, Merry E. 1989. 'Nuns, Wives, and Mothers: Women and the Reformation in Germany' in Sherrin Marshall, ed. *Women in Reformation and Counter-Reformation Europe: Private and Public Worlds*. Bloomington: Indiana University Press.

Welch, Sharon. 1985. *Communities of Resistance and Solidarity: A Feminist Theology of Liberation*. Maryknoll, New York: Orbis.

Wilkinson, John, trans. 1981. *Egeria's Travels to the Holy Land*, revised ed. Warminster, England: Aris & Phillips, and Jerusalem: Ariel Publishing House.

Williams, Bernard. 1976. *Descartes: The Project of Pure Enquiry*. Harmondsworth: Penguin.

Williams, Robert R. 1978. *Schleiermacher the Theologian: the Construction of the Doctrine of God*. Philadelphia: Fortress press.

Williams, Rowan. 1986. 'Balthasar and Rahner' in John Riches, ed., *The Analogy of Beauty: The Theology of Hans Urs von Balthasar*. Edinburgh: T&T Clark.

1991. *Teresa of Avila*. London: Geoffrey Chapman.

Williams, Selma R., and Pamela Williams Adelman. 1992. *Riding the Nightmare: Women and Witchcraft from the Old World to Colonial Salem.* New York: HarperCollins.

Willen, Diane. 1989. 'Women and Religion in Early Modern England' in Sherrin Marshall, ed. *Women in Reformation and Counter-Reformation Europe.* Bloomington: Indiana University Press.

Woods, Richard. 1986. *Eckhart's Way.* London: Darton, Longman and Todd.

ed. 1981. *Understanding Mysticism.* London: Athlone.

Yandell, Keith E. 1993. *The Epistemology of Religious Experience.* Cambridge University Press.

Zaehner, R.C. 1957. *Mysticism Sacred and Profane.* Oxford: Clarendon.

Zum Brunn, Emilie and Epiney-Burgard, Georgette. 1989. *Women Mystics in Medieval Europe.* New York: Paragon.

Index

Abelard, 84
active, *see* male
Adam, 45, 46, 47, 49, 66, 92, 114, 149, 223,
    227, 228, 229, 230, 232, 233
Ad nostrum, 258–9, 261–4, 266
Aeschylus, 29–30
affective mysticism, 87, 93, 106, 109, 118,
    123–33, 149, 152, 155, 286–290
Agnes, 220
Alberic of London, 226
Albert the Great (Albertus Magnus), 110,
    119, 259
Al-Ghazali, 305
Alpaïs, 208–9
Ambrose of Milan, 232, 233
Andrew of St Victor, 79
angels, 98, 99, 107
Anselm, 82, 83, 297–8, 300, 304
Aristotle, 29, 31, 41, 107, 115, 195, 275
Arius, 246
asceticism, denial of the body, 55, 121, 128,
    138, 149, 151, 196, 197, 198, 213, 247,
    248, 250
Athanasius, 246
Augustine, 43, 52, 71–4, 75, 78, 79, 80, 81,
    82, 83, 112, 113, 114, 123, 127, 194, 195,
    223, 227, 229, 232, 281, 283, 286
authority, 1, 12, 22, 24, 80, 83, 96, 99, 107,
    159, 160, 168–84, 214, 248, 251, 255,
    269, 325, 327–8

Bacon, Francis, 275–6
baptism, *see* sacraments
Basil, 196
Beatific Vision, 186
Beatrice of Nazareth, 134
Bede, 81
beghards, 203, 258, 263

beguines, 111, 134, 135, 141, 142, 146, 169,
    176, 203–7, 258, 259, 262–3
beguinages, 110
Benedict of Nursia, 84, 196
Benedictines, 124, 161, 199, 201, 264
Berger, Peter, 12
Bernard of Clairvaux, 7, 81, 85, 87, 95,
    123–32, 133, 135, 140, 141, 143, 145,
    149, 162, 184, 186–8, 236, 250–2, 280,
    281, 286–8, 304, 318
Black Death, 167, 182
Boehme, Jacob, 316
Bonaventure, 76, 81, 105, 123, 132, 281
Boniface, 69
Bouyer, Louis, 27
bride of Christ, 42
Bridget of Sweden, 158, 168, 169
Brown, Peter, 57
Bynum, Caroline Walker, 172, 173, 207,
    208, 211, 212, 213, 215, 216, 220, 221,
    222, 299

Cappadocian fathers, 70
Cassian, 196
Cathars, 199, 247–55
Catherine of Siena, 134, 158, 159, 168, 214,
    216–22
celibacy, 53
chastity, celibacy, 91, 92, 129, 151, 197, 198,
    201, 240, 291, 325
    see also virginity
Christ, *see* Jesus
Christina of St Trond, 204
Christina the Astonishing, 212
Chrysostom, 79
Cistercians, 124, 130, 143, 201, 208, 212, 297
Clare of Assisi, 199–203, 213
Clement of Alexandria, 53, 69

Clement VII, 221
Cloud of Unknowing, 123, 132, 191–2, 239, 242, 325
Cohn, Norman, 256, 267–9
contemplation, 93, 144
  see also union with God
Council of Elvira, 197
Council of Vienne, 206–7, 258, 259
courtly love, 136
cross-dressing, 57
crusades, 124

Damaris, 100, 108
Dante, 288
Davis, Caroline Franks, 328, 332–4, 336
deification, 139–40
Derrida, Jacques, 122, 351–3
Descartes, Rene, 103, 343
  Cartesian, 33
desert fathers, mothers, 54–7, 193, 195, 206, 208
detachment, 121
devil, demons, Satan, serpent, 46, 55, 56, 66, 89, 103, 131, 189–91, 203, 209, 219, 220, 231, 232, 233, 234, 244, 245, 246, 248, 249, 250, 258, 265, 266, 268–71, 275, 325, 327, 329
Dionysius the Areopagite, 85, 87, 95–109, 110, 111, 115, 118, 119, 120, 121, 124, 125, 127, 129, 130, 132, 138, 142, 143, 144, 281, 282–5, 290, 297, 319
Dominicans, 111, 112, 134, 218, 265, 266, 285
dualism, mind–body, 38–9, 86, 89, 139, 224, 238, 239, 248, 250, 251, 254
du Bois, Page, 28

eating, *see* food
Eckhart, 5, 7, 87, 109–22, 123, 124, 126, 129, 131, 132, 138, 139, 140, 142, 143, 144, 147, 148, 149, 151, 152, 188–9, 191, 281, 285, 286, 300, 319, 325, 332, 352
ecstasy, *ek-stasis*, 103, 106, 110, 121, 125, 128, 283, 284, 307, 316, 319, 331, 335
Egeria, 74–6, 159
Eleanor of Aquitaine, 291
Elsbet Stagel, 213
enclosure, 160, 196–207, 212, 237, 325
Enlightenment, 7, 9, 281, 307, 319, 334
Eriugena, John Scotus, 95, 109, 123
erotic mysticism, 126, 133–46, 165
eucharist, *see* sacraments

Eugene III, 184
Euripides, 29
Eve, 45, 46, 49, 66, 88, 92, 114, 131, 153, 170, 171, 228, 229, 230, 231, 232, 233, 235
Everinus of Steinfeld, 250–1
existence of God, evidence for, 2,9, 24, 308, 328–30, 341
experience, 106, 242, 245, 311–15, 324, 330–9, 341–2
  subjective, private , 2, 4, 5, 6, 10, 11, 17, 19, 20, 21, 24, 68, 80, 171, 243, 283, 304, 306, 318–21, 322
  see also visions

fasting, 207–16, 237, 240
Felicity, 49–52
female
  demonic, 55, 56; *see also* witches
  inferior, 53, 115
  linked with bodiliness, sexuality, 53, 56, 114, 196, 228, 237
  passive, 42, 43, 51, 53, 115, 196–7, 226, 273, 275, 292
  private, 275–7, 326, 345–6
food, eating, feasting, 136–8, 160, 207–16, 237
Foucault, Michel, 4, 13, 14, 15, 16, 26, 323, 326–7, 347, 348
Fourth Lateran Council, 201, 204, 253–4, 255
Fox, Matthew, 19
Francis of Assisi, 190, 199–203, 213, 239
Franciscans, Friars Minor, 142, 143, 200–3, 254
Frederick Barbarossa, 162
Freud, Sigmund, 16

Gerson, Jean, 80
Gertrude (the Great) of Helfta, 134, 159, 163–4, 165, 166, 169, 171–5, 210, 211, 280, 298, 299, 334
Gnosticism, 67, 246
goddess, 61, 64
Gregory of Nyssa, 54, 70–1, 75, 78, 94, 280, 319
Gregory VII, 247
Gregory IX, 253
Gregory XI, 221
Guibert of Gemblaux, 170

Hadewijch of Antwerp, 134–46, 147, 155,

Hadewijch of Antwerp (*cont.*)
  158, 159, 164–5, 166, 169, 175–6, 188,
  189, 204, 236, 280, 291, 292–6, 300,
  319, 334
Harvey, William, 273–5
Hegel, G.W.F., 122
Heidegger, Martin, 122
hell, 181, 183, 190, 288
Heloise, 84
Henry Despenser, 178, 182, 183
Henry of Lausanne, 247
Henry Suso, 213
heretics, heresy, 14, 79, 80, 134, 157, 158,
  183, 190–2, 193, 204–6, 214, 224, 241,
  243–64, 266, 269, 290, 325, 327, 328,
  331, 350
  see also Cathars; Lollards; Waldensians
Hesiod, 28, 35
Hester, Marianne, 271, 273–4
Hick, John, 6
hierarchy, 96–9, 107, 173
Hilda of Whitby, 198
Hildegard of Bingen, 45, 158, 159, 161–3,
  164, 165, 167, 169–71, 172, 173, 175,
  177, 184, 186, 224–38, 239, 240, 241,
  245, 280, 325, 328, 331, 339
Hilduin of Saint-Denis, 95
holism, *see* integration
homosexuality, 35, 44, 234–5
honorary males, 51–4, 327
Honorius III, 206
Hugh of St Victor, 109
Hughes, Gerard, 19
Hugolino di Segni, 201
Humbeline, 131
humility, 42, 153, 170, 177, 184, 220, 327
  see also passive
Huxley, Aldous, 243

illumination, 92–3, 105
image of God, 72, 74, 81, 112, 114, 115, 117,
  119, 120, 122, 123, 194, 227, 228, 290
ineffability, 9, 10, 24, 106, 278–321, 338–9,
  344
Innocent III, 199, 206
Innocent IV, 201
Innocent VIII, 265
inquisition, inquisitors, 14, 253–8, 259,
  262–4, 265, 269, 271, 275, 332
integration, 139, 145, 146–56, 182, 223–42,
  301–4, 319
intellect, reason, intellectual or speculative

mysticism, 87, 93, 94, 103, 109–22,
  129, 155, 191, 227, 286
Irenaeus, 70, 246
Islam, 59, 305

Jacques de Vitry, 134, 205–6, 212, 213
James, William, 3, 6, 7, 8, 24, 279, 305–7,
  309–11, 320, 330, 331, 341, 342, 343
Jerome, 54, 79
Jesus (also Christ), 48, 65, 67, 70, 77, 78, 79,
  81, 86, 112, 117, 133, 137, 154, 164, 203
  divinity and humanity, 71, 72, 140–1,
  142, 148, 150, 151, 214–15, 228, 236,
  246
  as Mother, 116, 297–304
  suffering, 166, 220–3, 236
Jews, Judaism, 43, 59, 64, 252
John of the Cross, 7, 15, 123, 280, 281, 288,
  305
Julian of Norwich, 7, 116, 146–56, 158, 159,
  165–8, 173, 175, 176–84, 185, 224, 225,
  238–41, 280, 301–4, 319, 328, 334, 337,
  339
justice, *see* social justice
Justin, 43
Jutta, 161

Kant, Immanuel, 7, 8, 16, 23, 105, 307–12,
  319, 338, 343, 344, 345, 347, 352
Katz, Steven, 7, 279, 336–7, 339
Kelly, Joan, 157

Leclercq, Jean, 131, 184
Levack, Brian, 269–70
Lollards, 178, 182, 185
Long, Asphodel, 63
Love, Lady Love, 135–8, 140, 141, 145,
  292–6, 300, 304
love, works of, *see* social justice
Luther, Martin, 77, 96

McGinn, Bernard, 5–6
McNay, Lois, 15–16
Macrina, 54
male
  active, 41, 43, 51, 116, 226, 275, 276, 292
  conceptualization of God, 64
  god-like, 116
  linked with mind, spirit, reason, 114–19
  public life of, 275–7
Malleus Maleficarum, 191, 265–7, 270
Margaret of Cortona, 214

Margaret of Ypres, 204
Marguerite of Oingt, 300, 302, 304
Marguerite Porete, 204, 259–64, 332
Martin V, 207
martyrdom, 49–52
Mary, mother of Jesus, 51, 91, 131, 164, 170, 208, 228, 229, 235, 296, 299, 300
Mary of Oignies, 204, 205, 212–13
Matthew Hopkins, 268
Matthew Paris, 205
Mechthild of Hackborn, 159, 172, 174, 299
Mechthild of Magdeburg, 133, 135, 174, 211, 294, 296
mendicants, 198–9, 200, 201
metaphors, 156, 186, 304
Miles, Margaret, 21, 50
modesty formula, 170, 173, 176
monasteries, convents, 84, 124, 196, 198, 208, 237
mortification, 95, 151, 172
Moses, 75, 94, 186
Moses Maimonides, 285
mystery religions, 26–30, 32, 33, 59, 60, 96, 97, 323, 331
    Eleusinian, 27–8, 60, 61, 68
    Mithraism, 27–8
mystical core of religion, 9, 24
mystical experience, *see* experience
mystical meaning of scripture, 59, 67–85, 86, 87, 93, 96, 97, 100, 102, 107, 117, 125, 126, 127, 133, 159, 171, 187–8, 191, 245, 280, 289–90, 297, 299, 318, 319, 324, 331
mystical path, 88–95, 99, 127, 141, 147, 189, 195, 260–1, 284
mystical theology, 87
    see also intellectual mysticism; affective mysticism
mysticism, true and false, 243–77, 306–7, 331

negation, negative theology, 105, 110
Neoplatonism, 98, 100
Newman, Barbara, 162, 170, 228, 231, 233, 238
nominalism, 263
Nouwen, Henri, 19

Origen, 43, 69–70, 75, 88–94, 99, 125, 126, 127, 129, 139–40, 142, 143, 144, 280, 319

Pachomius, 196

passive, *see* female; humility
Passmore, John, 10–11
Paul, Pauline writings, 45, 48, 65, 70, 95, 100, 107, 186, 251
Peasants' Revolt, 167, 182
Pelagia, 57, 196
Perpetua, 49–52, 56, 74, 159
Petronilla, 198
Philo, 43, 44, 51, 69
Pike, Nelson, 4, 5
Plato, Platonism, 29, 30–42, 43, 44, 52, 61, 73, 89, 94, 103, 119, 122, 139, 152, 352
Platonism, Christian, 23, 34, 43–54, 88, 89, 238, 286
Plotinus, 43
Poor Clares, 200–3
poverty, 200–3
Psellos, Michael Constantine, 252
purgation, 89–92
Pythagoras, 29, 31, 32, 41, 44

Raymond of Capua, 159, 218–19
reason, *see* intellect
resistance, 15–16
Richard of St Victor, 109
Richard Rolle, 190, 191
Richardis von Stade, 226
Robert of Arbrissel, 198–9, 247
Rorty, Richard, 348–50
Ruusbroec, Jan van, 5, 189–90, 191, 242, 325, 332

sacraments (eucharist, baptism), 86, 96, 97, 99, 101, 107, 135, 136, 172, 174, 175, 190, 209–11, 212–16, 219, 221, 222, 224, 234, 289–90, 294, 302, 324
sacred heart of Jesus, cult of, 174–5
Sappho, 29
Schelling, F, 316–17
Schleiermacher, Friedrich, 8, 311–20, 338, 343
Schüssler Fiorenza, Elizabeth, 48, 49
Scot, Reginald, 274–5
Scott Peck, M., 19
self-knowledge, 152–5
serpent, *see* devil
sexual encounter, passion, *see* erotic mysticism
silence, 278, 280, 284–5
    see also ineffability
sin, 153, 154, 179, 180
Smith, Margaret, 319

social construction, 12, 18, 24, 26, 60, 109,
    122, 156, 160, 161, 171, 192, 242, 244,
    278, 279, 281, 305, 309, 318–21, 322,
    323–8, 340–53
social justice, 17, 20, 21, 82, 141–5, 171, 204,
    294, 326, 347–53
Song of Songs, 88, 90–1, 92, 125, 127, 130,
    236, 251
soul, 136
    grammatically feminine, 40
    passive, 41
    see also dualism
speculative mysticism, *see* intellect
Spelman, Elisabeth, 39
Stace, Walter Terence, 279, 320, 333, 335–6
stages, *see* mystical path
Starbuck, R., 306, 320
Stoeber, Michael, 6
Swinburne, Richard, 7, 328
Synod of Whitby, 198

Taylor, Charles, 42
Teresa of Avila, 4, 5, 134, 158, 168, 169,
    333
Tertullian, 45, 91
Thecla, 56–7.
Third Lateran Council, 246
Thomas Aquinas, 80, 95, 110, 112, 119,
    194–5, 227, 256, 266, 270, 285, 305
Thomas, Keith, 267–8

Tobin, Frank, 121

Underhill, Evelyn, 317–18, 320n
union with God, 93–4, 103, 137–42, 145,
    148, 165, 186, 260, 263, 287
Urban VI, 182, 221

Valdes, 254–255
vernacular, 111, 134, 146, 159, 178, 204,
    286, 292
virginity, 53, 57, 91, 112, 113, 131, 153,
    223–41
visionary women, 23, 108, 146, 156, 159,
    281, 299, 318, 325, 332, 333, 339, 350
vision of God, 42
visions, 118, 121, 126, 161–8, 169, 170,
    185–91, 211, 219, 225, 226, 238–41,
    245, 307, 309, 324, 331, 333
Volmar, 159, 226

Waldensians, 247, 252, 254–8
Walter Hilton, 239
will, mysticism of, 94, 144–6, 155, 261
William of St Thierry, 131, 132, 236
William Humbert, 259–60, 261
Wisdom (Sophia, Hochma), 62–5, 104, 116,
    297
witches, witch hunts, 55, 161, 190–2, 193,
    194, 204, 241, 243, 244, 252, 264–77,
    325, 327, 328, 350

CAMBRIDGE STUDIES IN IDEOLOGY AND RELIGION

Books in the series

*A Theology of Reconstruction: Nation-Building
and Human Rights*
CHARLES VILLA-VICENCIO

Christianity and Politics in Doe's Liberia
PAUL GIFFORD

Protestantism in Contemporary China
ALAN HUNTER AND KIM-KWONG CHAN

Politics, Theology, and History
RAYMOND PLANT

Christianity and Democracy: A Theology for a Just World Order
JOHN W. DE GRUCHY

Pastoral Care and Liberation Theology
STEPHEN PATTISON

Religion and the Making of Society: Essays in Social Theology
CHARLES DAVIS

Theology, Ideology and Liberation: Towards a Liberative Theology
PETER SCOTT

Power, Gender and Christian Mysticism
GRACE M. JANTZEN

God's Just Vengeance: Crime, Violence and the Rhetoric of Salvation
TIMOTHY GORRINGE